Lawrence of Arabia

 P9-EJI-021

The publisher gratefully acknowledges the generous contribution to this book provided by The General Endowment Fund of the Associates of the University of California Press.

Lawrence of Arabia

A Film's Anthropology

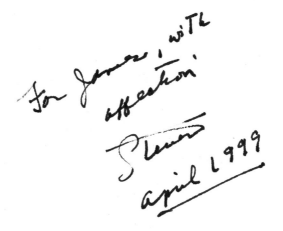

Steven C. Caton

UNIVERSITY OF CALIFORNIA PRESS
Berkeley · Los Angeles · London

University of California Press
Berkeley and Los Angeles, California

University of California Press, Ltd.
London, England

© 1999 by
The Regents of the University of California

Library of Congress Cataloging-in-Publication Data

Caton, Steven Charles, 1950–
    Lawrence of Arabia : a film's anthropology /
    Steven C. Caton.
        p. cm.
    Includes bibliographic references and index
    ISBN 0-520-21082-4 (alk. paper). —
    ISBN 0-520-21083-2 (alk. paper)
    1. Lawrence of Arabia (Motion picture)
    2. Arabs in motion pictures.   I. Title.
    PN1997.L353C38   1999
    791.43'72—DC21   98-3621

Printed in the United States of America
9 8 7 6 5 4 3 2 1

The paper used in this publication meets the
minimum requirements of American National
Standards for Information Sciences—Permanence
of Paper for Printed Library Materials,
ANSI Z39.48-1984.

In memory of my mother,
Hanni S. Caton (1912–96),
with whom I enjoyed many a movie
on the Late Night Show

Contents

Illustrations

FIGURES

DIAGRAM

Preface

Although this book is based on a great deal of research, it does not provide data from previously unpublished sources. Thus, I did not attempt to interview the surviving filmmakers of *Lawrence of Arabia,* nor did I rummage through out-of-the-way archives to ferret out new information. Both of these functions have already been served by recent and quite admirable publications on the production of the movie, particularly the work by Anderegg ("Lawrence of Arabia: The Man, the Myth, the Movie"), Silverman (*David Lean*), Morris and Raskin (*Lawrence of Arabia*), and Turner (*The Making of David Lean's LAWRENCE OF ARABIA*). There seemed to be no need to belabor what they have already done so well.

I see my book as more of a critical intervention than these other works. It is written with a somewhat different aim, and to some extent even for a different audience, though I like to think it is no less passionately involved with its subject matter. Readers looking forward to this critical intervention as long overdue in the discourses on this movie should also be warned, however. The kind of criticism they may be anticipating—what might loosely be termed an ideological critique—is not my project either. Exactly what that project might be and why I think it to be important, not only for film criticism but also for understanding the relationship between representation and power, is made clear in the introduction.

Finally, a word of explanation about the subtitle "a film's anthropology." I do not provide a model for the anthropological analysis of film, nor would I wish to; rather, I look at a specific film through what I deem to be an anthropological lens. I ask, for example, What would it mean for a film company to shoot on location in what are said to be "exotic" locales? What is this film's ethnographic gaze? How is that gaze linked, on the one hand, to the economics of the international film industry and, on the other, to certain themes of colonialism and world war preoccupying the West? How do I, as an anthropologist, view this film as itself an allegory of anthropology? How does one obtain readings of the film through an ethnography of audience responses in the context of the classroom or the movie theater? But the one thing that anthropology has taught me above everything else (and I make no claims here that one can learn this lesson only in my chosen field) is that one can look at the same thing or person or event from different perspectives, depending on whom one is speaking to in the field, or who one is as an anthropologist, as well as what the context might be. Thus, I keep shifting the perspective on this film in light of who is actually or only imagined to be the spectator, or in relation to the time period in which it is viewed and its larger historical contexts of spectatorship. I hope that as a result of such an analysis, the reader will come away from this book not so much with a definitive or necessarily coherent view of *Lawrence of Arabia* as with a richer, three-dimensional one.

Acknowledgments

I first got the idea for this book while teaching the film in an anthropology class on the Middle East. I want to thank all of my students for their insights, but especially Nick Alexander, James Lacoste, Alex (Fred) Long, Charlene Worley, Karen Kelly, Rosse Mary Taveras, and Kimberly Dumer. To Amanda Wilbur's alertness I owe the fact that I now own a copy of the original theater brochure of the movie. Through Randy Fischel's contacts I now own a copy of the issue of *MAD Magazine* that featured a parody of the film.

Portions of this book have been presented as lectures, and I want to thank audiences in various venues for their cogent criticisms and keen insights. I first delivered chapter 5 to the Department of Anthropology at Stanford University in the spring of 1990. The comments generated during the discussion period prompted me to think more seriously about anthropological practice as it is represented in this film, which resulted in chapter 4. I presented that chapter at the Department of Anthropology, Duke University, in the fall of 1992 and again at Williams College in January of 1997. One of the questioners at the Stanford lecture and another questioner at Duke asked me about representations of gender and sexuality, which made me realize how I might develop yet another reading of the film, which is found in chapter 6. The questions and comments at both venues were stimulating, but I wish particularly to thank David Edwards for encouraging me to deepen some of the discussion in chapter 5. Attending the talk was Alyce Dissette, who gave me the idea to incorporate the talk I gave to the junior high and high school students from North Adams as part of my epilogue. I am grateful to her also for giving me the opportunity to conduct focus groups with these students that helped confirm some speculations I had made about the reception of the film. I first presented chapter 6 to the Carolina Seminar "Gender and History," which was convened at the National Humanities Center in the spring of 1993. I thank all participants in that seminar for their wonderful comments, but especially Temma Kaplan and Marianne Hirsch for pushing me to think about masculinity as a topic in gender studies.

At the National Humanities Center (1992–93) I was the recipient of a fellowship from the National Endowment for the Humanities, where I began work on this book. I wish to thank the Center and the NEH for their generous support. At the Center, I participated in a stimulating, year-long seminar entitled "Autobiography and Subjectivity in Academic Writing," organized by Alex Zwerdling. Chapter 4 of this book was distributed to the seminar participants, who encouraged me to think about questions of autobiography in relation to my spectatorship of the film. I owe an enormous debt of gratitude to the following individuals: Kate Bartlett, Susan Porter Benson, Ed Cohen, Andy Debicki, Marianne Hirsch, Alice Kaplan, Temma Kaplan, Eleanor Windsor Leach, Lynn Roller, Richard Spear, Leo Spitzer, and Alex Zwirdling. My sister Janette Hudson also read the chapter, listened to the seminar discussion, and later helped me frame the autobiography in a larger family context. To her I also wish to express my thanks.

At Dartmouth College in the spring of 1994, I had the pleasure of presenting chapter 5 to the faculty of the Department of History. I want to thank especially Dale Eickelman for being a generous discussant of my work at the seminar, as well as Leo Spitzer and Gene Garthwaite for organizing the visit. I benefited greatly from the comments of all the participants and thank them for their encouragement.

William Lancaster read and commented on chapter 1 and gave me a very good historical perspective on the Jordanian situation. He may still not agree with my emphasis, but I did consider carefully his comments and thank him for them.

Among my colleagues at the University of California, Santa Cruz, I wish to thank Triloki Pandey, who read the entire manuscript and made copious suggestions for revisions. Richard Randolph also offered valuable comments on chapter 1 having to do with political pressures on King Hussein during the late 1950s. Lisa Rofel's critique of chapter 5 led to major rewriting, and for her suggestions I am most grateful.

Mary Murrell, editor at Princeton University Press, gave me the initial idea to turn what were lectures and notes into a book-length manuscript, but it was Lynne Withey of the University of California Press who ultimately saw the project through to completion. I thank them both. The anonymous readers of this manuscript for both the presses of the University of California and Princeton University were very helpful in their criticisms and suggestions for revisions. One of the early readers in particular provided valuable insights. As a result of their interventions, I considerably rewrote, and I hope thereby strengthened, the original manuscript.

For permission to cite from their brilliant parody of the movie, I wish to thank *MAD Magazine*. I am also grateful to the Department of Special Collections, UCLA Library, for giving me permission to cite from Joel Gardner's oral history of Michael Wilson, which came out of the UCLA Oral History Program. My special thanks go to Becca Wilson and Rosanna Wilson-Farrow for allowing me to quote from documents in the Michael Wilson Papers, which are housed in the Arts Collection, Research Library, UCLA. In particular, two long telephone conversations with Becca Wilson helped me enormously to put in perspective the problems that Hollywood writers like her father faced during the "Communist witch-hunts" of the 1950s. She shared with me little-known bits of information about her father that did not make their way into this book for the reason that I felt they were not directly related to my analysis of the film. From her, too, I saw more clearly what is at stake for her family in getting acknowledgment of her father's work on the screenplay. I hope I have lived up to her request to treat the materials in her father's papers with care and sensitivity. If my analysis might in the end differ from hers (which I cannot know), I trust it has in no way diminished the creativity or importance of her father's contribution to the making of the film.

For technical assistance on this project I am grateful to Kevin Hoshiko and Jon Kersey of the Media Lab, Social Sciences Division, University of California, Santa Cruz, and to Candice Gleim, Director of Faculty Computing Services, New School for Social Research.

Finally, Donald Scott has watched this movie with me more times than I think he would have wished, but he was too good-natured to protest. Besides being a sympathetic critic, he was also an unflagging supporter of this project. I thank him for his time, intellectual interest, and good company. The subtitle was also his idea.

The Teatro del Lago and After

The Teatro del Lago was a "movie palace" dating from the golden era of Hollywood.[1] Though not as expansive or ornate as many, with its heyday already long past by the time my friends and I frequented it as teenagers in the late 1950s and 1960s, it nonetheless possessed an impressive, if tarnished, splendor. The lot on which it stood was sandwiched between two suburbs on Chicago's North Shore, known locally as "No Man's Land," an appropriate name for a location in which celluloid dreams were shown. The theater has long since been razed, of course, and its place, inevitably, taken by an upscale shopping mall echoing its predecessor in name and style, if not in whimsy. Whenever I go back to the North Shore and drive past the lot, I still refer to it as "No Man's Land," though nobody except the old-timers remember it, and remember even less that a theater once stood there. I believe, though I am not absolutely certain, that it was in the Teatro del Lago in 1963 that I saw the film *Lawrence of Arabia* (1962) for the first time.

My reaction to the film was apparently enthusiastic in spite of its Wagnerian length. According to my mother, I couldn't stop talking about it for weeks at the dinner table, especially Peter O'Toole's performance. I couldn't persuade her to see it, however. The harder I tried to make the story clear to her, the more I realized that a simple retelling was quite beside the point for capturing the movie experience. Besides, she said, she didn't have the time. Who wanted to see a movie about a lot of sand and sun anyway? And who cares about the British?

When in December of 1989 the reconstructed version was showing in one of the Chicago theaters with a large screen, I reminded my mother of our conversation of more than twenty-five years ago. What excuse did she have not to see it, I asked, now that her children were grown up and her husband retired? She agreed, and we made the trek on an icy, blustery day; first by car to the suburban El station, then on the El to Chicago's Loop, and finally trudging several blocks to the theater. By this time I was starting to get nervous. Would she be bored? Would she get angry at the effort expended, the time wasted? As it turned out, I needn't have worried. Already by the intermission she was hooked. "God," she exclaimed, "it's nice to be reminded of how gorgeous O'Toole and Sharif were." When we left the theater, I was the one who was complaining. "We should have our heads examined, braving this god-awful weather to see a movie made over twenty years ago," I grumbled as I slapped my mittened hands together to get the blood circulating. I said this partly in sympathy for my mother, who was not in good health at the time and even in some pain. She would have none of my pity, however, whether directed at her or myself. She stopped and straightened. "Steven, have you forgotten what Lawrence said?" I gave her a blank look. " 'The trick is . . . not minding that it hurts.' " With that salvo, she pulled her muffler around her face as though it were her burnoose and walked resolutely into the wind, across her own wintry Nefud.

For weeks afterward, an image occasionally popped into mind. It was the Teatro del Lago with its white plastered walls, red-tiled roof, black wrought-iron grills, ornate gilt and brass railings, and wooden shutters. The image then became more complex. I saw a boy inside the theater who looked a little like I imagine myself to have looked at the age of thirteen, with a round face and red hair in a crew cut, sitting quietly in his seat. Dim reflections of light flickered on his face. I would attempt to shift the angle of vision in the daydream, to see the movie as the boy saw it. Why, for instance, did it fascinate him that Lawrence dressed in native garb? Why did he find the relationship between his two servant boys charming and then the friendship developing between Lawrence and Ali intriguing? Why, ultimately, was he simultaneously drawn to and repelled by the main character? What emotionally or psychologically might the movie have meant to him as a thirteen-year-old that it should have returned to him through the years like a lingering ghost? I have even wondered to what extent the film he saw in the Teatro del Lago inspired him to go to the Middle East.

The film critic Janet Maslin has written:

First love between a person and a film can be as intoxicating as first love between two people. It can mean just as much crazy behavior, just as many
sleepless nights. As a young adolescent, I became so desperately obsessed
with a certain film that I saw it over and over, spent years studying the life of
its hero, regarding him as a kind of role model and even dragged my family
on a long, dusty pilgrimage to a place where he had lived. If one measure of
a film's greatness is its power to affect the lives of those who see it, then
"Lawrence of Arabia" must be the best film I know.[2]

One woman, explaining how she felt when she saw *Lawrence of Arabia*
for the first time at the age of eleven, expressed similar sentiments. "It
was like having a crush on someone," she explained to me. "I drew pictures of Peter O'Toole and made little figurines of camels and Arabs out
of clay. It was my secret obsession." Partly, that is what I wish to understand in this book: the power of this film to have touched so deeply many
people's lives.

"I was transfixed," Spielberg recalls a quarter of a century later. "After the
experience of seeing *Lawrence of Arabia*, I never wanted to do anything else
with my life but make films." "I had never seen anything on such a breath-
taking scale that had real-looking people in it," says Scorsese, "people who
seemed as if they could have come out of the world I lived in."[3]

And here is film critic Stephen Farber, one of the most perceptive com-
mentators on David Lean's work:

When I first saw "Lawrence of Arabia" I was 19, and it was one of the films
that suggested to me what movies might attempt and accomplish, the special
power and excitement that made them the great art form of our time. It had
the same effect on many of my friends in college, and I still find in meeting
people who are close to me in age—young people who are not necessarily
film professionals or cineastes but love movies—that "Lawrence of Arabia"
is almost invariably one of the films they remember most vividly. . . .
"Lawrence of Arabia" was one of the few films made during the sixties that
touched the imaginations of a generation.[4]

I would have thought that a generation growing up after mine would
have difficulty identifying with this movie, and yet I have been surprised
by some of the responses I have heard from its viewers. When I once discovered *Lawrence* playing on the monitors of a local video store I frequent, I asked the manager who happened to be waiting on me at the
time why this movie was being shown. She blushed slightly. She confessed that it was her favorite movie, adding jokingly that she "inflicted"

it (because of its length) on her help from time to time. I asked why she liked it, explaining that I was writing a book on the movie and was casually interviewing people about it. "After all," I said, trying to provoke her with one of the standard complaints made by women, "there are no female characters in it." She nodded, observing, "I suppose the situation he was in precluded much contact with women." She became more reflective. "It's the Heart of Darkness theme that I find intriguing." By coincidence, we happened to be watching the scene in which Lawrence's guide Tafas is killed by Sherif Ali. Two other people in their midtwenties who had seen and liked the movie reiterated the Conradian theme, one of them comparing it to *Apocalypse Now* (1979), which he said was "sort of my generation's *Lawrence of Arabia*." Nor has a contemporary generation of filmmakers been left untouched by its influence. Anyone who has seen *The English Patient* (1996) will know what I mean.

While expressing enthusiasm for a film like *Lawrence of Arabia* might be unproblematical to some, it becomes disturbing to others. It is one of those movies that artistically high-minded cineastes hate to love as one of the most pleasurable Hollywood epics ever made and that the same critics might love to hate as a quintessential, orientalist discourse.[5] However, more than one academic has turned out to be a closet fan of *Lawrence of Arabia* and has blushingly confessed, "How I loved it!" after I had divulged my fascination with the movie. It is almost as though one were disabled from taking a complex position, at least in public, toward a work of art that is politically reprehensible on many counts, if one wants to remain loyal to the project of multiculturalism and sensitive to the cultural representation of others.

I have learned that a general problem of subjectivity emerges for the cultural critic who would interest herself or himself in a "repugnant" subject. For example, Tania Modleski found it difficult to explain herself as a feminist when she "liked" Hitchcock's films, knowing full well how they had been excoriated by feminists.[6] A similar risk was faced by Linda Williams, a feminist scholar who honestly admitted "enjoying" certain aspects of pornographic film. As she explains in her book:

> For a woman to admit to any . . . coincidence of scholarly and sexual pleasure undercuts her authority in a way that does not occur with a male scholar. It is not surprising, then, that I should want to protect myself against the perceived contaminations of a "filthy subject"—lest I be condemned along with it. At the same time, however, I feel it is important not to perpetuate the pervasive attitude among feminists that pornography is both the cause and the symptom of all women's problems. For even though I know that the slightest

admission that not every image of every film was absolutely disgusting to me may render my insights worthless to many women, I also know that not to admit some enjoyment is to perpetuate an equally invidious double standard that still insists that the nonsexual woman is the credible, "good" woman. Clearly, it is difficult to strike a proper attitude toward pornography.[7]

As a man who would like to enter into a conversation with scholars working on issues of gender and as an anthropologist who wants to be respected for his ethnographic work in the Middle East, I know that my fascination with a movie that seems to be yet another "buddy picture" ridiculing Arabs puts me in hardly a more enviable position.

The way Modleski expresses the dilemma, it is a matter of one's subjectivity wanting redemption. As a girl, she loved watching Hitchcock's films. Did her identification with them mean that she was herself "masochistic," which is to be placed in the victim position that perpetuates a subordination from which she and other women would wish to escape? Did her continued enjoyment of his films indicate that as an adult she was beyond redemption? What was the way out of the dilemma? Was it a matter of her being able to resist Hitchcock's patriarchal constructions by creating an alternative position from which to view and judge them? Or were the films themselves deeply ambivalent about the patriarchal constructions they were articulating, and was she then as a viewer able to work these contradictions into productive, alternative readings? I cannot imagine that, even as a teenager, I would have enjoyed *Lawrence of Arabia* if it had been as racist or sexist or orientalist as cultural criticisms inspired from many sources might condemn it to be. As a thirteen-year-old, I was in fact acutely conscious of the problem of cultural stereotyping and the damage it could do, having been subjected to it myself as a recent immigrant from Germany to the United States. I think I would have taken grave exception to it in any form that I could have noticed at that age and historical moment in film reception. Of course, that does not mean that "objectifications" of the "Arab" don't exist in the movie, but rather that they are more subtle and ambivalent than critics might presuppose of a product from Hollywood.

As is obvious from the comments of Modleski and Williams, I am not alone in my dissatisfaction with some of the currents of today's ideological criticisms. The problem is this: How does one get to an intellectually adequate criticism of such artistically complex and ideologically loaded works? I suggest that we may, in fact, be entering a new phase, which I will call "dialectical critique." In part this change of critical practice has to do with the way we now view dominant institutions as no longer necessarily monolithic or uniform, and therefore the works they produce as containing contradictions that become more, not less, problematical for hegemonic projects. Another related view of power suggests that the difference between center and margin, between dominant groups and subalterns, is not as stark as may have once been supposed; that, in fact, a subtle and complex collaboration has historically existed between the two. Yet another reformulation of margin and center, one that I will explore in this book, is to consider possibilities within the center of producing works that are critical of the hegemonic project they propose and of those individuals who perpetuate it. We might productively ask a set of questions of such works. What conditions encourage self-criticism, and what conditions stifle it? Is the moment sustainable or fleeting, and why? Works produced in such a moment would be read *dialectically*. One not only would hunt for the ways they construct cultural representations that perpetuate the domination of some over others—an important project that I would not want to block—but also would ferret out the unease of their producers in regard to such representations, an unease that may be a covert or explicit criticism of the center and its domination of the margins.

Although it is rarely called "dialectical" (sometimes a phrase such as "reading against the grain" is more common), one can see this approach emerging in a number of fields of criticism. In this introduction I will consider just two of these—feminist film criticism and postcolonial studies.[8] Let us turn our attention, first, to the way in which the feminist critique of the film spectator has evolved in the last twenty years into what I call here a dialectical critique.

As it was originally formulated, the spectator was not an actual person but a role or a position that the film constructed for its audience. Since the literature from which the concept emerged was primarily a feminist one, it is the issue of gender that the concept initially addressed. Its most influential formulation was given by Laura Mulvey in a now classic article that combined trenchant film criticism with an original application of psychoanalytic theory.[9] She criticized classic Hollywood cinema for presenting narratives and characters that demanded an identification with a male spectator's point of view, regardless of whether the actual viewer were male or female, in accordance with the patriarchal order dominant in the society at large. If one is female under such a regime, one has no choice but to identify with the male's "gaze." More is at stake here than sexist stereotypes in the way men represent women on the screen, however. The critique was meant to go deep into the cinematic apparatus, arguing that the camera is used to photograph women in countless, subtle ways that objectify their bodies as objects of male desire.

Over the years, Mulvey has modified her original formulation some-what,[10] and feminists in the 1980s have begun to doubt the hegemonic power of the patriarchal regime that her model presumes. Without at all wishing to downplay the power of the patriarchy, they have insisted that it may be more complex than originally supposed, in that Hollywood films contain enough internal contradictions to allow for subversions of the conventional male gaze or even constructions of an alternative "female" spectator with which women and some men can identify.[11]

Modleski's book on the films of Alfred Hitchcock, for example, is at heart a critique of the unidirectional way in which an earlier feminist theory has tended to read movies made by patriarchal film directors. She argues, "Feminist criticism has frequently tended to see only one aspect of female spectatorship—the complicity or the resistance; I have argued throughout this book, however, that woman's response is complex and contradictory and requires an understanding of woman's placement on the margins of patriarchal culture—at once inside and outside its codes and structures." [12] At another point she invokes the idea of a "characteristic" female spectator who, as a result of her subordinate positioning within patriarchy, is more than likely to develop a "dialectical" response to cinema (of the sort alluded to in the preceding quotation). Of course, Modleski would include herself within this category. It is understandable, therefore, not only that she would take the critical position she does but that, by the end of her book, she would be describing her project as "the ongoing development of female subjectivity," [13] both her own and that of other women who "like" Hitchcock's films but don't want to think of themselves as masochists. Therefore, to call her reading "dialectical," as I have done, does not depart too much from her own text and stated intentions. In a position somewhat analogous to Modleski is Carol Clover, who found herself enjoying horror movies in spite of the fact that they have a reputation for showing men as sadistic victimizers of women.[14] On closer examination, however, they seemed to offer a far more complex representation of both genders, often reversing conventional roles or blurring their boundaries, and overturning one's expectations of a mastering, voyeuristic male (audience) gaze when it identifies with a female victim.

Let us now turn to postcolonial studies to see whether what I call a dialectical criticism can be identified in it as well. To begin, it is necessary

to summarize Edward Said's critique of orientalism which is many respects the seminal work in this field.[15] According to Said, orientalism is
a structure of knowledge composed of "representations" (or what he
elsewhere also calls "stereotypes"). Some of these representations assert,
for example, that the Orient is a "mysterious" place, "decadent" and
"sensual," or that its peoples live in endemically "violent" societies and
understand only "force" in political dealings, or that its religions are
"fanatical" and their governments hopelessly despotic, incapable of
assuring a dignity of life for their citizens, and so forth. These representations presuppose a distinction between "us" and "them" or "self"
and "other," a distinction so binary and strongly drawn that it carries
with it hostile attitudes toward the non-West. Furthermore, because
these representations are produced by "experts" in the academy or by
"geniuses" in literature, they become authoritative for the reading public and have the power, as Foucault would put it, to constitute an object
not merely of study but of reality itself. The "episteme" of orientalism
has been in place for a very long time—for how long is a matter of considerable controversy, though, even within Said's own writings. It is even
more important to note that relatively little can be done to dislodge it,
in Said's view, because institutions of knowledge tend to operate as
closed systems—that is, as endless cycles of self-referring statements—
allowing for few counterrepresentations that might challenge authoritative knowledge. Significantly, Said charges that these representations
that pass for knowledge are tied to a project of power, and he specifies
what that project is: the ends of Western imperialism to dominate the
(post)colonial world.

Since the publication of *Orientalism* (1978), the examination of the
ways in which Western academic or scientific knowledge and artistic
production perpetuate the construct of the "orient" and are tied to Western colonial projects has continued at a furious pace, resulting in what
is now one of the most flourishing fields of cultural criticism. In the
process of expanding, however, postcolonial studies has also begun
the healthy process of questioning some of its own assumptions and
attempting new directions of criticism. In my judgment, nowhere is
this criticism more innovative and insightful than in the work of Homi
Bhabha[16] and Sara Suleri.[17] Let me review some of their work, and in
the process clarify what I mean by dialectical criticism.

One way of critiquing Said, while remaining sympathetic to his overall project, is to suggest that a text can be read more ambivalently than
he would, and then to ask what difference such a reading would make

for our understanding of representation, subjectivity, and power in the colonial context. Homi Bhabha says of Said's orientalist critique, for example, that "where the originality of this pioneering theory loses its inventiveness, and for me its usefulness, is with Said's reluctance to engage with alterity and ambivalence in the articulation of orientalist discourse." [18] Bhabha illustrates his criticism with an examination of the stereotype,[19] asserting that the stereotype, far from offering a secure point of identification for the colonizer, as Said would have it, is in fact "a complex, ambivalent, contradictory mode of representation, as anxious as it is assertive." [20] The ambivalence that the stereotype provokes in the colonizer consequently subverts the binariness of the "us" versus "them" distinction; that is, the "them" begins to look more and more like the "us" in colonial representation. How can such a resemblance come about? Bhabha's reading of colonial discourse would have it that the representation of the "them" is a "return of the oppressed [this, I gather, is an intended pun, not a typographical error] —those terrifying stereotypes of savagery, cannibalism, lust and anarchy which are the signal points of identification and alienation, scenes of fear and desire." [21] Bhabha urges us to include a "traumatized" colonizing subject in our calculation of the power/knowledge nexus in addition to the traumatized colonized subject that is more usually considered.[22] The reason for this insistence is, I presume, that such a subject, producing such ambivalent representations of the other, would tend to subvert, as much as it would impose, its will to power over the other, thereby rendering the hegemonic project of colonialism unstable.

This insightful and quite productive reading of orientalist texts, and the alterity they construct as inherently ambivalent, owes much to Freud, especially to his formulation of fetishism.[23] Freud's notion of the fetish, as I understand it, is specifically related to castration anxiety, which is projected onto a symbol whose very superabundance of meaning is supposed to conceal the "lack" that the subject fears within himself. The concept had already made its way into film criticism, of course, especially in the work of feminist critics such as Mulvey, who argued that the film spectator would gaze at the female as a fetishized object. What I think interests Bhabha is less Freud's explanation in terms of a universalist oedipal scenario and castration complex than the emotional *structure* of the fetishized sign—- an unconscious tension that it encapsulates between desire and disavowal, affinity and aversion.

With regard to Bhabha's reading of Freud, it is curious, however, that not much attention is paid to his famous essay "The 'Uncanny'" (1919), where we learn that the uncanny has a lot to do with ambivalence as concretized in the "double," among other symbols. This apparent elision of a crucial essay on ambivalence is interesting because the double has relevance to Bhabha's concern with mimicry in colonialist discourse.[24] Bhabha's examples of mimicry are almost all of the kind in which the colonized subject's persona, or the "other," is made to appear like the colonizer's "self"—appear like, but not be the same as, the self, for that is the nature of ambivalence—but I presume that he is at the same time concerned with the ways in which the mimicry would work in the other direction (as in "going native"). In either case, according to Bhabha: "Colonial mimicry is the desire for a reformed, recognizable Other, as *a subject of a difference that is almost the same, but not quite.* Which is to say, that the discourse of mimicry is constructed around an ambivalence. . . . the authority of that mode of colonial discourse that I have called mimicry is therefore stricken by an indeterminacy."[25] My reason for bringing up the connection between Bhabha's analysis of mimicry[26] and Freud's notion of the double as a manifestation of the uncanny is that Freud emphasizes an aspect of ambivalence that Bhabha ignores, an aspect that expands my notion of dialectical criticism. Not only is the double a supremely ambivalent sign in Freud's formulation of the uncanny; it is also what Freud calls the ego's "conscience," and in later essays will refer to as the ego ideal or superego. As he explains, the double "is able to stand over against the rest of the ego, which has the function of observing and criticizing the self and of exercising a censorship within the mind."[27] As an obvious example of mimicry through doubling, consider the character of Sherif Ali in the film *Lawrence of Arabia.* In roughly Part One of the movie, he is an ambivalent, fetishized object of mimicry *for* Lawrence. But as the story unfolds, his function as a double expands (especially so as Lawrence goes native), becoming in the end Lawrence's conscience, as evidenced in several scenes in which he admonishes his friend to avoid bloodshed. Thus I want to do more than point out the ambivalences in the orientalist representation of the other that operate to destabilize the colonial project; I also want to consider those moments in colonial discourse that allow for possibilities of self-criticism on the part of the colonizer and thus would further place in abeyance the colonial project or even subvert it.

A critic who in my estimation would be sympathetic to this approach is Sara Suleri. Like Bhabha, she too is concerned with breaking down the binarisms that have influenced the criticism of orientalist discourse. Regarding the distinction between colonizer and colonized, as well as between margin and center, she remarks that "the story of colonial encounter is in itself a radically decentering narrative that is impelled to realign with violence any static binarism."[28] She concludes that the discourse of Anglo-Indian history and literature "demands to be read against the grain of the rhetoric of binarism that informs, either explicitly or implicitly, contemporary critiques of alterity in colonial discourse."[29] The result of eschewing such a binary discourse, Suleri argues, is to view domination and subordination in less rigid terms as well; the colonizer is not monolithically powerful, nor the colonized correspondingly powerless. She would destabilize the power of the colonizer by suggesting ways of reading terror or horror into his or her colonial texts, a psychic trauma symptomatic of anxiety about dispossession of, or even aversion toward, the imperialist project. "The stories of colonialism—in which heterogeneous cultures are yoked by violence— offer nuances of trauma that cannot be neatly partitioned between colonizer and colonized."[30]

One can get a sense of the difference between Suleri's and Said's conceptions of cultural criticism by examining their analyses of Rudyard Kipling's *Kim* (1901), a story about an orphaned boy of an Irish soldier who grows up in the Indian city of Lahore. Because he is fully conversant, linguistically and culturally, with the city's "native" context, Kim is enlisted by a Colonel Creighton, an ethnographer, to collect intelligence information useful to the British.

Said is a great admirer of the text, though in the end, agreeing (with the American critic Edmund Wilson) that "the conflict between Kim's colonial service and loyalty to his Indian companions is unresolved" but adding (beyond Wilson) that it is unresolved "not because Kipling could not face it, but because for Kipling there was no conflict; one purpose of the novel is in fact to show the absence of conflict once Kim is cured of his doubts."[31] For Suleri, both Wilson's and Said's readings "seem unwilling to address" an irony in Kipling's story. Like Said, she remarks upon Kim's ostensible ability to "pass for a native," and not only that, but to transform himself into many *different* guises of "native" identity. For Said, this virtuoso cultural impersonation, this linguistic ventriloquism, is a delirious fantasy, a blatant expression of imperial control that seems to be saying "Isn't it possible in India to do everything? be anything? go anywhere with impunity?"[32] For Suleri, on the other hand, Kim's mobility is only apparent because, far from being able to choose, as Wilson suggests (and Said concurs), whether to play the Great Game, Kim's tragedy is that "[he] is the Game, and finally is unable to separate it from the parameters of his own history."[33] What she stresses, then, is the vicariousness rather than the supposed empowerment of Kim's ambiguous cultural positioning. Colonial messages for which Kim is a relayer are not transparently read; rather, they are fraught with possibilities of misunderstanding, which render the enterprise of intelligence gathering precarious and hence Kim's footing in the Great Game insecure. In the end does Kim have any choice but to join the colonial regime and betray his Indian friends? In other words, what appears to be a "choice" may be nothing more than coercion in disguise. For Suleri "The marvelous boy [is] an analogy for colonial casualty"[34] who has been thoroughly used (and one might say abused) by the colonial system.

Suleri's strategy of reading might be seen as the antithesis of Said's, which is to dispute rather than to grant to the colonizer his or her authority and unquestioned confidence in the Great Game. The "heart of darkness" in orientalist narratives, the panic or horror that they repress, confirms the sense of powerlessness of their producers. Imperialism is an inherently unstable project, which, if it believes in its absolute power, is *delusional* in that belief and therefore anxiously concealing its own doubts. It is far more enabling, in my view, to explore the possibilities of such ironic and ultimately destabilizing or decentering readings of the colonial tradition, much in the spirit of Suleri, than to foreclose them. Indeed, I think this is one of the most promising directions in which the field of postcolonial criticism can proceed.

If Kipling's apprehension about empire is largely intuitive or unconscious, it is far more self-conscious, far more overtly critical, in the case of Edmund Burke's indictment of the East India Company and its handling of affairs, as Suleri demonstrates in her splendid chapters on Burke's parliamentary rhetoric.[35] However, though specific colonialist practices might have been called into question, the notion of empire tout court was not. But there are always limits to criticism. The interesting question, it seems to me, is what those limits might be and the historical conditions that set them. Admittedly, that is too large a question to attempt to answer here. Less ambitiously, I would simply observe that the reading of colonial texts has advanced considerably since Said's pioneering work, and I would put forward the term "dialectical criticism" as a way to capture that kind of reading. That is, colonial texts not only represent the Other in the most disturbingly orientalist ways imaginable that Said was one of the first to criticize, but they may at the same time counteract those representations, either by the ambivalences (read also horror or terror) they betray or, perhaps more rarely, by consciously engaging in a criticism of colonial practices and regimes.

Something like this kind of criticism of Said's project has been made before, though in entirely different terms, by Marxists. Sadeq al-'Azm[36] and Aijaz Ahmad,[37] for instance, have noted that Said is virtually silent about the criticisms against colonialism that were voiced in the West almost from the beginning of the period of European expansion and economic exploitation. They claim that Marxist literature was particularly vociferous in such attacks. No doubt in response to such criticisms, Said attempted in his most recent book, *Culture and Imperialism* (1993), to include intellectual currents and political movements in European societies that countered imperialism during the nineteenth and twentieth centuries—only to dismiss them as small-scale, sporadic, and in the long run ineffectual. If his assessment is valid, it raises the more general question of the effectiveness of all such criticism, including Said's; or to put it differently, we have to examine the conditions under which political criticism becomes not only possible but also potent.

In an effort to give these emergent critical practices more theoretical grounding, I argue that we might profit—though not without important reservations—from the Frankfurt school's formulation of dialectical criticism. This is not the place in which to describe the history of this important group of German scholars (most notably, Max Horkheimer, Theodor Adorno, Walter Benjamin, Erich Fromm, and Herbert Marcuse) who achieved prominence in the days of the Weimar Republic and many of whom came to the United States in the Nazi period.[38] Nor is it necessary to explain the important differences between them regarding their specific concerns and approaches. Of the individuals identified with the school, probably Adorno and Benjamin are most relevant to the concerns in this book; the former because of his influential philosophical statement on (negative) dialectics,[39] the latter because of his formulation of commodity fetishism and the fact that he took works of popular culture extremely seriously.[40]

The Frankfurt school derived its idea of dialectical criticism from Marx, though perhaps the Marx who was most heavily influenced by Hegel. According to Marx, any cultural phenomenon such as a work of art not only expresses an ideologically dominant position in society but also reflects something of the contradictions latent in the material conditions at the moment of its production. Thus, every work or cultural phenomenon must be "read" or "interpreted" dialectically, as contain-

ing at the same time a representation of reality that is historically dominant and a representation or representations that contradict it, as though
anticipating a (not necessarily bright) future that will undermine the
hegemonic status quo. Adorno tended to favor an "immanent" dialectical critique: that is, he would push the presuppositions of a particular
system to their limits until their dialectical opposite would emerge.

Unfortunately, when it came to analyzing the products of what Horkheimer and Adorno called the "culture industry," they tended to be quite
*un*dialectical, seeing them as blindly reinforcing the status quo; in U.S.
mass culture, for example, as the totalitarian equivalents of the European fascist state. The beginning of their essay "The Culture Industry:
Enlightenment as Mass Deception" sets the pessimistic tone: "Films, radio and magazines make up a system which is uniform as a whole and
in every part. Even the aesthetic activities of political opposites are one
in their enthusiastic obedience to the rhythm of the iron system." [41]
Gone is the notion of internal contradiction. Complete is the hegemony
of the dominant ideological position. Even when the culture industry
comes up with novel forms, Horkheimer and Adorno argue that this
newness is only apparent, leading to reabsorption into traditional forms.
With regard to film specifically, they were most cynical. Thus, they asserted that in the movies "sustained thought is out of the question if the
spectator is not to miss the relentless rush of facts . . . no scope is left for
the imagination." [42] Such criticisms have to be taken seriously, of course,
and I will entertain them in chapter 3, where I discuss problems of reflexivity in film spectatorship, but in the end the criticisms of Horkheimer
and Adorno on the culture industry seem too one-sided. Perhaps Adorno
was overcommitted to the avant-garde as a critical-political force in society: compare, for example, his analyses of Schoenberg and the possibilities unleashed by atonal music with his far more disparaging account
of "decadent" jazz. [43]

Benjamin's writings on popular culture—though fragmentary and
elusive—offer a corrective to this one-sidedness. His formulation, at
least from my point of view, has the added advantage of synthesizing
psychoanalytical frameworks with a materialist Marxist theory of cultural production. The mass production of art, according to Benjamin,
may on the one hand destroy a work's "aura" (its distinction or value
arising from a particular placement in its originary context), [44] but in the
realms of photography and film it may also enhance what he called the
"optical unconscious." [45] Meanings might become associated with a
photographic or filmic image that could startle, charm, and disturb. As

a result, products of the culture industry might quicken rather than, as Horkheimer and Adorno predicted, deaden the imagination.

As long as the preceding qualifications are kept in mind, especially in regard to the remarks of Horkheimer and Adorno on the culture industry, I think the Frankfurt school's notion of dialectical criticism can be usefully employed in the analysis of films like *Lawrence of Arabia*. The challenge lies in understanding in what specific ways a work may be internally "contradictory." Here psychological phenomena can be of the utmost importance. For example, I have argued that the idea of ambivalence developed by Freud and lately recouped for postcolonial criticism by Homi Bhabha can be seen as a dialectic of the unconscious (that is, a *negation* of a powerful psychological identification). Alongside psychological phenomena such as ambivalence, I would put poetic figures such as irony, which, according to literary critic Kenneth Burke,[46] is another way of understanding dialectic. And finally, there is the form of counterargument or logical thought—what philosophers since Plato have mostly meant by dialectic—which I think also enters into a film such as *Lawrence of Arabia*. In other words, while works of the culture industry construct representations of reality that accord with the interests of a certain hegemonic position (however defined economically, socially, and so forth)—the contours of which should be exposed and traced by the critic—they also contain the dialectical negations of those representations, either implicitly and unconsciously or explicitly and consciously, whether in the form of irony or of logical syllogism, which the analyst is equally obliged to unearth.

Some people will disagree with this two-way critical practice. For them it will seem sufficient for criticism to expose the ways in which a work reaffirms a dominant ideology. It is at that point, I will argue, that earlier kinds of feminist film criticism as well as the Saidean formulation of orientalism and its critique have stopped. The result of such unidirectional criticism is to give the impression, ironically, that the work of art is impervious to criticism and change because of its monolithic quality. Why, in fact, bother to criticize it at all? But there is something deeper at stake in the dialectical exercise than exposing the weak points in the work of art or the stresses at which it is most vulnerable to critical pressure. It is also important to identify those aspects of the work—if any exist at all—where it seems to be engaged in a criticism of its *own* hegemonic project. To some, again, this may be rendering to Caesar more than he deserves, on the assumption that any work coming from the center is only "falsely" self-critical. The corollary of this view is that the only "genuine" or "authentic" criticism is the one issuing from groups that are the most oppressed or marginalized in the system. The conclusion might be, for example, that it is the workers more than the bourgeoisie who are capable of the most sustained and penetrating criticism of the evils of capitalism—the exception of at least Engels notwithstanding. The project of taking seriously the self-criticism contained in works produced by hegemonic institutions such as Hollywood should not be interpreted as uncritical approval of those works, and even less so as an effort to redeem those institutions; rather, it is to identify what, if any, critical awareness of the hegemonic project and its consequences exists in those works, making it the basis of positive transformation.

Having discussed one notion of dialectical criticism in the Frankfurt school—a critique immanent in the work of art containing its own contradictions—it is time now to consider another one connected to it, which is more usually understood as "materialist" in a narrow sense. It has to do with the relationship of the work of art to its economic contexts and technological production, questions that are particularly relevant to a Hollywood film like *Lawrence of Arabia*.

Lawrence of Arabia was an international and independently produced film of the sort that emerged in the 1950s after the studio system had collapsed and Hollywood was attempting to compete with television through large-scale productions involving stars from different countries. International film also commodified images of otherness, images that had to be more, not less, "authentic" as audiences in the United States and Europe became more knowledgeable and sophisticated in the postwar period through business travel and tourism. These and other themes are explored in chapter 1. For example, in the cinema of David Lean from the early fifties until his final uncompleted project, there was a continuous preoccupation with international themes such as tourism, war, travel, and colonialism, and this after a period of complete immersion in the British film industry as well as in British cultural subjects. As Hollywood realized that its films had to sell in international markets if it was to recoup its huge investments, it was also willing to accede to the demands of authenticity made by the countries into whose midst it was permitted to shoot its films. Even though these countries and their audiences were hardly on an equal footing with Hollywood, they were not without influence in shaping more complex and sympathetic images of their peoples and cultures. One could go further and claim that foreign countries sometimes saw it as within their political interests to collude in such projects of cultural representation. In the case of Jordan, for example, I argue that the government permitted the film company to shoot inside its borders not because of a generous financial settlement accorded to it by Horizon Pictures, which was probably small in any case and hardly compensated for the considerable heat it had to take from the state's opponents, but because it appreciated the power of popular culture to carry political messages at a time when the kingdom was hard-pressed by Egyptian and other Arab propaganda. And the message the film was supposed to carry, of course, was the story of Hashemite nationalism. Even the bedouin extras hoped, vainly as it turned out, to be able to control the way history was represented by participating in the battle scenes so often described by their grandfathers who fought alongside Lawrence in the Arabian desert.

Another way in which Hollywood competed with television was with the wide screen, *Lawrence of Arabia* being one of the most complex films ever made in this medium, a subject to which I turn in chapter 2. Lean's project of filming the desert "realistically" did not simply emerge at one particular juncture in the history of the industry, however; it was continuous with practices of the mechanical reproduction of reality going as far back as the beginnings of photography in the nineteenth century and leading up to today's experiments in IMAX screens and virtual reality. Horkheimer and Adorno had remarked of the culture industry, "The more intensely and flawlessly [the filmmaker's] techniques duplicate empirical objects, the easier it is today for the illusion to prevail that the outside world is the straightforward continuation of that presented on the screen." [47] To help us understand Lean's realist project on the wide screen, I employ a notion of embodiment that comes out of the phenomenological film theory of Vivian Sobchack. Such realist projects, however, are sometimes viewed by critics such as Colin MacCabe as totalistic and closed because it is presumed that they do not allow for contradictions or multiple spectator positions. I argue, to the contrary, that on the wide screen, even when the frame was fastidiously composed by a formalistic director like Lean, it was nonetheless open-ended. The eye had to rove, the head rotate, if the details were to be encompassed on such a large canvas, and even then they were often missed, thus increasing the possibilities not only for ambiguity but also for the oneiric and surreal. To help make the latter point, I have found useful Benjamin's notion of the "optical unconscious" as applied to a famous scene in the movie, the one in which Omar Sharif makes his appearance in a mirage shot by a special lens Lean had commissioned for the movie. In short, a certain kind of mechanical reproduction of reality could lead to a more active spectator and to a less totalistic visual control.

If screen images are apprehended through technological mediations, they must be interpreted through narrative structures and genre conventions, which will be explored in chapter 3. Without in the least wishing to contest Wilson's claims about his contribution to the screenplay, I nevertheless take exception with his criticisms of the movie as being either weak or confused in its politics because of the way it psychologized the main character. Wilson provided the movie with its basic narrative structure, but Lean was correct to feel that the result was too much like a nonstop action film, leaving little or no room for an audience to step back from the character and his epic situation in order to interpret both critically. Though Bolt is often credited with the script's witty dialogue and theatricality, he was far more important in providing a Brechtian critical distance, primarily through the motif of the performance-within-the-performance, as well as in creating subtle political significations through a dense parallelism of images. It was also because of Bolt, in collaboration with the film's star and the way he was photographed by Lean, that Lawrence was portrayed as a megalomaniacal "fascist" with sadomasochistic tendencies, thus linking deep-seated psychological disorders with political ambitions of empire. These psychological explorations questioned the will to power underlying the actions of Lawrence and the British in the Middle East, thereby strengthening the critical edge of the film. This criticism was also served by turning this grandest of all epics into an anti-epic, one of the first movies to do so in this second period of epic filmmaking.

While I was investigating the production history of this film, it became apparent to me that both multiple and critical spectator positions were encouraged by the filmmakers and also made possible by the technological and narratological mediations of wide-screen images. As Spiegel said in an interview, the filmmakers had wanted to make audiences coauthors of the film's interpretation. It is just as clear, however, that cuts by the distributors, particularly when the film was adapted for television, short-circuited that aim. Not until the reconstructed version came along in 1989 could these intentions be fully realized. Taking up the filmmakers' invitation to construct critical readings of Lawrence and his situation, I have entertained three different readings of the film in the last three chapters of this book.

Before I describe these chapters, however, some theoretical and methodological comments are in order. Although film theory at first assumed that the spectator was constructed by the filmic text, it soon became apparent that the process was more complicated, entailing an interaction between what was constructed by the film on the one hand and the audience on the other.[48] Alongside the notion of the spectator in the text, then, there has to be the idea of the spectator in the audience. I admit that my exercises in constructing differently positioned spectators are highly speculative. How Miriam Hansen[49] tries to understand the historical emergence of different kinds of spectatorship in the era of the American silent film has become a model for my own research into the history of the spectatorship of *Lawrence of Arabia*. I draw from letters about the film to various newspapers, critical reviews, parodies, advertisement and publicity, and a host of other sources to speculate about the possibilities of spectatorship. Yet another lead is provided by Elizabeth Traube,[50] who carefully examines changing patterns of work and family structure that have repositioned men and women since the 1960s and have created new expectations that may affect their spectatorship of various films of the 1980s. Analogously, I have tried to determine the historical social contexts in which *Lawrence of Arabia* emerged (and then reemerged in the late 1980s), especially political contexts in Britain and the United States but also in parts of the Arab world that were likely to have affected its reception.

I find it useful to distinguish between *reception* and *reading*. Reception is more closely connected to the experience of viewing a film in situ, with the immediate reactions that such an experience entails, whereas reading is more removed or distanced from the ongoingness of the event and proceeds retrospectively, perhaps in private contemplation of the film or in conversation with others about it. Of course, in practice the two are circularly implicated, especially when spectators go to see the film more than once. While viewing a film, one's reception of particular scenes is always influenced by readings one has already formed; in turn, a reading is always based on the details of reception and may be altered by them.

To get at spectator receptions, there has been no lack of audience research studies (surveys, questionnaires, and on-the-spot interviews), but to what extent they tell us anything of interest is a vexed question. Fieldwork can be conducted on audiences, whether in movie houses or private homes, to note viewing habits and reactions. Both techniques offer some clues regarding what audiences might or might not notice about a film. To a limited extent I, too, have depended on such ethnographic techniques as a way into the problem of determining spectator receptions. A reading is another matter, however, and is not a straightforward empirical issue in any sense. It is largely a construction by a film analyst of the way in which a film *might* be apprehended from a particular spectator position. The most one can claim is that the construction is plausible, given what one knows about specific audience reactions, what spectators have said in interviews about the film, what the historical practices of film viewing might be at any given period, and so forth.

The last three chapters of this book pick up the theme announced earlier—grasping the dialectical nature of the work of art produced by the culture industry. I will construct three dialectical readings of the film *Lawrence of Arabia,* trying to situate them within different historical periods of reception, ranging from the early 1960s until the present. Other readings are of course possible, but the ones I have chosen are far from arbitrary.

Throughout the book I have used snippets of my own life and career to help illuminate the film from a particular angle—I talk about what it was like to travel in the 1950s, for example, in order to show why this would become an important theme in the international film of the period, or I describe the way light in the desert can play tricks with photography as I remember from my days of fieldwork in Yemen—but this autobiographical approach has been nowhere more prominent than in the three readings I give in the second half of the book. I try to reconstruct how I might have viewed and understood this film as a child transported from Germany to the United States, and then again as an adult after I had made certain choices in life which it is not far-fetched to suppose this film influenced. In short, two historical moments of exhibition and viewing are privileged: the early 1960s, the date of the film's initial release, and the late 1980s, when the reconstructed version was shown in Great Britain and the United States.

In chapter 4 I read *Lawrence of Arabia* as an allegory about dilemmas of cross-cultural encounters, both while I was growing up and then in my career as an anthropologist working in the Middle East. I discuss many themes in the film that are part and parcel of my memories of childhood and my experiences as an anthropologist: the alienated self that is drawn to travel and the "other"; the complex process of entering into another culture through tourism, war, or migration; the so-called pitfalls of going native; the thorny question of cultural difference and its representation; reflexivity and introspection in life and ethnography; the difficulty, if not impossibility, of going home again; and so forth. There are very few films that take the anthropologist as the central figure of the narrative: most of these are either archaeologists or physical anthropologists; much more rarely is the protagonist a cultural anthropologist. Viewing Lawrence as one allows us to interpret the movie as a profound moral tale about the practices in which people of my profession are engaged.

The fact that this film is deeply involved in a project of representing the Other brings to mind the question not only of anthropology but also of orientalism in general, the subject of chapter 5. To be sure, this film is deeply orientalist, particularly in the way it reduces Arab to "tribesmen" (an old metonymic strategy in orientalist literature) and then infuriatingly attributes the failures of Arab nationalism to the supposedly never-ending feud of tribal politics. But the film is at the same time engaged in a critique of colonialism, and in such a way as to include U.S. colonial adventurism of the 1960s. It is this critique, combined with its depiction of the folly and sadism of warfare, that made *Lawrence of Arabia* powerful to watch during the Gulf War, when movie theaters were just ending their exhibition of the restored 1989 version. At that time, the media were constructing General Schwarzkopf as another "Lawrence of Arabia," and audiences were thus already primed to interpret the movie in light of the Gulf War. For example, during that war there were many complaints that our images were being controlled by the press, which in turn was being controlled by the state. In light of this criticism, the second half of the movie is particularly poignant when it reminds us that the Lawrence legend was created by a newspaper man hired by the U.S. government to portray World War I in its more "romantic" aspects and thus draw the nation toward war. The movie even points out indirectly how it is implicated in the very mythmaking process it critiques, and by implication asks the audience to do the same with all media.

The war hero and his questionable status lead into a final reading of the movie in chapter 6 that has to do with masculinity and sexuality. O'Toole's performance is crucial for understanding the treatment of these themes. There is at least one woman in his portrayal, not to mention two or more kinds of men. I explain how, as a teenager, I could have grasped and even appreciated this ambiguity. The complexity of gender in this film is due in part to the cultural climate of the late fifties and early sixties, in which dominant modes of masculinity were being questioned through, for example, the role of the "angry young man," as well as marginal types such as lower-class toughs and homosexuals portrayed by film stars Marlon Brando, James Dean, and Montgomery Clift, who had their own ambiguous off-screen sexual personae. But it was not only men who could identify with Lawrence. The early sixties was a period in which well-educated, middle-class women were beginning to enter the workforce at higher structural levels of the economic and educational systems. I argue that O'Toole's androgynous performance, combined with his sensitive and introspective characterization, allowed an identification with him *as* a woman. This is, of course, not the only kind of identification it allowed, for clearly he was also sexually attractive, but it was an identification that made the film more interesting. As for Lawrence's sexuality, or presumed sexuality, the filmmakers tried to explore it within the strictures of U.S. censorship, the hysteria in both Britain and the United States that led to the prosecution of homosexuals, and, of course, the producer's desire that this movie be a hit at the box office. The movie is powerful precisely in the way it talks about homosexuality obliquely and ambiguously. Because desire is repressed in the character, his forbidden sexuality is everywhere intimated and rendered visible. By the time the reconstructed version was released, the theme was overtly commodified in publicity posters deliberately intended to capture a gay audience.

Let me conclude this introduction with a word on why I think it is useful to adopt different spectator positions and to read the film dialectically from them. While I obviously have found Modleski's insight into dialectical criticism valuable to my own study, I disagree with her assumption that social groups, such as women, that have been historically oppressed "characteristically" take a contradictory (what I call "dialectical") stance as film spectators *because* of their position as subordinates in the patriarchy. Apart from the fact that this assumption has been proven wrong in specific historical instances, it also forecloses the possibility of dialectical reading by persons like myself, male and privileged, who have no reason to think of ourselves as victims or oppressed individuals even if we do identify ourselves with specific marginalized groups. The point to be emphasized, rather, is that dialectical reading is a critical practice that people at the center can adopt as readily as those at the margins, and that it is crucial for all of us, no matter what our subject positions might be, to insist on that fact and to foster its practice, if change in the system is to come from the top of the power hierarchy as well as from the bottom. The sorts of difficulties that might arise in the classroom when trying to teach this kind of reading are explored in the epilogue.

CHAPTER I

"Travelling Circus"

The Transnational in Film
Production of the 1950s

I always call it [a movie production] a circus. It *is* like
a travelling circus, the *last* of the travelling circuses.
David Lean, interview with Melvyn Bragg

International travel was close to the experience of many Americans in
the 1950s, when U.S. economic and political ascendancy in the world
had been assured after World War II. Though my childhood (born in Europe, raised there until I was ten, and thereafter living in the United
States) was hardly representative, it was not exceptional either. My father worked for a large international U.S. corporation, his assignment
after the war having been to go to a Germany-in-ruins to help reconstruct that branch of the firm. My mother, my sisters, and I spent sum-
mers on the North Sea or the storm-tossed coast of southern Ireland or
the more halcyon wine country of Switzerland, while my father toiled
away at his desk back at the office in the decidedly unscenic industrial
heartland of what was then West Germany. When it was his turn to travel
abroad, on business, not pleasure, we would receive postcards of his sojourns to Central America, Asia, and the Pacific, and I would spend what
seemed like hours staring at exotic images and luridly colored stamps.
He brought back gifts — a boomerang for me, a grass skirt for one sister,
a necklace of glass beads for the other — that were a link in our imagination to a world of "other," far-flung peoples. The ritual of "home" leave,
which we performed every three years, was supposed to reinvigorate our
connections with the United States, my father's homeland and my mother's adopted country. After a stomach-churning ocean voyage on one of
the great passenger liners that are now a nostalgic symbol of that bygone

era, we would land in New York, stuff our belongings in a train or a Ford station wagon, and make our dusty odyssey across a suffocatingly hot continent to visit my grandmother as well as other relatives and friends. My older sister made a tray as a memento of one "summer of 1955," consisting of a road map of the Southwest under a plate of glass with a picture frame around it. Black-and-white Polaroid snapshots are glued next to the names of popular tourist spots; they show various family members, looking a little tired and bedraggled, but nevertheless managing a brave smile before the camera, with a scenic backdrop behind them. In Germany that tray was a source of pleasant reverie and remembrance of a country that existed, for me, largely as a figment of the imagination. I have it still, in a kitchen that looks out to the Hudson River and the piers at which the ocean liner must have docked that carried us from Germany long ago, now a country I inhabit in memory.

It was in Germany that my family saw *Around the World in Eighty Days* (1956), a film that had a powerful impact on me as a child. That film and the experience of seeing it outside the United States are emblematic of everything I will talk about in this chapter: the international dimensions of film production and distribution. To see the film, we had to take a trip to the nearest big city, Düsseldorf, which had movie houses large enough to accommodate CinemaScope exhibition. I have a distinct memory, probably false, of sitting in the balcony directly behind a brass railing, which I clutched during the most suspenseful scenes, my knuckles turning positively white when Shirley MacLaine, an unlikely Hindi "princess," was about to be consigned to the flames of sati but was saved at the last minute by the colonial Phinneus Fogg, a role David Niven seemed born to play. Besides Niven and MacLaine, the picture also starred Cantinflas, a popular Chaplinesque comic actor of the Mexican film industry. That lurid scene became a recurrent childhood nightmare, but it was the sequences that took place in the American West that held me most in thrall; not surprisingly, given what I have said of our travels to the United States. Represented in the movie, at any rate, was nothing less than the *world*, a fantastic conceit to be sure, but not at all inappropriate for that era of global travel and business that my family, for one, experienced. I remember, too, though also more indistinctly, of being told that this was an "international" film, in a tone that was meant to impress me. In the words of one of the industry spokesmen of the times, "This is a picture . . . produced by an American company; but the labor that produces it is foreign, with the frequent exception of the director and two or three leading actors, and the film is shot in a foreign country." [1]

Curiously, film studies has neglected the international (or, as it would be called today, transnational) dimensions of filmmaking. Nor has transnational studies done much in the way of film research.[2] While there has been some research on the international side of Hollywood film financing and distribution, the more usual approach has been to study cinema in terms of national traditions. We have many excellent studies, for example, of the British "working-class" film, the American "western," the French "new wave" cinema, Italian "realism," and so forth. I argue, on the other hand, that particularly for the period that concerns us in this book, the 1950s, there is something to be said for examining film as an international commodity. The claim could be made that this approach is even more necessary for films produced after 1960, but that is beyond the scope of this book. For now, it suffices to show that there were compelling reasons in the decade after the war, mainly economic ones, that stimulated the production, marketing, and distribution of the self-consciously international film.

Given the global pretensions of a film industry such as Hollywood, it is reasonable to assume that its representations of the world were hegemonic. I will suggest, however, a more subtle view of the hegemony of American film than one that claims that its images were created without much concern for international reception, because the latter is supposedly automatically guaranteed by the brute power of Hollywood to impose itself on foreign distributors. Not only were foreign countries able powerfully to intervene in such productions, one has to take seriously the possibility that films produced by hegemonic industries were willing and able *themselves* to transform critically their representations of the world, especially if there were powerful economic incentives to do so. This notion is a result, again, of looking at film dialectically, a point that will be stressed throughout this book. To put it differently, one has to hold open the possibility of criticism coming from the center or the hegemonic, leading to transformed, if never entirely unproblematical, cultural representations. What are the conditions that make such self-criticism possible?

To put the argument in a nutshell, in the immediate postwar period Hollywood had to rely increasingly on the exhibition of its products abroad to make up for lost revenue in its competition with television at home, and that meant showing its films not just in European cities but also in Tokyo, Manila, Cairo, Johannesburg, Istanbul, Buenos Aires, Mexico City, and many other metropolitan centers of the so-called Third World. But why the international film? Why not export films on the usual American subjects, made by American artists and technicians? Making a film abroad could save money, although one cannot generalize this claim, as we shall see in a moment. The more compelling reason for shooting in foreign locations was to offer diverse audiences a taste of places and peoples that television at that time was not likely to supply. This commodification served two distinct audiences at once. The first was an American one, which, like my family, was traveling and seeing more of the world and was expecting a higher degree of ethnographic realism and authenticity than Hollywood had bothered to deliver in the past, while at the same time wallowing in the exoticism of the same images. The second, no less important, one was non-American, which often refused on "anti-imperialist" grounds the naive slice of an unproblematical America and expected more sophistication and sympathy as well when their countries and cultures were the object of the camera's gaze. The resulting images of the Other in Hollywood film were thus complex and contradictory, more ethnographically accurate or realistic, even at times quite sympathetic, while also exotic and paternalistic.

Changes in the structure of the Hollywood film industry in the postwar period will concern us in the first part of this chapter, in order to show the forces at work promoting international practices of filmmaking. Intertwined with the international film is the rise of independent film production, and I will illustrate the connection and its salience in this period through the career of Lawrence of Arabia's producer, Sam Spiegel. It would be a mistake, however, to concentrate solely on the Hollywood side of production for a movie that was shot in multiple locations. The word "location" is in fact too general to capture the ways in which the nation-state becomes a powerful factor in international filmmaking. The countries in which a film such as Lawrence of Arabia was shot have an ambivalent relation, at best, with the U.S.-centered film companies they host, especially when the United States was seen as an antagonist of socialism and a neocolonialist power in the eyes of many Third World countries. Permission to shoot was complexly negotiated, not automatically granted, a delicate diplomatic maneuvering. Once the film company located inside a country, the latter's politics was sometimes profoundly affected by the film company's presence, and vice versa, as we shall see in the case of Jordan, the primary location for the filming of Lawrence of Arabia (which included Morocco, Spain, and Great Brit-

ain). But the impacts of a film production on a nation-state go beyond
its ruling elite, including foreign technical crews as well as thousands of
extras and ordinary citizens who come into contact with the film company in more noncontractual ways. And in the case of Jordan, it is impossible to talk of a purely national perspective when the state's external relationship to other Arab states in the region, and of course to Israel,
profoundly affect nearly every important political decision. This story
of national and transnational politics will once again be told through
the lives and careers of a particular individual, the first being King of
Hussein of Jordan, who had only recently ascended the throne when
he granted permission to film the Lawrence epic in the Jordanian desert.
What might have been the king's motives for permitting a film to be made
within Jordan's borders on what surely was from his citizens' perspective
a controversial subject? What might have been the impact of film production on ordinary Jordanians, and vice versa? The second individual who
figures prominently in this story is Sam Spiegel, who developed a complex and ambivalent relationship toward Israel and Zionism. Why is it
that Spiegel was at once so nervous about filming inside Jordan and at
the same time willing to produce a picture that up until its time was the
most sympathetic portrait of Arabs to come out of Hollywood?

As for the artists involved in international filmmaking, directors, first
of all, had to be found who were willing to travel great distances, to remain separated from family and friends for long periods, and to work
under arduous conditions. Lean is a central figure in the history not only
of British films but more interestingly also in the history of the international film. This was not accidental. He had a peculiar psychological
penchant, as has been commonly noted, for filming in "exotic" locations,
as well as a fascination for international themes such as travel, world
war, and colonialism, which predominate in his post-1950 oeuvre. I will
try to explain this penchant through a bit of psychoanalytic detective
work. Though we will concern ourselves only with the narratives of
Lean's *Summer Madness* (*Summertime*, American title, 1955) and *Bridge
on the River Kwai* (1957)—in brief, the films immediately leading up
to *Lawrence of Arabia*—which contain what might be called a complex "international" theme and implicit criticisms of provincial Anglo-
American visions of the world, a similar observation could be made for
all of his films thereafter, which is that the international order is imagined in ways that are obsessive and go back to certain central experiences of Lean's childhood and young adult life.[3] In making this link between the global or international and the personal in Lean's output, we

might be able to answer auteur critics such as Andrew Sarris, whose reception of Lean's work has been chilly, to put it mildly, because of a perception of Lean as merely a dazzling technician without a personal point of view or unique style to impart. The yardstick of comparison for Sarris is the work of such directors as Truffaut, Bergman, and Fellini, all of them working within strong, distinctive national traditions and intimate, small-scale narrative frameworks. I consider his perception of Lean superficial because it neglects to see how his personal life was implicated in all sorts of hidden ways in his film productions' international peregrinations and global themes. I argue not only that they contain a vision of the world, psychological and moral, but also that its roots sink deep in Lean's personal history.

Actors from different nationalities and with different theatrical training and cultural backgrounds also had to be brought together and coordinated in the international film. If they wanted to become international film stars, they could ill afford to remain fixed in a specific theatrical and filmic tradition but instead had to negotiate complex careers that straddled several traditions at once. Omar Sharif is an interesting example of such an actor. A star in one tradition, Egyptian, he soon acquired international fame by acting in a string of big-budget Hollywood productions, while at the same time working in the "new wave" cinema of France. How he self-consciously constructed himself as simultaneously "Arab" and "cosmopolitan" in order to "travel" across artistic and cultural boundaries is by no means a unique story about actors in the international film industry, though it surprisingly remains uninvestigated in film studies.

Finally, there is the question of the film's distribution, which was certainly global in scope and deeply affected by the cultural politics of the countries in which it was (or, even more interestingly, failed to be) exhibited. In my examination of *Lawrence of Arabia,* I limit myself to three broad contexts of distribution, Great Britain, the United States, and the Middle East, particularly Jordan. In Great Britain, where critiques of colonialism and portraits of intelligent natives no longer led to automatic censorship by the colonial film board, the film had a more favorable reception than one might expect, largely, perhaps, because the left intelligentsia had grown steadily more disillusioned with the military and political establishment after the Suez Crisis of 1956. It was in the United States that the reception was more ambivalent, in large part because of the festering Arab-Israeli conflict. And in Jordan, anti-imperialist protest over the treatment of Arabs in the film led to its banning by the state altogether, though this result was not universal in the Middle East. Thus, a quite diverse global politics affected the film's distribution and success in complex ways.

Let us begin by seeing how Hollywood's film industry always depended on international production, though more so than ever when the industry was restructured after World War II. Because the history of restructuring is fairly well known, I will not comment on it extensively, except to emphasize some international dimensions of the story.[4] The career of Sam Spiegel (1901–85) illustrates well how American film companies began early on in their history to pay attention to an international market.

Spiegel had come to the United States in the 1920s after an unsuccessful debut in the cotton business in Poland. Because of his knowledge of the metropolitan cultures of Europe, not to mention fluency in many of their languages, he was hired by Metro-Goldwyn-Mayer to work in the script department. It had long since become apparent to American companies that they could not survive on domestic sales alone and, in order to compete in the international market, they could no longer export films on native and naive subjects such as small-town Americana. Film scripts with foreign interest had to be found or created, and people with Spiegel's background and taste could serve as advisers. His job was to discover contemporary European plays that might be successfully treated as film subjects. However, as explained by his biographer, in 1930 Spiegel was deported from the United States back to his native Poland. Universal's head of European production brought him to its headquarters in Berlin to recut and dub films intended for European distribution.[5] It soon became apparent that Spiegel also had impressive talents as a negotiator. After the fascist regimes came to power in Germany and Italy, he was assigned to persuade them—despite his Jewish background—to lift their ban on the showing of *All Quiet on the Western Front* (1930), at that time Universal's most prestigious production.

In the postwar years, the restructuring of the film industry had a profound impact on Spiegel's career. The first change had to do with the partial breakup of the vertically structured firm. Already in the late thirties, independent exhibitors, complaining of the monopoly major motion picture companies enjoyed, filed suit under the Sherman Anti-Trust Act. As a result of the Supreme Court's 1948 decision in *U.S. v. Paramount Pictures,* Hollywood's leading companies more or less severed themselves in two, giving up their monopolistic hold over theaters but retaining a parent company in charge of production and distribution. But it was economics more than legal challenges that battered the film industry. The overhead required to maintain huge lots and back stages became prohibitive. Downsizing began, and one of the casualties was the studio term contract under which everyone from stars to technical staff had been more or less permanently employed.

Another change to affect the industry, fostered largely by the breakup of the studio system, was the rise of independent producers who could now collaborate with directors and stars freed from the studio term contract.[6] Though they had existed since the beginning of the film industry, most notably, of course, in the formation of United Artists by Mary Pickford and Charlie Chaplin, it was only in the 1950s that independent producers became a force to be reckoned with in Hollywood.[7] A number of factors contributed to their rise, the most significant of which was explicable in terms of U.S. taxes. People like Spiegel who were willing to give up the security of a high-paying studio job to take their chances as independent producers could enjoy large tax advantages.

Spiegel already knew a lot about independent production by the time the latter gained ground in the industry, which is one of the reasons he became an industry leader in the fifties. He had produced several films, the most notable in artistic terms having been *Tales of Manhattan* (1942), after which he became one of the first producers to form an independent company with a major director—John Huston. Spiegel and Huston's company, Horizon Pictures, was responsible for the production of such notable films as *African Queen* (1951) and *On the Waterfront* (1954).

Of course, the main reason for the studio system's decline in the first place was poor sales at the box office, a fact that is often attributed to the growing popularity of television in the fifties. One of the industry's responses to television's challenge was to produce the "blockbuster" movie or epic, whose genre and accompanying wide-screen processes will be examined in detail in the next two chapters. Yet another response to television was to step up dramatically the international side of Hollywood's operation, specifically the promotion of the "international" film. Moreover, film exhibition was not restricted to the United States—far from it—but extended worldwide. It would appear that the rise in foreign-derived income had been steady and steep, amounting to approximately a third of the gross income of a company like Universal by the late 1940s and about half of the gross income a decade later.[8] Though available statistics are not absolutely reliable, a fair guess is that by the mid-1950s approximately half of a motion picture company's gross income came from rentals of U.S. films to foreign distributors and exhibitors. Part of this increase has been attributed to the rising standard of living in foreign countries in which television had yet to cut into movie theater attendance.

In order to attract foreign sales, however, the content of the movies had to change. As Irving Bernstein put it, "Another effect of the rising foreign market has been the emergent predominance of the film with an international rather than a U.S. appeal."[9] American films on American subjects were no longer doing as well on the international market in the fifties as they had in the past.[10] Foreign audiences were no longer satisfied with the novelty of seeing American slices of life on the silver screen. Moreover, these often sophisticated, urban audiences, or at the very least the elites who controlled the distribution of films inside their countries, were swept up by the nationalist, anticolonial ideologies characteristic of the postwar period, and they resented the exclusively American or European outlook that Hollywood films imparted. They did not have many filmmakers, nor film industries, secure enough to compete with the American giants. At the very least, therefore, they wanted to consume representations of their own societies that were sympathetic and desirable. Thus, I would argue that the deepening of the ethnographic "gaze"—and simultaneously making it more complex—was part of the Euro-American film industry's response to anticipated audience reception *abroad*. At the same time these images of other cultures could satisfy the taste of Western audiences who were traveling and seeing more of the world than ever before as a result of the globalization of U.S. capitalism. Insofar as the production side alone is concerned, this is what I have been calling the "international" film, but I am arguing that one might expect repercussions on the artistic side as well: more complex and perhaps even ambiguous thematic treatments of the Other because of marketing aimed at foreign audiences.[11]

Why was internationalizing the practices of film production profitable? We have already taken note of the tax advantages that accrued to U.S. filmmakers working abroad.[12] But Irving Bernstein, who was hired by some Hollywood studios to look into this matter, qualifies this generalization in ways that are quite important to our study of independent production. "The impact has been considerably greater upon the *independents* than upon the majors and the advantages to corporations have had more effect than the advantages to individuals."[13] It is somewhat clearer, then, why independent production and international filmmaking were linked. Even more important as a reason for the expansion of the international film, at least according to Bernstein, was the relative ease of foreign over U.S. financing of films. In the great boom economy of the fifties, U.S. banks could find safer investments than Hollywood films, ones that brought in a higher return as well. Consequently, only a fraction of the financing, perhaps as low as one-quarter, came from U.S. banks; the rest had to be raised from private backers, many of them from Europe. Though the sources available to me at the time of writing do not reveal to what extent Spiegel tapped into foreign funds, and even whether his extensive prewar experience in the international side of filmmaking gave him an advantage in establishing contacts with potential backers, it is certainly reasonable to *assume* that the latter was the case.

Another advantage of international filmmaking was reduced labor costs, though savings were not necessarily guaranteed if product quality could not be controlled. Shooting with a foreign film crew rather than with higher-paid, but also more skillful, Hollywood technicians could provide substantial savings only in the case of epic movies employing thousands of extras. It was observed that "Stanley Kramer, for example, hired a large chunk of the Spanish Army for the battle scenes in *The Pride and the Passion* (1957) for much less than it would have cost him to create an army with extras in the U.S." [14] Spiegel would adopt a similar practice in *Bridge on the River Kwai* when he employed Sri Lankan extras to play British prisoners of war, or in *Lawrence of Arabia* when hundreds of local citizens were hired in Jordan, Morocco, and Spain to play the Arab raiders in the larger battle scenes. Thus, a link was forged not only between independent production and international filmmaking but to the epic as well, a dominant genre of U.S. film in this period.

Shooting on location could be a mixed blessing, however, as Lean discovered when filming some of the scenes in *Summer Madness*. Some of the shopkeepers in Venice's Saint Mark's Square demanded steep compensation when they claimed that filming obstructed tourist traffic and caused business to fall off. It would have been preferable to have re-created the square on some back lot in England, if artistic quality were not sacrificed in the process. If the industry's received wisdom, that a film shot in "authentic" foreign locales could compete better with television, led to the commodification of authenticity, it was sometimes bought at too high a price.

Filming on location in a foreign country presented independent producers like Spiegel with stepped-up challenges. They had to mediate directly with foreign governments for permission to work inside the country, attaining a diplomatic status usually accorded only to official representatives of the U.S. government. As we know from his early professional history, Spiegel was no stranger to diplomatic wranglings with potentially hostile governments. Nor was he necessarily at a disadvantage being a Jew negotiating with an Arab state, for the real issue would not have been his religion but his Zionism. Just how ambivalent his ties were to Israel we will examine later, but they were certainly strong enough to have aroused suspicions. Spiegel needed an experienced diplomat whom the Jordanians could trust. Anthony Nutting (b. 1920) was his man. A former conservative member of Parliament and member of the British government in which he served as minister of state for foreign affairs and leader of the British delegation to the United Nations, he commanded the respect of the Jordanians because of his strong opposition to the British declaration of war against Egypt when the latter nationalized the Suez Canal. In fact, he resigned his governmental position in protest over the affair. Nutting had the kind of reputation that could work in the producer's favor.

It might now be helpful to consider the admonition of Armand Mattelart, a pioneer in the study of transnational culture, who said: "There is too much of a tendency to set up transnational firms as the only actors in the transnational process, consequently relegating the study of the national societies in which they are based to a minor level. What determines the particulars of this process in each national reality is the articulation of proposals of transnational firms with those of the groups and the classes that make up each national society." [15] Accordingly, who were the people in Jordan with whom the film company had to negotiate? And what were their motives for cooperating with this production?

But first, a word on why Jordan was chosen as a locale in the first place. Quite simply, it was one of the places, besides Saudi Arabia, in which T. E. Lawrence campaigned, and the latter was off-limits for on-location shooting because of the conservativeness of the state regime. Because "authenticity" was being marketed in the international film, efforts had to be made to shoot in some of the very places in which Lawrence saw action. That left Jordan.

The man with whom Anthony Nutting negotiated directly was King Hussein (b. 1935), head of the Hashemite Kingdom of Jordan. [16] Some historical background on Jordan will help to place in perspective the period of the 1950s and Middle East politics in which King Hussein was a leading player, all of which has a bearing on his decision to allow Horizon Pictures into the country.

The territory of what is now Jordan had existed under the shadow of Great Britain ever since Emir Hussein of Mecca, the present king's great-grandfather, had raised the standard of the Arab Revolt against the Ottoman Empire in 1916. T. E. Lawrence, of course, was sent out by the British army to help finance and organize it. After the war, the son of the emir known as Feisal, who had campaigned alongside Lawrence in the Hejaz, became king of Iraq, then a British protectorate, whereas another son, Abdullah, the grandfather of King Hussein of Jordan, became the leader of the League of Nations' Mandate Transjordan. It remained under the "tutelage" of Great Britain, and it was really the British high commissioner of Palestine who ran the country through the British Resident living in Amman. Though Jordan was granted independence in 1946 and Abdullah became king of the Hashemite Kingdom of Jordan, the country still depended heavily on British military support and financial subsidy.

In particular the throne leaned on the Arab Legion, a bedouin army of several thousand formed from the remnants of the insurgents of the 1916 revolt and trained by the British "Glubb Pasha" (Lieutenant General John B. Glubb) to become a formidable desert fighting force. It not only kept the peace inside the country but also protected the borders against Saudi Arabian incursions as well as hostilities with the growing Zionist population in Palestine. During the Arab-Israeli War of 1948, only the Arab Legion distinguished itself among the armies of Egypt, Syria, and Iraq in the offensive against the state of Israel, preventing the Zionists from seizing Jerusalem, and in conjunction with the Iraqis securing the West Bank. Nevertheless, Abdullah was vilified, on the one hand because of his policy of negotiation and compromise with the Zionists and on the other for the continued support he accepted from the British, for which he was branded an "imperialist lackey."

The future King Hussein had a different education from the sons of the emir who led the Great Revolt of 1916. It was no wonder that his detractors would paint him as westernized and Anglophilic. Hussein's education began at Victoria College, Alexandria, one of the finest British public schools anywhere, which was reserved for future leaders of the empire. Then, after the murder of his grandfather Abdullah made Egypt unsafe for him, he attended Harrow and Sandhurst, the famous English military college. He grew up into a debonair young man, with the reputation of an international playboy. He was intrigued by Western technology, particularly sophisticated military hardware and fast cars and planes, which he loved to race. Yet his grandfather made sure that Hussein was tutored in Arabic, learned Islamic ritual and law, and felt at home in the bedouin traditions of his country. The combination of educations turned him into a complex cosmopolitan, but he also definitely remained an Arab figure, one who could "travel" through several, sometimes mutually hostile, worlds at once.

Only seventeen when he ascended the throne in 1952 after his deranged father, Talal, was forced to abdicate, Hussein fended off assassination attempts, severe internal pressures from the refugee Palestinian population, pro-Saudi religious conservatives and communists, a worsening economic situation, and relentless criticism from President Gamal Abdel Nasser of Egypt, by far the most charismatic Arab leader in the post–World War II period. It was the challenge from the latter quarter that makes particularly puzzling the king's decision to allow the production company to film a story about T. E. Lawrence, arch-colonialist, inside Jordan.

In the late 1950s and early 1960s, radical Arab nationalism (*qawmiyyah*) under Nasser was at its height, deeply influencing the internal politics—and even threatening the internal stability—of the countries of the region. Saudi Arabia competed for this mantle of authority by being the keeper of the sacred cities of Islam. Where Jordan was concerned, it could be said that the first modern and politically potent expression of Arab nationalism in the twentieth century was the revolt against the Turks in 1916, which was proclaimed by the sharif of Mecca, a descendant of the Prophet (hence, a Hashemite), and led by his sons. In the ideological warfare that characterized the relations between Egypt, Saudi Arabia, and Jordan/Iraq in the late fifties and early sixties, King Hussein of Jordan and King Feisal II of Iraq, as the great-grandsons of the sharif of Mecca, represented themselves as the obvious inheritors of this "great revolution" (*ath-thowra l-kubra*). Over and over again, often in mass cultural venues such as the press, television, and schools, the Jordanian state alluded to that epic event and its significance for the future of Arab nationalism. But trouble was brewing for the Hashemite thrones. The populace of Arab countries, only in part because they were inflamed by Nasserite rhetoric, saw these "inheritors" of the Great Revolt as corrupt monarchs, little more than lackeys to European imperialist powers, and hardly deserving the labels of patriots and nationalists. Hussein's cousin in Iraq was murdered in a 1958 coup that ushered in a socialist regime in Baghdad, strongly supported by the Soviet Union. Because of his British upbringing and Jordan's dependency on Britain, Hussein too was vulnerable, though he had acquired a certain legitimacy in the eyes of radical nationalists when in March 1956 he chucked out the British head of the Arab Legion and expelled all but a handful of the British advisers from his country. Yet Cairo was still doubtful that the Hashemites had at long last rid themselves of Western imperialists, for it was clear that if the British had been ushered out, the Americans were waiting in the wings. Within the context of an unstable Jordanian state and the fiery nature of Arab nationalism during the period 1952–62, it is therefore an understatement to call Hussein's decision to allow Horizon Pictures to film inside Jordan provocative. Why did he do it? Was it another instance of his "Anglophilia"?

One might conjecture that the reasons were economic. Though still comparatively weak in the 1950s, the Jordanian economy was starting to take off, and tourism was seen to be an essential ingredient of its success. Among the more popular tourist spots in the country is the "rose red city" of Petra, a beautiful Hellenic site carved out of sheer rock in the desert. If it was indeed Lean's intention to stage a battle scene there, nothing came of it, however. The forbidding scenes that appeared in the final product could hardly have inspired a tourist stampede either. In fact, the only solid benefit accruing to the Jordanian state was a hefty charge to Horizon Pictures of a million pounds sterling for a badly needed army hospital.[17] King Hussein was always in need of cash to pay his Arab Legion, on which he counted to bolster his regime, particularly in the frequent crises during these early years of his reign.

As for stimulating expenditures inside the country, it is doubtful whether local business gained very much from the production. L. Robert Morris and Lawrence Raskin boast that "in twelve months the company would spend more in Jordan than the sum total of a year's income [in] tax revenue!"[18] They fail to mention, however, that tax revenues had never amounted to much in a relatively poor country like Jordan, whose extremely mobile populations could readily evade tax collection in any case. Moreover, the personnel of the company lived barrack-style on their own compound built on the shores of 'Aqaba and did not pay rent to landlords. Some basic supplies were purchased locally, but production accounts always play up the sumptuous foods and wines flown in daily from Europe: one did not buy haddock in downtown Amman. For the most part, the technologically sophisticated equipment needed for the production was purchased outside the country.

It is thus hard to imagine that economic reasons played much of a factor in Hussein's decision to allow Spiegel and Lean to film their spectacle inside Jordan. I would suggest another explanation, having to do with the propaganda power of popular media, which the king had learned to appreciate not only in the Egyptian barrage against his regime but also in his family's claims of Arab nationalist authenticity. Since he was constantly invoking the Arab Revolt to affirm his position as a pan-Arab leader, perhaps he thought of the Hollywood screen as an arena in which to narrate to the world his family's and his nation's saga, one that could compete with Nasser's loudly trumpeted nationalist narratives. It would be one of the more stunning examples of the conjuncture of state politics and global popular culture in modern history.

The film company's presence in Jordan had almost immediate, and one might have thought predictable, repercussions on national politics. Protests were reported in the Jordanian press. One of the publicists for the film overheard the following: "Lawrence, so said some of the Arabs, was no friend of the Arab cause. He had helped to betray Prince Feisal and he had not really played any practical part in the Arab revolt at all. In fact, the grumblers claimed, the whole presence of an alien film company in their midst was an insult to the Arab people and some of those working for Horizon Pictures might well be investigated by the Arab Boycott Committee." [19] By approving the project, King Hussein appeared to be collaborating with the neocolonialists, as Nasser had been intimating he had been doing all along.

Matters were not helped by the impression that the film company's arrival in the country made on the local citizenry. It seemed like a foreign invasion. Horizon Pictures established its headquarters in Amman, while a base camp was set up at 'Aqaba for the cast and crew. The latter was half army installation, half safari encampment. Pictures show barbed wire encircling the perimeter and a big sign at the entrance warning "off limits" to all but authorized personnel. Soldiers paced up and down in front of the main gates. From the point of view of the nationals *and* their government, such cultural quarantine might have been effective in keeping the film company inside the compound's perimeters. Muslim countries differ in the degree of xenophobia their religious elite express, and it could be argued that Jordan was far less conservative than, say, its neighbor Saudi Arabia; nonetheless, it would have had to have taken steps to reassure some elements of the local population that alcohol consumption, displays of affection between the sexes, or the appearance of inappropriately clad women and men would be restricted to the "European quarter." From the point of view of the filmmakers, the fence may have been instrumental in keeping the nationals outside the compound. One could sit in deck chairs by the sea or lounge in the shade of ample awnings. The food was apparently outstanding. "Thanks to a jovial lump of a man named Phil Hobbs, amazing meals were served day in, day out, even in the most remote spots. For my first breakfast at the Beach Camp, after a preliminary canter with fruit juices and cereals, I was offered a range of main dishes, including a smoked haddock."[20] Wine was available, and, according to Omar Sharif, the selection was nearly as good as Maxim's.[21] For recreation, one could attend open-air film shows, play bingo, table tennis, and darts, and of course swim in the Red Sea. Drinks were served by an Arab waiter referred to in the literature as a "batman," a term used in the British army for the servant of an officer.

The description of 'Aqaba base camp reminds one of a makeshift colonial administrative town, and in fact Morris and Raskin caught the parallel by printing on opposite pages of their text photographs of the 'Aqaba "tent" city and British army headquarters set up on the same beach in 1917, shortly after the time that T. E. Lawrence had taken the port city with the Arab army.[22] Upon seeing these pictures, I was reminded of the compound for foreign employees of the Arabian-American Oil Company (ARAMCO) located in Dhahran, Saudi Arabia, with its large chain-link fence through which could be seen ranch-style houses with green lawns, cement walks, and mailboxes on street corners: in brief, a modern, middle-class, American suburb in the middle of the desert. Similarly, in the remotest and most forbidding location in which shooting for *Lawrence of Arabia* took place, Eddie Fowlie, Lean's right-hand man, put down a square of artificial grass in the midst of the sand dunes, so that the director could have tea on the "lawn."[23] Something of "home" (in terms of both family and class in the metropolitan culture) is re-created "away from home," a nostalgia commonly awakened by international travel.

To be sure, the Jordanian state was keeping a close watch on the film company in spite of its apparent self-containment. Production photos show a number of "Jordanian assistants" of indeterminate status working with British and American technicians. On the one hand, these might have been employees (three hundred in all), which Horizon Pictures might have been required to hire in nearly every department, the aim being to train Jordanians for jobs in an emerging Jordanian film and television industry, a nationalistic practice in many countries that contract with foreign companies. When I worked for the Department of Antiquities of the Saudi Arabian government, for example, archaeologists were required by law to train Saudi Arabian counterparts as a way of nationalizing the workforce. Then again, and not incompatibly, the assistants on the movie set, like the trainees on the archaeological site, might have been working for internal security. How otherwise would the state be able to keep its eyes on the Western technical crews while they were on location?

Falling under suspicion is an ineluctable part of the experience of travel and what one might call the culture of the contact zone. As an anthropologist doing fieldwork, I was cast in the role of the "stranger" and "foreigner," always being watched. Not without reason, of course. There are enough historical precedents of espionage, unfortunately, to make such suspicions entirely warranted. In the case of the production of *Lawrence of Arabia,* they seem even more plausible for a number of reasons.

The first has to do with a precedent for what Spiegel attempted to do in Jordan. In the 1930s Alexander Korda, a Hungarian-born British producer and director of historical dramatic films, had negotiated with Hussein's grandfather, Emir Abdullah, for permission to film his version of T. E. Lawrence and the Arabian campaign in what was then Transjordan. He got as far as shooting some scenes in the desert when the deal was aborted, not by the emir, according to official accounts, but by Winston Churchill, who apparently anticipated that the portrayal of Turkish atrocities would offend the Turkish government, precisely at a time when he was counting on its alliance against the rising threat of European fascism.[24] The explanation seems a bit far-fetched, and years later it was revealed that Korda had been awarded a medal and a knighthood in recognition for his espionage services during the 1930s— precisely the period of the failed production of Lawrence.[25] It is entirely possible that Korda was engaged in clandestine operations in the desert, which, once accomplished, no longer needed the cover of an international film production. Though the government of Transjordan might not have had hard evidence of Korda's espionage activities, it certainly would have been suspicious, and it is more than likely that Jordan's internal security of 1960 would have been aware of that history.

Admittedly this is conjectural, but one has to raise the possibility of Spiegel's company, too, having come under suspicion for espionage activities while filming *Lawrence of Arabia.* The offending power would not have been Britain in this instance so much as Israel, which might have sent its agents to infiltrate the crew. Tensions between Israel and its Arab neighbors were at their height in this period. Horizon Pictures not only had its base camp a few miles from the Israeli border but also was shooting on location deep in the interior of the country, all the way to the Saudi Arabian border; indeed, it may have illegally crossed that border during the shooting of some of the scenes. Reconnaissance of military installations, defenses, troop deployments, and training camps would have been possible. It appears that bedouin extras in the production still remember a somewhat eccentric assistant by the name of Eva, whom they referred to as "the Jew" (Nicholas Alexander, personal communication).[26] Although this is not evidence that she was a spy, the point is that suspicions in such a situation of proximity between hostile nations are almost inevitable.

Another reason for such suspicions has to do with the producer's political commitments, which can be illuminated through something of a digression. Spiegel's family had fled southwestern Poland (Galicia) in the wake of pogroms against Jews. While his brother Shalom and parents settled into their new milieu in Vienna (eventually to migrate to the United States and then return to Israel), Sam made his aliyah to Palestine in order to explore his Jewish identity in his own way. For a while he worked on a kibbutz in the Jezreel Valley. As was the case with some of the early kibbutzim in Palestine who were trying to displace Palestinian Arab peasants, Jewish settlers often had a great deal of contact, much of it "friendly," with Arab neighbors. There is no reason to assume that Spiegel did not also experience something of life in Arab villages or that he was not sympathetic toward the Arab culture. He certainly learned Arabic, though how well is unclear. When the grinding labor on the kibbutz in time proved too taxing, he spent the early 1920s living out the trope of the wandering Jew: first as a tourist guide in and around Jerusalem, then returning to Poland to broker the cotton trade. By the time he clandestinely emigrated to the United States, he had become an atheist. Moreover, his connections with big business obviously meant that he had turned his back on the spartan socialist utopian experiment of the kibbutz, though not necessarily on the political aims of Zionism.

As this brief synopsis suggests, Spiegel's relationship to Israel, Judaism, and Arabs was at the very least complicated by a certain ambivalence. He had fled Europe because of anti-Semitism and sought refuge in the socialist Zionism of Palestine, only to discover that it wasn't what he was searching for. Out of the experience of being neighbors with Palestinian Arabs in the pre-state years, he may have found them to be less Other than many Americans who have not lived in their midst. I find it entirely plausible that such a man could produce a representation of Arabs that was more sympathetic than anything Hollywood had come up with—so sympathetic, in fact, that from the retrospective accounts I have gleaned from some American Jews who saw the film in its initial release, the portrayal seemed falsely and dangerously attractive. At the same time it is perfectly reasonable to suppose that he was complicit with Zionist aims, perhaps by permitting Israeli agents to infiltrate his movie company while it was in Jordan.

Evidence, all of it circumstantial to be sure, comes from Spiegel's behavior while the film was in production in Jordan. His fears of his Jewish identity and Zionist past coming to light during his negotiations with King Hussein have assumed the dimensions of high farce in the stories of the production, and they tend to be dismissed as part of his eccentric, high-strung personality. I think, however, they deserve to be contextualized a bit. Spiegel went through an elaborate charade of being Christian during a dinner with the king, for example, even though he must have known that the king would have been briefed about his background. Though "Anglican" was stamped in Spiegel's passport to allow him to pass through immigration (as I had "Christian Science" in mine when I went to Saudi Arabia), this would not have fooled internal security. Yet, as a Jew, he was not persona non grata in a country that was technically at war with Israel. What was at issue for an Arab state like Jordan, which supported the Palestinians, was not whether Spiegel was Jewish but whether he was Zionist, for Jews, like Christians, are a "people of the Book" (that is, a people who have received part of the divine revelation in their Torah and their New Testament) and are therefore protected in the Muslim community. It is highly likely, given Spiegel's prior knowledge of Muslim culture in Palestine, that he would have known these facts. When I was in Saudi Arabia, for example, it was more or less an open secret that the head of a branch office of a very important American firm was Jewish and that the authorities looked the other way as long as he was discreet in his religious observances. Spiegel's extreme nervousness would be more explicable, however, if he were worried that his production company was infiltrated by Israeli spies.

But the fraught issues of Jordanian nationalism where the production of *Lawrence of Arabia* is concerned cannot be plumbed by focusing exclusively on state-level politics or international espionage. One must also consider the point of view of the bedouin extras, many of whom were the sons and grandsons of the men who fought alongside Feisal and Lawrence in the Arab Revolt. What, besides a salary, was at stake for them in participating in the film?

Shooting took place in three locations inside Jordan, from May to

October 1961. At two of them, Jebel Tubeiq in the remote southeastern corner of the country near the border with Saudi Arabia, and Wadi Rumm, due east of ʿAqaba, hundreds and at times thousands of bedouin extras were used in what were some of the most spectacular scenes in the movie: Feisal's encampment at Wadi Safra and the attack by the Turkish planes; the exodus of Feisal's army from Safra to Yenbo; the raiders' arduous trek across the Nefud; the donning of Lawrence's Arab robes for the first time at Auda's wells; Auda's encampment at Wadi Rumm; and the departure of the Arab raiders for ʿAqaba, a scene involving many women emitting their shrill, eerie trills on the sheer cliffs above the floor of Wadi Rumm, where the raiders are seen riding in resplendent regalia.

At this point I rely on information provided to me by Nicholas Alexander, a former student at the University of California, Santa Cruz, who had the chance to spend 1992–93 in Jordan taking Arabic language and literature courses at one of the national universities. As it turned out, he spent some time in the areas in which filming took place—not Jebel Tubeiq, for that was too distant, but the areas in and around Wadi Rumm—where he had the opportunity of meeting bedouin who claimed to have been extras in the film. They had been given the impression that they would have the chance to reconstruct the battles just as their fathers and grandfathers who fought in them had narrated those battles to them, thereby ensuring the historical accuracy of these sequences. Authenticity raised its head again, only this time from the members of the indigenous culture.

But the opportunity for collaboration passed when Sam Spiegel decided to pull Horizon Pictures out of Jordan in the fall of 1961. He was getting more and more uneasy about the political storm building in the country around the production and nervous about the huge expense of maintaining cast, crews, and a great many extras in remote desert locations. Spiegel decided that a set built on the southeastern coast of Spain, near Almeria, could be made to resemble ʿAqaba, where the famous battle would be staged. The bedouin, of course, felt betrayed. Many told Nicholas that they *had* seen the film but were dismayed that "Lean hadn't gotten the battle scenes right." Not only had their hopes of reliving their history through the powers of modern spectacle been dashed, but they were shocked to see how much of that history focused not on Lawrence—which was to be expected of a British film company—but on Auda Abu Tayyi, head sheikh of the Howeitat. He had been only one of several tribal leaders in the desert revolt, they explained to Nicholas. Viewing the film from their own segmentary politics—in which each tribe had its honored leaders but none was paramount—they resented the undue prominence given to Auda in the story of Arab nationalism.[27]

Having examined *Lawrence of Arabia* as an international film of the 1950s from the perspectives of the producer, foreign government, and national technical crews and extras, let us now turn our attention to some of the more important artists who were involved in the production. As can be imagined, the latter were many—too many, in fact, to discuss them all here—and came from all over the world. I will focus on the director, David Lean, and on one of the non-Western actors, Omar Sharif.

An interesting fact about David Lean's biography that is not stressed as much as it should be is that around 1949, with the release of *The Passionate Friends,* he developed into a rather different sort of director from what he had been in Great Britain between the wars.[28] The transformation was gradual, not abrupt, but still discernible. I have in mind less his adoption of the epic style in the 1950s than the global arena of his on-location shooting and certain international themes that circulate throughout the later oeuvre. His films prior to 1949 had been made exclusively in Britain, concerned with British themes, and derived from the British literary tradition, most notably his adaptations of two of Dickens's novels (*Oliver Twist* [1951] and *Great Expectations* [1946]) and several Noël Coward plays as well as Coward's famous melodrama *Brief Encounter* (1945), which the critic Richard Dyer has called the most "British" of films.[29] After 1955 Lean would never again film exclusively in England. The places in which he worked were almost all former colonies of Great Britain, though. At the same time that Lean entered into an international arena of filmmaking, the themes from his earlier, more "British," subjects did not so much disappear as become displaced onto the landscape of the British Empire—not coincidentally, at a time in the fifties and sixties when it was rapidly collapsing.

Why did Lean make this shift from a homegrown industry to an international cinema? The explanation in part has to be economic. British filmmaking was undergoing a crisis in the 1950s because of competition from Hollywood, and many successful directors like Lean were having difficulty finding work. Some of them went to Hollywood, but this was not a particularly attractive option when the studio system seemed to be in decline after 1950, so another strategy was to hitch up with independent producers. It was not long before Lean went into partnership with Sam Spiegel. As we have learned, independent producers saw filmmaking in international locales as necessary to the economic well-being of their industry, and Lean ended up working in Ceylon (Sri Lanka) for his first collaboration with Spiegel, *Bridge on the River Kwai.*

For Lean, however, making a movie in a foreign locale represented much more than economic necessity; it was an obsession. And in this obsession lies a clue to the psychological dimension of his films that certain critics have overlooked. Like Andrew Sarris,[30] they have espoused the notion of the director as an auteur, that is, as an artist who forges a unique style or projects his own personality into his films, and they have accused Lean of being merely a dazzling technician with no "voice" of his own or distinctive point of view. Steven Ross has ably defended Lean against such a charge.[31] I would argue that one may not be able to truly appreciate, on the one hand, the psychology of Lean's films and, on the other, his pursuit of international filmmaking and the themes of foreign travel in his films unless one bears in mind his childhood experiences, which led to a peculiar conjunction of interests in photography, travel to lands with beautiful scenery, and the themes of frustrated erotic desire and marital as well as familial dissolution. In other words, by filming in foreign locales, accompanied by stories about Europeans traveling in such locales, Lean revisited some of the primal scenes of his childhood. But there is another reason besides auteur criticism for making this link between Lean's psychological makeup and the study of his transnational filmmaking. Too often the individual personality falls out of the analysis of what is today called the transnational perspective: commodities, cities, borders, regions, or diasporic communities are usually the units of analysis; more rarely are they individuals. I shall try to demonstrate the links, however speculative, between Lean's psychology and the global arena of his filmmaking in order to show just how deeply connected the two were.

It was said of Lean by Betty Spiegel, the producer's wife, that: "David is at his happiest living in an adverse environment, and he flourished like an orchid in Ceylon [the location for shooting of *Bridge*]. It was hot, it was humid, people were dropping like flies, and he was happy." [32] These feelings became even more pronounced while Lean was working on his next picture, as he himself confessed in an interview: "I love travelling, going to strange corners of the world, and *Lawrence* gave me the opportunity of seeing places I could never possibly have seen in similar circumstances in private life. I was living in the desert and it was a wonderful experience. In order to travel this way you have to be physically very tough and I haven't got so many more years to do that kind of thing. So if I can find the subjects, I would like to do another film in some strange place." [33] To be sure, one has to read these passages as constructing a youthful and above all masculine self, with filmmaking as a physical challenge of manhood and the land of the "other" as its proving ground. We will explore this reading in another chapter that discusses gender and orientalist constructions in more detail. Here I would add an explanation that is perhaps more psychological in nature.

In biographical sketches of the director, it would appear that his love of travel had been shaped by his childhood experiences. He himself has claimed that some of his happiest memories are of his vacation trips to Switzerland, France, and the Mediterranean when he was a teenager, carrying with him at all times a camera. [34] His favorite photographic subject was magnificent scenery, which he developed and printed in his own darkroom. Upon the heels of his family's Continental sojourns, but coincident with his introduction to and growing enthusiasm for photography, the teenage Lean went through the unsettling experience of watching his parents grow apart and finally separate when he was fifteen, the father falling in love with another woman. Lean's mother, who was deeply hurt by the divorce, never fully recovered emotionally. The sons remained loyal to her, and their father eventually became a remote figure to them. The teenage Lean in turn felt ashamed about what happened to his parents, a shame made more acute by his Quaker upbringing, but it was difficult for him to verbalize this emotion, even to his brother, from whom he was estranged. "The fact was that I was a terribly lonely young man and wrapped myself in a lot of dreams and eventually confided them to the camera." [35]

The camera as confidant enters as a trope for the first time in the films of Lean's "international" period. There is the shy, introspective, homely Jane Hudson in *Summer Madness* taking pictures of everything and everyone in Venice with her movie camera, which is put aside only when she meets her holiday romance. And the reporter Jackson Bentley in *Lawrence of Arabia* is more than a thinly disguised representation of Lowell Thomas; he is an allusion to the director himself. Both snap pictures of their respective "heroes," T. E. Lawrence in one case, Peter O'Toole in the other, in order to have a resounding success with their shows. The magnificent scenery of Lean's teenage travels, coupled with the awe it stirred in him, is directly translated into the fantastic geography of the lands and cities through which the travelers wander in his later films. The canals of Venice, the jungles of Sri Lanka, the deserts of

Jordan, Spain, and Morocco, the rugged Irish coast, and the Ganges: these are the backdrops of his later, international pictures.

According to one biographer, "David was unusual for his generation in that he felt that sex should be central to life, and not a furtive pastime, carried on outside the normal course of activity."[36] But it was difficult for him to realize sexual fulfillment with one woman. He had six wives and countless liaisons on the set, with everyone from film stars to continuity girls. One of his wives, the actress Kay Walsh, observed, "He [Lean] was so attractive to women and women were so attractive to him, but you don't keep on and on and on. What was he searching for? I always think he was searching for something inside himself."[37] There were probably many reasons for this endless succession of women, and Lean actually underwent psychoanalysis for a few years to discover some of them.[38] Perhaps he was neurotically enacting an emotional conflict, the seeming irreconcilability of erotic passion with bourgeois marriage, which he had seen demonstrated in the relationship between his mother and father. Their eventual separation and the great unhappiness it caused many people were among the traumas of his childhood. Only partly in jest would Lean confess that his life was lived for his movies, for they, shot in locations ever more distant from his home in England, were both a pretext for escaping the problems of marriage and at the same time the context for falling in love all over again. Was it merely coincidence that when he shot *Lawrence of Arabia* he was a married to an Indian woman, the most "exotic" of his wives, with whom he also had the most psychologically strained relationship? The other troubling tableau of childhood was that of the father remaining a remote figure to his sons. Lean would hardly see his son Peter from his first marriage in large part because of his busy work schedule which, moreover, took him to places where it was difficult to maintain regular contact with family and friends. Though they managed to remain on good terms after the divorce—I suspect largely because of the good-naturedness and generosity of the son—the relationship between father and son was never close.

We have been concerned with the practices of international filmmaking—shooting in exotic places, travel away from home—with which Lean may have had psychological associations because of the unhappy circumstances of his childhood. Let us now take note of the way the camera was confessional of these associations by turning to the three movies of the 1950s that epitomize Lean's international theme. Yet, it would be an impoverishment to interpret their meaning solely in terms of Lean's individual personality. These films construct a type of trans-national individual who passes like a phantom through the world, gone half or wholly mad by cross-cultural confusions of travel as well as the horrors of war and colonialism. The central figures in them, far from finding in such travel a resolution to their personal problems or a satis-faction of their political ambitions, are shaken to their foundations, to the point of being nearly or completely destroyed. It is useful at this point to consider how this representation of the international is dissonant with a certain ideology of internationalism of the 1950s.

According to anthropologist Liisa Malkki, "Internationalism is fruit-fully explored as a transnational cultural form for imagining and order-ing difference among people . . . and . . . one of the moral underpinnings of dominant discourses of internationalism is the ritualized and institu-tionalized evocation of a common humanity." [39] To illustrate her point, she examines two very different discourses of internationalism, one a Hollywood film—Bob Hope's *A Global Affair* (1964)—the other her correspondence with a young man in an East African refugee camp whose existence depended on many, albeit slender, threads to the inter-national community that surrounded and to some extent overwhelmed him. She is ultimately interested in the forms of "romantic internation-alism" [40] that both of these discourses express, in which distinct nations are seen to exist harmoniously with each other because their cultural and political differences are "domesticated." Roland Barthes made a similar observation in his critique of the *Family of Man* photographic exhibition that toured the world.[41] That the international theme is an important element in the cultural imagination of peoples in the twenti-eth century is, of course, a valuable point to make. To have isolated a theme of romantic internationalism and to have critiqued it for its sim-plistic view of diversity without adversity is no less significant. I would only add the caveat that romantic internationalism may have also had a more complex and contradictory representation in popular culture. By looking at Lean's oeuvre from 1955 to 1962, we can see how the theme twists and turns and eventually negates itself. This conclusion is only pos-sible, however, if we read his stories of travel and war as ironic and deeply ambivalent.

The theme of *Summer Madness* can be seen as a continuation of a story Lean had told in his earlier, more British period, *Brief Encounter* (1945), in which a married woman with children casually meets a doc-tor in a train station and falls in love. They have their romance but not without guilt and emotional turmoil, particularly for the woman. In the end she resists his entreaties to go away with him and returns to her pallid but sweet and gentle husband, Fred. The doctor decides to start life over again in Johannesburg, as if the kind of emotional happiness he is looking for is impossible in England and can only be found through travel to the colonies. This was the stark cost of middle-class marriage, according to Lean: one chose either erotic love and romance or domestic stability, middle-class respectability, and the happiness of children. Not only could one not have both in British culture; it was far better to choose the latter of the two options if one had to. Since it is to a film that takes place in Italy to which I compare it, it is interesting that when film critic Richard Dyer showed *Brief Encounter* to a class of Neapolitan students, they hated it. He noted, "They couldn't understand why Laura and Alex didn't just get on and have sex, and why indeed she didn't leave Fred for him."[42] *Summer Madness* is about the clash between these two irreconcilable cultural constructions of desire and respectability. But the film does not only gesture to Lean's earlier output. Seen from the perspective of the later oeuvre, it can also be interpreted as the first film to explore international themes, a story about a whole host of moral, psychological, and erotic difficulties necessarily arising in cross-cultural contact, none of which is smoothly ironed out. The vehicles for exploring these confusions are tourism and romance, but rather than a man at the center of the story in *Summer Madness* there is a woman, and a middle-aged spinster at that. Irony is used heavily throughout to call into question uncritically held cultural pieties. Because this movie, as an international film, was supposed to have an audience multiply positioned with respect to worldview and political perspectives, whose pieties and with what attitudes they get expressed and criticized become complex issues.

The main character of *Summer Madness,* Jane Hudson (Katharine Hepburn), is made to represent a certain female type of 1950s America. She is an old maid who is something of a fifth wheel at social gatherings, and in Venice loneliness presses in on her like a fog. In spite of her isolation, she is intrepidly determined to have what she saved her hard-earned money for—an "experience" that will bring her out of her shell and make her connect with life. Her ubiquitous movie camera is as much a vehicle with which to get at the experience as it is to keep it safely at bay, but unlike her "ugly American" but well-meaning compatriots the McIlhennys, she eventually allows herself to be touched and transformed by Venice's magic.

She arrives on a train, also central to the plot of *Brief Encounter.* Once comfortably ensconced in her pension, she befriends a charming street urchin named Mauro who becomes her guide. Though a kind of Italian Oliver Twist, Mauro is far less innocent and far more mischievous. He smokes cigarettes, tries to sell Jane pornographic pictures, and is paid by a married American artist to arrange secret trysts with the lady owner of the pension. A far cry from the angelic children in the British movie. Stumbling upon the boy while he is voyeuristically keeping guard over the couple, Jane comes horrifyingly face-to-face with the moral ambiguities and emotional dilemmas of her impending romance with a handsome but also married Italian shopkeeper (Rosano Brazzi). She lashes out at the boy for being little more than a pimp. Taken aback by her vehemence, he cries out, "Are you crazy, lady?" Indeed, the strain of trying to reconcile beauty and romance in Venice with the sordidness of adultery is almost too much for her. The theme of madness precipitated by moral and cultural confusions (brought out explicitly in the British title of the film, which was inexplicably changed for its American release to the blander *Summertime*) is explored even more fully in Lean's subsequent movies.

The symbolic function of the adulterous American couple does more than mirror Jane's confusions, however. They prevent an American audience from jumping too smugly to the conclusion that only Italians are "immoral." The movie makers criticize American mores far more than they moralize about Italians. They also call into question the sexual uptightness and rigid moral conventions of 1950s Anglo-American society, suggesting that there may be alternatives to its concepts of love and marriage of which we may not approve but which in their own way are comprehensible and sane.

Jane's suitor explains to her that, though married with children, he does not love his wife. His wife knows and accepts this, and they have an arrangement that permits him (though, of course, not her—that would be too fortunate for the wife) to have his romance on the side. Jane is resolved finally to risk an affair. In the process, she literally refashions herself. She buys a black dress, red high-heeled shoes, and a white diaphanous scarf. When the hotel maid sees her thus transformed, she exclaims that Jane looks like a *bella donna italiana*. These words hint that more than her wardrobe has changed. The theme of "going native," which is muted in *Summer Madness,* becomes pronounced and dire with consequences by the time of *Lawrence of Arabia.* It is, of course, a theme of the international and intercultural order. Though Jane's affair is portrayed as wonderful, perhaps because it operates under moral and amorous constraints quite different from the ones to which she is accustomed, it ends nevertheless. She resolves to go home. The reason for the decision is never made clear, though one might presume that she does not wish to remain a "mistress" or that she is simply a creature of her own culture after all and wants to return to its more linear moral perspectives. The final scene has her waving from a train that pulls ever more quickly away from an incandescent Venice and the lover she has left behind. That she has had her "experience" is clear; that it has changed her life upon her return to the United States is less so. Indeed, what exactly will become of her now?

In *Bridge on the River Kwai*,[43] filmed directly after *Summer Madness*, the cast is even more international in scope, headed by the superb character actor Alec Guinness in the main role of Colonel Nicholson. He is ably supported by two others: William Holden, who was then one of Hollywood's highest-paid leading men, portraying the American Shears (sounding, appropriately enough, like "jeers"); and the veteran Japanese and American movie actor Sessue Hayakawa as Colonel Saito, in what is surely one of the screen's most memorable performances. The cast is made up almost entirely of men (a minor part was written at the last minute for Shears's lover, to be played by a woman who was apparently a protégé of a Hollywood mogul), thereby gendering the narrative as a male story about war and militarism, with one small exception: the Burmese women bearers who help the British commandos hack their way through the jungle to the River Kwai. Present but not dominant in Lean's previous picture, irony now becomes overriding and destabilizes notions of authority, discipline, heroism, and other masculinist concepts associated with military life and warfare.

The theme of conflict between cultures is continued but made more complex and engrossing. In the characters of Nicholson and Saito, we watch two major militaristic-colonial powers confront each other across a cultural divide, with an ironic commentary provided by the diffident American Shears, a sort of Humphrey Bogart cynic (in fact, Spiegel tried to get Bogart for the part). Colonel Nicholson and his British soldiers have been interned during World War II in a Japanese labor camp deep inside the Burmese jungle. The camp's sadistic commandant, Colonel Saito, has been assigned the task of building a bridge over the River Kwai for a Japanese railroad that will eventually connect Malaysia with India, thereby threatening the British Raj. Saito makes it clear to everyone that he will stop at nothing to meet his objective on schedule, and he orders even the officers to help in the construction of the bridge. The

British colonel has the temerity to contradict the commandant's order on the grounds that it violates the Geneva conventions, an appeal, if you will, to the idealized international order of which Saito is contemptuously dismissive. Following the Japanese warrior code of honor, Saito is of the opinion that once defeated, a prisoner of war has lost all honor and deserves no better treatment.

Eventually the Japanese commandant realizes that his own engineers are unable to build the bridge, and he shamefully and angrily concedes to Nicholson's demands; namely, that the officers may be allowed to abstain from working on the crew. The relationship of Saito and Nicholson is now reversed. Saito becomes passive, seeming in the end even to contemplate ritual suicide as a way out of his dishonor, while Nicholson becomes the personification of the fascist leader in his ruthless and perverse determination to build a bridge that will last the centuries—"as long as London Bridge." The ultimate irony is that in order to meet the deadline set by the Japanese, he orders not only his own men to work but eventually also his officers, as well as the sick and wounded, whom even the Japanese had exempted. His explanation to his men is that a job well done boosts morale and discipline, thereby inadvertently echoing Saito's fascist admonition in the beginning of the film to "be happy in your work."

Meanwhile, the British have learned of the building of the bridge and send a team of commandos to destroy it. They are joined, reluctantly to be sure, by the cynical Shears, who has made good on a narrow escape from the camp. The commandos are even more international in composition than the prisoners of war. The leader, Warden (Jack Hawkins), is a Cambridge don, a specialist in Asian languages, and an expert in explosives (shades of Lawrence). A young and inexperienced Canadian lieutenant named Joyce (Jeffrey Horne) joins the expedition who turns out to be on an "initiatory" journey into manhood.

By the time the team of saboteurs has arrived at the river, a solid, permanent bridge has been built. Nicholson is standing on it and, unbeknownst to the would-be saboteurs, expressing his admiration of its beauty to Saito. "Yes, a beautiful creation," the Japanese commandant agrees, but because he is looking at the sun setting in the hills we are not sure whether he is referring to God's or Nicholson's creation. By now, perhaps, the distinction is blurred in Nicholson's mind too. Thankful that his army career should culminate in such a magnificent achievement, he is suddenly cut short in his valedictory speech when he inadvertently drops his stick—which has served as his baton while he ordered his men in the building of the bridge—into the river. Lean is fond of props like Jane Hudson's camera or Lawrence's compass, whose displacement or disappearance at a crucial moment takes on the symbolic meaning of a character's psychological imbalance.

That night the commandos set their plastic explosives under water. However, when the river level falls the next morning, exposing the charges, disaster strikes. Nicholson, accompanied by Colonel Saito, decides to inspect the bridge one last time before the arrival of the train. He uncovers the main line leading to the detonator, which Joyce has been assigned to activate as the train passes over the bridge. Fearful that the entire mission will be jeopardized if the detonator is discovered, Joyce finally overcomes his qualms about killing and leaps out of his cover to cut Saito's throat. Watching from his own hiding place, Shears cheers the youngster who has finally become a "man," miming his knife slashing as he becomes swept up in the ritual of killing. Nicholson is horrified at what has happened and begins to yell to the Japanese for help, while struggling to prevent Joyce from getting to the detonator plunger. Shears yells to Joyce to use his knife to kill Nicholson too; but it is too late and the younger man dies in a hail of bullets fired by the Japanese. Now Shears, insane with a rage that has been building ever since he met Nicholson, races toward his victim with a knife—because now he too wants to become a hero? or because his hatred for Nicholson is stronger than his keen sense of his own preservation?—but is gunned down in the river and expires on the embankment at his enemy's feet. They have a final moment of mutual recognition—"You?" says Nicholson in astonishment, "You!" says Shears disgustedly in his last breath—each, as it were, mirroring the other (the theme of the double). At last Nicholson realizes his mistake, but before he can do anything about it, an explosion throws him to the ground. Stunned but not unconscious, he manages with his last strength to get up and stagger forward, falling onto the plunger just as the train, with whistle blowing, passes over the bridge. In a tremendous explosion that left audiences breathless the first time they saw it, the bridge collapses and the train plunges into the river. The British medical officer who has been in the hills watching the whole scene dumbfounded has the last words. Madness, madness, he exclaims, half mad himself as he picks his way through the wreckage and carnage.

Made a little more than a decade after the war, *Bridge on the River Kwai,* having raised certain genre expectations about the war hero in the first third of the movie, unsparingly interrogates them in the rest of the narrative. It may be distressing nowadays to see the non-Western Other portrayed in such unremittingly dark tones, but at least Saito's character is psychologically complex and in the end no more sinister than Nicholson's. Indeed, it is the British officer who winds up being the fascist, with the internees as his adoring and unquestioning followers. The possessor of rational, technological means who perverts his knowledge by trying to control the world with it, is clearly criticized, and certainly more fully and damningly than in any Lean movie. As Andrew Sinclair astutely observed, "The [Suez War] Crisis [of 1956] seemed a running commentary on the film itself, a dedicated examination of the inflexible military mind, which believed in the superiority of Western methods even if put to the wrong use."[44] A favorite trope of the war movie is also mocked: the boy's "coming of age" story as symbolized by the younger Joyce, who finally learns how to kill—though by that point in the narrative his victim is the wrong man—and then, in a double irony, is himself killed immediately after having "achieved" manhood. Being an international movie, it was important to forestall American audiences from exempting themselves from the moral dilemmas depicted on the screen with the smug, self-satisfied conclusion, "O well, that's the British for you." In the end, the amusing, seemingly human, and attractive Shears succumbs to the very madness he had mordantly criticized. In the heart of darkness, no one is immune from obsession, masochism, and megalomania, precisely the themes to be explored further in *Lawrence of Arabia.*

In that film, the "international" theme becomes even more pronounced, not only in the way it combines many of the thematic elements that occurred in the previous pictures—travel, war, and fascism—but also by adding a complex and, as I shall argue, critical view of colonialism, not to speak of a more subtle representation of the Other. In many ways, Lawrence's character is an amalgam of Jane Hudson and Colonel Nicholson—a romantic attraction for the native Other combined with a fascistic personality—and though one could draw out the parallels in specific ways, it is important only to note that he seems to be a woman (perhaps more than one) in a man's persona. This immensely complicates the view of gender and sexuality and further destabilizes complacently held cultural views about the figure of the international traveler.

Ever since the days of silent cinema, a star's international appeal was a key ingredient to his or her success. Charlie Chaplin achieved international fame by rising through the Hollywood studio system at a time when the latter dominated the industry worldwide, becoming internationally famous as a result of its hegemony. But there were other routes to international stardom, ones that depended on transnational careers.

For example, Peter Lorre, a masterful actor in Germany's successful and internationally renowned expressionist cinema of the 1920s and 1930s, went to Hollywood, where he ended up playing mostly villainous character roles in what became film noir classics. He moved from one culturally, linguistically, and artistically distinct cinematic tradition to another. In *Lawrence of Arabia*, Peter O'Toole provides an example, if less illustrious, of a career such as Chaplin's, whereas Omar Sharif's more transnational trajectory mirrors the path of Peter Lorre. For the purposes of this chapter, Sharif's career is more germane; we will consider O'Toole's elsewhere.

Omar Sharif was not the only non-Western, transnational actor in the film. There was also his countryman Gamil Ratib (playing Majid), I. S. Johar, a star in Indian cinema, playing the important part of Gasim and, above all, the Pakistani stage and film actor Zia Mohyeddin in the role of Tafas. The latter had created Aziz in the London stage adaptation of Forster's *A Passage to India* (1960–61) before joining the production. Of all of Sharif's fellow actors, Mohyeddin would have the most work in Hollywood movies—for example, a stunning cameo role in *Khartoum* (1966), starring Charleton Heston as General "Chinese" Gordon. Though, like Omar Sharif, they moved back and forth across different national cinemas and theatrical traditions, negotiating a transnational, international stardom, none of them achieved a stardom that rivaled his.

It was a complex and risky bit of casting to place an actor like Omar Sharif (b.1932), virtually unknown at the time outside of the Egyptian film industry, in one of the most demanding supporting roles in Hollywood history. Some of the production accounts make much ado out of the fact that an "Arab" was chosen to play the role of an Arab, thus seeming to bestow a cultural integrity on a part that is rare in traditional Hollywood cinema (though, as we have seen, fetishizing authenticity had its own commodity value by this time in cinema). In fact, however, Lean was much more insistent on this type of ethnic casting than the producer.

Yet the selection of Omar Sharif as representative of "the Arab" is not without its ironies. He claims in his memoir to have been born Michael Shalhoub, a Catholic. Rumors in the Egyptian film industry suggest that he concocted this story of his Catholicism during the turbulent Nasser years in order to conceal his birth into a wealthy, highly cosmopolitan Jewish family from Alexandria. Then again, these rumors might have been apocryphal and circulated by persons jealous of his success. Whatever the truth may be, the story he tells of his name change is revealing, and not only of his sense of humor:

> The name Michael annoyed me. I tried to come up with something that sounded Middle Eastern and could still be spelled in every language. OMAR! Two syllables that had a good ring and reminded Americans of General Omar Bradley.
>
> Next, I thought of combining Omar with the Arabic sherif [i.e., a descendant of the Prophet and considered high-born in most Muslim countries] but I realized that this would evoke the word "sheriff," which was a bit too cowboyish. So I opted for a variant—I became Omar Sharif.[45]

Already he was carefully constructing himself as a star with a transnational identity; that is, not primarily as an actor associated with a specific culture who then appears around the world (an example is Maurice Chevalier, who was never other than a quintessentially "French" actor and entertainer) but who is ambiguous with respect to nationality and ethnicity, seeming to straddle multiple such identities at the very outset. This characteristic is seen as a key ingredient of the star's movability and subsequent success. Surely a sociolinguistic analysis of the industry's invention of stars is overdue, especially in the case of transnational film stars with their array of names and accents. "I spoke French, Greek, Italian, Spanish and even Arabic," explains Sharif, somewhat immodestly, ". . . with an accent that enabled me to play the role of a foreigner without anyone knowing exactly where I came from, something that has proved highly successful throughout my career."[46] In brief, his appeal is supposed to be based on cosmopolitanism.

The construction of this transnational identity runs deep in Sharif's memoir, *The Eternal Male*. By the time he was a young man, he had become, in his own words, a "Europeanized Middle Easterner,"[47] as the result of having gone to the elite secondary school of Victoria College in Alexandria (which King Hussein had attended), where he learned to speak three languages fluently, acquiring a deep love for French literature along the way, and dabbling in amateur theatricals as a result of his fascination with English drama. When he has talked about his cultural identity, it is also ironic, but not surprising perhaps, that he echoes the very sentiments and ideas of orientalism that today are criticized in Western discourses on the Middle East. For example, he speaks of his "Middle Eastern fatalism," his Middle Eastern "laziness,"[48] and claims that during the filming of *Lawrence* "my Islamic atavism surfaced"[49] —and this after his self-professed Christianity. On the occidental, or to be more precise the Francophone, side of his identity, he tends to stereotype his thinking and acting as "Cartesianism." "David Lean had looked all over the United States and Europe for 'Ali, the Arab,'" Sharif muses, no doubt with a tone of irony and self-mockery.[50]

Unlike Peter O'Toole, Sharif had no formal training as an actor when he began his film career. The pictures of him as a young man show a face of rare beauty, however, which won the attention of film people like Youssef Chahine, who was to become one of the most interesting and distinguished of Arab film directors.[51] "I was *his* discovery," Sharif emphasizes, echoing the themes of invention and proprietorship that are so much a part of the industry's discourse.[52] Chahine cast him in *The Blazing Sun* (1955), costarring the nationally revered Egyptian actress Faten Hamama. Because the film was nominated for a prize at the Cannes Film Festival, Sharif acquired instant worldwide recognition, if not immediate work in the international film industry. Jean Cocteau saw the film and, according to Sharif, was impressed by the latter's performance. By the time Sharif was cast in *Lawrence of Arabia,* he had made a name for himself in Egyptian movies and was breaking through the barriers of the international film industry.

The transition required some modifications in his acting style. Egyptian movies, Sharif says, were "geared to two imperatives: speed and money." [53] Of course, that would not necessarily distinguish them from most cinema, including Hollywood, but he adds that the acting style is sentimental, pitched to an "emotional" audience. "Arab film actors use lots of mime and grandiose gestures that come more from silent movies than talkies," he explains.[54] While this assessment of Egyptian acting as melodramatic is made from a Eurocentric point of view and fails to provide a deeper analysis of its integrity as a cultural style (an analysis of which has yet to be made, in fact), the point is that Sharif had become proficient in one tradition of acting, only to have to make an adjustment into another when he started work on *Lawrence of Arabia.* In some of the production accounts, a humiliating story is told of Lean standing next to him with a stopwatch in an effort to speed up the pace of his delivery.[55] That was only the beginning of his disciplining and Lean's refashioning of him. "He would have a preponderant influence over my career," confessed Sharif, for the director would later cast him in the lead role of *Doctor Zhivago* (1965).[56] After becoming known for his performance in *Lawrence of Arabia,* he not only went on to play in English-speaking parts but also made several French movies. In the latter, the challenge was to disengage from an epic style of film acting that he had learned from Lean and to become proficient in yet a different

form of self-presentation that might be described as more interiorized
and more economical.

With the film industry once again in trouble in the early 1960s due in
large measure to the rise in popularity of television, overseas sales were
critical to *Lawrence of Arabia*'s financial success. There were hopes for
long runs in movie houses in Great Britain and the rest of Europe, the
United States, Latin America, Asia, and the Middle East. The global extent of the film's distribution was affected, however, by a complex politics of reception. How audiences would relate to the movie, if at all,
depended on what was happening in the political culture of the country in which the movie was exhibited, the historical relationship, if any,
of that country to the legacy of British colonialism, and the politics of
varied kinds of nationalisms. Because the reception of the movie was
bound to vary depending on political circumstances, it required different marketing strategies (promotion and advertising) on the part of the
distributors.

Our story of the film's reception begins at a highly publicized performance before the queen at the Odeon Theatre, Leicester Square, on December 10, 1962. This was not just a publicity coup on Sam Spiegel's
part. It was a way of co-opting part of the political establishment's support for the film. One has to bear in mind that the characterization of
Lawrence was part of a revisionist movement within Great Britain, not
only of Lawrence as a historical figure and cultural icon but also of the
British army and (post)colonial politics. Since the fifties, British biographers had begun to reassess the claims put forward by Lawrence and
others regarding his role in the Arab Revolt (see chapter 3). Concomi-
tantly, the military and political establishment had come under heavy
fire since the Suez Crisis, when it became patently clear that Britain's
empire was finished but that it had no commensurate role of importance
to play in the postwar world. Hence, the establishment would have
tended to be on the defensive with regard to the film's representations of
Lawrence, the military, and British colonial politics, whereas the left intelligentsia and a countercultural movement burgeoning in the sixties
would have regarded the film more ambivalently.

An angry exchange of letters was in fact published in the *Times* between some defenders of the establishment and the filmmakers. "They
have used a psychological recipe: take an ounce of narcissism, a pound of
exhibitionism, a pint of sadism, a gallon of blood-lust and a sprinkle of
other aberrations and stir well," complained Arnold Lawrence, brother

of the war hero.[57] It was not just the reputation of his brother that concerned him, however. "A Machiavellian element in the character (of Allenby) was introduced. . . . The film shows him so intent on an imaginary political advantage that he lets Demascus [*sic*] burn (ignoring a staff officer's protest) instead of ordering the repair of the water and electricity supplies, and leaves wounded prisoners unattended in a hospital (ignoring a medical officer's protest)."[58] Not surprisingly, a cry of outrage was also heard from Allenby's descendants. "Sir, Is there any way in which a film company can be stopped from portraying a character so inaccurately as is that of the late Field Marshall Allenby in the version of *Lawrence of Arabia*? . . . Could an injunction be taken out?" asks Daisy Allenby of Megiddo, obviously distressed.[59] But the film's anticolonial stance, coupled with its relatively more sympathetic portrayal of Arabs, was made possible by the more relaxed attitude of the British Board of Film Censors, which in the past had been concerned about the effects that colonial representations in film would have on Britain's colonial possessions but could look the other way now that they were insignificant.[60]

The movie's American premiere took place on December 16, 1962, at the Criterion Theater in New York City. If the filmmakers' jaundiced view of the establishment's war and colonial heroes was the context for understanding the film's reception in Great Britain, a film about Arabs and their fight for freedom could not be presumed to be a success in the United States when the Arab-Israeli conflicts were still lingering in the public's memory and resentment toward, if not fear of, Arabs was barely, if at all, repressed. In order to counteract such negative reactions, Abe Kronenberg of Columbia Pictures (the company with which Spiegel had contracted to distribute the film), in conjunction with Rand McNally, visited a hundred top high schools across the country to talk to young people about Lawrence, World War I, and the film.[61] However, it was not until the movie won seven Oscars (Picture, Director, Cinematography, Editing, Art Direction, Sound, and Musical Score) that attendance in movie theaters picked up and the producer could relax.

There was another concern of a racist kind, one perhaps more subtle than audience's negative reactions to Arabs, that is evident in the U.S. public's reaction to the movie's early poster. It showed a man's head with traditional Arab headgear pulled in front of his face, plunging it in deep shadow. This image was in keeping with one of the movie's motifs, that of the enigmatic hero, and was suggested by the resemblance of the face to the outlines of a theatrical mask on the one hand and to a sphinx on

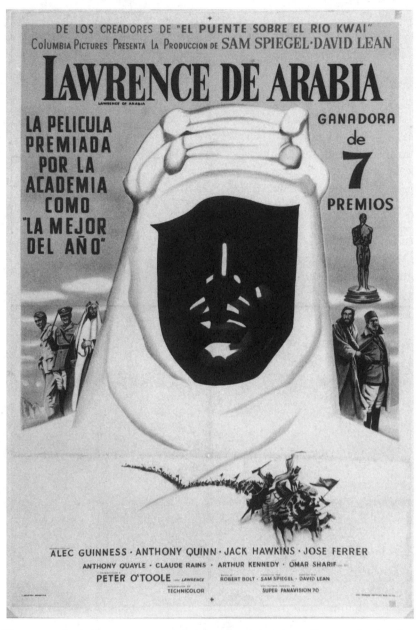

Figure 1.   Argentinean poster advertising the 1962 release (from author's collection; photo by Jon Kersey).

the other (see figure 1). Audiences, however, who knew nothing about the film or the story interpreted "the almost completely shadowed face in the ad art [as] . . . a black man." [62] As a result, they stayed away from the movie. An even more interesting spin is thus given to the American public's interpretation of the film, especially in light of the burgeoning civil rights movement of the 1960s. Might the repressed "other" for white U.S. audiences have been "black" Americans, leading their own struggle for liberation, and might this repression have been the reason for their aversion to the poster? As for African-Americans who had seen the movie at the time of its release, it would also be interesting to know how, if at all, they identified with the character and his story. Assuming that white audiences would not come to see a movie about a "black hero," the studio cynically changed the image on the posters, lightening the face and over the years making it appear more and more like Peter O'Toole once he had become a star. Omar Sharif, who had been virtually absent on the original posters, also began to be featured.

Whether the film's distribution extended much beyond audiences in Great Britain, Europe, and the United States is not clear to me. Evidently, it was shown in Buenos Aires, if the evidence of the poster shown in figure 1 is any indication. Whether or not it was released in cinemas in other Latin American capitals is a question I have yet to answer. My information is even less trustworthy for Asia. Let me therefore concentrate on the Middle East.

As can be readily imagined, the reception in this region of the world would have been even more sensitive to problems of cultural representation, not to mention the politics of British colonialism and Arab nationalism. The official reception was bound to be chilly, though perhaps no one could have predicted just how chilly, for on January 13, 1964 — a little more than two years after its release — Jordan's Council of Ministers voted to ban the film. [63] Though the official registry of Jordanian laws does not give reasons for the ban, the *Guardian* reported the next day that, according to the Committee for the Boycott of Israel, "Arabs in the film were presented 'in a comic way and favourable Arab attitudes in modern Arab history converted into ridiculous attitudes.'" [64] The film was also banned in Beirut but not, in all places, Cairo (according to one Egyptian filmmaker who recalls having seen a badly cut version of it). Turkish reaction may have taken a different form but was no less severe than that of the Jordanian government. According to the *Times* of January 18, 1963, the Turkish government issued an official protest against the film's depiction of Ottoman soldiers. [65] I am not certain, however, that the film was actually banned in Turkey at the time. I do know of Turks who have subsequently seen it in Istanbul.

Never, as far as I know, did the filmmakers go on record to defend themselves against Arab and Turkish accusations of misrepresentation, the way they did against criticisms from the British establishment. I don't think we can jump to the conclusion that they didn't care how the movie would fare in Third World countries, for the industry generally hoped that the so-called international movie would have global box-office appeal. How the obsession for authenticity was mediated by processes of wide-screen filmmaking will be examined next.

CHAPTER 2

Lean's Lens

An Embodiment of Vision

I begin with Lean's story of his scouting trip in early 1960, deep into the interior of Jordan, where he was searching for possible locations in which to shoot his film.[1] It was a profoundly moving, almost transcendental experience for him, which he recounted in a twelve-page, single-spaced typed letter, dated April 24, 1960, and sent to his then scriptwriter Michael Wilson. This was several months before they had their bitter falling-out, and so the tone is intimate and friendly.

The letter is remarkable for what it reveals of the creative process through which Lean came up with the images in his film. It gradually became clear to him that the romantic desert of his childhood, gleaned from boys' books and magazines as well as Hollywood movies such as *The Sheik* (1921), had created a nostalgic and magical place in his imagination, which the "reality" he now saw did not match. Though he was at first sad about the discovery, he realized that the desert he was traveling through was more thrilling than, if still quite different from, what he had imagined it to be. His understanding of his task as a director was to make his audience see the desert as he had seen it—to experience his awe of it, his wonder and excitement—and to achieve those responses, it was equally clear to him that wide-screen processes were essential.

Besides his production manager, John Palmer, the director was accompanied by two other men, a British expatriate named George Littledale, with many years of experience in Jordan, who served as interpreter and escort, and a bedouin guide on loan from the Jordanian army, whose name was Aloysh and was said to know the desert like the back of his hand.[2] As it turned out, the party was reenacting the story Lean was hoping to film—of a man in the company of bedouin guides, searching for something and someone to devote himself to and through which to enhance his own reputation.[3]

Lean had declined King Hussein's offer of a helicopter, confessing that he was "the original cowardly flyer," and so the party proceeded by car, heading southward from the capital of Amman to the famous "red rock" Hellenic city of Petra. The vehicles taking the sharp curves at an alarming speed made Lean complain of vertigo. His discomfort only increased when they changed over to the horses needed to negotiate the narrow defile into the valley leading to the ancient city. "The horse bumps up and down with merciless regularity," prompting Lean to lament. "What do you *do* with them? You can't stand up in the stirrups for two hours. . . . It's the only time I wished I were a woman." When they arrived at Petra, it was nighttime and too dark to see anything. Lean shivered from the cold. To make matters worse, the party arrived too late to secure rooms in the tourist "hotel" and had to spend a fitful night sleeping in tents.

Like nearly every traveler to Petra before him, however, Lean did find his reward, even if he had to wait for it until the next morning. "The rocks *are* rose red," he exclaimed to Wilson, "and the whole place is much more impressive than any pictures we have seen in any of the books. . . . what sights! what colours!" Lean's sense of the shortcomings of pictorial representations of the desert is plainly revealed. To help plan the shooting of what he hoped would be a more satisfyingly realistic portrayal, he took numerous color slides as well as black-and-white print film, hoping that "if I've done a good job they should give a pretty good idea of the things we saw." "The trouble is one needs Tod [*sic*] A.O.," one of the film formats widely in use for wide-screen productions of the 1950s, a telling remark, given that Lean planned to make one of the greatest epics of the wide screen. The point, however, is that the screen's gigantic size was not to be simply gratuitous for Lean's subject. The medium was integral to his visualization of the desert.

As magnificent as Petra is, it was not its beauty that was so tantalizing to him. It was rather the indistinct strip of desert beyond that beckoned his gaze:

> I think the most impressive sight was from way up behind the hotel near a second temple. From the top we could look downwards towards the Wadi Araba over precipices of jagged rock. You could see it was distant desert but

couldn't really define it. A blurred line of dazzling off-white merging slowly into the deepest blue sky.

It was at the outpost of Abu l-Lissan—two hours away by car from the port city of 'Aqaba, the site of Lawrence's greatest military triumph and the party's destination—that Lean found what he was searching for. "For the first time we saw the real desert," he explained. He experienced a kind of epiphany.

> It practically took my breath away. The hill is about 3,000 feet above, and one looks down on a vast plain out of which hills and mountains spring up like sugarloaves. The desert is off-white, and the hills and mountains are of every colour you can think of.

Lean's gaze is painterly and abstract: shades of color and light; shapes and volumes; perspective and depth. It is also in many ways an orientalist gaze, for the "real" desert lay beyond the towns, "dirty, broken down and untrustworthy," a conceit about oriental civilization in decay that is only too familiar in the literature of the nineteenth century. By contrast, "the desert is *wonderful*." To his credit, Lean gradually became aware of the fact that his gaze was powerfully mediated by representations not of his own making, which now appeared to him to be hackneyed and false:

> It gave me a shock as [the desert] wasn't at all what I had expected from my boyhood diet of "The Sheikh," "The Garden of Allah" and "Beau Geste." . . . I was terribly worried by not finding what I expected. I thought I would find miles and miles of flat sand and oceans of rolling sand dunes—and they're just not there.

Initial disappointment gave way to elation, however. He began to think that he was seeing the desert in images that were novel and fresh. "I suddenly came to and realised that what I was seeing was better than what I had hoped to see."

Besides the movies, another but much later source of Lean's impressions of the desert was Lawrence's memoir, *Seven Pillars of Wisdom* (1935), a copy of which he is said to have taken along on his reconnaissance trip. A film director like Lean would appreciate Lawrence's acute visual and mimetic powers, the exercise of which is nowhere more obsessive than in his depictions of the desert. Here, for example, is Lawrence on Wadi Rumm, Jordan, which was to become one of the filming locales:

> The ascent became gentle, till the valley was a confined tilted plain. The hills on the right grew taller and sharper, a fair counterpart of the other side which

straightened itself to one massive rampart of redness. They drew together until only two miles divided them: and then, towering gradually till their parallel parapets must have been a thousand feet above us, ran forward in an avenue for miles.

They were not unbroken walls of rock, but were built sectionally, in crags like gigantic buildings, along two sides of their street. Deep alleys, fifty feet across, divided the crags, whose planes were smoothed by the weather into huge apses and bays, and enriched with surface fretting and fracture, like design. Caverns high up on the precipice were round like windows; others near the foot gaped like doors. Dark stains ran down the shadowed front for hundreds of feet, like accidents of use. The cliffs were striated vertically, in their granular rock; whose main order stood on two hundred feet of broken stone deeper in colour and harder in texture. This plinth did not, like the sandstone, hang in folds like cloth; but chipped itself into loose courses of scree, horizontal as the footings of a wall.

The crags were capped in nests of domes, less hotly red than the body of the hill; rather grey and shallow. They gave the finishing semblance of Byzantine architecture to this irresistible place: this processional way greater than imagination. . . . Landscapes, in childhood's dreams, were so vast and silent.[4]

Lean's initial response to this description was to demur. This is a desert Petrafied, made grand by its allusions to antique and now decayed civilization, precisely what Lean was fleeing from. "At first I was a little disappointed," he ruefully notes. And though he was to come around at least insofar as Lawrence's awe of Wadi Rumm was concerned, admitting that he "found it the most exciting place of all," his description playfully inverts the passage in *Seven Pillars,* with its striving for Byzantine splendor. "Again, it's vast. . . . It's red rock rising straight out of the plain and going up to God knows what, and some prehistoric giants had a game and poured a sauce on top of the pudding giving it a grey-white top." In Lean's imagination this is a land anterior to civilization, a landscape, as Lawrence proclaimed in his final haunting allusion, that exists in childhood dreams. Lean's description is less lyrical than whimsical, in the tone of a children's storybook, complete with giants pouring pudding into mountains. Traveling in the desert may have resonated with supposedly prelapsarian moments of his childhood, that is, before the breakup of his parents' marriage, when the teenage Lean had snapped pictures of beautiful scenery with his camera, except that the geography of his imagination had now been displaced from Europe onto Arabia.

His enchantment was immediately checked by another shock. "I was really carried away by this desert stuff," he remarks with a trace of embarrassment, for neither John Palmer nor George Littledale shared his enthusiasm. Their lukewarm reaction ushers in another moment of doubt and introspection. Is he mad, Lean asks himself, for being so enthralled? Is he being obsessive? No, he concludes: a representational tradition found in the boys' magazines of his childhood may have been "a cliché-ridden lot of nonsense" but it nonetheless instilled in him "the magic of distant places," a magic reawakened in his intense, personal experience of *seeing* the desert for the first time. His aim is not a nostalgic one of re-creating those places from his children's books, along with their clichés. Rather, his project is realist, in the sense that he wants audiences to see the desert as he now thinks he sees it for the first time. He anxiously wonders, "Can I make audiences share my thrill?"

'Aqaba. Lean loved the slightly dilapidated port city, suggesting that his attitude toward Arab towns was not uniformly negative. But he especially marveled at the wadis in the vicinity, at their variety, telling his production manager that he could probably shoot the entire film in their environs—if he had to, which he hoped he would not, for he wanted to photograph as much of the desert landscape as possible. "There are numerous ravines down which camels could charge," and he notes that they "are the most desolate you can imagine. . . . Hardly a bit of scrub and *pitiless*. Makes the kite scene in [*Bridge on the River*] *Kwai* look quite cosey." Climbing to the top of the ravines, Lean could look out to sea. "The sun shining on the gulf makes it stand out like a glittering mirror," an image he was to exploit in the movie after Lawrence has taken 'Aqaba with the help of the Arab army and tries to savor his moment of victory in solitude by the shore. Lean was also mesmerized by the sandstorms drifting like ghosts over the islands. "They are constantly crossing the sea and add an out-of-this-world effect to a staggering landscape." He gushes to Wilson, rather gratuitously by this point in his letter, "I *loved* it." The sandstorm—transferred from the sea to the desert, transformed from an isolated squall into an encompassing whirlwind—would become symbolic not only of Lawrence's character but also of the larger structure of the film's narrative. Lean pronounces the desert "ever changing. From one point one gets 4 set-ups. Go around the other side of the hillock and you get 4 more. You can just take your pick." It was that variety he tried to capture in his film.

From 'Aqaba Lean's party proceeded to Mudawwara, where a fort still existed at which Lawrence had holed up and beyond which he had harassed the Turkish railway. But something far more shattering than the traces of Lawrence's exploits was in store for him. On their way to Mudawwara, the party had to proceed through the mudflats of al-Jafar.

"There's a terrible loneliness about these mud flats," Lean confides with a shudder. "They are more deserted than any desert I've seen or read about." A gruesome incident gives Lean the idea of how to film the climactic scene of the movie, the massacre of a Turkish brigade ordered by Lawrence in revenge for the rape and destruction of a bedouin village. Lean is the involuntary, if fascinated, witness to an impromptu hunt of two gazelles, beautiful and graceful creatures that are said to cry when they are mortally wounded and are now unfortunately extinct in the Arabian Peninsula. "Once out in the open mud flat nothing's got a chance if you can keep it from reaching the shore on either side. . . . One [gazelle] escaped but the other went spinning over and over after a ghastly chase." In accordance with Islamic dietary law, the creature's throat is cut. Lean is disgusted at the sight, swearing that "these ancient prophets must be roasting in some animal hell." And then he sees how to shoot the massacre of the Turks. "I think, Mike, the great trick in this is to take a leaf out of the poor gazelle and make it a panic scene of the Turks trying to disperse in different directions, and all directions ending in F.A. [fuck-all] and the gun and the knife."

It was in the mudflats, too, that Lean saw the mirages that would become such a haunting image in the film. To Wilson he divulged, "The light is the strongest I've ever screwed up my eyes against." If the waters in the gulf served as a mirror for that light, waves of heat rippling on the desert floor acted as its distorting lens, producing the fabled fata morgana. In an almost scientific tone, he notes that it is difficult to tell the nature of distant objects seen through these mirages. "Half the effect," he notes of their powers of distortion, "comes from movement. I've taken stills—and you can see it even on the black and whites—but the real thing is the movement and colour." I made a similar discovery when I tried to reproduce images of a mirage from the movie: even when one placed consecutive frames next to each other, they failed to capture adequately the flamelike flickering of the image. This shortcoming was even more pronounced in black-and-white reproductions. Color is indispensable to the effect. "For some reason the mirage seems bluer than the sky and therefore gives the impression of a lake," Lean observes. But his experience of the mirage was even more profoundly unnerving than these clinical observations might suggest, for something seen through a mirage is not simply distorted but momentarily unrecognizable, unintelligible, unknown. "What is it?" one might ask unconsciously and perhaps apprehensively. And then Lean had his brainstorm. "I found myself thinking of introducing Ali this way," he tells Wilson. "There could be a

certain amount of tension about such an appearance because you really
don't know what's coming towards you." Just how this effect complicates
and deepens Lean's realist project will be explored later when we consider
it in relation to Walter Benjamin's idea of the "optical unconscious."

In the rest of his letter to Wilson, Lean describes the final leg of
the journey, which included finding the remains of the Turkish railway
Lawrence and his raiders had wrecked, but the tone is anticlimactic. By
then he had understood his project. He would make audiences see the
desert as he (and they) had never seen it before, whether in Hollywood
films, travel magazines, or even Lawrence's memoir, and he would communicate his thrill for this "magical" place through equally magical
wide-screen processes of the day.

The idea of wide-screen viewing being more "realistic" was one that the
film industry, of course, encouraged in the 1950s as part of its hype about
CinemaScope. Every time, in fact, there is a technological advance in visual representation or aural projection, it is promoted by boasts of enhanced realism. Take, for example, the impending commercial release of
high-resolution television and ads which proclaim that the images will
be as sharp as "natural" vision, as if seeing everything with the detail of
an object held about six inches from one's face were a standard of the
culture. But the 1950s were also a time in which realism in film and its
connection to the technological breakthrough of the day, CinemaScope,
was theorized, and it is ironic that the critic who did so most compel-
lingly was perhaps most responsible for constructing and advancing the
agendas of the new French cinema of the 1950s that would displace
Lean and his cinematic practices at the pinnacle of film art. "The narrow, traditional screen," wrote André Bazin in a 1954 article on Cinema-
Scope published in the influential journal Cahiers du cinéma, "is an accident which most of the great cineastes have tried to overcome."[5] Abel
Gance's Napoleon (1927), with its multiple screens and projectors, was
perhaps the most magnificent of such attempts, and Bazin speculated
that such experiments with big screens might not have been aborted if
sound had not revolutionized the medium. When CinemaScope came
along in the mid-1950s, he was curious to see whether that great early
experiment might now be successfully completed. His enthusiasm was
also shared by a few American critics such as Charles Barr. There was
thus a brief moment in French and American film criticism and theory
when wide-screen processes were applauded as having potentially revo-
lutionizing effects. If the euphoria was short-lived, having almost entirely

subsided by the 1960s, when critical opinion turned sharply against wide-screen filming, it is nevertheless important to understand why it was taken seriously at the time—why, that is, the connection between realism and an emergent technology seemed so clear in the minds of critics and audiences alike.

As a way into that discussion, it might be useful to review some of the technological innovations that underpinned wide-screen processes of this period. The pre-1953 screen (1953 being the release date of the first CinemaScope movie, *The Robe*) was almost square, with an aspect ratio of 1.33 (length) to 1 (width), or with proportions we would describe informally as 4:3. With experiments in the 1950s, the screen's shape began to change. It not only became more oblong through widening, but also became curved (outer edges toward the audience), thereby giving the spectator a greater sense of depth (a consequence also of opening up the frame)—at least if he or she were seated in the center and toward the front of the screen. To take advantage of the wider screen, filming and projection processes had to be changed. With a standard 35 mm film, a cinematographer would have to use a special anamorphic lens to encompass a scene approximately two and a half times as wide as it was high. The lens would then take an image and squeeze it into the frame of the standard negative size. If shown on the screen with a standard 35 mm projector, however, the now greatly shrunken image would look rather like a face squeezed between two hands; therefore, another anamorphic lens was required on the movie projector to stretch the image back to its original size. Schematically, this was the CinemaScope method that eventually was used in most movie houses around the country.

There were two serious hitches with the method, however. A grainy image was one of them. To correct it, a number of solutions were tried, including Todd-AO and Super Panavision, the latter used for *Lawrence of Arabia*. In these formats the image is exposed on a 65 mm negative, which is printed onto a 70 mm positive, leaving room for the sound track. But this method was not without its own glitches. The wider the angle of the lens's field, the greater the distortion of the image, with lines off of center frequently appearing bent on the screen. Those of us who grew up in the 1950s may remember one of the more hilarious moments in the movie theater when an object, say a car, was seen passing but would suddenly appear crooked on the screen. To prevent such image distortion, the object or actor moving in the upper or lower part of the screen had to be shot by the camera man at a diagonal. But the correction of one problem seemed to produce another, for if sharpness of image was finally gained, a peculiar "flutter" effect was produced during projection, a blurring of the image so pronounced that it was intolerable to human vision if left uncorrected.[6] The method of correction could be a bit trying for actor and director alike, as Fred Young (b. 1902), the cinematographer of *Lawrence of Arabia,* explains: "When this problem occurs with movement across the front of the lens, the director must slow the actor down or give him a more diagonal movement where the flutter is less likely to occur. . . . Some tests are necessary so that everyone becomes acclimatized to the wide-screen medium."[7]

As for improved sound, it was basically the same as stereophonic sound that had been developed commercially for record players, radios, and so forth.[8] In the older monaural system, sound was recorded as though it were being heard through one ear. Now microphones (in most cases three) were placed at different positions on the set, recording the sound separately (in other words, as they receive them from their own positions). The audio tracts are then projected through separate speakers in the auditorium (usually three), the effect being a reproduction for the audience of the *relative* positions of the sounds as they occurred in the performance. It was said in industry publicity materials that this effect made the listening experience vivid and intimate, or that one could overhear the performance as if one were in it. In other words, it was a kind of audial voyeurism.

What Bazin saw as *theoretically* exciting about CinemaScope, however, was less the widening and deepening of the field of vision, or even its stereophonic sound, than the prospect of its displacing montage editing. Montage constructs an intelligible scene by assembling separate shots into a sequence. It was, of course, developed to a fine art in the formalist tradition of film associated with Sergei Eisenstein and other directors. Because of the narrowness of the pre-CinemaScope frame, it was difficult to shoot an entire group of actors from head to foot in such a way that the audience could discern subtle facial expressions and other gestures, let alone the larger physical context that enveloped them. Thus, close-ups showing crucial facial reactions or gestures had to be spliced together with wider shots of the group as a whole. "Montage," writes Bazin, "which one wanted, wrongly, to believe was the essence of cinema, is in reality relative to the exiguity of the classical image, condemning the director to morseling reality piece-by-piece. From this point of view, CinemaScope is part of the logical evolution of cinema."[9] If "reality" is morseled and then artificially reassembled in montage, CinemaScope, by contrast, seemed to allow the audience to apprehend it "whole," very much as it would have without the mediation of film editing.

Another great champion of CinemaScope, the American film critic Charles Barr, spoke in even more pointed terms than Bazin when he connected the greater space through which action could be represented on the wide screen with a certain narrative realism. Here, for example, is Barr on a segment from Nicholas Ray's *Bitter Victory* (1957):

> The scene is taken in a series of full or medium close-ups, each of the three in turn, as they talk, sometimes two together. The normal theoretical attitude is that this would be fine on the old-ratio screen but clumsy if not impossible in Scope. If anything, the reverse is true, and it works brilliantly *because* it is in Scope: the cutting does not disorient us, the close-ups do not wholly isolate the characters, we know where we are all through. At the edges of the frame there is decor and space and perhaps some casual detail; thus when the camera is on one of the men, Richard Burton, we can see a couple dancing, and an Arab guard, and a general background of the room; we are completely situated at each moment, and accept the scene as real, while getting the full concentration of each face.[10]

On the wide screen the background of a figure, shown in close-up, would still be visible, thus keeping the figure in context. Rapid cutting (as in the earlier montage style) was considered disturbing on the wide screen as opposed to longer and more fluid takes, though Barr conceded that the latter required more planning by the director and more rehearsing by the actors. Nevertheless, the supposed gains of enhanced "realism" were worth the extra effort on the set:

> It is much easier to put together a complex scene synthetically out of separate details . . . than to organize and film the scene in its integrity. But you sacrifice the possibility of *real* conviction, of *real* subtlety.[11]

Bazin was to embrace wide-screen processes even more rapturously in an article published the year following his "Fin de montage," this time on Cinerama. He was bowled over not by the screen image's depth of field but by its overwhelming sense of space:

> For the first time, or almost (this reservation applying to rare images in CinemaScope of which I will speak shortly), I was aware of the limitations of all images known to this day in that they all were powerless to render space, being confined to translating it by the geometrical symbolism of perspective. I am not in a position nor have I the competence to analyze the causes for this discovery, but one at least seems certain: the angle of vision. At 146 degrees in Cinerama it is thus nearly equal to that of natural vision. Likewise one is in effect physiologically incapable of synthesizing all the elements of the image: to look one must not only move one's eyes but also the head.[12]

Then he pointedly connects these effects of space with documentary film: "We may dream what Flaherty would have been able to do with Cinema-Scope or Cinerama, he for whom the spatial relations of man and nature constituted the infrastructure of the mise-en-scène." [13] Unfortunately, the point Bazin makes about documentary filmmakers such as Flaherty who took space, more than anything else, as the subject of his realism is something of a red herring, for it narrows the notion of realism to a certain kind of subject matter or content—which is, to be sure, one of the ways in which it has been traditionally understood—but this seems less interesting than a notion about the *experience* of film perception per se. [14] The latter, I believe, gets us to the heart of what is interesting about CinemaScope and its offshoot Panavision. When Bazin does get to talking about *perception* of the screen image, and the difference in that perception between CinemaScope and previous methods, he obscures the issue even more by employing two outworn metaphors of film criticism: that of the (picture) frame and that of the window. In pre-CinemaScope movies, according to Bazin, images are carefully composed in relation to an imaginary frame constituted by the edges of the screen, similar to the way in which a classical painter composed a picture. In CinemaScope, on the other hand, the frame (almost) disappears because of the great width and curvature of the screen, thus making the experience of vision more like standing by a window and gazing out onto the world.

The trouble with talking in terms of frames and windows is that, as the phenomenologist film critic Vivian Sobchack argues, they make vision passive—in other words, always removed and at a distance from an action or object represented by the film—as opposed to an active experience in which the spectator's body is involved, not to mention that it appears to be integral to the space-time dimension of the screen image. [15] In many ways, film technicians and industry spokesmen understood this point well. These technological innovations were said to be experienced in direct psychophysical terms. They emphasized the ways in which a person was *physically* drawn into the scene, a sensation of palpable connectedness with the event being represented. Because of the curved screen that tended to envelop peripheral vision, the viewing experience was felt to be more vivid or, as people liked to say, "more real." Leon Shamroy, cinematographer of *The Robe*, added that because of the curved screen, which "gives the viewer a feeling of being surrounded by the action and, therefore, participating in it," he was "immediately aware of the disappearance of the proscenium." [16] In other words, the classical frame seems to, though never quite does, disappear. Here again is invoked "the realism of the big screen, its ability to project a life-like illusion," as Jean Negulesco, director of *How to Marry a Millionaire* (1953), explained. "The new process brings the audience into the action, makes them feel they are in the same room with the performers." [17] Of course, there is the question here of which came first, the chicken or the egg: Was there a palpable difference in perception, which the discourse tried to represent; or did the discourse predispose the viewer to perceive a technologically produced image as different and more "real"? I think both are true. That is, it is undeniable that a new kind of seeing was effected by widescreen processes, but at the same time audience attention had to be oriented to these effects, their bodies disciplined to assimilate them. For example, the head had to move around the screen in order to encompass the scene, and the eye had to wander around in the detail to discern a visual pattern. This is a motor habit that a younger generation of filmgoers is unused to, having grown up with rapidly edited television images that require different corporal training, namely, that of the head remaining steady in front of the screen.

Following Sobchack, one could speak of the realism of film viewing phenomenologically, or in terms of embodiment. That is, one feels as if one's own body were continuous with the space inhabited by the image on the screen. One experiences the image more as one would if one were simply *in* the world of the object that the image represents, a feeling of coexistential connectedness that is enhanced by the fact that the sense of the frame that marks the limit of the screen begins to disappear. More radical still is Sobchack's insistence not only that the viewing subject must be understood to be more dynamic but also that the image on the screen is in turn a subject because it appears to be embodied (or made incarnate) in the spectator.[18] It is not that the film image is a human subject but that it is not without any subjectivity at all. The impression of subjectivity is produced, first of all, by the realization that what one is seeing is an intentionally produced object (the product of a director, a screenwriter, actors, cameraman, and so forth). In addition, the impression of subjectivity is enhanced on the wide screen because of our sense of the visual representation exceeding one's perception, at least on first viewing. We seem to have to interact with the film image, in different ways and on multiple occasions, in order to grasp it, but the grasp is never complete, much as it wouldn't be if we were trying to get a handle on a person.

I would suggest, then, that it is in terms of such a notion of embodiment that we must understand Lean's realist project when filming the desert in Super Panavision. At the film's most intense visual moments, the wide screen would allow the frame to virtually disappear, with the result that one felt one's own body to be coterminous with, and not outside of or removed from, the action represented on the screen. Phenomenologically, the desert is a subject acting upon the viewer, who feels as though he or she were being watched by it. Jacques Lacan asks somewhere in his writings, is it the fisherman who sees the tin can bobbing up and down in the water or is it the tin can that sees the fisherman and through its glint catches his eye? It is only fair to point out that critical opinion eventually looked down on the "experiments" of the wide screen. For example, in an excellent overview of wide-screen processes, David Bordwell, a leading figure of film theory, concludes that "Hollywood's widescreen filmmaking was but another instance of trended change, a new set of stylistic devices brought into line with the classical schemata."[19] But this is to miss the point about embodiment that I have been making. What may have changed was less a narrative form than a visual *experience*. It is also this point that I wish to underscore in Lean's realist project.

As a final note, it is useful to recall that these issues are still alive today. CinemaScope, Todd-AO, Super Panavision, not to mention Cinerama, were antecedents of the giant IMAX screens and technologies of "virtual reality" that are the commodity fetishes of the 1990s. Viewing *Lawrence of Arabia* on the big curved screen might not be alien to today's younger generation of moviegoers after all. Indeed, one could argue that, because of their familiarity with today's technologies, these audiences would have a clearer understanding and better appreciation of the experiments of vision Lean and his generation of wide-screen directors strove to achieve.

If the previous chapter helped us understand why and how Lean transformed himself from a national into an international filmmaker, we must now come to grips with the other momentous change in his long career. He had mastered the traditional montage style of filmmaking; he was considered by many to be the finest editor in the film industry. In the 1950s, first with *Bridge* and then with *Lawrence,* he made a transition to wide-screen processes that not all directors managed successfully.

Lean's filmmaking prior to his work on the wide screen can be encapsulated by the metaphor of the "frame" used by Bazin to describe the traditionally narrow screen. His scrupulous attention to formal composition and camera angle is one of the reasons that he, according to his own admission, was considered a "classic" or "formalist" director.

In fact, it was the formalism of classical cinema, he has said, that attracted him to this art form in the first place. As a young man in the early 1920s, he would escape from his humdrum activities as an accountant by watching the silent films of director Rex Ingram (1892–1950), noted for his *Four Horsemen of the Apocalypse* (1921) and *Mare Nostrum* (1925–26). Watching those films, Lean realized that "somebody was actually guiding [the camera]": "Ingram's images had such power. I knew that they were thought-out images. It wasn't that the camera just happened to be there. . . . It was a view of what was taking place. And he had staged it. . . . This I found tremendously exciting." [20] Before we can understand how Lean arranged the desert in order, like Lawrence, to "write" his cinematic will upon it, it is helpful to briefly review his career.

Lean himself has constructed it as a kind of Horatio Alger story. Through his father's connections, the nineteen-year-old managed to get an interview with the production manager of Gaumont Studios (a French-based firm with production units in London that became British-owned in 1922). He started out by serving tea to the production crews, sweeping the studio floors, cranking the hand-operated cameras, and even standing in for the mistress of the wardrobe. It was in part because of his multifaceted experience gained while climbing up the industry ladder that he later became known as a director with total control of his medium.

He excelled especially in film editing. It was his work in the editing room, in fact, that made his reputation in the industry, after he had successfully edited newsreels in the early 1930s and then switched over to feature films. In the estimation of some prominent directors, he was the best editor in England; a few argued that he was the best in the world. He retained his fondness for the process all his life and edited his own films throughout his career. In his filmed self-portrait Lean talks about the quasi-sensual pleasure he derived from running the celluloid strip through his fingers, as though he could not quite imagine the final product unless he made palpable contact with it.

As Lean's responsibilities on the set grew, his work began to rival in importance that of the directors he was supposed to be assisting, until he gradually took over from them. He got his first real break while working with Noël Coward in his World War II propaganda film *In Which We Serve* (1942). More important perhaps than his directorial debut was the practice he adopted for capturing the big action sequences in this film, a practice he would continue to adopt for works he directed in their entirety. Sitting down with the writer, he developed a production script, precisely visualizing every action and reaction shot in terms of camera angle and range, gestures, expressions, props, sound effects, and so forth. He referred to the script as a "blueprint," and he claimed to deviate from it while shooting only in the slightest details.[21] It was this kind of preparation, this exact attention to detail, that earned Lean the reputation of a perfectionist. While admirable in some respects—he garnered the sobriquet of the thorough "professional"—his practices have also been called too controlling and even patriarchal by performers and critics alike.[22] The important imaginative thinking, in Lean's opinion, had to come before the shooting ever started, which would tend, of course, to make actors feel excluded from a creative process dominated by the director and screenwriter. If anything, wide-screen filmmaking exacerbated these tendencies, but in his defense Lean would argue that the kind of "big" filmmaking in which he was engaged—involving as it did huge and complex equipment, not to mention sometimes thousands of technicians and actors, to be transported halfway around the world— was too costly and complex to allow for vagary, chance, or even lengthy experimentation on the set. Paradoxically, however, this same perfectionism could become tremendously expensive as well, when he would insist, for example, on having only the right kind of equipment or location for certain kinds of shots. For the sake of his realism, after all, Lean would have preferred to have stayed in Jordan for the entire filming of *Lawrence of Arabia,* even though this was financially prohibitive and politically precarious.

Let us now consider the sorts of changes Lean would have needed to adopt as part of his film technique, once he began working in the wide-screen format. Two directors of very different CinemaScope movies, one an epic, the other a bedroom comedy, wrote brief comments about their experiences. Henry Koster, the director of *The Robe,* pointed out that "the composition technique of a first-rate painter (because he is working on a large canvas)"[23] was still required of anyone who worked in CinemaScope. He best captures the ambiguousness of the space occupied by the CinemaScope director when he describes it as "somewhere between the stage and the screen technique."[24] That is, a director must pay more attention to staging a scene because more of the scene is visible to the viewer, as it is on stage. Actors, even whole crowds, now moved more, either toward, away from, or across the camera, rather than remaining more or less stationary before it, with the camera moving if necessary.

Because the total scene could be photographed much nearer to the action, actors' faces were clearly visible, even at considerable distances, and close-ups were unnecessary. They could appear distorting or simply superfluous if not used with care, though this did not mean that close-ups were not extremely effective when narratively motivated. For example, Leon Shamroy, the cinematographer for *The Robe,* was proud of the enormous close-up of Victor Mature gazing rapturously at the cross. "Close-ups are more dramatic than ever," he proclaimed.[25] Because the new screen could literally take in more space, a shot of space *as* space could be exciting in and of itself. "No director has the power to portray with montage or long shots the magnitude and spirit of New York City as we have done in this picture with a single shot of the city's skyline at dusk," says Negulesco of *How to Marry a Millionaire,* who claims that audiences applauded at the image when they first saw it "as though it were a symphony orchestra."[26] Of course, this use of the wide screen to capture a vastness of space would be especially tantalizing to someone like Lean working in the desert.

One of the results of being able to shoot a whole scene without having to insert close-ups, according to Shamroy, was not only that the director would have to become more of a stage director but also that "actors will have to memorize more lines and more action, and the timing of scenes will have to be precise, as cutting to other angles will be less frequent and more difficult."[27] The takes would be longer and in a sense more fluid. Also affected was perhaps the cinematographer's most interesting and vexing challenge: lighting. Since more area could be photographed, huge arc lamps would be needed to light a range far from the subject that nevertheless was part of the narrative context. Because Lean found the light in Arabia the strongest he had ever "screwed his eyes up against," it was ironic that his cinematographer had to use even larger arc lamps, the problem being that contrast in desert light was so stark that shadows had to be lightened if they were not to appear opaquely black on the screen. "On this broad canvas," Shamroy exulted, "we can paint with lights, highlighting actors and scenes both in the foreground and the background which we want to dominate."[28] Lean would find precisely such a painter in his cinematographer Fred Young.

Since *Lawrence of Arabia* was shot in Super Panavision, Lean had an even larger "canvas," as everyone was fond of calling the camera frame, on which to visualize the story than was available on regular 35 mm film. The "window" on the world may have widened, but now he was faced with perhaps the greatest problem of all: how to fill the window, laterally

Figure 2.   Frontal view of Gasim shedding his dagger and cartridge belt.

as well as in terms of depth of field, when he was shooting something—
a desert—that was seemingly empty of details. In part, this would require
a kind of painterly or compositional art, which he had already mastered
from an earlier style of directing. But he was faced as well with the problem of how to embody that world for the spectator. He had constructed
an abstract geometry of planes and lines according to what he had learned
from the cinema of Rex Ingram. Now he would have to add a mastery
of a different kind.

One of the sequences that reveals Lean's sense of geometry and depth
of field on a huge but virtually empty canvas is Lawrence's rescue of
Gasim, a bedouin lost in the Nefud Desert. Sky, sun, desert, and human
figure on the horizon: these are virtually the only compositional elements
on the screen. In the beginning of this sequence, Gasim is seen trudging
in the direction of the rising sun. The feeling of isolation is almost abstract
in its purity and made more terrible by the vastness of the screen. We
watch the lone figure trudging on a perfectly level plane, its flatness un-
relieved by vegetation or stones, his shadow extending to the right. Then
he sheds pieces of apparel one after the other (figure 2). On the one hand,
this makes good narrative sense, but what Lean does with these items
also cleverly solves the problem of depth of field, for they form a line on
the desert floor, stretching behind and away from Gasim (figure 3). Moving along this line, our eyes apprehend how far and how fast he is walking. Then there is the opposite effect: a flattening of the field, when Gasim
is shot from above (the angle of the sun), or horizontally at the line of
the horizon as in a silhouette. These images of flattening, too, make good
narrative sense, for as Gasim succumbs to the agonizing effects of heat

Figure 3.   A lesson in depth of field: View of Gasim in far background, with his gear strewn in a diagonal line.

and thirst, he seems to have come to the end of his tether and moments later sinks to the ground, apparently lifeless. Gasim's ordeal is shot pretty much in a series of fluid takes interrupted by rapid cuts to a more and more blistering sun, but at the moment of his collapse there is a straight cut to a watering hole at which camels are noisily drinking, the idea of the thin line between life and death thereby dramatically underscored.

In the scene in which Gasim slowly succumbs to the sun's heat, we see how Lean applied the lessons he had learned from an earlier cinema, that of Rex Ingram. But the question remains of whether he captured something novel about the experience of visual perception on the wide screen. In other words, are we still operating as though vision were bounded by a frame? The images are for the most part static indeed, rather like figures that move into a frame and then freeze in a huge tableau vivant (or perhaps, in this case, mourant). The editing pattern involves views of Gasim trudging, the sun growing more intense, Lawrence riding, and Daud watching. What follows in this sequence, however, goes beyond montage editing. A rhythm of motion and speed is embodied for the spectator. The viewer, I would argue, is kinetically pulled into the action in a way that is possible perhaps only on the wide screen.

Take the static image of the boy servant Daud, who is waiting for Lawrence in this same scene, perched on a camel that stands motionless on the right side of the screen. The boy peers bleary-eyed at the horizon from under a tentlike structure he has fashioned out of his cloak to protect him against the sun. He looks at the horizon, dazzlingly white and empty except for what appears to be a whirlwind faintly visible in the distance. Out of this whirlwind Lawrence now appears, an image that is again not without narrative significance, given the allusions to Lawrence as riding a whirlwind (Dryden's remark at the end of Part One) and the earlier appearance of Sherif Ali in a mirage (the difference being, of course, that the Englishman brings life and hope, whereas the Arab brought only death and despair). When Daud sights Lawrence and tentatively prods his camel forward, his image slowly comes to life. Lean brings the audience into the movement of the boy's camel by showing the ground from the rider's perspective, passing with accelerating speed underneath the camel's feet. For a moment, *we* feel as though we are sitting on that camel. Small black pebbles (probably distributed by the film crew) are visible on the white surface of the desert floor, and when we look down at them, they seem to be rushing toward and underneath us in a blur. As the camel gallops at breakneck speed, the wide screen is used to show Daud and Lawrence racing toward each other from its periphery, as if to collide in the center. Because they start at opposite ends of a curved screen, it is as though they come into our field of vision, which is more thrilling than stepping into a frame. In any case, from almost complete immobility the movement on the screen changes into a rhythm of forward propulsion, in both the figures on the screen and the spectators in the audience, creating enormous exhilaration after minutes of suspense. Daud's forward momentum is further conveyed by having him overshoot his goal and continue rushing past Lawrence, the excess of speed symbolic of his exuberance and joy at finding Lawrence alive.

As we now understand, filmmaking practices for the wide screen—the longer takes and deep-focus photography, combined with wide-angle lenses that encompassed more of the narrative situation—allowed a director to think of the set as more like a theatrical stage and to encourage actors to think in those terms as well. Of course, if the medium allows for such possibilities, this does not mean that directors took advantage of them, nor that they had actors who could work dexterously with them. If actors were encouraged to conceptualize the set as a kind of stage, they nonetheless were also told to move differently on it, often at a diagonal to the camera and sometimes slowing down. Thus, if O'Toole's training as a stage actor could be exploited by Lean, it would also have to be adapted. A collaboration emerged, with Lean often taking O'Toole literally behind the camera to peer into the lens so he could see for himself how he would appear; thus he could keep that image in his mind's eye as he was acting on the set, adjusting his movements accordingly. Conversely, Lean had no directorial experience in the theater and was willing to entertain O'Toole's suggestions regarding a stagelike acting.

It is worth reviewing O'Toole's theatrical training and career up until the time he was cast as Lawrence to put his acting in *Lawrence of Arabia* in perspective.[29] After graduation in 1955 from the Royal Academy of Dramatic Art, one of England's finest acting schools, he became a repertory actor with the Bristol Old Vic. By its practices and roles he was shaped into the kind of actor that Lean would tap into. He had to learn to work, for example, with a talented and dedicated ensemble, to learn an enormous variety of roles, and to accept the fact that a walk-on one night is as important to the company's success and to the practice of the actor's art as a lead role the next. As can be expected of a newcomer, O'Toole began by acting in bit parts. Though the experience may have caused his ambition to bridle, it also challenged his ability to invent a presence and "stage business" that would make him intensely visible, at times perhaps even an annoying scene-stealer. In this kind of performance where the lines are few and the action sparse, he learned to use his entire body, producing maximum effects out of small details.

I mention this acting practice because of its importance to O'Toole's performance in *Lawrence*. He is visible on the screen in the obvious sense most of the time, but his presence could have become dull, had he not been constantly inventive in gesture and bodily movement, vocal inflection and facial expression. His body is often photographed in full, so that one can see how a particular step, a swing of the arm, or a turn of the body is executed for some specific dramatic effect. For example, if he trips in the famous scene at the Masturah Well, in order to express bodily the sense that he is thrown mentally off balance by the appearance of the "mysterious" stranger, he skips with arms slightly akimbo toward some fellow British officers whom he greets shortly after his return from Deraa (the scene of his beating and presumably also his rape by Turkish soldiers) in a movement that suggests "gayness."

In time, O'Toole was to become one of the most talented young Shakespearean actors on the English stage. The role in which he asserted his own vision of Shakespeare was the critically acclaimed 1958 Old Vic production of *Hamlet*. The director interpreted the character as a moody young rebel, very much in keeping with an emergent, transatlantic construction of masculinity called the "angry young man," most popularly represented in Britain by John Osborne's play *Look Back in Anger* (1957), whose main character, Jimmy Porter, boorish and self-pitying,

O'Toole had already played at the Old Vic. In his interpretation of Hamlet, O'Toole decided to do away with the melodious voice and the stilted delivery. He wanted to break free of conventional, stereotypical, and overly studied performances of the prince: "Shakespeare's a theatre man, for Christ's sake, not a deity. His people are real. You can smell their breath. They piss against the wall. That's the way I play Shakespeare."[30] As one critic noted, this "is a restless interpretation, crudely staccato in diction and gesture, yet blessed with uncommon energy and power."[31] And according to Nicholas Wapshott, his biographer, "O'Toole's Hamlet was . . . easily understood by a new generation of urgent, serious, intense young theatregoers for whom O'Toole would remain a life-long representative of their generation."[32]

In 1959 O'Toole was in rehearsal as Shylock for a new production of *The Merchant of Venice* that was being mounted not by the Bristol Old Vic but by Peter Hall's ambitious new company at Stratford-upon-Avon. At twenty-six he was the youngest leading man in Stratford's history and therefore something of a phenomenon.[33] Here again is his biographer: "He was to play [the role of Shylock] in an original way, as an individual Jew who tries to persuade the audience that his commercial logic is correct and appropriate. He was not going to play the Jew as an old-fashioned avaricious moneylender but as a go-ahead sixteenth-century entrepreneur, out to maximize his legitimate profits."[34] O'Toole's performances at the time made critics think he had the talent to become one of England's most compelling stage actors. Inevitably he was compared to Olivier and placed in an older tradition of grand and passionate acting that went as far back as Edmund Kean (1787?–1833), of whom Coleridge once said, "To see Kean act is like reading Shakespeare by flashes of lightning."

Although the credits to *Lawrence of Arabia* claim that Peter O'Toole was being "introduced" in this picture, this was not his first feature-length movie, though it was his first major film role.[35] He was nevertheless a relative newcomer to the screen. There were precedents in the way O'Toole was making himself into a film star, however, the most notable up to that time having been the career of Lawrence Olivier. (Kenneth Branaugh and Ralph Fiennes are arguably the latest in this tradition.) Talent was only one ingredient in the success of these Shakespearean actors turned film stars. Knowledgeable about a repertoire of canonical plays and trained in a dazzlingly virtuosic style, they were charismatic in film partly because of their association in the public's imagination with the core of the elite cultural tradition on both sides of the Atlantic—not to mention even the former colonies. It was a tradition that had been successfully commodified in the period of the late fifties and early sixties, as in Richard Burton's Broadway *Hamlet* (albeit its public notoriety abetted by his sensationalized affair with Elizabeth Taylor) or Marlon Brando's performance as Anthony in the Hollywood film version of *Julius Caesar* (1953). One woman who tried to explain to me one reason that *Lawrence of Arabia* made such a deep impression on her when she saw it as a teenager in the 1960s said, "Things were becoming deeply conflicted in the U.S. Civil rights was producing mass unrest. There was the beginning of big U.S. involvement in the Vietnam War. And then we began to discover the Beatles, and all things British seemed tantalizing."

It was particularly his Shakespearean training that stood O'Toole in good stead in the wide-screen medium in which he was to work, with its fluid takes and more carefully staged acting. To get a sense of the way O'Toole's theatrical training spills over into his performance on the screen, there is perhaps no better scene to watch than the one in which he exhibits himself for the first time in the robes of a sheikh of the Bani Wejh.

The robe is dazzlingly white and, to Western eyes, makes him appear more like a blushing bride than a military hero, with Sherif Ali standing before him like a proud husband or father. The image makes sense in terms of the dialogue between the two friends in the previous scene, in which Lawrence had admitted that he was illegitimate and Ali had decided that Lawrence should therefore reconstitute himself as an Arab, starting by taking an Arab name "el-Aurens." O'Toole's face simultaneously expresses shame and gratitude. In the next scene, Ali reassures him that his outfit makes good riding clothes. Encouraged by the vociferous proddings of the bedouin and a smile from Ali, he rides off to be by himself in the desert.

An outcrop of rock, against which has piled a large mass of beige sand, forms a majestic backdrop. The sky is a deep blue. Having dismounted from his camel, O'Toole walks on a flat white surface, perhaps a salt pan, as though he were an actor making an entrance onto a stage for the first time. Now he enacts a comical, if silent, soliloquy of the body. Only at the end of this scene are words uttered, yet by the way O'Toole moves, gestures, and utilizes his costume, the contradictions and ambiguities of the character he is portraying—and, above all, the latter's self-consciousness bordering on exhibitionism—are subtly conveyed.

Turning toward the camera, O'Toole takes out his dagger in a gesture of mock aggression, which seems even directed against himself, as the point of the blade is turned toward his own breast. Then he uses it in an unwarlike manner to gaze narcissistically at his own reflection. Satisfied with the way he looks, he jams the dagger back into its sheath. Now he grabs the folds of his robe so that they billow out behind him. He turns in the sun and catches sight of his own shadow on the ground. O'Toole salaams his own shadow, bowing deeply and reverentially, and then rises, giggling at the preposterousness of this charade. The schizophrenic quality of Lawrence's attitude toward himself—self-mockery/self-aggrandizement—is economically captured. Rather than pausing in embarrassment, he decides to intensify the play. Spreading his arms like the wings of a bird, he races as though he were trying to take off from the ground, an Arabian Icarus, his eyes directed toward his flitting shadow on earth. Lawrence, the actor, continues to admire his own performance. As it turns out, however, he is not alone; there has been an audience watching him all along. While the camera pans with O'Toole dashing across the stage, it catches the back of a man on a black horse (Anthony Quinn, playing Auda). At the same moment, O'Toole catches sight of the front of the figure from the corner of his eyes and is startled. He stops running and looks at his intruder with barely concealed embarrassment. With a look of utter astonishment, Anthony Quinn asks, "What are you doing—Englishman?" At a loss for an explanation, Lawrence can only weakly reply, "As you can see."

To some spectators, O'Toole's acting comes across as "stagey" but that, I submit, is precisely what he and his director had in mind. Because the acting is theatrical, it draws attention to itself *as* a performance. Though it may be entranced by the performance, the audience can also step back or distance itself from it long enough to scrutinize critically what it sees.

Joined by Peter O'Toole, Zia Mohyeddin playing Tafas, and bedouin extras, Lean began on-location shooting on May 15, 1961. When I worked for the Department of Antiquities in Saudi Arabia, the archaeological teams always *returned* from the desert no later than May. To have begun work after this time, when the summer heat was fiercest, would have been considered the height of folly. There is no shade except perhaps in the early morning hours or near dusk, when the shadows are longer and the sun moves behind rocks. During the hottest part of the day, temperatures climb to well over a hundred degrees Fahrenheit. A stone is like a fired brick to the touch. Being near a sand dune can be like standing at the open door of a furnace, where engulfing waves of heat induce nausea, retching, and at times dizziness. Under such conditions, dehydration is, of course, a danger. "You start to worry when you no longer can piss," I was once told by an archaeologist with long experience digging in Arabia. As one of the movie's publicists observed, "Only by having drink after drink of water or squash, and by taking regular doses of salt tablets, were the actors and the crew able to stand up to the heat, day by day." [36] While keeping drinking water always available on the set solved the problem of thirst, albeit at tremendous cost in equipment and crew, it created another: hundreds of thousands of tiny white plastic cups blowing about. [37] The crew had quite a job picking up the litter. Occasionally a plastic cup would be tossed by the wind into the middle of a take, giving lie to Lawrence's contention that the desert was "clean." There is in fact one shot in the movie of a whirlwind that seems to have a piece of paper caught in its draft. One wonders how much rubbish the production left behind after it moved to its next location.

It has never been adequately explained why the director pushed ahead with this torturous schedule. There had been fears that competitors like the British film producer Herbert Wilcox were mounting rival productions, but by March of 1961 Spiegel had neutralized these threats by buying up the rights to practically every major biographical source on Lawrence's life that could have become the treatment of a screenplay, including Terrence Rattigan's highly successful stage play *Ross*. There had to be other reasons. Sadomasochism? Overidentification on Lean's part with his film subject? Arrogance? Testing of manhood? The best explanation may very well be Lean's stubborn determination to uphold realism. Lawrence's surprise attack on the Turkish-held port of ʿAqaba from the landward side took place, after all, in the middle of June.

In any case, Lean wanted to catch the desert as his audience would have expected to see it, and then to challenge these highly romantic expectations with other kinds of views. Indeed, the first film location at Jebel Tubeiq would turn out to provide the audience with its first glimpse of the desert, in the scene in which Lawrence and Tafas appear atop majestic sand dunes. Jebel Tubeiq is an arid region with black, pyramidal basalt rocks that jut above vast empty planes or between massive, razor-backed sand dunes that in a certain light appear bloodred. It was something of a joke that production crews were sent out with giant rakes to sweep the footprints off the sand before O'Toole and Mohyeddin started another take. A traveled desert was not in accord with the image of a wilderness, a desolate world, uninhabited, unexplored, removed from "civilized" life—and therefore ripe for colonization. In actuality, however, tracks abound in what we might consider to be the remotest areas, and more so today than ever before because of the accessibility provided by car, jeep, and Land Rover. I was astonished to come across tread marks in the sand in the middle of the Empty Quarter. A guide like the one Lawrence is depicted as having in the movie would almost certainly have followed well-worn tracks to Prince Feisal's camp. It is interesting, therefore, that Lean was positively fastidious in the way his desert should appear pristine. Was orientalism reinscribed by these practices?[38] Maybe so, but given what we know of the contents of Lean's letter to his scriptwriter, there is reason to believe that more is involved. I would argue that the initial images of the desert are made thrilling by Lean because he wanted audiences to be caught up in its magic; but then these scenes give way to others, in which the desert appears quite different, more menacing, and in the final scenes even flat and uninspiring. Just as it seemed in the end to defy Lawrence's will to power, so did it Lean's ambitions to shoot the entire film within Jordan. From an inert object upon which Lawrence writes his will, the desert seemingly becomes an agent in its own right. This impression is reinforced by the cinematography of the wide screen, in which the visual experience is more intensely embodied in the viewer and, phenomenologically speaking, the image itself therefore seems to become an acting subject.

Assisting the director in creating this experience was Fred Young, recognized by this time as one of the world's great cinematographers.[39] This, his first collaboration with Lean, was also the first time he shot with a Panavision camera, a big, cumbersome apparatus with slow lenses. This technology had to be deployed under difficult conditions. For purposes of photography, the desert is best seen in the morning and the late afternoon light, for at any other time of day the sun is directly overhead, bleaching out the colors and the contrast. One suspects many of the desert shots to have been taken early in the morning or in the late afternoon (with the exception, perhaps, of some of the scenes that are supposed to take place in the Nefud). The wind is stillest at these times, and it is easier to keep the huge equipment clean. There is little time in which conditions are optimal for filming: a minute too soon and the colors are not yet at their brightest; a minute too late and they have faded. To avoid squandering precious daylight hours, rehearsals with the director and actors were required at night. Even with all this preparation, O'Toole complained that shooting might take place for only a few minutes each day and then start all over again if Lean was dissatisfied with the takes.

Young once said about his cinematography that shooting is "the same as painting. Both are about light and shade and colors."[40] Young's palette in *Lawrence of Arabia* is both lush and subtle. Yet there are important scenes in which color is nearly drained, leaving a chiaroscuro; or else part of the frame appears in brilliant color and the rest is set off by pastels, grays, and off-whites, depending on the effect that was sought. Young not only depended on existing camera equipment for his needs but also had to design a new kind of lens to shoot the mirage that had dazzled Lean on the Jafar flats. For years afterward, the lens was supposedly borrowed by other cinematographers who were striving to capture similar effects, over time becoming known as the "Lean lens."[41]

I have been arguing that the desert becomes a protagonist in this film, but the paradox is that the director is at the same time striving to exert a total, even obsessive, control over it, which would seem phenomenologically closer to an "object" than a "subject" relation to the image. However, on the wide screen there is always more space, and hence more details filling it, than a spectator can possibly absorb, at least in one or perhaps even more than one sitting. It may be strategic for a director to try to exert total control over the details to create the unconscious impression that that space contains a *surplus* of meaning or design that eludes spectatorial encompassment. No other scene so clearly demonstrates Lean to be a formalist director than the one in which Sherif Ali makes his appearance: the placement of the figures, as of every visual element within the camera's frame, is planned as carefully as the details in a painting by Velázquez. And yet, at the heart of this scene, there palpitates another sort of image, one of ambiguity and mystery, which talks back to the camera and the audience.

We are looking up the dark walls of a deep, round and stony well shaft. At the center are a circle of blue light and two figures opposite each other (figure 4). One is Tafas, holding onto a rope, at the end of which is attached a leather water bucket. The other is Lawrence, with his compass dangling from a strap around his neck, which we see for the first, but not the last, time as a symbol of his rationality, of his ability to orient himself in the desert. These characters are contrasted through parallel postures: the Arab relying on little more than his body, his unaided sight, and his almost intuitive knowledge of the terrain (thus, like the noble savage, he is closer to nature); whereas the European, whom we have seen to be physically helpless, nevertheless is powerful by virtue of mechanical instruments like his revolver, binoculars, and compass (which make him further removed from nature and thus civilized). On another

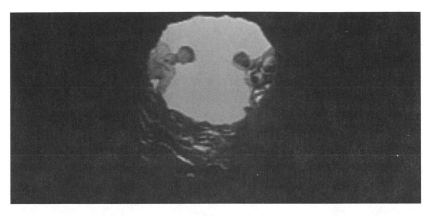

Figure 4.   Tafas and Lawrence, in soft-focus background, peering down
a well shaft.

level, we can read the opening of this scene as being about the film experience. Like Lawrence with his compass, so Lean looking through the
lens of his camera tries to orient himself and us in the world.

When Tafas lets go of the rope, the bucket plummets, the sound of its
impact on the surface of the water, not coincidentally in this scene, re-
sembling that of a gunshot. The view now widens from a narrow hole
to an expansive wasteland, flat and featureless (this scene was shot in the
mudflats of al-Jafar), except for a few stone cairns and a bit of dried
brush scattered by the film crew at strategic intervals away from the well,
providing the viewer with the sense of depth so essential on the wide
screen. A faint white path in the sand recedes to a vanishing point on the
horizon: "John Box and members of the crew scattered by hand tiny
black pebbles across the sand, in the shape of a wide 'V' that narrowed
as it closed in on the feet of Lawrence. This, says Box, was symbolic of
Lawrence's meeting a mysterious figure who would forever change his
life. For added dimension—and to provide Sharif and his camel a sort
of guiding track—Box spray-painted a straight white line on the sand." [42]
If you pay close attention, you will notice that the two figures—but
especially Tafas—look cautiously at the path and then all around, as
though anxious at the possibility of detection. The visual clues are thus
arranged in such a way as to give a foreboding of tragedy: after all, we
have already been informed that Tafas is in enemy territory.

It has been observed, correctly up to a point, that the next series of
actions delay the arrival of the long-expected menace in order to enhance
the dramatic suspense.[43] They do much more, however. While Tafas at-

tends to the watering of the camels, Lawrence moseys over to a low hillock on which he stretches his tired frame for a few seconds. His army
cap lies inverted in front of him. Caps, *kufiyyahs,* and other headgear
are important in this film, symbolizing both the power and the personality of their bearers, as well as their cultural identity. By taking off his
cap, Lawrence has momentarily displaced his own identity, precisely at
the moment that the stranger, whom I will argue throughout this study
is his psychological double, appears. Now Lawrence takes his army compass and begins cleaning it, while absentmindedly whistling a popular
ditty of the day, "The Man Who Broke the Bank of Monte Carlo." He
looks through the compass sight to check for dust. While peering at the
horizon, he is suddenly startled by the same sound we had heard at the
beginning of the scene, the sound of the bucket hitting the surface of
the water in the well. Looking over his shoulder, he peers quizzically off-
camera at Tafas, who is made to appear as though *he* were looking directly over Lawrence's body in the direction at which the latter had been
gazing. To be emphasized is the fact that the stranger appears in the direction in which Lawrence had all along been squinting through the sight
of his compass, even though Lawrence does not actually *see* him there.
It is Tafas, his guide, still holding tightly onto the rope that disappears
into the "depths," who sees the stranger for the first time. The significance of this fact, I would claim, is that we are supposed to feel that the
stranger is in some uncanny way connected to Lawrence, but precisely
because his appearance is uncanny, as Freud has taught us, the connection is through the unconscious mind. This idea will seem less far-fetched
when we actually see the stranger enter in a mirage, an image that is
almost hypnotic in effect and certainly phantasmagoric in appearance.
Fred Young, who filmed this sequence using the special Lean lens recalls:
"It was a tiny pinprick. . . . We put Omar, oh, I don't know, about a quarter of a mile away, and David told him just to come riding toward the
camera. We shot a thousand feet of him coming closer and closer and
closer. It was fantastic watching him coming toward us, sort of this swirling wave. It looked like a sea on the desert." [44] Eventually, the "swirling
wave" is recognizable as a lone rider furiously whipping his camel as it
bears down on the well. If not from the unconscious, this apparition
could come out of hell—or perhaps, the two are indistinguishable.

    According to Walter Benjamin, the mirage image brings to the surface
of apprehension our "optical unconscious." It is a phenomenon he connects with realism, though a realism captured not by the naked eye but
by the camera. "For it is another nature that speaks to the camera rather

than to the eye," he states, "other in the sense that a space informed by human consciousness gives way to a space informed by the unconscious."[45] He goes on: "Whereas it is a commonplace that, for example, we have some idea what is involved in the act of walking, if only in general terms, we have no idea at all what happens during the fraction of a second when a person *steps out*. Photography, with its devices of slow motion and enlargement, reveals the secret. It is through photography that we first discover the existence of this optical unconscious, just as we distinguish the instinctual unconscious through psychoanalysis."[46] Benjamin expands upon these ideas elsewhere: "The enlargement of a snapshot does not simply render more precise what in any case was visible, though unclear; it reveals entirely new structural formations of the subject. . . . Evidently a different nature opens itself to the camera than opens to the naked idea—if only because an unconsciously penetrated space is substituted for a space consciously explored by man."[47] It is important to note in Benjamin's idea of the optical unconscious that reality is made more intensely visible as a result of technological mediation. Nor is it unimportant that the optical unconscious connects up with Freud's unconscious. Though what is perceived may be dependent on a sophisticated technological apparatus, it is not apprehended primarily through the conscious or rational, as it is through the unconscious and oneiric, mind. "The camera introduces us to unconscious optics as does psychoanalysis to unconscious impulses."[48] In seeing the mirage on the wide screen, one does not say to oneself: oh well, that's just a reflection of light passing through layers of air of different densities; but, by God, that's a demon rushing out of hell. We do not really forget that we are watching a technologically mediated image—that was the whole point of astonishing Hollywood and the public at large with a special effect—but at the same time we cannot help but apprehend that image unconsciously. Because we cannot resist the optical unconscious in the moment of seeing an image through a technology that makes it intensely visible, it may be that we endow that image with magical value, for it is as though the image could speak to us and reveal who we are. Benjamin reports the reactions of the first viewers of the daguerreotype: "We . . . believed that the little tiny faces in the picture could see *us,* so powerfully was everyone affected by the unaccustomed clarity and the unaccustomed truth to nature of the first daguerreotypes."[49] Phenomenologically, the image in the photograph as well as on the screen seems to possess a subjectivity of its own.

Lean taps into the optical unconscious on other occasions in the movie. Take, for example, a scene that ends with Lawrence blowing out a match. There is an immediate cut to a flat, empty horizon. The bottom third of the screen is dark. The sky is a pale orange. This image is etched in our minds for a couple of seconds. Then, slightly to the right of center the rim of the sun appears. We see it rise until half of it is visible, filling the sky with light. Its ascent takes a long time, however, at least several seconds, and so it appears on the screen like an object rising in molasses. The paradox is that the film has been speeded up in order that the sun's movement can be seen at all, and yet it appears to be moving in slow motion. Once again, reality is made visible, and intensely so, by technological mediation, but the image is apprehended unconsciously. It is an image of birth. At the risk of overinterpretation, let me suggest that the very next fade into Lawrence and Tafas coming into view in the hollow between two huge sand dunes intimates that birth.

Lean had extended the project of realism to its limits by making nature visible on the screen in ways it had never been before. Yet it is not by rational or logical knowledge that the images are apprehended, but instead by unconscious, hallucinatory processes. The mirage and the sun release in the spectator the dream (or nightmare). The argument, of course, still leaves the optical unconscious too unmediated by narrative structures and cultural conventions of seeing. If Lean had presented his clip of the mirage in a different context—a convention of cinematographers, for example—then the audience's exploration of the image would have very likely been informed by rational, conscious thought as well as by scientific discourses of photography and optics. In the context of a fiction film, however, the audience is asked, implicitly, to narrativize the image in terms of allegory, metaphor, irony, and so forth. The other issue left unaddressed has to do with politics. Benjamin saw revolutionary potential in the optical unconscious, but clearly this result is nowhere guaranteed; and nowhere less so, it would seem, than in a Hollywood epic. The salient structures of narration as well as the politics that mediate the image for the audience will be explored in the next chapter.

For a film theorist like Colin MacCabe, all this control by the director produces a "closed" realism.[50] He takes exception with Bazin's "naive" view of realism, particularly the idea that a more open frame with less montage editing would necessarily lead to ambiguity, openness, and contradiction.[51] In other words, a realist director like Rossellini, even when he examines life from different angles, some of them contradictory, in the end settles on a perspective or perspectives that unify the contradictions.

Otherwise, it would seem as if there were competing realities, a situation that would give the lie to unity and coherence. Ambiguity must be resolved, the narrative contained, and interpretation given closure. If, for Bazin, the wide screen could be liberatory, it is because reality itself is always richer than any one representation of it. For MacCabe, on the other hand, the control that realist directors such as Lean had to exert over the wide screen is totalitarian; resistance, to the degree that it is exercised at all, is only possible in the spectator.[52]

Also in keeping with MacCabe's theory is the notion that for realism to work, the camera has to remain invisible, for if the camera calls attention to its own apparatus the suspension of disbelief is broken. I believe, to the contrary, that this is a particular *convention* of realism, not one of its inherent traits, a convention that in fact no longer holds for audiences today. The paradox is that audiences are more likely to believe that a representation is true, or at least one that they can trust to be true, if they can see that it has been constructed. Thus a representation of reality often contains within it either an allusion to, or a direct representation of, the means by which something is made visible or the conventions by which something seen is to be interpreted. One reason for this paradox is that some portions of our culture today subscribe to a notion of reality as being always already mediated. Film characters caught up in a realistic situation will refer to characters or situations in other films, an intertextuality that not only does *not* undermine the realism of the scene but actually seems to secure it, in large part because contemporary audiences have different expectations about the boundary between what is film and what is not film than did audiences of two or more decades ago.

Lawrence of Arabia alludes to its technical apparatus at several key points, but the self-referencing is more sublime because it is connected with embodiment.[53] It is not that the camera is visible per se but that it seems to be an extension of the spectator's body. This self-referencing would be one way to explain a series of linked scenes that on one level have to do with Lawrence's journey into the desert for the first time, and on another constitute an elaborate allegory about vision in film. The scene that has just ended shows Lawrence looking through his binoculars at a party of hostile bedouin riding in an immense plane. They are being pointed out to him by his guide Tafas, unaided by any technology of sight. If we, the audience who are not in this scene, are to see the bedouin at all, we too will need a mechanical apparatus. The dissolve into the very next scene shows our stalwart pair proceeding on their journey—with Lawrence about to receive instruction on camel riding.

Figure 5.   Lawrence and Tafas in the desert (framed by a black rim), the parallel of the scene from the bottom of the well.

Oddly enough, however, this image is framed for an instant by the rim of something black and circular (figure 5). It is a puzzling dissolve. Presumably, Lawrence is the only person in the desert with binoculars, given that the Arabs are constructed in a whole series of scenes linked to this one as not only "barbaric" but also "primitive," not only bereft of Western technology but innocent of its workings. Is this an accident by a director who was known to be fastidious to the point of obsessiveness in his composition and editing? Or do we assume that it was deliberate and has significance? I wish to entertain the latter possibility. The black circle, I would argue, stands not for the binoculars—for they are with Lawrence in the image in front of us—but for the eyepiece of the camera. And because of the wide-screen image's extension with the space-time dimensions of our own bodies, the eyepiece of the camera becomes the eyelid of the spectator's body. We can only see the image, the metaphor seems to imply, because there is a mechanical apparatus that mediates it for us, but at the same time that apparatus is coexistential with our own bodies and hence is as real as our own bodies are.

This subtle allusion to the camera recurs a few moments later in the transition into the very next scene, the famous one in which Sherif Ali makes his first appearance. For the end of the scene leading up to this one, Lean employed a helicopter, which pulled back from the two riders, Tafas and Lawrence, as they enjoy a rollicking race and then disappear from view. The dissolve entails the opposite image: rather than looking down from the sky, the camera is looking up into it from the bottom of a dark well shaft, our riders leaning over the rim. The shot echoes the earlier image of Tafas and Lawrence going down a sand dune framed in the rim of binoculars or the eyepiece of the camera. That is, the shaft of the well looks rather like the long barrel of a camera. And because the figures are staring straight at us, the audience, it is we who are peering through the Lean lens, the device that Fred Young had made in order to capture the mirage on film. Through a series of linked images— Lawrence peering through binoculars, bedouin in the distance framed by his binoculars, Lawrence and Tafas framed by the camera eyepiece, Lawrence and Tafas seen through the shaft of the well or the barrel of the lens—the technological mediation of vision is simultaneously re- ferred to and embodied.

Lean loved the desert, or so it has been stated in the production accounts. "When told that the shooting could not go on forever, [he] had asked, 'Why not?'"[54] By the early 1960s, shortly after *Lawrence of Arabia* was released, the age of the "big film" was over, cut short by escalating costs and dwindling theater audiences. It is not surprising, though rarely pointed out, that the material contradictions of the industry are appar- ent in the film's production. The requirements of authenticity in the context of the so-called international film, combined with expensive on- location wide-screen production, brought Lean's realist project to a pre- mature and, for him, undesirable end.

When the production company moved to Spain, the filming of the des- ert had to change. From an open frame—the hallmark of wide-screen filming—the camera was now kept close to the action (as in the derail- ing of the Turkish train that begins Part Two), which blocked out sky- scrapers or television antennae that might destroy the illusion of realism. Extras for the large crowd scenes were hired from among the Andalu- sian Gypsies. In an effort, I presume, to rescue the commitment to real- ism, compromised by moving the production outside Jordan, we are told that "most of [them] are descendants of the Moors and are Arabic in ap- pearance."[55] At the same time, the "desert" shrank to the size of a post- age stamp. The hutments at the Suez Canal, the emotional climax of Lawrence's crossing of the Sinai, were constructed from an abandoned farm building on the plains of Almeria.

These measures may have been highly regrettable to Lean from an artistic standpoint, but the tighter camera work, along with the ruse of "sandstorms," ironically made the "desert" more intriguing than the ar- restingly sweeping images in Jordan. Had he continued to film inside the country, the majestic visual rhetoric he had forged might have become

heavy-handed. Material constraints faced by the production thus arguably turned into an artistic boon. Lean regretted this happenstance, but
in some ways the more closed frame created a claustrophobic intensity
in Part Two that is in keeping with the more introspective mood of
Lawrence's character as well as the escalating desperateness of his situation. And what of realism in the film and the experience of vision for
the spectator as embodiment? I would argue that the results were the dialectical opposite of the project as developed by Lean in Jordan: realism
gave way to surrealism, embodiment to disembodiment.

We can see how Lean's realist project was affected in the scene depict-
ing Lawrence's crossing of the Sinai Desert after he has taken the port of
'Aqaba. As the journey begins, we see strange rock formations looking
like statues in a surrealist landscape. The absolutely bare, rugged hills
have an otherworldly, lunar aspect. Dust devils become for Lawrence
"pillars of fire," but Daud, not catching the note of irony in Lawrence's
voice, corrects him pedantically, "No, lord, *dust.*" The two servant boys,
not he, sound the note of reality. Almost immediately into the scene,
while caught, significantly enough, in a blinding sandstorm, Lawrence
loses his compass, the symbol throughout this movie of his rational self,
as perhaps conveyed most obviously in the shoot-out at the Masturah
Well. No matter, he reassures the boys, so long as they ride into the setting sun they will be heading west, where the Canal lies. On another
level, this scene could be interpreted as an allegory of Lean's lens. Adapt-
ing his vision to a necessarily artificial canvas, he now had to create a
makeshift, if still convincing, realism.

The direction of the setting sun, of course, is also the land of death.
Though the boys complain of fatigue, Lawrence insists on continuing
onward, pushing them beyond their endurance. As a result, when Daud
falls into "quicksand," he is too weak to extricate himself even with the
help of Lawrence, who has thrown him a lifeline. Lawrence is now so
demoralized by the death of his beloved servant boy that he continues
on the journey as though he were in a trance. Once apparently a master
of his fate, he now seems entirely subservient to it. As though mortify-
ing his own body, he plods along on foot, while Farraj is slumped on his
camel. The boy protests gently, coaxing his master to climb on board
with the perfectly reasonable observation, "Why, Lord? It serves no
purpose—there is room for both." There was a pair on a camel alone in
the desert once before, but now it is Lawrence's turn to be rescued, and
by his servant no less. We see him next sitting passively behind Farraj.
Lawrence's face is covered with a mask of fine white sand. We will see

the same expression in his eyes—the look of peering blindly outward because his vision is seared by what he sees within—when he poses for a photograph taken by the newspaper reporter Jackson Bentley just after the Turkish massacre, a massacre Lawrence has ordered. A blind Oedipus, he fails to respond when Farraj yells, "Look, Auens," pointing to an abandoned army outpost. As in other instances in this film, it is auditory rather than visual clues that first announce the presence of something. There is an incessant banging, which turns out to be a door swinging on creaky hinges. It is followed by a repeated tapping that is later discovered to be caused by a halyard buffeted against a flag pole. These are the only sounds except for the moaning of the wind. The temporary disassociation between image and sound effectively re-creates the state of Lawrence's disembodiment. The camera now photographs him in semiobscurity (a strategy used again at the end of the movie, but through other visual cues such as reflections and shadows, to convey the sense of his insubstantial and enigmatic character): he is seen through a screen, the opening of a doorway and from behind.

In a desperate attempt to bring Lawrence out of his comatose state, Farraj splashes water on his face. Slowly it comes to life, and its eyes focus on the boy, as if seeing him again for the first time in a long while. "It's all right, Farraj," he murmurs. The two solitary figures pass through the entrance with the banging door, and in the next instant we are startled by a loud, monstrous, and not immediately identifiable sound, which like all the other sounds in the last few minutes is disassociated from the image it accompanies. There is an immediate cut to a smokestack looming above a sand dune. It takes us another instant to realize that we are seeing a steamer and to conclude that the two have arrived at the Canal.

On the opposite bank a motorcyclist happens to be passing, looking rather like the motorcyclist we saw at the beginning of the movie. Seeing Farraj's gesticulations, he stops and yells, "Who are you?" In spite of the fact that the stranger repeats the question, Lawrence says nothing. The camera lingers on his face, with its dazed expression, while on the sound track we hear a trolley's ringing, marking the transition into the next scene, a crowded Cairo street. But we do not see that street yet, and so the ringing of the bell, matched by a close-up of Lawrence's masklike face, evokes the psychological alarm within.

The surrealism of this scene, conveyed through image as well as sound, has a narrative function of representing the disoriented mind of the protagonist. It is at the same time quite effective in the way it makes us experience his disembodiment. But it is obvious that the images are not the images of the desert, which awaken our optical unconscious because they are mediated by the technology of the wide screen. In the shoot-out at the Masturah Well, Lean had pushed this technology of realism to its limits, making intensely visible the thingness of this world, which had not been previously perceptible on the screen. One did not need 70 mm Panavision film to experience the imagery of the Sinai.

The negation of the wide screen did not stop here, for when the movie was released for television, the rival of the film industry, it was in effect cannibalized through brutal cutting, not to speak of constant interruption for commercial advertising, which destroyed its pacing. It is particularly difficult to talk about *a* film in the case of *Lawrence of Arabia* because it has undergone so many transformations in the course of its rerelease and distributions.

In an interview with Gerald Pratley, Lean talks about the problems of small-screen projection of his larger films: "We take a tremendous lot of trouble over composition, and very often, I go to a theatre and the screen is quite a different shape. Quite unnecessarily so. It just takes the theatre manager's fancy, I suppose. Or the projectionist's, I don't know. . . . They also find it very hard to keep it in focus. You can't really see it. You know, it's particularly painful in long shots." [56] As Janet Maslin has pointed out, "There are some films that should never be watched on television under any circumstances and 'Lawrence of Arabia' is arguably one of them." [57] The whole point of filming in Super Panavision was to allow Lean the opportunity to paint on a broad canvas. It is not just that the details that make the formal composition of each frame so arresting are indiscernible, nor that the subtlety of the performances is lost. Above all what is missing is the embodiment in the spectator of the image which the technology of the wide screen had made possible. Nevertheless, it was the television version that many viewers, particularly ones who came of age in the seventies, saw, and it probably adversely affected their reception of the movie. Yes, the cinematography was beautiful and the battle scenes exciting, but it was almost impossible to see how this movie provided a different *kind* of visual experience from any other complex film.

The most recent versions on video and laser disc are based on the film's restoration and reconstruction, one of the most formidable undertakings in cinema history. Lean had wryly warned the restorer Robert A. Harris about the obstacles facing him: "You know the way they kept

hacking away at it, I'm afraid the rats have gotten to it." [58] Help was provided by the director, Jim Paiten (Harris's coproducer), the original
coeditor of the film, Anne V. Coates, and the still-surviving principle actors, who redubbed many scenes. O'Toole quipped that now he finally
understood how the lines should have been delivered in the first place.
The film was then fine-cut by Lean (accomplishing what he had intended
to do twenty-five years earlier), leaving a final restored version that is
217 minutes in length. Soon after the release of the restored version in
movie houses around the country, a video was marketed in "letter-box"
format to re-create the wide-screen shape, followed by a laser disc version that is crisper in its colors and sounds, and now a "Thirtieth Anniversary Commemorative Video" (1993), with original theater trailer
and a short documentary on the film production. But the contradiction
of a movie made for a particular mode of viewing that is all but moribund has never been overcome.

CHAPTER 3

Riding the Whirlwind

Scripting the Political in the Spectacle

"Credit, at Last, for 'Lawrence of Arabia.'" announced a headline in a 1995 issue of the *New York Times*.[1] The article reported that the Writers Guild of America had determined that credit for the screenplay must be shared by the two writers, Robert Bolt and Michael Wilson. Several important articles have been written about the Michael Wilson affair that supposedly were instrumental in influencing the Writer's Guild's decision.[2] Some of these—including the *Times* article—have placed Wilson's long-standing struggle to win screen credit in a larger context than a battle over intellectual property rights. At issue was Wilson's blacklisting by the House Un-American Activities Committee (HUAC) in the 1950s, as a result of which he could neither be hired by the studios nor receive screen credit under his own name. The film thus becomes implicated in a more significant story about Hollywood's ignominious political history. In other words, we are to presume that Wilson was denied screen credit by the producers on account of their fears of HUAC.

Exactly what had Wilson done on the script? Besides the two detailed treatments he had prepared for Lean, he had written and revised three versions of the script in accordance with the director's detailed suggestions and criticisms. After having reviewed the scripts, I am convinced, along with Hodson, Turner, and others, that Wilson's contribution was quite substantial. Nonetheless, Lean had claimed the reverse. Indeed, Bolt insisted until his dying day that he had never had knowledge of, let alone seen anything done by, Wilson prior to completing his own script. Wilson sent him drafts which proved conclusively that he had worked on earlier versions and that these provided the structural edifice of the screenplay. The controversy surrounding the Michael Wilson affair is complicated, much more so than an explanation in terms of an anti-Communist scare might suggest, and it may never be possible to get to the bottom of it.

In my view, however, the stumbling block was less HUAC than Lean. After Wilson's death in 1978, his family appealed for screen credit to Columbia Studios, which now owned the rights to the film, citing an earlier nonbinding ruling by the British Writer's Guild that had upheld Wilson's suit against Spiegel and Horizon Pictures.[3] Notwithstanding the fact that by this time HUAC had become a nonissue, the studio declared that it would not reinstate Wilson's name because the director was adamant in refusing to acknowledge his claims.

The rest of this chapter develops a point regarding the representation of this affair, one that in my view is important for film theory. It has been argued, by Wilson first of all and by others talking about his case secondarily, that Bolt's screenplay not only weakened the political vision of the original treatment but did so primarily because of the way it psychologizes the character of Lawrence and his situation. It is this view that I think is damaging not only to understanding the ways in which the contributions of the two scriptwriters are linked in this particular project but also to a certain notion of the political in the art of film writing more generally.

In a 1964 interview published in the French journal *Positif*, shortly after he had put his case before the British Guild of Screenwriters in regard to the writing of the script for *Lawrence of Arabia*, Wilson made these telling remarks:

> I like the film, but with reservations. I think there is a confusion of themes. My version of the character of Lawrence was more sociological and political than that of Robert Bolt, who prefers [to stress] the psychoanalytic side, the sadistic, masochistic, and homosexual aspects of his character. I believe that at the end of the film these two conceptions are confounded and it [the end] is not clear to most spectators. Many people have said to me: "Lawrence is mad." Not at all, Lawrence was not crazy. He was a very complex and interesting man. His was the tragedy of a man who tried to follow two masters. On one side, he wanted to become Arab but could not, and on the other he was ashamed to remain English. And it is this which is tragic for Lawrence, and not the violence [he suffered at the hands] of the Turks.[4]

Notice how Wilson's criticism of the film entails certain (by now perhaps outmoded) assumptions about the political. According to his view, the political is located in the public realm, not in the private, and certainly not in questions about a person's sanity or sexuality. With regard to the former, to name just one influential exception to this kind of thinking, psychoanalyst Erich Fromm of the Frankfurt school had argued in the late 1930s and early 1940s that a link existed between a sadomasochistic personality and fascistic tendencies in some twentieth-century Germans.[5] With regard to the latter, we need only point out recent feminist and queer theory scholarship that has attempted to link political projects such as nationalism with problems of sexual identity;[6] psychoanalytic film critic Kaja Silverman has done something similar in her study of T. E. Lawrence.[7] The filmmakers, quite deliberately as we shall see, were making a similar point about Lawrence, implying that he was both a sadomasochist and a fascist. It is thus perhaps with hindsight that we can see today the insightfulness with which the psychological and the political were imbricated in this film's representation of Lawrence. It is ironic that in his comments on the film Wilson focuses on a psychological trait to which Lawrence's "tragedy" is ascribed—the problem of divided loyalties that his going native (or mimicry of the other) provoked in his psyche—a problem of ambivalence that postcolonial critics have now been arguing has everything to do with understanding processes of the political in the colonial context.[8]

Building on Wilson's critique, one might suppose that Bolt and Lean sacrificed the clarity of the political issues, particularly of colonialism, for the sake of a psychological investigation of Lawrence's character. This is, for example, the implication of the following remarks by critic Joel Hodson in his article "Who Wrote *Lawrence of Arabia?*" which has played a key role in rekindling interest in the Wilson affair: "Each [Lean and Wilson] wished to pursue a fundamentally different approach to the subject [of Lawrence]. Lean's interest in Lawrence was primarily psychological . . . whereas Wilson wanted to situate Lawrence's exploits within the broader political context of Anglo-Arab and other international relations of the WWI period. As a filmmaker, Lean had never been interested in social and political themes."[9] To claim that Lean was indifferent to social and political themes is somewhat rash in light of films such as *Hobson's Choice* (1953), with its exploration of patriarchy and feminism, or *This Happy Breed* (1944), with its portrayal of class sympathies toward Communism in the 1930s, not to mention the antiwar film *Bridge on the River Kwai*. Nor was Lean uninterested in the political as far as *Lawrence of Arabia* was concerned, insisting to his filmmakers, including Michael Wilson, on the need to incorporate a critique of colonialism in the film. It would be hard to miss such a criticism, even in the final product in which Wilson had no hand.

The problem with Wilson's statement and those of critics like Hodson, who wonders how the film might have turned out had Wilson had a freer hand in the production, is that they hold a view of the political that makes it seem to be incompatible with the psychological. Yet Wilson's portrait of Lawrence was hardly unpsychological, if he understood the character—as the passage quoted earlier indicates he did—to be torn between conflicting *identities*. Nor does Bolt's more psychologically nuanced rendering of Lawrence's character necessarily distract or distance us from the latter's politics; in my view it actually leads to a deeper critique of them. Further, I will try to show that Lean desired a script that would construct a more reflexive spectator than the one Wilson's treatment allowed, a spectator who would be induced to form his or her own critical interpretations of the hero. I claim that Bolt enabled this reflexivity, or at least the degree to which Lean wanted it, largely through devices he adapted from Brechtian theater. Rather than think of the contributions of Wilson, Bolt, and Lean as disjunctive, I suggest we see them as linked political projects.

To gain some purchase on the various notions of the political that Wilson and Bolt brought to the film and on the artistic practices by which they endeavored to realize them, let us review the careers of the scriptwriters. I will focus more on the former's life than on Bolt's, in part because it is not as well known but also to show that the kind of political person Wilson became was altogether more psychologically ambivalent than we might assume and in that respect resembles more the figure he was to write about in his screenplay. Above all, we shall see how Wilson struggled to gain clarity on what it meant to be a political writer of films.

Michael Wilson (1914–78) grew up in San Francisco, the son of a fairly prosperous businessman. Quite religious as a boy, he was inclined toward the priesthood and credits his deep faith in Catholic doctrine—to wit, that all people are created equal before God—with his early feelings of indignity and outrage toward any form of racism. "I simply would not join in the racist slurs that many of my companions had about Negroes or Filipinos or Japanese and the rest. . . . I can't say that I fought racism in any articulate way; I simply refused to join it." [10] These attitudes alienated him from his often anti-Semitic father, a distance compounded by the sense that "I did not like the philistine life represented by [him], the Babbitry." Though he adds that "this was a world I wanted to shun," Wilson was hardly a rebel. Not, I think, for lack of courage so much as love of family combined with a deep sense of social tact.

Blessed with uncommon intelligence and more than average talent, he was by his own admission a "golden boy," a top student and a successful athlete—a robust, handsome youth who was not only admired by but also popular with his classmates. Below the surface of a conventionally successful adolescent career, however, there smoldered an unarticulated discontent. As his faith in Catholicism began to wane in his senior year of high school, he was searching for a higher moral purpose in life, one that would replace religion.

In 1932 Wilson entered the University of California at Berkeley, without the blessing of his father, who never had a college education and did not see the point of one. He nevertheless recognized his son's scholarly aptitude and agreed to pay for school tuition and other expenses. In his first two years of college Wilson's reading of literature, which had never been slight, grew by leaps and bounds. "I used to spend hours [in the university library], by the day and by the night. And in no organized way, just kind of a feast of reading." In spite of his literary interests, which included editing a literary magazine, he decided to major in philosophy, a choice he interpreted retrospectively as a desire "to find out why we were on this earth and what man's role was in the universe, if the answers were not to be found in the Catholic faith." It is interesting, and not insignificant in light of the characterization of Lawrence he would help to forge, that Wilson continued to lead what he called a "double life," expressed this time by joining a fraternity of which he became president in his senior year, at the same time that he began to show an interest in the larger political movements of his day. The mid-1930s saw a number of important labor strikes in California and the country at large, which, Wilson commented, "demonstrated to students like myself that . . . the working class, led by maritime workers, were ready to fight back against the bosses." The San Francisco longshoreman strike of 1936, for example, inspired Wilson to write a short story that was published in *Esquire*. But the call of political activism was still relatively faint.

In spite of the fact that he was an excellent student and was encouraged by his college professors to go into college teaching, Wilson had decided by his senior year that he wanted to become a writer. Following the example of one of his adolescent idols, Ernest Hemingway, he went to Europe and made his base in Paris in order to get a new perspective on his life and country and, he hoped, to find themes for his writing. He traveled widely, eventually making his way to Moscow, where he tried unsuccessfully to obtain a job as a newspaper correspondent. As was the case for so many of his generation who were disillusioned by capitalism and fearful of fascism's rise, the politics of the Soviet Union held a special fascination for him. On his return to Paris, he stopped briefly in Berlin, where he visited the Museum of Communism, which the fascists had defaced with anti-Communist and anti-Semitic slogans. He came across glass cases stuffed with insignia worn by former Party members, executed or left languishing in prison, and, when the guards were not looking, managed to open one and steal a memento. He clung to it like a fetish to ward off the growing threat of fascism. Back in Paris he read radical literature, chiefly Marxist. He tried enlisting in the Spanish brigade; he attended a few Communist rallies. Most of all, he wanted to write socially aware fiction without having it turn into political tracts.

In regard to his growing sense of his own artistic "activism," it is significant that Wilson began to frequent the movies in Paris. To our expatriate it seemed that films had been taken seriously as works of art by the French critical and intellectual establishment long before they had been in the United States. Watching French cinema, the artistically ambitious Wilson may have had an inkling that writing for the movies could be not only a political act but a rewarding artistic one as well. He was most impressed by Renoir's *Grand Illusion* (1937). Not coincidentally, the antiwar film would become one of Wilson's staples, first in his treatment of *Friendly Persuasion* (1956), a complex Civil War story about a farmer played by Gary Cooper who is torn between his Quaker religious conviction and secular loyalties of various kinds, but most spectacularly, of course, in *Kwai*.

When Wilson returned to the United States in 1938, his political radicalism, if anything, had deepened. He joined the Communist Party, with which he would remain affiliated until 1956. His commitments were once again ambivalent, however. It was not love of Communism or socialism that motivated him "so much as . . . a hatred of Babbitry, chauvinism, racism, and economic exploitation in a capitalist society. I . . . felt that fascism had to be stopped." He played at first an educational role by taking a graduate post in Berkeley's Department of English. "I was teaching classes in Marxism, primarily to students, undergraduate or graduate, who, we felt, were close to the party, moving in that direction. And so I gave them some courses in basics."

Party work was time-consuming, however, and after attending rallies and meetings, Wilson did not have much energy left over for his fiction. Nor was college teaching an attractive option either. He tried some odd jobs—working for a year in Alaska on the salmon run, for a brief time on a socialist or collective farm in Baja, California, where he got the idea of doing a series of short stories about minority workers—and then decided to try his luck in Hollywood. He moved there in 1940.

Like many earlier writers with high aspirations, Wilson had a snobbish attitude toward the film mecca. He saw employment there purely as a way of making a living, so that he could then become financially independent in order devote himself full-time to writing the great American novel. He changed his attitude soon enough. "Although I . . . after my arrival read Nathaniel West's book *The Day of the Locusts,* . . . I really didn't share his gloomy view of Hollywood or his hatred of it." He had no track record as a scriptwriter and somehow had to learn his craft. He solved this problem by going to the movies, even B movies, for he reasoned that he could learn by figuring out how to write better ones. He also volunteered to work for next to nothing on low-budget productions that were willing to take a chance with beginners. For his first movie he had to crank out the scenes one day before they were shot on the set, a nerve-racking experience from which he nevertheless acquired an iron discipline.

Wilson, meanwhile, got to meet some of Hollywood's political radicals like John Howard Lawson, author of a number of screenplays.[11] Lawson had a profound influence on Wilson's developing understanding of himself as a writer for films, especially in connection with the problem of political expression in works of art intended for mass consumption:

> He often spoke of the struggle for content in motion pictures, by which he meant that although it was extremely difficult to do a truly progressive and honest film in Hollywood, we, as radicals and Marxists, had an obligation to try our damnedest to do so; and that one could accomplish certain things, even in the pictures which thematically seemed silly or vapid. And I don't mean by that the oversimplification which his enemies would say this is, the injection of Communist propaganda. That isn't what he meant at all. He meant the injection of honesty and humanism in the pictures which lacked it.

As an example of what Lawson meant, Wilson wrote for one of the Hopalong Cassidy pictures of 1942 a screenplay called "Border Patrol," in which he used stories he had heard years earlier in Texas about Mexican migrant workers who were exploited after crossing the border. Those episodes were some of the most popular in the entire series.

In the meantime, World War II intervened, and Wilson volunteered as a candidate in officer's school. Though he could stomach the rigors of training, the social attitudes of the soldiers sickened him. "What I was unprepared for was the racism and chauvinism and general ignorance both in my fellow candidates and in the instructors and the officers. . . . there were certain officers or noncoms I wanted to kill, literally murder . . . because they were such dirty anti-semitic bastards." These experiences would deeply inform Wilson's biting satire of army mentality in both *Kwai* and *Lawrence.* Stationed in the Pacific, he saw action as a marine lieutenant in the invasions of Kwajalein, Guam, and Saipan, experiences that proved invaluable when it came to writing about war in Burma.

After the war, he returned to Hollywood. Things went well for him at first. He wrote the script for Frank Capra's *It's a Wonderful Life* (1946) a year after his return. His screen adaptation of Theodore Dreiser's *An American Tragedy,* which came to be called *A Place in the Sun* (1951), was a great success, starring Montgomery Clift and Elizabeth Taylor, and directed by George Stevens. Wilson was brought into the production specifically to preserve the spirit of Dreiser's social criticism. He received an Academy Award for his work on the film, a clear sign from the industry that he was now a top writer. But HUAC had already begun its investigations of Hollywood figures suspected of being Communist sympathizers, among whom were Wilson's closest friends and colleagues such as Dalton Trumbo and John Howard Lawson. They were part of the "Hollywood Ten" who were given prison sentences for refusing to testify to the committee and name names. By 1951 Wilson, too, had been called to testify before HUAC, a summons he courageously declined. His Academy Award for *A Place in the Sun* was deemed a "mistake." By now he was dropped by MGM and was considered anathema in the industry. When William Wyler, the director of *Friendly Persuasion* (1956), dropped Wilson's name from that film's credits, Wilson stubbornly fought back by seeking arbitration from the Guild of Writers in America. The guild ruled in his favor, but the studio decided to omit entirely the mention of a screenwriter rather than to reinstate Wilson's name.

In protest of the McCarthy hearings, Wilson decided to go into independent production with another blacklisted artist, Paul Jerrico. The result of their collaboration, *Salt of the Earth* (1953), was to become a cult classic among the left. In his script Wilson told the story of a strike by badly exploited Mexican American laborers. He used some of the stories he had heard in Texas about the plight of migrant workers for his material. But as he had learned from his friend Lawson, the point was not to propagandize for this or that creed but to show the struggles of people against inequalities and injustice in their human dimensions. We are treated to an intimate portrait not only of the strikers but also of their mostly female and protofeminist supporters, who hope that a brighter future for the community will include women as well as men. When one of my classes watched this film recently, most of the students, but particularly the students of color, noted how compelling it was and, above all, how relevant its themes still were today (see also the epilogue). One of the lines that struck them as particularly moving was uttered by the wife and narrator of the film to her husband, who bridled at the fact that the strike had been taken over by the women in the community, leaving the men to tend to the children and the household chores. "Why can't I be your friend," she asks him simply when he refuses to open up to her, preferring to go hunting in order to bolster his imperiled masculinity.

Because the film is such a clear indictment of international capital, not to mention a clear incitement of labor to resist it with the help of socialist or Communist organizations, it was blacklisted in the United States. Tremendous pressure was put on distributors not to carry it and on movie theaters not to show it. Wilson had achieved his goal of writing a film with a powerful political message having to do with the working class, gender, and race or ethnicity, and yet it would not be seen widely, if at all, in the United States. How, then, was he to script the political into films with mass circulation and appeal controlled by a conservative, even timid industry? It was clear that if he were to continue working in Hollywood, Wilson would have to throw in his lot with independent producers, some of whom operated within a complex international framework that transcended the borders of a chauvinistic America.

This was not altogether a bad proposition for Wilson artistically either. As described in an earlier chapter, independent producers were behind some of the best pictures released in the 1950s. Furthermore, a respected scriptwriter like Wilson could have considerably more input into an independently produced film than would be possible in a studio production. As he explained in an interview with the French journal *Positif*:

> An evolution has occurred in the last fifty years in the situation for the American screenwriter with the decline of the major studios and the appearance of "independent" companies. . . . Those [screenwriters] who have been employed by the "independents" have profited from a somewhat elevated position. I don't want to say by that the screenwriters (at least being equally producers) had control over the production; but I am of the opinion that

American screenwriters have more influence on the film than their European colleagues. It's very difficult for me to explain this to some Frenchmen. In France, with a few exceptions, the director engages one or several screenwriters to assist him in the preparation of his own ideas; in America the scripts are sometimes completely done before the director is chosen.[12]

It is not altogether surprising, then, that Spiegel and Lean would have hired Wilson to work on the script for *Kwai*. Since the final version resulted from a collaboration between Wilson and Foreman, it would not be until *Lawrence* that Wilson would have the chance to produce his own script, with some influence on the production, or so he hoped.

The story of Wilson's life and career, as I have told it, is the story of a writer who learns to become political in his art but also learns the constraints placed upon that art by industry and government censorship. If he went the non-Hollywood route, he risked having his work not seen at all. If his work was purchased by Hollywood, he knew he would have to make certain kinds of compromises. But as his mentor John Lawson taught him, the "humanism" of the situation through which the political was expressed mattered more than an explicit political message per se.

From his Parisian home in "exile," Wilson sent to Spiegel and Lean an initial film treatment dated September 20, 1958, with the title "LAWRENCE OF ARABIA: Elements and Facets of a Theme."[13] Wilson's talents as a scholar, honed as a student at Berkeley, are fully evident in it. It is important to place Wilson's screenplay within a particular discursive "field"—that of the travelogue, travel memoir, and especially biography—in order to understand his political take on Lawrence. In other words, it would be a mistake to assume that he developed it independently, given that he was living in a time of critique and revisionism where the Lawrence legend was concerned, not coincidentally after World War II, when the British Empire began to crumble. Where Wilson was original in his revisionism was his acute sense of the historical constructedness of Lawrence's biographies; that is, that they were not simply reflections of facts—deeds that Lawrence performed—but construals that served particular political interests at the particular historical moments in which they were written. The film, as Wilson quite acutely understood, was thus also a construction of the Lawrence legend at a certain moment in the latter's discursive history, a moment when the legend was coming under attack.

Lowell Thomas's famous travelogue "With Allenby in Palestine and Lawrence in Arabia" toured America, Great Britain, and some of the

British colonies from roughly 1919 to 1923. It turned Lawrence into one of the first mass media stars. On the heels of the spectacular success of Thomas's show came his memoir *With Lawrence in Arabia* (1924), which was published in several editions and sold tens of thousands of copies. In the twenties and thirties, a series of highbrow biographies followed, most distinguished among them being Robert Graves's acclaimed *Lawrence and the Arabian Adventure* (1927) and B. H. Liddell Hart's assessments of Lawrence as a guerrilla leader and military strategist in his *Colonel Lawrence: The Man Behind the Legend* (1935).

In spite of the many biographies written in his own lifetime, Lawrence was not innocent in the manufacture of many of the most important ones that solidified his legend. As Wilson astutely observed in his document outlining his treatment of the screenplay, "The prime mover in the creation of the legend was, of course, Lowell Thomas. But wittingly and/or unwittingly, Lawrence himself contributed heavily to the myth. In this sense, he helped to perpetrate a fraud." For example, though Lawrence tried publicly to distance himself from the "vulgar" American who was turning him into the most popular war hero in the world, it was revealed after his death that Lawrence had willingly posed before Thomas's camera in Arabia. The same game was coyly played with his other biographers, on the one hand insisting that they derive their portraits independently of him for the sake of historical "objectivity" and on the other subtly amending the final manuscripts before they went off to the publishers to reflect his own sense of himself. One of the great lines to come out of this affair turned out to be Lowell Thomas's, to the effect that Lawrence had a genius for "backing into the limelight." [14]

Biographical representations of Lawrence began to change radically in the 1950s, however. "Countermyths" were being entertained. The one with the most impact in changing the way Lawrence was to be examined by biographers was Richard Aldington's incendiary *Lawrence of Arabia* (1955), less a biography than what the author termed a critical "enquiry." It is clear that Wilson had read this book carefully. "Richard Aldington's appraisal of Lawrence is not a balanced judgment, but on this score Aldington is perfectly correct: Lawrence needed the legend; he fed on it, and he found that the best way to perpetuate it was to plant conflicting or baffling stories about himself in order to keep controversy brewing and the enigma unsolved." Aldington's meticulously researched book attempts a point-by-point rebuttal of every aspect of, and claim about, Lawrence's life and achievements. It concludes that Lawrence had been a pathological liar. Not surprisingly, the book created a sensation and was considered scandalous by Lawrence mythographers, who ended up branding its criticism excessive and the motives of its author neurotic. Before Aldington, however, there had been Arab revisionist historians of the Arab Revolt, lesser known to Western historiography perhaps, such as George Antonious's magisterial *The Arab Awakening*, published in English in 1938, which did not so much dispute Lawrence's claims as replace him with Emir Hussein of Mecca as the central figure in the revolt. The most significant work to follow in this vein of Arab revisionist scholarship was Suleiman Mousa's *T. E. Lawrence: An Arab View*, which, however, would not appear in English until 1966, four years after the film was released. It is difficult to judge how much of the Arab revisionist view of Lawrence Wilson and Lean knew when they began work on the script. They may have had much greater inklings of it by the time filmmaking began in Jordan, where they must have caught wind of the criticism directed at the film project. But there can be no doubt that the filmmakers' treatment of their subject is at least in tune with the British revisionist view of Lawrence emerging in the 1950s.

One can begin to see in Wilson's remarks the outlines of a political project for the film. "Our story should develop as a slow revelation of the man behind the myth—a probe, a gradual exposure of the failure that lay at the core of a triumph." The ending would have to be anticlimactic, taking on the quality of farce (as Lawrence himself had acknowledged in his memoir), "a parody of great hopes," as Wilson puts it. He explains: "Lawrence had lied, cheated, stolen and murdered to reach Damascus, yet he entered its gates not as a modern Saladin, not as an infidel Messiah, but as a puny masquerader, no longer in control of his destiny and no longer the master of events—an adventurer who, having deceived others, finds himself deceived."

Thus, what intrigues Wilson about Lawrence is his "contradictory character," as evidenced by his trying to serve two masters, neither of whom he could satisfy, and in the end becoming disillusioned with both. I think Wilson may have identified with Lawrence's character because of his own history as a youth leading a "double life," being at once brilliant in a conventional social career (top student, successful athlete, fraternity president) while all the time searching for higher ideals—Catholicism, Marxism, activist filmmaking. This was the so-called humanism of the situation. Thus, Lawrence yearned for an ideal that would raise him above his bourgeois English life; he eventually found it in his fight for Arab freedom, though he was naive not to realize that he was a pawn in the Great Game, not to mention also in Arab politics. Why is Lawrence a pawn in the Great Game? Here Wilson puts forward the thesis that Lawrence's legend was created in order to serve Anglo-American colonial interests: "In the general disillusionment and cynicism following World War I, the western world needed an authentic hero to shore up the ideals for which the war had allegedly been fought. . . . A shining symbol was needed. . . . The Lawrence legend was created to fill that need. One can even say that if Lawrence had never existed, it would have been necessary to invent him." Wilson then pinpoints the source of that invention in Lowell Thomas. There is thus an implicit critique in the use of media and media-constructed heroes for political purposes.

It is interesting that when Wilson turns to what might be called the human interest of the story, he dwells on the "dramatic necessity" for the character of Ali and his relationship to Lawrence. Wilson is not forming this opinion independently of his director. "David's notes on this character are extensive, and I will not repeat them here." He summarizes by saying, "David Lean believes . . . that S.A. [the initials in the dedication attached to Lawrence's poem at the beginning of his memoir] was Sherif Ali ibn El-Hussein," one of the leaders of the Arab campaign. It is Lean, however subtly and tentatively, who makes the homoerotic and possibly homosexual connection. Wilson, on the contrary, is skittish about the question of their relationship and Lawrence's sexuality: "I leave aside for the time being the question of homosexual attachment. . . . Let us assume for a moment that it is a David and Jonathan relationship, of two blood-brothers dedicated to a common cause. . . . To Lawrence's mind, the relationship was perhaps a model of what human intercourse could be, a prototype of a brotherhood to come." However Wilson chose to construe the personal in Lawrence, it is clear that it was not divorced from the political; his understanding of his own script treatment undermines the assumptions of his subsequent criticisms of the film, in particular that the political in Lawrence's project is somehow incompatible with the psychological motivation of his character. This sense is deepened when we realize what Wilson intended Ali to stand for in the picture. "It seems to me that S.A. might represent what is wholesome and uncorrupted in the Arab mentality—even if that position is objectively reactionary." The orientalist reference to "Arab mentality" might make us cringe, but Wilson was not altogether essentializing. He warns the filmmakers: "We must avoid careless generalizations about the 'Arab point of view'. . . . This said, let us examine the character of S.A. in relation to an Arab point of view. . . . S.A. would epitomize the free desert nomad, opposed to modernity in any form, a man who tries to return to and safeguard what he considers to be the pristine nobility of the traditional Bedouin way of life. In that sense, S.A. wants to turn back the clock." Of course, that description fits Auda Abu Tayyi in the final version of the film far more than it does Sharif Ali.

I would maintain that Wilson's screenplay is in general far more critical of Arab politics than the final version prepared by Lean and Bolt. "The feudal Arab world," writes Wilson rather cynically, "had its own form of corruption. . . . The cash nexus would replace the ties between equal nomads. Arab leaders who had pursued an idea would now pursue fortunes in oil, and sell their brethren at the bidding of a western master." Wilson's understanding of the Arab Revolt—a liberation movement that was parochial and chauvinistic in its nationalist ambition—is basically a conservative one and is usually attributed to Lean and Bolt's treatment, but since it is not so extreme in the final version of the script, I must assume that the latter toned it down. Wilson's script also emphasizes that tribal conflict and bloodshed are supposedly endemic to Arab politics and are commonly said to have stood in the way of Arab nationalism. Though present in Bolt's script, this theme of tribal feud is deeply ironized by showing it in the context of a bloody European war as well as being fueled by Lawrence's sadomasochistic personality. Nor is Ali a reactionary in the version of the script prepared by Bolt. In his albeit reluctant acceptance to pursue a career in politics in which little honor will accrue to him, Ali tries his hand at parliamentary democracy. His failure is not all his fault or the fault of a supposedly feuding Arab politics. The machinations of the British have a lot to do with thwarting his nationalist ambitions. And while Wilson tended to see the Hashemites as essentially toadies of the British, his script portraying Prince Feisal as a weakling and a puppet of Lawrence and the allies, Bolt's characterization strengthened Feisal and rendered him far more complex. In Bolt's treatment he becomes a witty, insightful, and urbane man, though at times deeply cynical about human motives, including his own (as revealed in his final lines about Lawrence).

So much for Wilson's initial treatment, which outlines a political vision for the film story: Lawrence is to be at odds with two different masters and a pawn of both, and his legend is to be created by the press and fostered for purposes of empire. It is important to bear in mind that Lean sent to his scriptwriter his own statement of ideas dated October 1959, entitled "Possible Scenes, Sequences, Characters or Visuals,"[15] in which he urged Wilson to be uncompromising in his political criticism of colonialism. Lean dwells at length on the introductory chapter of *Seven Pillars of Wisdom,* in which Lawrence complains that the aspirations for freedom unleashed by the Arab Revolt were quashed by Western colonialism. "I do implore us all to consider what we can say about this important aspect of Lawrence's beliefs," Lean exhorts his team. "They are the main-spring of the story we are going to tell." Whether rightly or wrongly, Lean considered Lawrence ahead of his time in the way he criticized Europe's colonial system. He states, "We weren't—as is so often thought—driven out of the colonies by the subject race. We had people at home who were pushing hard as they were," and he goes further than either of his scriptwriters in claiming that Lawrence was one of those who tried to resist the colonial system from within. One might take exception with Lean's reading of that chapter of *Seven Pillars* as being overly generous to Lawrence's anticolonial sentiments, insofar as they still advocate a tutelary relationship between Western powers and nascent Arab states to be realized in the form of "protectorates," a more benign form of colonialism, perhaps, but hardly anticolonial. Nevertheless, Lean wanted to tell a story that was about the machinations of colonialism that thwarted Arab aspirations for independence, and thereby make a film critical of the colonial project.

In December of 1959, in a single-spaced, ninety-two-page synopsis of Lawrence's memoir, Wilson proclaimed triumphantly, "Whoever said that there is no motion picture in SEVEN PILLARS OF WISDOM is mistaken."[16] In his view, the work contained an inherent narrative structure, which he hoped to foreground by carefully selecting dramatically significant material. In the final product he did not limit himself to the memoir, of course, for he began the screenplay with Lawrence's death as announced by the media, which is then commented on by various celebrities, and not always flatteringly, as if to underscore the fact that Lawrence's legend was very much a construction and a controversial one at that. Bolt had inherited this structure whether he was aware of Wilson's treatments and scripts or not; but as we shall see in a moment, he fine-tuned it by eliminating, rearranging, and in some cases introducing new material. This is not the place to analyze in detail the differences in the scripts, which has already been done by others.[17] Rather, let me first clarify the structure of the final screenplay, which is for the most part Wilson's contribution, before I go on to describe Lean's reservations about his treatment and Bolt's innovations in dramatic form, which, I believe, strengthened the possibilities of a political critique of Lawrence and his situation.

The narrative structure may be grasped in the form of one of the film's central images, the whirlwind (see diagram). This is my way of understanding the structure, not Wilson's, or Bolt's, or any of the other filmmakers'. On the one hand, this could be a metaphor for a man riding political events that are ultimately out of his control (as when Allenby says of Lawrence at the end of Part One, "He's riding a whirlwind"); on the other, it perfectly captures the psyche of a man with contrary impulses that chase each other around a hollow center. Or consider the resemblance between the shape of a whirlwind and a question mark, for Lawrence is asked throughout the movie—and in turn asks himself—"Who are you?" In one image, the political and the psychological, which I do not want to keep separate from each other, are yoked together.

At the risk of being pedantic, let me trace in some detail the brilliant structure of the reconstructed 1989 version that Wilson initially provided and Bolt fine-tuned. What I call the beginning is actually two scenes, Lawrence's death in a motorcycle accident, followed by his memorial service in Saint Paul's cathedral. Bolt omitted the newsreels and celebrity interviews in Wilson's script (which in my view seem a little too much like *Citizen Kane*). He figured out another way to allude to the idea that Lawrence was a construction of the media, which was more organically tied to the memorial service by showing a newspaper reporter interviewing various personalities on the steps of the cathedral, all of whom give contradictory statements about this world-famous figure. What I call the ending is the "chiasmus" of the beginning: Lawrence "interred" under the dust kicked up by a speeding motorcyclist. Bolt added that motorcyclist to Wilson's ending, thereby realizing more completely the sense of the movie as having come full circle. The motorcyclist at the end is an allusion to the motorcyclist at the beginning, reminding us of Lawrence's death, and thus the movie loops around itself, the end returning to the beginning.

Starting at the top left-hand corner of the accompanying diagram, the plot as it was written in Bolt's production script is drawn linearly in four "curves" and ends at the bottom left-hand corner. Imagine each curve as the completion of a full plot cycle—beginning with an interview between Lawrence and some important military officer or political figure, then a

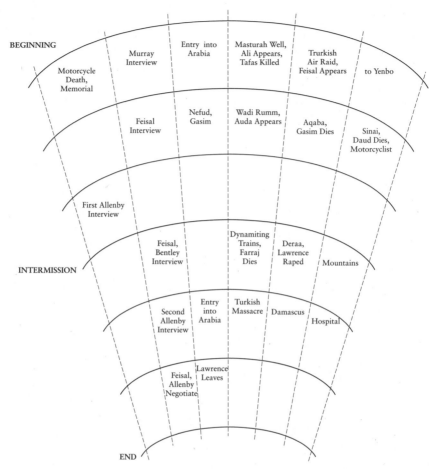

BEGINNING

Motorcycle
Death,
Memorial

Murray
Interview

Entry into
Arabia

Masturah Well,
Ali Appears,
Tafas Killed

Trurkish
Air Raid,
Feisal Appears

to Yenbo

Feisal
Interview

Nefud,
Gasim

Wadi Rumm,
Auda Appears

Aqaba,
Gasim Dies

Sinai,
Daud Dies,
Motorcyclist

First Allenby
Interview

INTERMISSION

Feisal,
Bentley
Interview

Dynamiting
Trains,
Farraj
Dies

Deraa,
Lawrence
Raped

Mountains

Second
Allenby
Interview

Entry
into
Arabia

Turkish
Massacre

Damascus

Hospital

Feisal,
Allenby
Negotiate

Lawrence
Leaves

END

Structure of *Lawrence of Arabia* (1962, 1989)

journey by Lawrence (back) into Arabia, followed by an act of "cultural"
violence, a political denouement (of triumph or defeat), and finally a retreat or withdrawal from the situation—there being four such cycles in
the "whirlwind" of this narrative, interrupted by an intermission at the
structural (if not temporal) halfway point. Let us now consider each rotation or cycle in a bit more detail. The events plotted in the rotations are
roughly parallel to each other. For example, looking down the columns
in the diagram, one can read as parallel the following events (even though
each event occurs in a different cycle or rotation): Masturah Well scene

(in which Tafas is killed by Sherif Ali); the wells and tents at Wadi Rumm (at which Auda confronts and challenges Lawrence, Ali, and the raiders); blowing up and raiding the Turkish trains; and the massacre of the Turks ordered by Lawrence. In each of these events certain key elements of the plot are repeated, so that we have a sense of having visited them again, even though they are explored in slightly different ways each time (hence a cyclic structure). In the case of the four events in question, the themes might be the so-called violence of Arabs and the European's complicity (or participation) in that violence. Now consider the column next to it. Here we find the following parallels: bombardment of Feisal's camp; the taking of 'Aqaba; Lawrence's beating and rape in Deraa; and the Arab nationalist meeting in the town hall in Damascus. I admit that it is harder to claim these to be parallel to each other—the four seem to be slightly mismatched—but are they not about leadership, its successes and failures, and hence represent a political denouement?

The reason I prefer this more formal representation of the film's structure is that it stresses repetition and circularity, if you will, a kind of Freudian "repetition compulsion" that captures this movie's obsessive quality. For some viewers, however, this way of looking at the structure will appear *too* formal. In that case, consider the structure more loosely as two cycles represented by Part One and Part Two. This movie turns in on itself roughly around the time that 'Aqaba is taken. It then works backward to undo or subvert itself. Part One reveals a man, who is alienated from the army and his cultural identity, seeking an adventure as a form of escape from his humdrum life. Gradually we see him become a hero. True, things already start to go awry for him in Part One, shortly before his greatest triumph at 'Aqaba, when he discovers to his horror that he not only has to execute the man he saved in the Nefud but enjoys doing it; and then again in the Sinai Desert, when he loses his beloved servant Daud in "quicksand," largely due to his own—that is, Lawrence's—negligence. But as Part One ends we confidently hope, I think, that these are temporary setbacks from which our resilient hero will rebound to achieve even greater glory in Part Two.

However, as Part Two unfolds, slowly but inexorably our expectations are disappointed and we are treated instead to a spectacle of anti-heroism. It is as though the movie now enters into a downward, rather than an upward, spiral. If in Part One Lawrence was able to gather the Arab forces together, in Part Two they slowly melt away. If in Part One he is shown as becoming overly identified with the "Arab," in Part Two he slowly disavows him. If in Part One he is supposedly rational and compassionate, in Part Two he becomes increasingly merciless, driven by unconscious forces.

What were some of Lean's dissatisfactions with Wilson's artistic treatment? Continuity was one.[18] How did Bolt provide it? The concept of parallelism is useful for understanding his solution to the problem.

As a theoretical term, parallelism has been employed most extensively in the analysis of poetry[19] to describe alliteration, rhyme, meter, metaphor, and so forth, not to mention the larger architecture of verse structures such as strophes.[20] It has also been applied to cinema by film theorists such as David Bordwell and Kristin Thompson.[21] Parallelism is a regular repetition of equivalent (though not necessarily identical) units. A word such as "table" is parallel to the rhyming word "able"; a metrical foot composed of a stressed syllable is parallel (that is, equivalent, not identical) to an unstressed syllable, and if next to each other in the verse, they may form a metrical foot; one stanza is parallel to another stanza, and together they may constitute a whole poem or part of one; and so forth. The function of parallelism is not only to form structural linkages between separate units of a work of art but also to suggest *meaningful* relationships that bear on the work's interpretation. Thus, the lines connected by the rhyming words "table" and "able" will be compared to each other and a common meaning or some sort of relationship between them suggested or sought. When it comes to film, continuity may be established by matching the positions or actions of an actor from one scene to the next or, more subtly, by having similar events recur in scenes that are less contiguous to each other. The point that Bordwell and Thompson make is that a well-crafted film like *Lawrence of Arabia* is bound to contain dozens of such parallelisms, linking one scene or segment with another, as well as crossing over them, to produce a dense texture of significations.

Crucial to the film's continuity, for example, is the parallelism of the motorcyclist, which is only hinted at in Wilson's scripts but is accentuated in Bolt's. In Wilson's third and final script, Lawrence is seen riding his motorcycle to his death and then again later in the movie when he races with Farraj through the streets of Cairo just after having crossed the Sinai. In Bolt's version, however, the motorcyclist spots Lawrence at the Suez Canal and shouts, "Who are you?" He is not literally but figuratively Lawrence—that is, his double—and it is the same motorcyclist whom Lawrence holds in his gaze from the back of the truck as it makes its way through Cairo. The parallelism does double duty, so to speak, establishing continuity between one scene and another as well as suggesting Lawrence's disassociated state. At the end of the film, he appears one last time when the protagonist is morally and spiritually spent, the mere husk of a human being. In front of a dusty windscreen we can see the outline of Lawrence's head as he is being driven out of Arabia. At that instant a motorcyclist overtakes the car and roars past, presaging Lawrence's death in an accident years later. In Bolt's treatment the motorcyclist is both a structural and a thematic device, linking beginning, middle, and end.

As the goggles on the motorcyclist reveal, one of the most important motifs of this film has to do with masking. At the Masturah Well, when Sharif Ali presents himself to Lawrence for the first time, he pointedly drops the end of his headdress that covers his face as though to unveil himself, like a bedouin woman. What he reveals, I will later argue, is that he is one of Lawrence's doubles. A couple of scenes later, Lawrence encounters Prince Feisal for the first time. Elegantly clad, the gallant prince is seen galloping on a magnificent white charger into the midst of a badly panicked camp, exhorting his men, "Fire back at them!" and riding recklessly in the path of swooping Turkish aircraft. A bomb explosion leaves a thick wall of black smoke and yellow dust, before which Feisal reins in his horse as the airplanes roar off. He sheathes his sword dejectedly and with lowered head closes his eyes, almost as though he were looking deep into his own anguished soul. The camera closes in. Moments later he looks up to see Lawrence peering down at him. It is as though Lawrence were a figment of Feisal's own wishful thinking, an answer to his silent prayer. Lawrence's face, obscured by smoke and dust, is like a mask. A bit startled by the young man's sudden appearance, Feisal asks, "Who are you?" The question is supposed to be matter-of-fact, as per the snide directive in the script: "straightforwardly interrogative— no 'significance' please." However, it is clear that the interrogative— parallel to similar interrogatives such as the one shouted by the motorcyclist—alludes to the enigma of Lawrence. The masking motif recurs during Lawrence's crossing of the Sinai Desert, where we see his face literally caked white with sand and, of course, most dramatically at the end of it, when he finally reaches the Suez Canal and the motorcyclist reappears. Another double, this time in Part Two, is a Turkish officer, wounded in a train wreck, who shoots at Lawrence but succeeds only in grazing his arm. The officer's face looks to be of the same age as Lawrence's and has somewhat similar features, though obscured (that is,

Figure 6. Close-up of Turkish soldier, one of Lawrence's "doubles."

Figure 7. The revolver Lawrence gives as a "gift" to his guide Tafas.

Figure 8. The revolver continues its circulation, this time as Lawrence prepares to execute Gasim.

masked) by grime and sweat (figure 6). Oddly enough, Lawrence does not seek cover but stands in front of his would-be assassin, seemingly seeking his own execution. Once again, the Turk takes aim and fires, but because he is seriously wounded and frightened, he repeatedly misses Lawrence, who looks straight into his assailant's terrified eyes. In that young man's eyes, I would argue, he recognizes his alter ego. Loathing himself for his sadism, Lawrence in a sense projects a death wish onto his murderous double.

Besides masking, another subtle parallelism is to be found in the circulation of a pistol through many scenes of the film. Though the germ of this parallelism is already present in Wilson's script, it is accentuated or intensified by Bolt, who extracts political meanings, and not just irony, from it. At first the pistol is Lawrence's. When he wants to reward his guide Tafas for his faithful service in leading him to Feisal's encampment, he gives him a revolver. We see it for the first time in an abrupt cut, filling the entire screen, so that we might remember it (figure 7). At the Masturah Well, Tafas pulls the revolver from his saddle bag when he attempts to shoot the approaching stranger. The revolver falls at Lawrence's feet, its muzzle pointing like an accusatory finger at him. Having killed Tafas, Sherif Ali appropriates the gun for himself, and it is at Ali's waist that we see it next, when he is standing beside a seated Lawrence in Feisal's tent. Many scenes later, it will be from Ali's waist that Lawrence will take the pistol with which he then executes a criminal (figure 8). When he is horrified to discover that he enjoyed killing the man, he tosses the gun like an evil fetish back into the crowd of bedouin who are seen scrambling madly after it. The European has thus reintroduced the instrument of death back into the rounds of violence. After this point in the film, the director did not bother to establish strict continuity between the pistol we had seen in these scenes and the revolver Lawrence carries in subsequent ones. No matter; for parallelism depends on structural equivalence, not identity. When we next see the pistol, it is in a brief scene when Lawrence and the Arab army have stopped on their march to Damascus to observe the heavy bombardment of Turkish positions by the British. Lawrence feels no sympathy for the enemy, having just been a victim of their brutal treatment in Deraa. He spins the bullet chamber of his gun like a homicidal maniac (figure 9). In the very next scene, a massacre of a Turkish brigade ordered by Lawrence, we see him shooting the enemy at point-blank range with his pistol, a demented look of glee on his face (figure 10). And again in the next major scene, the town hall in Damascus in which the Arab army tries to constitute itself as a nation, Lawrence

Figure 9.   Lawrence, like a homicidal maniac, spins the bullet chamber of the revolver as he watches the Turks being bombarded by British artillery. A night-time scene.

Figure 10.   Lawrence shooting a Turkish prisoner who tries to surrender.

calls the assembly to order by slamming the butt of the pistol onto the table like a gavel (figure 11). After what it has come to symbolize, the gun's use in this scene thoroughly undercuts all of Lawrence's expressed intentions of working for peace, justice, and brotherly love.

Mindful of what I have said about parallelism, that it not only stitches scenes together but also creates a kind of subliminal meaning across them, we might ask what meanings the appearance of the revolver has in the movie overall. In my view, what it signifies is an old theme in Lean movies—particularly evident in his *Bridge on the River Kwai*—having to do with technology and the West's perverse use of it. In other words, here is a case where the political enters the poetic structure of the screen-

Figure 11.   Lawrence, in the Damascus town hall, tries to call the Arab assembly to order with the butt of his revolver.

play. At the time that Bolt was writing the latter, this theme also must have been uppermost in his mind, for he had just been jailed for civil disobedience in a London antinuclear rally organized by Bertrand Russell and other left-wing intellectuals and artists. Bolt once explained, "I am absolutely opposed to the possession and making of atomic weapons."[22] Spiegel had to bail him out of jail so that work on the script could be completed.

Having tightened the continuity of the screenplay at the same time that he managed to explore certain psychological and political themes, Bolt had to address Lean's next major criticism of Wilson's screenplay. In a letter to Spiegel dated January 5, 1961, written while Lean was already in Jordan scouting for film locations, the director explains why he was dissatisfied with the script: "The basic flaw is that in the present construction there is no margin for comment or kick-back off the main character. He just keeps on doing things and the audiences watches and draws their own conclusions."[23] I interpret Lean's comments as meaning two things: one is that the script should contain room for both the filmmakers and the audience to construct differing interpretations of Lawrence; the other is that these interpretations should to some degree be critical of Lawrence and the colonial situation. Of course, to achieve such effects requires building an audience expectation of reflection and criticism, not merely passive entertainment of nonstop action. It is the solution of this problem of reflexive and critical spectatorship, I would argue, that was Bolt's single most important and original contribution.

Let us look at the British theater out of which Bolt emerged to understand this aspect of his screenwriting.

The British theater of the 1950s was marked by three dominant trends:
social realism and criticism as exemplified in John Osbourne's *Look Back
in Anger;* the brilliant drama of Harold Pinter's *The Caretaker,* which
was deeply indebted to Samuel Beckett and the Theatre of the Absurd;
and Brechtian "Epic Theatre," by which Bolt's big hit, *A Man for All
Seasons* (1960), can be seen to be influenced.[24] To be sure, his indebted-
ness to Brecht did not lie so much in the treatment of themes as it did with
form. "I love the chunky classical four-square quality of Brecht,"[25] Bolt
confessed, adding elsewhere that "I think it is form that is missing [in
film productions] and form is, and must be, the province of the writer."[26]
What Bolt does not mention about his playwriting, and which I have
found to be a compelling basis of comparison with Brecht, is his use of
a Brechtian "alienation" technique.[27] Through this technique Brecht had
hoped to distance audiences from the epic action on stage long enough
to get them to think critically about what they had been seeing, rather
than be swallowed up in their identification with the characters and
their predicaments. Such distancing can be achieved through a variety of
means: set design and lighting, choruses or actors who directly address
the audience, and, most significantly, a distinctive mode of acting and line
delivery. Reminded that they were seeing acting or representation, not
being, audiences would hopefully step back from the play long enough
to evaluate its political lessons.

In the film *Lawrence of Arabia,* Bolt achieved a similar alienation effect through the motif of the performance-within-the-performance. To be
sure, this motif captures something of the historical character's acute self-
consciousness, which is why it does not seem artificial to those who know
the autobiography. "There was a craving to be famous: and a horror of
being known to like being known," T.E. Lawrence confessed.[28] Addition-
ally, however, the motif is used, or so I would claim, to get the audience
to think critically about the character. Consider the scene in which Lawrence goes off into the desert and capers about in his new robes, only to
be caught playacting by Auda Abu Tayyi, who asks in astonishment,
"What are you doing—Englishman?" The narrative-internal audience,
the sheikh, abruptly makes the viewing audience step back and recon-
sider Lawrence's heroic qualities: he is, of course, amusing, childlike,
and charming, but is he not also rather vain and slightly "off"?

The recurrence of the motif reminds the audience that what they are observing is an act, a representation, which calls for scrutiny and evaluation. Here is another example. After his guide has been killed by Sharif Ali, Lawrence proceeds by himself to Wadi Safra, where he knows Feisal to be encamped. The view is of a gorge, a huge amphitheater of stone. He is on camelback, twisting around in his saddle to admire its grandeur. Appropriate to his stagelike surroundings, Lawrence begins a performance, singing at the top of his lungs the same ditty he whistled in the well scene. He listens with delight to the sound of his voice bouncing back and forth between the sides of the towering sandstone cliffs, as if it were filling a void. Once again, we are made aware of a scene-internal audience: the camera pans from the top of a cliff face to a British officer sitting on a boulder below, watching Lawrence's performance with a jaundiced eye. The officer begins clapping, a sound that becomes derisive as it echoes in the gorge, somewhat like the clapping of a single audience member at a play. Lawrence, of course, is caught off guard and appears embarrassed. Eventually the officer stands and shouts "Hey, you." Lawrence is not only surprised to hear himself addressed in English; he is disconcerted to hear "you" reverberate all about him—an aural image of hollowness that sums up the problem of a self that will claim multiple identities and loyalties. Lawrence is being addressed by Colonel Brighton (Anthony Quayle), on loan from British headquarters in Cairo as military adviser to Prince Feisal. We see him now from Lawrence's perspective, a tiny speck at the base of a gigantic outcrop of rock. The image is held for several seconds in order to give the audience time to see him on the wide screen as well as to convey the sense of space in the desert, its hugeness and emptiness, which is an integral part of drama's epic situation.

As the analysis of these scenes reveals, it was not only Bolt's writing or Lean's directing that was a key ingredient to the success of this alienation technique—not to mention the fascistic meanings which the play-within-the-play motif constructs by the end of the film—it is also Peter O'Toole's acting. I would argue that the theatricality of O'Toole's performance, due in no small measure to his training as a classical, and especially a Shakespearean, actor, enhanced the motif of Lawrence's playacting on the historical stage. An examination of the way his life intersects with his film career will also clarify what he brought to the characterization of Lawrence that could be interpreted as fascistic. He confided to Rebecca West in an interview, "I compared him [Lawrence] once—and I've never been forgiven for it—to Hitler." [29]

Peter O'Toole (b. 1932) came of age during the war in Europe, which he poignantly remembers from the perspective of a child in the first volume of his autobiography, *Loitering with Intent* (1992). A startling element of this memoir is its folding of a biography of Adolf Hitler into itself, a biography that is not just an impressionistic account, casually related to provide some wider historical context, but stems from a lifelong obsession on O'Toole's part.[30] With his future wife, the actress Sian Phillips, for example, he would make a trip to Linz, Austria, the birthplace of the future Führer, "there to indulge my prating of and peering at matters Adolf."[31] At Nuremberg she would suggest to him that he read Geoffrey Household's *Rogue Male,* a thriller published in 1939, "which describes the predicament of a man determined to assassinate a vicious dictator, head of the totalitarian government of a European country, and at once avert a possible war in Europe while avenging the slaughter of his Jewish lady love."[32] O'Toole would wind up playing the part in a television movie, the work on which, he noted, "had given me a sensation of somehow resolving a chord which had hummed in my mind since boyhood."[33] If Robert Bolt has said that he interpreted Lawrence as a "romantic fascist," it is not farfetched to think of O'Toole as embodying this quality in his performance's gestures and inflections of words.

The combined contributions of screenwriter, director, and actor produced a scene such as the following, which illustrates brilliantly Brechtian alienation technique joined with a fascistic interpretation of Lawrence's character. The performance-within-the-performance returns in abbreviated form in many scenes of the movie but nowhere as powerfully as in Part Two when we are introduced to Jackson Bentley, the American reporter who has been sent by his government to find a "hero" whom the public would find glamorous and thus draw the country into war. Bentley joins Lawrence on one of his expeditions dynamiting Turkish trains and asks whether he can take his picture. Lawrence not only agrees to the request but actively poses for Bentley's camera, an allusion to Lawrence's participation in the construction of his own myth as revisionist biographers such as Aldington had stressed. Moving swiftly along the length of the wreckage, a shout of "Aurens" goes up among the bedouin as if they were hailing a leader at a political rally. Mocking himself while secretly enjoying the adulation, Lawrence gets on top of the train to strut high above his admirers, who have unfurled great bolts of cloth and are waving them like banners at a parade. The Lawrence theme is struck but in a brassy, dissonant form. It is interesting how Lean now

Figure 12.   Lawrence walking on the roof of a train with bedouin cheering him in background (shades of the fascist leader).

photographs O'Toole's body (figure 12). We see mostly his boots, stomping in great strides across the roof of the train like the jackboots of a general; then his silhouetted figure turns in the sun, his robe fluttering in the wind, much like when he first donned his robes; and finally his elongated shadow undulates over the sand. These are the gestures of a man on stage—a demagogue or dictator—who is at the same time insubstantial and ephemeral. Bentley, pleased with the marvelous pictures he is getting, grins from ear to ear. "Yes sir . . . that's my baby," he says cynically to himself, a quotation from another song of the period.

Clearly, the filmmakers wanted the audience to identify with the character, yet through the performance-within-the-performance to make it possible for them to step back from it as well, long enough to evaluate it critically, and in particular to think about Lawrence's politics. When the reporter is taking Lawrence's picture, for which all the while Lawrence is carefully posing, the audience should grasp how the legend of Lawrence of Arabia came into being in the first place   on the one hand by the media, on the other by imperial forces that exploited the media for their own political purposes, and finally through Lawrence's collusion with both. When the newspaper reporter is creating a "hero" out of Lawrence, the moment of his heroism has of course already passed, for he is now seen to be sadistic and megalomaniacal, thus rendering the performance-within-the-performance deeply ironic.

Alienation technique does not exhaust the means by which Bolt created the critical spectator. Just as important is his use of irony. The literary critic Kenneth Burke treats irony as a form of dialectic.[34] Simply put, irony requires the audience to take a perspective on a situation that is different from, or at odds with, the view held by one or more of the characters in the drama. What is represented as A, the audience is asked to consider as Not-A. Burke adds an important caveat, however: "True irony, humble irony, is based upon a sense of fundamental kinship with the enemy, as one *needs* him, is *indebted* to him, is not merely outside him as an observer but contains him *within* him, being consubstantial with him."[35] In this kind of irony we do not feel superior to the protagonist because we know his or her problems to be our own.

To gain a sense of the complex use of irony in this film, let us consider once again the memorial service held for Lawrence in Saint Paul's cathedral. Jackson Bentley's cynical remark—to wit that Lawrence was a shameless exhibitionist—is overheard and challenged by a belligerent little gentleman in a bowler hat. "Did you know him?" Bentley asks. "No, sir," replies the man in the bowler hat, "I can't claim I knew him. I had the honour once to shake his hand in Damascus." In fact, he meets Lawrence twice toward the end of the story, but we, the audience, cannot know that the gentleman's statement is in error until then, another instance of how the narrative works by coiling around itself like a snake. In the beginning, then, we are put in the same ironic position as the obnoxious gentleman (or, Kenneth Burke would say, we are consubstantial with him); being used to looking up to Lawrence as a hero and staunchly wanting to think of him as one, even though we have to lamely admit that we cannot claim to know him. But by the end of the film, we do know him, or at least a great deal better than the gentleman in the bowler hat. Thus, our perspective in relation to him shifts when we see the gentleman again, and this time it is he who appears ironic to us. We now see that his construction of Lawrence as a hero is deeply problematical.

Let us then look at the complex irony in the two encounters between Lawrence and this odious little man. The first time they meet is in a Turkish military hospital inside Damascus where Lawrence, in sheikh's outfit, his face masked by his headdress, wanders horrified among the Turkish dead and wounded. The officer approaches a man whom he takes to be a bedouin and shrieks, "Outrageous! Outrageous!" in reaction to the conditions in the hospital. Lawrence starts to laugh uncontrollably at the fact that he is blamed for a situation that was caused by the British in the first place; namely, their refusal to give medical assistance to the bedouin army. Incensed by the laughter, which he takes to be a sign of callousness, the officer shouts at Lawrence, "Bloody little wog," and slaps him with such force that Lawrence is toppled to the ground. He lies there crumpled up with laughter, overcome by the irony that he has been mistaken for an Arab, or rather, I should say, *finally* mistaken for an Arab—for that had been his ambition all along—only to be vilified for it. His headdress comes loose, exposing him as the Englishman that he is, but the officer has already moved on and therefore cannot recognize him. For the audience, the irony works to temper our judgments of Lawrence, to feel if not quite sympathy for him, then at least that he has been unduly blamed. This nasty little man's second encounter with Lawrence is in British headquarters in Damascus, just as Lawrence has been dismissed from Allenby's office to return to England. Once again the scene is doubly ironic. The beefy officer gushes over a British uniformed man whom he recognizes as the "war hero" Lawrence, proudly pumping his hand. Lawrence is certainly not a hero in his own eyes, and is not one in any uncomplicated sense in ours either. Lawrence then pointedly asks, "Haven't we met before?" To which the officer chortles with absolute confidence, "No, sir, I should have remembered *that.*" In other words, though he thinks he recognizes Lawrence, he really doesn't, and therefore ends up lionizing the very same man he had formerly vilified. If, in the one encounter, he was not supposed to rush to judgment, in the other he was not to rush to hero worship either.

If, in scenes such as these, irony can be seen to work on such a subtle level, it is no less effective in the narrative as a whole. In Part One an identification is established of Lawrence as the kind of hero with whom we, or perhaps certain ones among us, might identify. People who cannot understand how a movie that is supposedly critical of the hero and the colonial project can begin on such an unabashedly romantic note may miss the point that if we do not feel "consubstantial" with Lawrence, we end up feeling too removed from his problems and therefore cannot see them as also our own. But then the question arises as to how to reorient the audience from unmediated identification to a questioning of the character's identity (and ultimately of their own). One way, as Bolt tries to do, mirroring Lawrence's memoir, is to make the questioning of identity part of the protagonist's character, so that as we identify with him we begin the process of our own self-reflection or autocriticism. "Who are you?" we ask of him; and of ourselves we ask, "Who are *we?*"

There is reason to doubt, however, that this aim of critical and reflexive spectatorship—whether executed through the script, the director, or the actor—was satisfactorily fulfilled. For one thing, we know that the movie underwent considerable cuts, and just as these damaged the wide-screen effects, they also greatly impaired the construction of a desired spectator, not to mention an intelligible narrative. The version that premiered before the queen lasted 222 minutes. Spiegel explained to his director at the time of the opening that the movie was not doing well at the box office in part because of its unusual length. For the distribution in movie theaters in December 1962, Lean took out twelve minutes at the producer's behest. In response to exhibitors eager to make more money by squeezing in another show per day, "Spiegel just went with some cutter they [the exhibitors] hired and cut it"[36]—by another 8 minutes, to be exact, leaving a film for redistribution in January 1963 that was 202 minutes in length. Almost ten years later, in April 1971, the movie was re-released for a national theater run and cut an additional 15 minutes (making its total running time 187 minutes). Stephen Farber reviewed the film for the *New York Times,* complaining that besides countless small cuts that disturbed the film's rhythm, three entire scenes had been lopped off that were essential to the intelligibility of the plot and the persuasiveness of the characterization.[37] Particularly affected was Part Two. For example, the scene where Lawrence tries to exhort the remnants of his exhausted and exasperated Arab army to enter Deraa had been omitted, leaving the motivation behind his sudden appearance in the city's precincts totally unexplained. The second and more serious deletion is the conversation in which Allenby succeeds in persuading Lawrence to resume the desert campaign for the final offensive against the Turks. At one moment pleading with the general to be released from duty, Lawrence is seen in the next moment, unaccountably, leading his army against Damascus. Finally, the gruesome scene of the Turkish prisoners in the military hospital was cut, where Lawrence has to confront the obnoxious military gentleman and his last failure. "Some people may feel that 15 minutes of a three-hour film is an insignificant proportion to be lost," Farber observes, but "in a work as carefully structured and designed as 'Lawrence of Arabia' . . . a cut of even three minutes would be noticeable and damaging."[38] On top of all these alterations, the versions prepared for television and then video release were based on an erroneous 1966 Technicolor positive that had the image reversed in several sequences. As Janet Maslin amusingly points out, "Peter O'Toole's wristwatch, in the scene where Lawrence first sees Ali ride out of the desert like a mirage, . . . switches abruptly from one hand to the other."[39]

The film's lacerations undermined a spectator position that the film-makers were trying to construct. Their stated intention was to create a spectator who would not just passively receive a view of Lawrence and the epic spectacle, but who would try to construct such a view from as much information given in the film and from as many angles as possible. The producer, ironically enough, given his role in cutting the original, was most emphatic on this point:

> We want the audience to become *co-author* with us, contributing its own im-pressions of what Lawrence was like as a human being and a human dilemma. It is this emotional involvement that makes a picture successful. . . . Just as Bolt and Lean and myself began with a friction of viewpoints that had to be talked out, we like to think now that any three people leaving the cinema after seeing the picture will have three different attitudes toward it. The im-portant thing is that everyone should be sufficiently intrigued to want to sup-ply an answer. *So we have not tried to resolve the enigma of Lawrence but to perpetuate the legend, and to show why it continues to haunt us after all these years.*[40]

But the cuts were damaging to such an extent that it was unclear whether any spectator could have become coauthor of the construction of Law-rence. If a scene is cut that motivates the plot in important ways, the spectator is left bewildered and eventually will give up trying to follow the narrative closely at all. But something more subtle is lost when shots are removed that construct the (self-)questioning spectator, which Spiegel says the filmmakers were striving for.

Consider the cuts in the following scenes, for example. As we know, the movie opens with Lawrence's death in a motorcycle accident. Law-rence loved the exhilaration of riding his motorcycle at high speeds, and Wilson exploited this aspect of his personality in order to portray him as gripped by a death wish. The last shot is of his goggles dangling on a branch. It is precisely this shot that was often cut from the version shown in movie theaters or aired on television, perhaps on the assump-tion that Lean was simply being long-winded. But the close-up of the goggles, as if suspended in midair, obviously suggests a mask through which the *spectator* is asked to penetrate. From the dangling goggles with daylight visible in their eye slits, the film cuts to the symmetrical in-verse of this image: "the blind stone eyes of Lawrence's bust" in Saint Paul's cathedral, suggestive of opaque identity and problems of its pene-tration that lie ahead. The role of the (self-)questioning spectator is re-stated in the next scene, which was also often cut. Organ music is faintly audible. Next we see Brighton (Anthony Quayle) in civilian clothes standing beside a cleric. Both of them are looking up at Lawrence's bust. In reverential tones Brighton exclaims, "He was the most extraordinary man I ever knew." Almost immediately, however, this glorification and canonization are placed in doubt by the cleric's question: "Well *nil nisi bonum* [nothing but the good (should be spoken of the dead)]. But did he *really* deserve a place (pause, looking up at the ceiling of the cathedral) in here?" Brighton appears contemplative, perhaps a bit disturbed by the question, but he says nothing to counter the cleric's skepticism. In a few seconds the logic of the spectator's position has been announced: we are confronted with the construction of a "hero," a construction that we should call into question. Of course, not all such scenes were removed, only some of the shorter ones, but the effect is cumulative and may have precluded certain interpretive possibilities on the part of viewers. The cleric's glance at the ceiling serves as a transition to a view of the cathedral spire, the camera slowly panning down its ornate facade to the entryway far below, where people dressed in black are filing down the stairs. A young newspaper reporter is seen scurrying from one eminent personage to another—General Allenby (Jack Hawkins), Jackson Bentley (Arthur Kennedy), and General Murray (Donald Wolfit)— trying unsuccessfully to elicit a consistent story from these luminaries about the dead war hero. The scene tells us what the rest of the movie is about—the construction of a man's identity by the news media—and it warns that the task will be difficult.

The cuts made in the various releases of the movie were reinstated in the film's 1989 reconstructed version. Were the aims of spectatorship now finally achieved for contemporary audiences? Unfortunately, the answer is equivocal. Asking the audience to fill such a spectator position is, to say the least, risky, if not perhaps impossible, for a movie three hours and forty minutes long, demanding a power of concentration that would test the limits of anyone's patience and endurance. Here are some reactions from of my students who saw the 1989 reconstruction of the film for a class on the Middle East:

> I felt a little overwhelmed, just trying to absorb the movie, [to] get an idea of what it was about, since I was not at all familiar with the story line. I wasn't in a position to analyze it while watching it, I was too busy being drawn into the music and characters and setting. [female]
>
> Truthfully, when I think back on the film it seems like a big blur. Maybe that was due to the length. I did get the impression, however, of Lawrence's demise as a leader and his inability to realize exactly who he was, or maybe he realized who he was to an extreme extent. [female]

Without any prior knowledge of Lawrence's biography, or of the specific period of Middle Eastern "history" depicted in the film, I came with almost no expectations. But the representations of Lawrence were more textured, with more psychological depth, and more pathos, than I had anticipated. The contradictions and internal ambivalences, both emotional and political, played out in Lawrence's character were both moving and thought-provoking—but with, I felt, too many gaps or loose ends. [male]

As their comments suggest, these students had come to the movie "unprepared" by any information on Lawrence, the Middle East, and the history of World War I. An "intelligent" spectacle or a "thinking person's" epic, though it may be, this big picture sometimes produces a sensory overload that can short-circuit the critical faculty.

Anticipating such a problem, the filmmakers hoped to intervene in the reception process through the text of a lavishly produced movie brochure that was sold in theater lobbies during the film's original release. The brochure was quite informative, containing a biographical sketch of Lawrence's life, a brief history of the Arabian campaign complete with a map, background on the production and the actors, and, most important of all, explanations of the filmmakers' artistic intentions. Tucked away in the margins of the brochure were photographs and illustrations of Lawrence, including an early newspaper cartoon of him pulling away a mask. Yet another clue to how the filmmakers wished the audience to read their film, this presages images of masking in the film that I have already discussed. It is interesting that the most recent video release of the movie (1993) includes a small booklet—much more modestly produced than the original theater program—that provides some of the important background information that simultaneously facilitates and directs audience spectatorship. And to return to my students, when I ask them to see the movie again after having learned more about the region, its history, and the role colonialism played in it, their reaction is more in line with what the filmmakers intended.

The cuts to the movie were damaging to be sure. Had they not been made, however, it remains to be seen whether another factor would have precluded the sort of reception the filmmakers desired. I am thinking here of the turn influential critics of the 1960s took away from Lean's kind of filmmaking, especially the epic. Bolt explained to audiences before the opening that "the situation of Lawrence as revealed in [his memoir] is an epic situation."[41] There was no way to use the term "epic" innocently where film audiences of the period were concerned. They had been watching epics since the early days of cinema with a hunger that never seemed to be surfeited. It had become a powerful genre in terms of whose conventions *Lawrence of Arabia* would be watched and judged. Now, if the narrative structure and the use of parallel images not only reproduce a story of heroism but also get us to reflect upon it, and to some extent even criticize it, is all of this reflexivity jeopardized by the epic genre in which the story is also cast?

When *Lawrence of Arabia* was released in 1962, it was difficult for many, though not all, film critics to take the work seriously. Andrew Sarris, the influential critic for the *Village Voice,* excluded Lean from his pantheon of "auteur" filmmakers,[42] which he justified on the basis, specifically, of the epic genre in which Lean worked: "The sheer logistics of *Lawrence* and *Kwai* cannot support the luxury of a directorial point of view. Lean is even more of an enigma than Lawrence, but the cinema as an expressive art form is not receptive to enigmas. Now that Lean has been enshrined in the various Academies [Sarris is writing these words in 1963], whatever artistic sensibility he once possessed is safely embalmed in the tomb of the impersonal cinema."[43] The views of the epic Sarris promulgated have not substantially changed. With few exceptions, cultural studies and film criticism have tended to neglect the epic.[44] This is somewhat surprising, for as a genre, epics from *Birth of a Nation* (1915) to *Dances With Wolves* (1990), *Malcolm X* (1992), and *Braveheart* (1995) have been crucial not only for the economics of the culture industry but also for the cultural life of the nation, constructing notions such as individualism, society, the state, nature, freedom, primitivism versus civilization, and many other themes that are then exported to other countries. Insofar as epic filmmaking seems to be making a comeback in recent years, it is probable that *Lawrence of Arabia* will continue to be a reference point for filmmakers working in the genre.

There is a purpose, it seems to me, of subjecting *Lawrence of Arabia* to the kind of critical scrutiny that it never enjoyed, in order to go beyond negative assumptions about the epic's lack of self-criticism. I want to grasp some of the complexities of the genre and its dialectical relationship with *Lawrence of Arabia*—that is, working within inherited conventions but also extending them to the point where the epic was undermined as a stable form. I argue, in fact, that *Lawrence of Arabia* was one of the first "anti-epic" epics of Hollywood. The contradictions apparent in this movie's relationship to the genre are in part the result of the economics of the film industry in the 1960s, to be sure, but also, I would claim, to Lean's direction and Robert Bolt's vision of the screenplay, in both artistic and political terms. We have seen how Wilson criticized the media for its construction of Lawrence as a hero, but Lean and Bolt go further in the way they point to their own film as colluding in that mythmaking in scenes that are covertly about filmmaking itself.

To begin with, it is helpful to place this film within a brief history of the film epic. Hollywood, along with the Italian film industry, has dominated the production of the epic, the first period of which occurred during the silent era, from 1915 to 1927, when early film was competing economically with nineteenth-century popular theater. The challenge was to create a viewing experience that theater might aspire to but not effectively achieve—namely, spectacle. With the Great Depression, however, big-budget productions became uneconomical. Even more important, with the introduction of synchronized sound, the epic lost out to more popular forms of entertainment in which witty or highly dramatic dialogue and music predominated: sophisticated comedies, melodramas, and musicals. Epics, of course, appeared sporadically after the twenties, but it was not until 1950 and stretching roughly to 1963, sometimes known as the golden age of Hollywood, that the epic rebounded, largely in response to competition from television. After only a decade, however, from *The Robe* (1953) to *Cleopatra* (1963), epics had become not only economically unsound but an anachronism to many audiences. *Lawrence of Arabia* was clearly in the tradition of epic filmmaking in its grandest and most lavish style, but, released in 1962, it came toward the end of the second cycle of epic filmmaking. The film reflects a sense of its own historical moment through its ambiguousness as a genre film. It seems to know that it has pushed the artistic possibilities of the big-screen epic as far as they can go. At the same time that it had reached these limits, particularly in regard to the story, it seemed to have become another sort of film, an "anti-epic" epic.

Spectacle is, of course, a key ingredient of the epic, and it is effected through sets and costumes as well as through grand entrances of personages of state in imposing amphitheaters and mass audiences of people. Lean's film is most obviously epic in the way the desert setting is captured. The extent to which locale or geographic milieu becomes a central element in many of his films has already been remarked upon. And it should be borne in mind that the desert is more than a magnificent backdrop for the hero's actions: as we have seen in the previous chapter, it is a constantly shape-changing protagonist in its own right. It is noteworthy, too, how Lean creates through the desert the sense of massive scale that is a significant part of the enjoyment of any epic spectacle. Figures stand on dunes or in rocky chasms dwarfed by their environs, or they are seen as dots scattered on a vast plain. Alternatively, they may appear indistinct on the horizon and then move ominously or mysteriously toward us, as when Sherif Ali materializes in a mirage. Vastness is conveyed through image as well as sound, as when Lawrence rides into Wadi Safra and hears his voice thrown back at him from the towering cliff faces.

If setting is one source of spectacle, so, too, is pageantry—but mostly during certain sequences of arrival and departure of the *Arab* army. This spectacle is never invoked merely for the sake of the ocular satisfaction it provides—though to say this is not to disparage the latter in the least— for Lean is careful to vary the pageantry as he does the desert, integrating details and moods into the progression of the narrative. Let us look at some examples.

The first of these is the somewhat modest departure from Feisal's camp of fifty men, who begin the trek across the Nefud Desert, the most arduous leg of the army's expedition to the port of 'Aqaba. Quickly the groaning camels lurch into the air and the raiding party assembles, with Ali and Lawrence at its head, exchanging rivalrous glances. Colorful banners unfurl in the breeze. We hear on the sound track a brisk marching air, composed of intricately interlocking Lawrence and Arab themes, lyrical but disjointed at the same time, showing that the forces are commingled but not quite in unison. O'Toole's face registers boyish glee, verging on the manic, and he cannot suppress his giggles of excitement as he absorbs the impressive sight of the proud young men on their magnificent mounts. Then the camera pulls away to show the expedition riding into a vast but beautiful desert landscape, the two mischievous boys, Daud and Farraj, far in the rear of the train, trying not to be seen, for they are joining the expedition without Lawrence's knowledge or permission.

We are once again treated to spectacle when the raiders enter the vast and beautiful Wadi Rumm. Heading into camp, they are greeted by hundreds of galloping Howeitat horsemen furiously circling around them, shooting their guns in the air for joy, and emitting mock war cries. The mood is quite different from the scene of departure from Feisal's camp: grand but also slightly ominous. In spite of the fact that we know Feisal's raiders to be under Auda's protection and therefore safe, we nonetheless feel uneasy with what we see; I think this is due in part to the way the "violent Arab" has been constructed in previous scenes as well as to the polyrhythmic music that accompanies this one, conjuring up a "savage" or "barbaric" image.

The departure from Wadi Rumm the next morning is the most imposing of all, though Lean imparts to it new emotional overtones. Particularly evocative is the sight of women dressed in black and veiled from
head to foot, lining the sheer, stupendous cliff faces, with the eerie but
thrilling sound of their ululation echoing throughout the valley. They are
saying farewell to their male folk, who in the meantime are chanting
poetry on their mounts far below. Lawrence and Ali, who are friends
now, exchange glances of pleasure at these thrilling sights and sounds.
By switching views several times between the women and the men, an
interestingly gendered polyphony is created. One aerial shot at the end
of the scene makes the raiders appear tiny in the vast amphitheater of
Wadi Rumm.

In the last of the processionals, the movie pushes the genre of the epic to
its limits, especially in the way it alludes to itself in the mythic construction of the hero. Contrast earlier treatments of the epic situation with the
following scene, which occurs toward the end of the story. The voices we
hear on the sound track ending the previous scene are the voices of the
Arab tribesmen who have assembled at Lawrence's command for the
push to Damascus. As in the views of Wadi Rumm, verticality is stressed.
This impression is created by a corridor formed by sheer sandstone cliffs
down which Lawrence will soon pass. The music is even more "atonal"
and polyrhythmic than in the scene in Wadi Rumm. Sharif Ali, along
with Jackson Bentley sitting on top of a bakery truck, are discussing
Lawrence's identity as they wait his arrival along with the assembled
tribesmen. Bentley suggests that Lawrence has changed and coyly asks
Ali, "What did that Turkish general *do* to him, in Deraa?" Ali, still loyal,
insists that "he was the same man after Deraa . . . the same man *hum-
bled!*" He then deftly parries Bentley's question with one of his own:
"What did the *English* general do to him, in Jerusalem?" By drawing an
analogy between the sadistic bey and "Allen-Bey," the English general,
Ali suggests that Lawrence has been abused by both father figures. We
now see the "son," Lawrence, dressed once again in his pure white robes
and golden headpiece. There is a coldness in his look, a hardness in his
manner that contrast with all previous processionals. Quite subtly, the
scene now becomes reflexive. The bakery truck on which Bentley is pre-
cariously perched to take pictures tries to keep up with Lawrence's pro-
cession but veers erratically while the exhaust coughs and then back-
fires (figure 13). Bolt tells us in the script that "Bentley is the vitalizing
point of disturbance in this epic atmosphere which he will enrich, not

Figure 13.   Bentley, atop a bakery truck, taking pictures of Lawrence and his
troops on their way to Damascus (the movie alluding to itself).

destroy, if we use him bodily. Nothing like a streak of low comedy running through a scene of high drama." The sight of Bentley with his camera propped on a moving truck reminds one of a tracking shot in which
a camera is affixed to a dolly and then moves with the actor on the set
(the dolly shot in fact having been crucial to the making of this and other
scenes). The filmmakers, I believe, are telling us not only that the representation of Lawrence as a "hero" was the construction of the culture
industry but also that this film is colluding in it.

Of course, an "epic situation" would not be complete without a hero
at the center of the action. Most important in the definition of this hero
are certain cultural conventions of male sexuality—that he be physically
strong or imposing, handsome, courageous, and, above all, heterosexual—as well as social and moral ones dictating extroversion, and, of
course, goodness. As with almost all epic heroes, the action reduces
more or less to that of a duel or contest, between the hero and the forces
of nature, the hero and the evils of society usually embodied in other
men, or the hero and the gods or other mythical beings and fantasti-
cal creatures; but it is almost never directed inward between warring
selves of his own nature, for this would make the hero introverted and
to some extent morbid. And, of course, he must be victorious in the end
or must at least achieve some sort of apotheosis, otherwise the audience
that has been made to strongly identify with the hero would feel sorely
disappointed.

It is perhaps in regard to the hero that Bolt and Lean's epic is most ambiguous, responding, as they were, to the discrediting of the Lawrence

legend of the 1950s. Qualities of hardihood and endurance rather than sheer physical strength predominate in Bolt's characterization. Lawrence is handsome, of course, but with his brilliantly blond hair and enamored, as he is, of his gorgeous tribal costumes, he appears somewhat like a dandy and therefore dubious as an epic hero, at least in the eyes of American audiences who might miss allusions to a cultural "type" that Lawrence personified for Britons in the period between the wars, probably best exemplified in the poet Rupert Brooke.[45] The trouble with this sort of representation of Lawrence as a dandy, unless it is a disguise for some other, more masculine identity to be revealed later in the story (as in the epic of Zorro), is that it mightily contradicts the image of the epic hero. And where is the woman who will become his mate as a reward for having successfully completed his heroic tasks? The characterization becomes even more incongruous in terms of the epic tradition when the audience realizes by the end of the movie that Lawrence was not after all morally good or even redeemable. As we know, Bolt includes sketches of sadomasochism and megalomania in his characterization. In the first paragraph of the *New York Times* article introducing the movie to the public, Bolt said that he "was brought up to disapprove of figures like T. E. Lawrence as being the colorful ornaments and stalking horses of imperialism."[46] Later, he was to make his condemnation even stronger. Lawrence was a "romantic fascist," he revealed to an interviewer.[47]

Of course, Lawrence is attractive to audiences not simply because O'Toole is sexy but because his character is self-aware, and O'Toole subtly captures Lawrence's moody introspections. But then again there is a problem. Who has ever heard of an introspective epic hero? And this is not all, for Bolt will not let us know who or what this hero finally is; there is no stable, firmly grounded sense of self developed in his character. And this, we are to presume, is a flaw—from the modernist point of view. The question of "Who are you?"—either uttered by various figures such as Feisal, Sharif Ali, and the motorcyclist at Sinai, or posed metaphorically through various forms of masking and masquerade—persists until the end. An epic hero must know who he is and what he stands for and believes in, but Lawrence's interior dialogues do not lead to a clearer understanding of himself.

Lean and Bolt's movie cannot, then, be an epic in any conventional sense, no matter how sensitive the filmmakers were to the film genre in which they were working. On the one hand, nearly all of Part One, up until Lawrence's raiders successfully seize 'Aqaba, fulfills our expectations of a classic epic film, even in regard to the heroic stature and actions of the main character, but then almost everything afterward goes awry for him. Right after 'Aqaba, the filmmakers raise doubts about the hero's essential goodness, doubts that deepen during Lawrence's disastrous crossing of the Sinai Desert with his two servant boys, and in every scene thereafter until the end of the movie. By that point, an action-packed epic becomes more and more interiorized, as Lawrence duels with his multiple and contradictory selves, and not just his outer enemies, the Turks. We may even begin to wonder whether the oppressors of the Arabs are in fact the Turks or the British who arrive in Damascus as occupiers. Perhaps Lawrence was fighting the wrong foe after all.

If Part One is full of light, of open spaces, of grand vistas, and a hero with a robust, exuberant, and optimistic personality, Part Two is preponderantly full of darkness, shadows, and pale reflections, of moonlight, of cramped and dingy quarters in caves and prisons, and a hero who is morose, morbid if not actually insane, and by the end broken in spirit. If the taking of 'Aqaba is glorious and relatively bloodless, the major battle scene in Part Two, the massacre of the Turks, is horrific and evil. Contrast the exuberant and innocent leave-taking of Lawrence and the bedouin raiders on their way to 'Aqaba with the cynicism and evil of Lawrence and his body guard of cutthroats on their way to Damascus. So antithetical are the two parts that, far from continuing the story of Lawrence, the second part ironizes more deeply the first, turning Lawrence's heroism into a sham. Indeed, Part Two almost seems like a different film. I have known people to stop viewing the first half and concentrate solely on the second because they find the latter more consonant with their own disenchantment in heroism and war.

Obviously, this film intends to be a revisionist history of Lawrence, and this explains in part its reversals. But it is a fascinating film precisely because it uses the genre of the epic, the conventions of its kind of filmmaking, simultaneously to construct Lawrence's heroism, indeed making the audience strongly identify with him, and then to deconstruct it, deliberately subverting their identification. But I would argue that the film does much more: in the process of creating a disturbance in the audience's expectations of Lawrence as a hero, it also disrupts what they expect this film to be as a *genre*. That is, I want to claim that the film repositions itself from an epic to an "anti-epic" epic. To express the point more abstractly, Lean and Bolt's film is subtly about a certain kind of filmmaking and its power to create myth.

Just how powerful the movie is in its construction of the hero was confirmed in a letter I received from a student in Jordan (Nicholas Alexander, personal communication). He said that he had met a Howeitat, a member of the tribe of which the great Auda Abu Tayyi was sheikh. When asked if he knew who Auda was, the man replied that of course everyone knew that redoubtable fighter. And what about Lawrence of Arabia? That was another matter, Nicholas was told, for the tribesman had not heard of "el-Aurens" until he had seen the film! But the myth-making process can also work the other way, for until he had seen the movie, Nicholas hadn't heard of Auda either.

In a nutshell, my argument has been that Lean and Bolt were in fact deeply committed to a script that would construct a reflexive and critical spectator. As I see their creative process, they built on the foundations provided by Wilson's earlier treatments. For that reason I began this chapter by examining Wilson's work on the initial script, or rather scripts, and Lean's contribution to them. Then I analyzed the changes and additions Bolt (one assumes in collaboration with Lean) made to Wilson's baseline treatment, suggesting that Brechtian "alienation" techniques and heavy doses of irony were crucial devices in creating the kind of spectator they wanted. An essential element of this collaboration was Peter O'Toole's acting, in terms of both its theatricality, which drew attention to the performance, and its fascistic undertones.

In important respects, however, audiences failed to respond to the film in the reflective and indeed critical manner that the filmmakers intended. One reason for this failure, I suggest, lies in the fate that the film had in its editing and distribution. Another lies in the way it worked ambiguously within the established Hollywood genre of the "epic" picture, at once pushing that genre to its limits and then undermining it. The fact that Lean was falling out of favor with certain powerful critics who were unable to appreciate what he was doing with the epic genre on the wide screen did not help the situation either. Indeed, until this day a complex critical reading of the film has been largely missing.

In the next three chapters, using the 1989 reconstructed version of *Lawrence of Arabia*, I want to take up the invitation of the filmmakers to "coauthor" their work. I start with a chapter in which I explore, frankly and critically, my consubstantial identification with Lawrence as he was constructed in the movie.

CHAPTER 4

An Allegory of Anthropology

One discovers that allegory arises in periods of loss, periods
in which a once powerful theological, political, or familiar
authority is threatened with effacement.

> *Stephen Greenblatt,* Allegory and Representation

In 1959 I had arrived in the United States from West Germany, and the
adjustments, linguistic, and cultural, were difficult, at times traumatic. I
was teased by my classmates for mispronunciation of English words like
"three," an embarrassment that made me acutely self-conscious about
speech. I marched home from school one day and announced tearfully
to my parents that I wouldn't utter another word of German. It was
not only language that betrayed me as "different." There were dozens of
seemingly innocuous rules in the classroom that I either failed to obey
or innocently contravened or mixed up with ones from my own background that were entirely inappropriate, like the time I was called on by
the teacher, shot up from my seat to bark out the answer to the question, and promptly sat down. After a moment of stunned silence I was
greeted by uproarious laughter from the entire class. I seemed to have
been Adorno's caricature of the authoritarian personality. Not merely
different, I was "repellent"—a Nazi.

This story about my entry into the culture of white, middle-class
America might help explain the impact the movie *Lawrence of Arabia*
had on me when I saw it in 1963, four years after I had landed in the
States. I could sense parallels between the figure on the screen, moving
from one cultural stage to another in an effort to become the "native,"
and my own faltering attempts to become "American," as my father,
himself a U.S. citizen, had wished his children to be when he moved his
family to this country. When I ask myself thirty years later why I became

an anthropologist who wanted to study the Middle East, a question that has become more insistent in the wake of the Saidean critique of orientalism, I think back on this time of my childhood and also on this movie as formative experiences.[1]

It is perhaps obvious that such a film would awaken a desire to study the Middle East, but is there any reason to suppose that it also quickened an interest in practices that I would in college identify with cultural anthropology, once I began to take courses in that subject? In those courses it seemed that I had found a professionalization (through fieldwork) of the predicaments of cultural liminality and travel that had been part of my childhood. Their subject matter seemed painfully self-evident to me: there were norms of behavior and symbols and fairly stable patternings of both that differed from place to place. Hadn't I hit my head against *that* wall before? Now in my academic major I had a name for it: cultural relativism.

I propose in this chapter that *Lawrence of Arabia* can be read as an allegory about anthropologists, their ideas, and particularly their practices. Though allegory has been discussed lately by anthropologists[2] and by anthropology's critics,[3] and is of course a staple of literary criticism,[4] I do not mean by it anything more complicated than a narrative that can be used for didactic purposes. Using reflexive writings by anthropologists as well as my own memories of fieldwork, I want to show how the film operates like an anthropological text, and in the next two chapters I will look at different cultural representations (British and Arab) that the film constructs and some problems these representations entail. At the same time I will show how the film operates as a story about anthropology, and a deeply moral one at that. There are, in fact, very few films that talk about the experience of being a *cultural* anthropologist: an archaeologist, yes, as in the Indiana Jones series; or a physical anthropologist, primarily as a result of charismatic (Jane Goodall) or tragic (Diane Fossey) women who have captivated the imagination of the American public. To avoid misunderstanding, I should stress that the filmmakers almost certainly did not have anthropology in mind when they conceptualized the main character of the film and its plot, nor would most audiences interpret the film as being about an anthropologist. But the point of this chapter is to suggest that the film unintentionally spectacularizes the figure of the anthropologist in ways that we perhaps have not yet fully appreciated. Furthermore, the points I will make in this reading of the film are also more general ones that could apply to narratives about travel into the cultural worlds of other peoples besides the kinds of stories anthropologists have told of themselves. The text of the film becomes emblematic of the perils of cross-cultural collision.

I have another aim in keeping with the larger agenda of this book, which has to do with reading and interpretation in general. The reading of anthropological works that specifically interests me comes out of a heated but profound and ultimately highly constructive criticism to be found in writings by George Marcus, Michael Fischer, and most of all the intellectual historian James Clifford, to mention only a few. As I understand it, the general aim of this reading has been to destabilize the project of anthropology in order to create a space for alternative practices and objects of study that have not actually found their way into much anthropological research and writing even to this day. For instance, this critical reading suggests that the practices of modern anthropological fieldwork are not that far removed from the work of nineteenth-century missionaries, explorers, travelers, and colonial agents (like Lawrence), with the result that the too convenient cordon sanitaire that has been thrown up by anthropologists between themselves and these other, now perhaps discredited, practitioners has crumbled. The effect has been salutary, prompting a more honest, searching appraisal of their own discipline as having been and continuing to be racist and colonialist. Or consider the way in which the writing of ethnographies has become complicated, as the boundaries between science and art, fact and fiction, objective and subjective have been blurred, thus heightening our awareness of what Clifford Geertz over two decades ago called the *fictio* of ethnographic writing—its intricate constructedness. Finally, the concept of culture as a static, bounded, and holistic object of study—long the theoretical foundation of the discipline—is all but moribund in the wake of criticisms that have stressed its processual nature, porousness, hybridity, discursiveness, and fragmentariness.

In one sense, I am in sympathy with this kind of reading, because by using *Lawrence of Arabia* to talk about anthropology I inevitably raise issues of travel and colonialism in anthropological fieldwork, as well as of fiction versus fact in the representation of the Other, not to mention, of course, orientalism and other fraught subjects. But I suggest more than that this film is expectably orientalist, colonialist, racist, and sexist. I want to explore the unexpected in this Hollywood epic, for the reason, as I hope to show throughout the book, that I believe this film is profoundly self-critical and hence anticipates the very critical reading that its appearance as an overblown Hollywood extravaganza would belie. In other words, like all texts of intellectual complexity, moral depth, and artistic vision, this film has to be read dialectically, as both containing a project that is problematical for all kinds of reasons adumbrated earlier and at the same time distancing itself from that project in order to interrogate and criticize it. That I think much critical reading of anthropology is not dialectical enough is implicit in this whole exercise.

The film opens with a scene that is now famous: Lawrence riding on his motorcycle and then fatally crashing when he swerves to avoid hitting some bicyclists who are in the wrong lane. There is a cut to his goggles, symbolic of a mask, dangling from the branch of a tree, suggesting that the enigma of the man is left behind for us to unravel, if we can.

Stephen Farber thinks this opening scene encapsulates the tragedy of Lawrence's life, an individual wanting to break free of stuffy social conventions, which are as claustrophobic to his spirit as the hemmed-in quality of the country road down which he hurtles to his death.[5] But people who defy their own societies pay a price, as Farber notes: "The frightening thing is that Lawrence's urge to break free of English domestic life is also demonic and self-destructive; in this scene it is quite literally suicidal."[6] This interpretation might seem far-fetched unless one knows something about Lean's other movies in which we see the individual trying to go beyond his or her own world, only to get caught in a confusion of identities and loyalties and as a consequence suffering mental breakdown, ostracism, or death (for example, *Breaking the Sound Barrier* [1952], *Bridge on the River Kwai,* and *Ryan's Daughter* [1970]).[7] In essence, this is the theme of the outsider, and perhaps it should not be surprising to find it emphasized in the output of Lean's postwar period, since it is resonant with the then popular interpretations not only of Lawrence but of men in British society in general.[8]

The theme of the outsider, of the individual who does not feel comfortable in his or her own society, is developed in the movie's early scenes. At this point, Lawrence seems only a bit eccentric, lighting matches that he extinguishes with his own fingers, though it is clear that this trick, performed for the amusement of his cronies, signals a streak of masochism and occasions the warning remark by one of the onlookers that he is "barmy." That Lawrence is indeed an odd creature in other respects as well is explored in subsequent scenes. For example, he is a maverick in the military ranks and rebellious: he wears his cap in the officers' mess when he's not supposed to and then, like a trickster, deliberately upsets the officers' game of billiards. He's socially maladroit and physically clumsy, knocking over a table and causing tea to be spilled on another officer's lap. He is also impudent, for when he meets General Murray to be informed of his Arabian assignment, he first forgets to salute his superior (apparently a formality the actual Lawrence tended to overlook, to the annoyance of his fellow officers) and then cheekily parodies the salute upon exiting the general's office. His thinly disguised contempt for those around him is heartily reciprocated, of course. The officers dismiss him as a "clown," and General Murray, the commander of British forces in the Near East, tells him point-blank that he can't stand his "type"— meaning that he is effete, perhaps even effeminate, arrogant certainly, and hopelessly undisciplined.[9] He can't stand his "type" for the deeper reason that Lawrence thumbs his nose at precisely those conventions on which military authority rests. He is in short subversive and therefore potentially dangerous. Brighton will later call him a "traitor" for disobeying orders and siding with Feisal in his dispute with the prince over the British navy and its shelling of the port of 'Aqaba.

Once Lawrence has entered Arabia, he tries to explain to his guide Tafas where he has come from and what sort of land England is. He tells his new friend that England is a "green" and "fat" land with "fat" people. "You are not fat?" he is asked by his guide. "No, I'm different." The word "different" had the connotation at one time of someone who was "odd" or "strange" or just not quite "normal," all of which apply only too well to Lawrence after what we have seen of him in these early scenes; but in the discourse of "difference" of the 1980s the word also takes on the meaning of cultural marginality and alienation. It is a conviction of difference that propels Lawrence out of his own society, that makes him seek, or rather positively ache for, a rupture with his own culture. Later, in a poignant conversation with his friend Sherif Ali by a campfire, we find out in part why Lawrence sees himself as an outsider when he confesses that he is the bastard son of an English lord. Like the two servant boys whom he adopts and learns to love, Lawrence is a social outcast. How much more damning the sense of ostracism as a bastard would be for audiences in the sixties than today is perhaps self-evident.

What might be the relevance of the theme of the outsider to a representation of the anthropologist? Like the bohemian artist, the anthropologist has been constructed in various discourses as an individual who as a child felt alienated or even excluded from parents and family or, as usually goes with such rebelliousness, from certain norms or conventions. If they have any genuine artistic talents, these individuals might become artists; or if inclined to scholarly pursuits, historians, and when combined perhaps with a yearning for adventure, anthropologists.

Consider, for example, the introspective ruminations of Claude Lévi-Strauss in the chapter "A Little Glass of Rum" from his ethnography cum memoir *Tristes Tropiques*. "One can very probably discover in his [or her] past certain objective factors which show [the anthropologist] to be ill-adapted to the society into which he [or she] was born." [10] Clyde Kluckholn said in his widely read textbook *Mirror for Man* that "The lure of the strange and the far has a peculiar appeal for those who are dissatisfied with themselves or who do not feel at home in their own society." [11] And Hortense Powdermaker, one of the first anthropologists to think reflexively in any deep way about her reasons for going into the profession and the manner in which she practiced fieldwork, claims in her book *Stranger and Friend*, "A feeling of personal or social discomfort (or both) have been a prelude quite often to anthropological and sociological curiosity and interests in my generation, and, I think, in that of my teachers." [12] Anthropology, or so it is maintained, is one of the vocations an alienated individual in society might imagine himself or herself pursuing because its practice—known as fieldwork—has, however temporarily, taken the person out of his or her own milieu. More unacknowledged, I think, is the naive hope harbored by many first-time fieldworkers that the group into which they have been "adopted" can become another home, a substitute family, rather like Lawrence, who thought he could find a home among the bedouin in the desert.

I must emphasize the fact that this representation is a cultural construction of and often by anthropologists, not a personality type that is necessarily based on psychological tests or any kind of empirical studies.[13] Nor does such a representation necessarily accord with the backgrounds and experiences of all or even many anthropologists I have known. Even if these same anthropologists were to admit to feeling such childhood alienation, it is not clear that they felt more alienated than anyone else or that they now think such feelings were important to their becoming anthropologists. My point is that this construction of why some people become anthropologists is evident in various influential writings by anthropologists, indeed becoming a cliché and, for that very reason, important for an allegorical reading.

After their interview with General Murray, the diplomat Dryden and the intelligence officer Lawrence remove themselves to a beautiful antechamber, Dryden's office located somewhere within the vast chambers of Cairo General Headquarters. It is filled with exquisite Orientalia—papyri-looking wall mountings, marble statuary, brass and pottery vessels, and bits and pieces of ancient objets d'art bought and probably pilfered from the tombs of the ancient Near East.

Unless one has seen this film several times, one is not likely to pay attention to the office's interior, nor for that matter notice the significance of a momentary action on Lawrence's part; he sees on the other side of the room a large, dark green pharaonic sculpture of a godlike cat, says to Dryden with evident approval, "Oh, that's new," and swiftly walks toward it to appreciate its beauty up close. In one sense, of course, this scene alludes to Lawrence's own interest in the archaeology of the Middle East, which he practiced professionally before the war. On another and probably unconscious level, however, the scene constructs an idea about the Orient that humanists like Edward Said in his book *Orientalism* have justly criticized; namely, the presumption that the Orient exists in the form of beautiful and exotic specimens to be collected, extracted, and removed from their own local contexts, and ultimately to be possessed for aesthetic contemplation or classified for scientific scrutiny. In other words, the scene literally objectifies the Other, who exists not in his or her own right and by his or her own definition but essentially for the West's imagination and pleasure. It is a crucial attitude, which critics like Said claim can be found in practices ranging from curio collecting to anthropological research, classification, and theorizing.

It is also important to note that the scene is set in the seat of colonial power and becomes associated with its selfish and obsessive enterprise, to absorb Arabia within the British Empire. Throughout this movie, it is the British, the Western colonizers, who occupy and move through the sumptuously ornate spaces of urban civilization, whereas it is for the most part the Arabs, the colonized, who tent and travel through the vaster if emptier but equally beautiful wastes of the desert. A set of symbolic oppositions is thus created between city/civilization/colonizing West and desert/nature/colonized Arab. Hence, a seemingly innocent act of aesthetic contemplation on Lawrence's part is fraught with political implications.

This is a perfectly plausible critical reading of the movie but is it dialectical enough? To what extent, in other words, is the film conscious and critical of its own orientalist presumptions? On the face of it, hardly at all, and yet I think one could make a plausible argument that at least Robert Bolt had his misgivings. For the moment, I would like to delay the arguments for a more dialectical reading of orientalism until the next chapter.

To me it is not entirely coincidental that I should have seen *Lawrence of Arabia* (in which the wonders of Cordova are extolled) in a movie theater called the Teatro del Lago on Chicago's North Shore. When I was still a child in Germany, my parents took a vacation trip to Spain from which they returned laden like the magi with gifts for my sisters and me. If I remember correctly, my present was a miniature toreador outfit, complete with black hat, a sequined satin vest and pants, a red sash for the waist, and black slippers. I think there was a small red cape, too, though I seemed to have been less intrigued by it than I was by one of the presents for my sister, a pair of castanets, which I can still remember trying to work with my small fingers because I was fascinated by the sounds they made. I pored over beautiful coffee-table books on the Alhambra. I came across photographs of my parents in smoke-filled Spanish nightclubs being entertained by beautiful, long-necked flamenco dancers, and I would try tirelessly to elicit from my mother descriptions of "Moorish" Spain. (Like Italy and Turkey, Spain is one of Germany's "others.")

Clearly, "dressing up in native costume" was an important game of my childhood, and I suspect in that of many others in our culture. We smile with recognition when we see Lawrence playfully running across the dunes in his newly acquired Arab outfit. The sight is also disturbing, however, for we are aware of the fact that Lawrence is not a child, after all, but a powerful political agent and military leader. The Great Game, as it has been called by Kipling and others, is not literally a game. However, the extent to which identifying with the Other gave my child's imagination many hours of pleasure, not to mention the likelihood of it having instilled in me a fascination with other cultures when I started to study anthropology, has to be acknowledged. This identification would be complicated, or so I now surmise years later, when I moved from Germany and became an Other in the United States. On the one hand, the (false) idea in my child's mind that this was another "game" of cultural impersonation gave me a certain confidence, at times even a cockiness, in coping with cultural collisions; and yet this was clearly not a game, or at least not an innocent one, when hardly a day went by that was free of small but countless frustrations as I was "otherized" by my peers. Hardly less innocent was I when as an anthropologist I wore bits and pieces of "native" tribal clothing. Like Lawrence I was not a child, dressing up. This was not a game, however deep may have been the practice's associations with my own childhood. In fact, I feared a regression to a neurotic state in which I would be enacting childhood fantasy and trauma. All kinds of questions were raised, almost too painful to contemplate: What obsession was driving me to place myself in an analogous position I had occupied as an immigrant child, a position that had proved painfully humiliating? By succeeding in fieldwork did I somehow think I would finally triumph over, and put behind me, these childhood anxieties? By acknowledging the "return of the repressed," was I invalidating the entire enterprise of cultural representation on which I had embarked now for more than five years? To call what I was doing a "game" would be demeaning not only to my Yemeni friends but also to the painful realities that impinged upon me as a fieldworker, the full extent of which we shall see at the end of the chapter. In the movie *Lawrence of Arabia,* the character is tragically "caught" in his own game: at the end of the Turkish massacre (a massacre he has ordered) we see him in his blood-specked robes staring vacantly into the blade of his dagger in a gesture that recalls the earlier scene of innocent playacting.

Another key idea about the relationship of the westerner to the exotic has to do with adventure, signaled in the interview with Dryden. When Lawrence receives his instructions to look for Prince Feisal, he is bubbling over with boyish exuberance: "Oh, thanks Dryden. This is going to be fun!" Dryden tries to warn him: "Only two kinds of creatures get 'fun' in the desert, Bedouins and gods. And you're neither." But Lawrence, to his ultimate cost, is deaf to the admonition: "No, Dryden, it's going to be fun," he insists. This remark could have been said by the adolescent Kim to his mentor Colonel Creighton in Rudyard Kipling's classic novel about espionage, ethnology, and the Great Game. When Lawrence ignites the match, rolls up his sleeve, and extends his arm as if to perform his trick, Dryden caustically observes, "It is recognized that you have a funny sense of fun." This bit of dialogue, of course, reinforces the interpretation of Lawrence as a masochist, but it also announces and simultaneously denounces the thrill of adventure that propels Lawrence into Arabia.

Adventure, by its very definition, is set off from the quotidian; it is discontinuous with what deadens and disturbs, and is therefore alluring to the alienated and disaffected. It was Simmel who realized the connection between adventure and the work of art, for an adventure has, like the latter, a form—there is a beginning and end, and it can be encompassed whole by a narrative—and it seems to be marked by an overarching design or pattern, a guiding system or imaginative hand, that turns accident and historical contingency into plan and necessity.[14] For Lean, making "big" pictures, especially in what he described as "exotic" locales, was also an adventure that stood in contrast to his ordinary domestic life, since the forces required to produce an epic were so multifarious and complex, the obstacles that stood in the way of those forces so gargantuan and unpredictable, that only a monumental will, it is presumed, could shape them into a coherent and compelling product.[15] In this sense, filmmaking is an adventure in the way that Lawrence's campaign in Arabia was also, and it is not serendipitous that critics have seen parallels between Lawrence and Lean as "adventurers."[16]

The lure of anthropology for some of its students has been the sense of adventure promised by travel to faraway and exotic places where one might have some "fun." I dedicated my first book to my parents, whom I say taught me a sense of adventure by the example of their own somewhat offbeat, wandering youths. Can the reader fail to surmise that anthropology was supposed to provide adventure for its practitioners? In other words, the critics would say, once again the locale and life of the Other become a source of diversion for a bored westerner. To some extent, perhaps, that criticism is true, but I hardly think that is all there is to the experience of adventure. Just as Dryden problematizes for Lawrence his sense of impending fun, so our enthusiasm for adventure often wanes in the face of travails and the general exhaustion of fieldwork. Some of us give it up altogether. By the end of the movie, the adventure has turned into a nightmare for Lawrence.

Feminists have also picked up on adventure as a quintessentially masculine story that leaves women largely out of its account or, if not omitted, then assigned a passive role (though in Arabia as in other parts of the Middle East the "lady" Victorian traveler, explorer, and writer was hardly uncommon either). With regard to *Lawrence of Arabia,* I argue in the chapter on masculinity that the protagonist is ambiguously male and that women could in fact identify with him. The critique of adventure as a result becomes more complicated when women are included in the picture, as we shall see when we examine a woman's tale of "adventure" fighting in the Gulf War.

It is an interesting coincidence that at the time Lawrence was living on and off among the bedouin (1916–18), the British anthropologist Bronislaw Malinowski, widely acknowledged as one of the architects of fieldwork practices, was living among the Trobriand Islanders in Melanesia (1914–18), creating what would become a role model for future generations of anthropologists. As we now know, he kept a diary of his

experiences, which was not published until 1967, twenty-five years after his death. In the entry for January 9, 1918, he wrote:

> I know that if I had had to go to war, I would have gone calmly and without
> too much inner fuss. Now: place my everyday life in that heroic frame; be
> ruthless in relation to appetites and weakness; not to yield to depressions and
> such digressions as the inability to take photos. Shake clumsiness, yearning,
> sentimentalism.[17]

For Malinowski, fieldwork had become a military exercise. The anthropologist was the Lawrencian-type soldier, the foreign culture his field of
battle. Just as important to notice is that the reverse had occurred in
Lawrence: that in the course of waging war, he had turned himself into
the anthropological fieldworker, becoming proficient in Arabic, living
with the bedouin according to their own customs, and sending back dis-
patches to the Arab Bureau that contained detailed ethnographic information on how to rule the natives, all of which are represented in the
movie, including writing that is continuous throughout the desert campaign and, we are to assume, are his field reports. One can see a fateful
convergence of two conceits, as it were, that were being constructed at
the same moment in history: the war hero and the anthropologist.

I am no military historian, and therefore cannot say whether this convergence occurred for the first time in the career of Colonel T. E. Lawrence, guerrilla fighter. There is no question, however, that it is very
much with us to this day, perhaps even more so than ever before, now
that the American military is bent on adventurous intervention in a number of different political cultures (Somalia, Iraq, Haiti). It is a fascinating story that can be traced in a number of military memoirs, most recently in General H. Norman Schwarzkopf's autobiography, *It Doesn't
Take a Hero* (1992). This linguistically gifted soldier prides himself on
his ability to move almost as effortlessly as Rudyard Kipling's Kim between linguistic and cultural communities. While stationed in Germany
in the early sixties, he went native:

> I spoke mostly German with my girlfriend, and my command of the lan-
> guage was so fluent that Berliners had difficulty pegging me as an American
> if I wasn't in uniform. I was a very effective go-between.[18]

Action in Vietnam followed.

> Once in the field we lived as Vietnamese: we ate what they ate, slept where
> they slept, wore the same uniform, and suffered the same hardships. We were
> much more involved with our Vietnamese counterparts than many of the U.S.
> advisers attached to regular units.[19]

He then tells a story that underscores how going "primitive" was a critical strategy of war in the field.[20] The operation involved rebuilding bridges that had been blown up by the Vietcong. The American officers had been invited by South Vietnamese engineers to a bridge-blessing ceremony. The Vietnamese slaughtered a pig as part of the ritual, added its blood to glasses of scotch, and then passed them around for a toast. Schwarzkopf remarks, "My year [as a child] in Tehran had taught me what was expected, so while the engineer battalion's U.S. adviser wouldn't touch his drink, I gulped mine down, toasting the completion of the bridge." And then, of course, follows the clinching argument for going native. "Simply by drinking that toast of scotch and blood, I'd begun building ties that would prove vital in battle."[21] As we shall see, Schwarzkopf identified with the film *Lawrence of Arabia* at the time of the Gulf War, remarking that when he had received a traditional Arab male outfit from one of his Kuwaiti friends, he had to think of Peter O'Toole and the first time he dressed up in native costume. Schwarzkopf has identified with the film *Lawrence* in ways that serve his own interests. I will try to suggest that there are ways to read the movie that undermine that identification.

And what is it exactly that an anthropologist does when having his or her "fun"? The name for this pursuit, "fieldwork," is almost magical in the fantastic images it conjures up in the popular imagination. The early desert scenes of *Lawrence of Arabia* provide the most obvious parallel to this anthropological experience and also capture some of its humor. For example, Lawrence learns from his charming guide, Tafas, to ride a camel; to harden himself against thirst; to eat "bedouin" food, which he doesn't like very much but knows better than to refuse, and to drink the brackish water from the wells, which he finds hardly more to his taste; to sleep on the sand under the stars; and in a conversation with Tafas, of the sort every anthropologist has had in a foreign culture, to try to explain where he comes from, what kind of land Britain is, what kind of people the British are, and how he may be similar to or different from them—in brief, the problem of representing the self to the other.

Almost every anthropologist has had to rely on a guide to enter a foreign culture, a friend and principal informant who teaches him or her almost everything that is necessary to know about a given society and its customs. Victor Turner had as his mentor the brilliantly philosophical Muchona.[22] Marjorie Shostak, living among the !Kung peoples of the Kalahari Desert in southern Africa, was very close to a charismatic woman by the name of Nisa, who became the subject of a now classic biographical study by that title.[23] For his insights into trance and possession among Moroccan Arabs, Vincent Crapanzano depended on Tuhami, a member of a religions cult, who also became the subject of a full-scale biographical study.[24] Like these anthropologists Lawrence has his own friends and tutors, among them Tafas in the early scenes but principally Sherif Ali, who bestows upon him his Arab cultural identity.

My friend and consultant in the field was Muhammad al-Hijam. When I crossed his path one day, he recognized me from a television interview and asked, "Are you the fellow who wants to study tribal poetry? Then I want to help you." I thanked him politely for his interest, did not believe he would visit me to discuss the project (which I took to be a show of politeness on his part), and forgot about him as I went on my way. Several hours later he knocked on the door to my house. He had under his arm a bunch of *qat* leaves (a mild narcotic or stimulant like betel nut), for he meant to chew them with me as is the custom in Yemen in the afternoons. Along with him were several friends, and together they regaled me with proverbs, poems, jokes, and stories.

Fairly quickly, Muhammad and I became friends. Because of trouble in the village where I was living, he was a frequent visitor who came with a group of regional dispute mediators trying to resolve the conflict (which they eventually did). In the afternoons, he would share with me the poems that had been composed in the latest round of negotiations.[25] At one point fighting did break out, however, and Muhammad came to take me and all my worldly possessions safely to his own village several miles away. He did me the singular honor of introducing me to his mother and wife, usually completely off limits to strange men. It was a sign of his extraordinary trust in me. He also pointed out to me the woman who had been his childhood sweetheart. He couldn't marry her because she wasn't from the right family. They smiled and exchanged a few pleasantries before continuing on their separate ways. Sharing this confidence with me once again showed his extraordinary trust in me.

Eventually I returned to my own village, only to be taken by national security agents into the capital for questioning: What was a lone American who spoke pretty good Arabic doing in the midst of a tribal war zone? Was he really who he said he was? Could he be stirring up trouble in order to embarrass the central government (after all, the United States did not approve of Yemen's policy of rapprochement with communist South Yemen in the early 1980s)? These were all reasonable questions, even in my judgment. Notes were impounded, along with tapes and photographs.

Security forces tried to take Muhammad from his village for questioning, too, but according to his family and friends, he said he would fight them if they tried, warning them that he would not be taken alive! But when I was released from prison, Muhammad came to the capital to meet me and to swear that he had done nothing to get me into trouble with the police. He said he would redouble his efforts to help me finish my project, and he did: wedding poetry, interviews with famous poets, meetings with men who could explain local history, and so forth. As I was on my way out the door to go to the airport to leave Yemen, he still wanted to give me a last cycle of poems.

I cannot say that ours was an easy relationship, however. The strains were caused mostly by the difficult circumstances under which we had to live and work. I respected him enormously for his intelligence and linguistic gifts, and I liked him for his frankness and loyalty. But because he was a reserved man, even at times austere, it was difficult to get close to him emotionally, and for his part it must not have been easy to have been friendly with a foreigner. Once I overheard someone ask him, "Now why do you want to get involved with an American? Huh, Muhammad? What do you hope to gain from it?" "Nothing," was his answer. "But you wouldn't believe that, would you? I have to want money or power or just a trip to America, don't I, in order to be friends with him. Seif [the name I was given] likes poetry, I like to talk about poetry, and we have some good conversations together."

The relationship with the informant/friend in *Lawrence of Arabia* evolves into an interesting and also troubling friendship, which is one of the more moving parts of the film's narrative. Sherif Ali in a sense allows Lawrence to be "adopted" into bedouin society, much as anthropologists have said they have been incorporated into the kinship systems of the cultures they have studied. He also gives Lawrence his Arabic name, el-Aurens. While el-Aurens feigns sleep, Ali throws his British army clothes one piece at a time onto the campfire, symbolizing the shedding of his former cultural identity; in the next scene he gives Lawrence the brilliant white robes of a sharif of the Bani Wejh. Uncertain at first whether he ought to wear them, he is reassured by an elder that "he for whom nothing is written may write himself a clan." In other words, Lawrence appears to be capable of anything, including transforming himself into the image of the Other and creating a society (an Arab nation) for himself in which he can feel not only at "home" but honored as one of its leaders. Here, the parallel with anthropology breaks down, I think, and I will return to it at the end. I will also have more to say about the fact that "Lawrence writes himself a clan."

The last we see of Sherif Ali, after a bittersweet parting with Lawrence, is when he is having an argument with Sheik Auda Abu Tayyi. He leaves in a huff, tears in his eyes, looking back over his shoulder at Auda while striding offstage—into total darkness. The image is arresting because of what Auda next tells Ali and how it reminds us of the history of Arab nationalism in the postwar period: "I tell thee what though! Being an 'Arab' will be thornier than you suppose—Harith!" For me, the image has now become even more haunting and fearful. After I left Yemen, I never heard from Muhammad again. I never knew whether my tapes and letters got through to him, and for reasons having to do with a peripatetic career as an "underemployed" younger academic, I never returned for a revisit. Two years ago, however, I found out that he had been killed in a tribal war. Major confrontations of that sort cannot be comfortably dismissed as "local" matters, for they are always enmeshed within the snares of national, and even more global, political processes. Nor, as I will show in the next chapter, can we take refuge from our guilt in the comforting orientalist construction of the "violent" and ultimately self-destructive Arab.

An anthropologist is expected, of course, to write an ethnography, some sort of description and analysis of the culture in which he or she has been living. Is there any parallel here in the movie? I am free-associating with the important metaphor of "writing," and in particular the interesting phrase "to write oneself a clan," uttered by an elder in the scene in which Lawrence assumes his new identity. "He for whom nothing is written may write himself a clan."

As we all know, a culture becomes "objectified" in anthropological accounts, just as Arab bedouin ways are "objectified" in this movie in countless scenes of ceremonial, eating, feuding, religious worship (the call to prayer), and so forth. Though the anthropologist does not, of course, try literally to create a society, and would be appalled even at the idea of what Lawrence attempted to do by constituting an Arab nation, nevertheless he or she does create a society in the metaphoric sense, through his or her ethnographic writings, and the end result may have similar consequences and may be just as disquieting. For example, it is now becoming more common for anthropologists to be called in as ex-

pert witnesses for the defense of Native American tribes submitting legal claims to ancient homelands (such as the court testimony of one of
my colleagues, Triloki Pandey, on behalf of the Zuni) or to serve as advisers to peoples who want their traditional rituals reconstituted according to ethnographic accounts of a presumably "authentic" past (such as
the intervention of Deborah Battaglia in the Trobriand Islands). As anthropologists discover the extent to which their ethnographies are no
longer, if they ever were, innocent, in that they are involved in a process
of representation that can "write" a clan and thus objectify society, and
as they appreciate the extent to which this process implicates them in
power relationships that render their enterprise fraught with moral dilemmas and self-doubts, their position does not seem too dissimilar to
Lawrence's, if perhaps less extreme.

Though Lawrence is not depicted in the film as writing about the bedouin, the film of course does represent them, and the filmmakers not
only were acutely self-conscious of this fact but also went to extraordinary lengths to make this representation ethnographically accurate.
There is only one glaring error that I have discovered: Lawrence accepts
and then eats with his *left* hand the food that has been offered by his
bedouin guide. In other words, if the filmmakers have taken such pains
to be accurate, what then is their representation of Arabs that they wish
us to take seriously? How do they write a "clan"? Furthermore, what are
the dangers of such representation, and does the film realize and make
them apparent?

An antique, romantic, surprisingly rich and complex world is pic-
tured that includes generous hospitality (Auda's feast for the bedouin
raiders); fiercely loyal friendships (Sherif Ali's devotion to Lawrence
even to the bitter end); intensely poetic or vivid personalities (Auda); patriarchal pride (Auda's relationship with his young son); feuding honor
(the actual duel between Tafas and Sherif Ali, the verbal one between
Auda and Sherif Ali); a resigned and sternly puritanical faith (the for-
mula "it is written," which reverberates like a cliché throughout the
movie); physical hardiness tested by elemental harshness (the crossing of
the Nefud Desert); pastoral self-sufficiency (the camels in the desert); no-
madic freedom (the raiders leaving Damascus to melt back into the
desert); and eye-for-eye retribution (the massacre of the Turks in revenge
for the butchering of the bedouin village).

Lest we assume that this film is interested only in the representation
of the Arab as noble savage, we should take note of its account of evil in
this nearly idyllic world. This evil is portrayed as the violence that is sup-

posed to erupt in a feud-driven, tribal society, epitomized by what is perhaps the most artistically successful scene of the movie and one of the most famous in cinema: what I have called the "shoot-out at the Masturah Well."

In the Masturah Well scene, certain us/them distinctions are relayed that are fundamental to this movie's ethnographic gaze. The first is that the westerner possesses technology and the rational outlook that goes with it (symbolized by Lawrence's compass, which he will lose during his crossing of the Sinai, the same scene in which he goes temporarily mad), while the Arab possesses only his body (Tafas does the menial work for Lawrence, like hauling the water, taking care of the camels, and so forth), a body that can erupt at any moment into violence (as Tafas does when he runs to grab his pistol in order to shoot the stranger advancing menacingly toward the well). An opposition is established that continues to be elaborated throughout the movie: the westerner who is powerful because of technology, particularly military weapons, and the "oriental" who is weak without it.

Tafas then indulges in some of his own us/them thinking, a kind of internal orientalism, when, shivering in disgust, he says, "This is a Harith well. Ah, the Harith are a dirty people." Almost immediately his remark is made to appear ironic when he noisily slurps water with his own hands. Meanwhile, Lawrence giggles quietly at this slight and silently drinks the same water out of a cup, this act of delicacy distinguishing him as civilized. The filmmakers will reinforce this distinction during a brief bit of dialogue between Lawrence and Sherif Ali when the latter drinks from Lawrence's cup, thereby arrogating to himself civilized status, like Lawrence had before him, but which is undermined by the heavily ironic remark, "I have been to Cairo. I can both read and write." Under the circumstances, of course, his claims to be civilized seem preposterous, given his callous reference to the murdered guide as "that." Nor does Lean let us forget that there is a body lying at the edge of the frame or in the immediate space off-camera.

If I believed that these were entirely gratuitous slights at the Arab Other, intended to make a Western audience feel smug about themselves, I would not have been grateful for their reconstruction in this movie. But that is not all there is to this scene. First, let us remember that the pistol Tafas uses against Sherif Ali has been given to him as a "gift" by Lawrence, a reward for conducting him to Prince Feisal's camp. This complicates the guilt of the murder, because Lawrence is to some degree responsible for Tafas's death. His complicity is suggested by a tiny detail, which, however, is given prominence by a close-up. The moment that Tafas is shot, his hand jerks the pistol it has been holding into the air, and it lands at Lawrence's feet, the muzzle pointing directly at the British officer. We should be mindful of the fact that this detail recurs in a later scene when Lawrence's servant boy Farraj is mortally wounded by the accidental explosion of a detonator. It is decided that it would be more merciful to kill him than to risk letting him fall into the hands of the Turks, who would treat him as a rebel. But the man who has been designated to carry out the mercy killing refuses to do the job and instead flings the gun at Lawrence. It lands once again with the muzzle pointing directly at his feet. This time he cannot distance himself from a death in which he has been clearly implicated. He decides to execute the boy himself. Going back now to the scene in which Sherif Ali, taking the gun that lies at Lawrence's feet, asks him, "Is this pistol yours?" and Lawrence responds, "No, his" (referring to Tafas), we know his answer to be disingenuous. And, of course, Lawrence's arrogant remark ("so long as Arabs fight tribe against tribe, so long will they be a little people") is undermined at the same instant that it is pronounced, unless we forget that he is a European officer serving in the most barbaric conflict in world history.

Finally, let us also note that Sherif Ali is constructed in this scene as Lawrence's double. That is why his appearance in a mirage is powerful, not simply because it panders to an audience's taste for the "mysterious Orient" but also because it comes across as something uncanny, something repressed. After Ali unveils himself to Lawrence, we see that he resembles the British officer to an extraordinary degree: same age, height, intense eyes, handsome face, and lithe physique, except of course that he is Lawrence's racial "opposite." Lean underlines this significance of the double by shooting O'Toole and Sharif side by side and in profile. But what implications do we draw from this theme of the double? As Freud reminds us in his essay "The 'Uncanny,'" the theme of the double appears frequently in works of fiction. Not only do such works contain "characters who are to be considered alike [but] this relation is accentuated by mental processes leaping from one of these characters to another—by what we should call telepathy—so that one possesses knowledge, feelings and experience in common with the other."[26] A line has been crossed separating what we comfortably call reality from phantasmagoria, and we are not sure how to distinguish the two, an experience that heightens the sense of the uncanny. In the scene at the Masturah Well when the mysterious stranger is sighted, O'Toole conveys the sense in which Lawrence feels caught off guard by tripping slightly as he edges for security toward Tafas and then, in a voice that mixes curiosity with dread, asks, "Who is he?" This, as we know, is the question everyone will ask of Lawrence, which only reinforces his commonality with the stranger. As Freud goes on to remark about the double, "[It] is marked by the fact that the subject identifies himself with someone else, so that he is in doubt as to which his self is, or substitutes the extraneous self for his own." [27]

Into this scene we can read the danger that besets all fieldwork and ethnographic writing, a danger that can never be entirely evaded: self-projection. We have been prepared to see Lawrence as an "odd" creature who enjoys inflicting pain on himself and others. The barbarism that he projects onto others, the Arab, is what now describes his secret self. But the filmmakers want the audience to understand that they too are vulnerable to self-projection, and do so through the unusual opening of this scene in which we look up a well shaft as though peering from deep within our own, dark self.

I learned the lesson of self-projection under more humorous circumstances in the field. The war that broke out in my village had conjured up my worst fears about Arab violence, nurtured mainly, I regret to say, by the anthropological literature on tribal society in the Middle East.[28] My fears worsened when I realized that marksmen were crouching on my rooftop and taking aim at the enemy. My house was in the immediate line of fire. At one point I heard a voice ask me whether they could have some tea. "Tea?" I asked incredulously. "If you don't mind and it's no bother," was the rejoinder from the rooftop. One should not underestimate the Yemeni's fine sense of the absurd, but it seemed as though the request were being made in all seriousness, and so I complied with it. Minutes later, fumbling up the dark stairwell to the roof and then crouching as low as possible to avoid being hit, I made my way to the marksmen with a pot of tea and porcelain cups rattling on my tray. Now it was their turn to be astonished. "Why are you so frightened? This is very ordinary. They're not trying to kill you, or us, for that matter." Indeed, though I had heard gunshots, I had not noticed that the bullets were way off their mark. This was, at least for the time being, a "game" of violence, a way of staging honor that I came to distinguish from actual or brute force intended to maim or kill.

The film is quite explicit in making Lawrence out to be unique among his fellow officers in wanting to go native. None is willing to go to such lengths, not even Brighton, the English officer who accompanies him on many of his campaigns but who never wears Arab clothes. I have already remarked on the fact that Lawrence's success in allegedly organizing the bedouin to fight in the Arab Revolt has been attributed in part to his knowledge of their culture and, more important, to his ability, and worse his desire, to become the Other.

In one scene Allenby and Brighton are together in the general's office in Jerusalem. While Brighton is assessing the accuracy of a report Lawrence has submitted to the general on the progress and success of the Arab army, Allenby interrupts to ask, "Think he's going native, Harry?" After a brief pause Brighton admits, "He would if he could, I think," but then quickly distances himself from this uncomfortable prospect with the disclaimer, "not my line of country this, sir." If for the anthropologist the danger of "going native" is the supposed loss of distance and therefore objectivity, both of which are thought to imperil the scientific project, then for a political agent and representative of Western civilization like Lawrence, it represents the betrayal of country, cause, and even culture.

One of the worst taboos that can be committed in the colonial outback, or for that matter the field, going native is a theme that Somerset Maugham explores with considerable complexity in his short stories set in Malaya and the South Pacific.[29] It is perhaps surprising that so little has been written on the subject of going native by anthropologists, though it has come to the attention recently of the literary critic Marianna Torgovnick and the art historian Abigail Solomon-Godeau.[30]

The theme is explored with great subtlety in those scenes where Lawrence returns from Arabia, from "out there" (as his fellow officers refer to it), in order to report back to his superiors. After the taking of ʿAqaba, Lawrence explains to Ali that he personally must go to Cairo and tell the generals the news, otherwise they would not believe it coming from the mouths of the bedouin. Ali bristles, but not because of the suggestion that the English would take the bedouin for liars:

> I see. In Cairo you will put off these funny clothes; you will wear trousers and tell stories of our quaintness and barbarity. And then they will believe you.

The reaction must be painfully familiar to many anthropologists. At times my Yemeni informants would grow skeptical of my ethnographic project, for example, and would defensively confront me with the accusation that I would tell Americans how backward and poor their country was. When Lawrence returns to Cairo, however, he remains steadfast to his newly acquired "Arab" identity in spite of, or perhaps even because of, the negative reactions it elicits from his British colleagues. "What do you *think* you look like?" a soldier asks rhetorically, as he watches Lawrence in full Arab dress escorting Farraj, his servant boy, into the officers' club. At first, Lawrence is mistaken for an Arab and treated with racist contempt, but once he gives Brighton his news of victory the tone changes.

In the next scene Lawrence has his interview with General Allenby, who at one moment asks to see Lawrence's headdress, apparently intrigued by the idea of assuming another cultural identity. But Allenby quickly retreats from the possibility when Brighton remarks that he would look "damned ridiculous, sir." (Odd, isn't it, how General Schwarzkopf receives this film.) The general returns the headdress to Lawrence and retreats to his side of the desk. Allenby knows who he is and does not want to be anyone else, least of all someone of another culture. And that is one important source of his power over Lawrence, who is vulnerable precisely to the extent that he seems to belong to both cultures and yet to neither one. When the two figures leave the office to return to the officers' bar, the general dons his British army cap, Lawrence his Arab headdress.

At the end of the interview with Allenby, the theme of "going native" is once again raised. In a marvelous bit of acting, O'Toole sweeps up the train of his robe and marches resolutely toward the somewhat menacing-looking group of officers. It is his guise as an Arab that puzzles and disturbs them, and it looks for a moment as if they will make an issue of it. They appear to be intent on blocking his exit, but then their mood instantly changes from belligerence to jubilation. Crowding around the hero, they congratulate him by pumping his hand and thumping him on the back. As long as he is triumphant in what they perceive to be their own cause, they will tolerate, perhaps even applaud, his assumption of otherness.

Immediately after the conversation in Jerusalem between Allenby and Brighton about Lawrence's "going native," the theme is raised in a scene in which Lawrence, now at the nadir of his powers as the leader of the Arab Revolt, tries to persuade the remnants of his ragtag army to come with him and enter the Turkish-held, fortress-town of Deraa. The idea seems preposterous to his followers, one of whom scoffs, "Aurens! Can you pass for an Arab in an Arab town?" Upon this admonition follows one of the most controversial and disturbing scenes in the whole movie, one that is symbolic of the loss of Lawrence's sexual innocence: it tells of his imprisonment, beating, and implied rape by the Turks inside the Citadel of Deraa. It would be a mistake to read this scene as only about sexuality (I return to it in chapter 6). It is also about race and cultural identity. When the bey refers to Lawrence's whiteness with the remark "You have blue eyes" and then admiringly pinches the skin of his chest, can we presume to know what exactly causes Lawrence to strike out at him? Is it only the homosexual nature of the bey's advance? Certainly, this is the meaning most often attributed to the scene, as we shall see. But could it be something other than or in addition to homophobia? In other words, does not the bey unmask Lawrence for what he is, a white man who is not Arab, and then proceed to "unman" him as punishment for presuming he could merge his identity with that of the other? In fact, the movie deliberately asks the spectator to entertain this interpretation. When in the next scene Lawrence talks to Ali about what happened in the Citadel, he takes hold of his own flesh in a gesture that is reminiscent of the bey's and says, "Look Ali. Look. That's me. What colour is it? . . . That's me; and there's nothing I can do about it." And he continues a little later, "[A man] can't want what he wants. (He touches his own flesh again). This is the stuff that decides what he wants." Here the movie seems to lapse into a kind of racial theory of volition much closer to the one held by the colonial society Lawrence had despised and rejected, and which would not strike a sympathetic note with contemporary anthropologists. Indeed, he thinks he is now called back to his "own kind." At the conclusion of his conversation with Ali, Lawrence exhorts the Bedouin to "trust your own people! . . . and let me go back to mine."

The return, however, is futile, conveyed swiftly in one of Lean's evocative cuts. The production script reads: "CUT . . . By way of the answer the screen is filled with shining brass and brass music crashes into the sound track." The effect is jarring.

Hailing some fellow officers, Lawrence asks them what is happening at headquarters in Jerusalem, and he is told proudly that they have a new squash court. These are the people he returns to. Ever attentive to formalities, they notice Lawrence's ill-fitting uniform. If before he would have been indifferent to his Western clothes, he is now somewhat embarrassed by his appearance and explains that he had to borrow someone else's uniform because his own had been stolen. "Bloody wogs" is the reaction from the officers, and Lawrence, after a moment's hesitation and deliberation, decides not only to overlook the racist remark but to actually acknowledge its truthfulness. "Yes, probably." Such is his desperate need to rejoin his own kind that he is willing to collude in their racism against the people he has loved. As Ali predicted, he would eventually take off those "funny" clothes and speak of the Arabs' greediness. Ironically, the officers do not see the extent to which Lawrence is accommodating himself to their point of view. They mistake his reticence for a reproach, and he overhears them comment behind his back, "Lays it on a bit thick, doesn't he?" The scene of return has hardly begun when it is obvious that the native is to be rejected.

In the next scene Allenby makes this rejection certain by refusing Lawrence's plea to live like "an ordinary man," thrusting him back into Arabia for the final push to Damascus. By the end of the movie, the Arabs (or rather Prince Feisal) reject Lawrence, too. He realizes that the condition of being an outsider is permanent and inescapable. It is one of the tensions that wear down his spirit and leave him, as Bolt tells us, a "burnt-out" case,[31] which is conveyed in the last few segments of the movie by filming O'Toole in pale reflections and retreating shadows.

For me the problem of "going native" was complicated by very real exigencies of fieldwork and at the same time connected to biographical questions I have raised earlier. Like many anthropologists, I worked hard at learning the spoken language so that I could converse without interpreters on a wide range of topics, but it was impossible to communicate effectively without also simultaneously being *in* the society (living among native speakers, shopping with them, attending public events with them, and so forth) and, little by little, day by day, turning my appearance into that of the "other" (which, of course, is never *the* other—which doesn't exist—but only one's own imaginative construct of him or her). I did not want to fool anyone into thinking I was Yemeni or perhaps more plausibly Lebanese, nor for a moment was anyone gullible enough to be fooled. I am reminded of the scene in the film where Sheik Auda Abu Tayyi remarks to Lawrence when he sees him cavorting like a "native" in the desert, "What are you doing—*Englishman?*" Nor do I honestly think that the Yemenis I met supposed I was *trying* to "pass" for one of them.

No Yemeni I knew took offense at my appearance (the complaint heard at the end of this chapter came from a Syrian who wanted to make a political statement against Americans), and indeed many of them encouraged my dressing in "native" clothes. They understood my attempts to speak their dialect and to live among them as an appeal to take my project seriously. For example, when I appeared in headdress, they would ask, only half in jest, why I didn't wear the rest of the ensemble: the men's skirt (*futah*), the button-down shirt, the woolen jacket, and sandals? And they would smile approvingly when they next saw me in public. I consumed local products because I was part of the local economy. I chewed *qat* and smoked the water pipe, both of which I enjoyed immensely, but they were also the prime leisure-time activities performed by groups of Yemenis, male and female, which I had to join in order to speak Arabic and learn new things about the local culture. One of the Egyptian schoolteachers in the village once asked me why I engaged in that "filthy" habit of chewing the leaves of a plant. I told him that if he tried it, he might like it, but one is reminded of the scene at the Masturah Well in which Tafas tells Lawrence, "Ah, the Harith are a dirty people." And, of course, there were boundaries that I tested all the time: "How about if I pray with you in the mosque?" "Only if you become Muslim," I would be teased in return.

It turns out to have been more my boundary than theirs. They would have welcomed my joining their faith if my conversion had been sincere, but religion has never meant very much to me and would not have in this context either. In other words, "going native" is rarely, if ever, a unilateral decision but is bilaterally negotiated, and there is plenty of space for rejection or resistance on both sides.

The blending of cultural differences creates tensions in Lawrence's character that he cannot sustain without losing his sanity. To be sure, there are other, and for a general audience perhaps more obvious, causes for his madness—megalomania, war trauma, and masochism—but to anyone who has traveled extensively in the worlds of other peoples, "the movement toward otherness," as Dorinne Kondo has called it,[32] can produce disorientation, at times psychological conflict akin to neurosis, and possibly even nervous collapse. For each person the experience will be stressful in different ways and with different outcomes. The movie explores the psychology of the situation with unusual depth and subtlety.

Lawrence, as we have seen, is prepared to reject his cultural identity and assume another's, a process in which, at least in the beginning, his Arab friends are enthusiastic accomplices. The process of identification is gradual and subtle. For one thing, it is not the same throughout the movie, his identification in the beginning being with the "nobler" aspects of bedouin culture, but by the end with cutthroats and mercenaries. He also overidentifies, wanting to submerge himself in Arab otherness in order to set himself up as their "prophet" or "miracle worker" and "nation builder." His overidentification, of course, is ambiguously motivated: on the one hand by his love for Arabia and Arabs; on the other by his ruthless ambition and his need for adulation. By virtue of who he is—that is, a political and cultural broker whose very identity depends on straddling two worlds—Lawrence cannot remain wholly one or the other, Arab or English, regardless of what either the Arabs or he wants. His is a position analogous to, if perhaps more severe than, that of the anthropologist's. By virtue of what we do, we too must exist in a culturally liminal state, long after we leave the field.

According to the movie, the cost of living with such a split cultural identity for a man like Lawrence is madness or burnout. This view is very much a modernist one, expounding the need for a stable, grounded, and holistic subject, no matter how complex and ambiguous that subject may be. The idea that a person could contain many different identities, depending on the context of action, some of them contradictory, is something that we are only now beginning to entertain as sane and perhaps even desirable in a "postmodern" world. But that portrayal of Lawrence would be a very different construction and a very different movie.

For me, the problem of the fragmented self did not lie in different cultural selves that I was unable, but wanted, to reconcile. Perhaps because of my cultural migrancy from Germany to the States (and, within this country, living for long stretches of time in distinctly different regions) and from there to Arabia, I have grown used to the idea of never feeling completely "at home" in any culture or ever resolving the discrepant traces of my past identities. The problem, rather, stemmed from a different but still quite acute psychological process, which has its precise analogue in *Lawrence of Arabia*.

Throughout the movie, the desert is like an enormous amphitheater, and Lawrence is a self-conscious actor in it. The stage metaphor and the motif of playacting become more overt as the movie progresses and more gruesome by the end. The idea of being on stage, of playacting, has its parallels in fieldwork for many anthropologists who assume to some degree or another alien dress, manners, language, and even modes of thought and feeling, constructing a role of what *they* think it means to be a "native" in a given society. They are constantly being watched, coached, and asked to "perform" the roles they and their friends have constructed before audiences who do not hesitate to criticize or applaud them. I found it to be an uncomfortably exhibitionist experience, more than once acutely embarrassing.

But there is much more to this "playacting" than simply assuming a (dis)guise, a role, a mask. When I was doing some theater work in college, I once had a quasi–"out-of-body" experience while concentrating very hard on a comedic role that required complicated stage business and some careful timing. Suddenly, I became two people: one was on stage saying his lines fluently, going through his paces gracefully, the other was in the wings observing the performance with a look of terror as though everything would soon go badly wrong. While it was frightening to think that I was both these people at once, I also knew this to be absurd—rather like holding to the conviction that A is equivalent to Not-A. Though never to the same degree of intensity, this heightened self-consciousness, this unflagging effort to watch oneself, hardly ever left me during fieldwork. I was always aware of the *effect* I was having on others (the house lights do not go out on the audience), not out of any excessive narcissism I can detect in myself but because I was anxious to please and to learn whatever I could pick up from the subtle clues dropped by my interlocutors. It's not only exhaustion that sets in after a while. There is a desperate feeling that madness is not far behind. The escapes are few—one's room, a week in the capital with American friends—but the performance never really stops.

In the final scene of the film we hear the driver in his Cockney accent congratulating Lawrence upon finally going home. "Mm?" he asks absent-mindedly, and the driver repeats with a mixture of envy and delight: " 'ome, sir!" It is a moment of pathetic irony, for Lawrence knows there is no home for him. The movie constructs the sentimentality of going home and at the same time slyly mocks it. In their final meeting Feisal parodies a nostalgia for England that Lawrence, in fact, doesn't feel: "He longs for the greenness of his native land. He pines for the Gothic cottages of—'Surrey'—is it not. Already in imagination he catches trout . . . and all the activities of the English gentleman." Allenby rightly observes, "That's me you're describing, sir, not Colonel Lawrence." In an earlier scene Allenby had been shown in his office, casting an imaginary fishing rod and reeling in the line in the middle of the chaos of Damascus. Lawrence, on the other hand, had rejected his country as a "fat" land with "fat" people, asserting that he was "different."

The nostalgia of "going home" was a significant theme in colonial culture and is frequently spoken of in its literature. In a short story entitled "Masterson," Somerset Maugham has a character in Burma say:

> I don't want to be buried out here. I want to be buried in an English courtyard. I'm happy enough here, but I don't want to live here always. I couldn't. I want England. Sometimes I get sick of this hot sunshine and these garish colours. I want grey skies and a soft rain falling and the smell of the country. I shall be a funny fat elderly man when I go back, too old to hunt even if I could afford it, but I can fish. I don't want to shoot tigers, I want to shoot rabbits. And I can play golf on a proper course. I know I shall be out of it, we fellows who've spent our lives out here always are, but I can potter about the local club and talk to retired Anglo-Indians. . . . It's a dream if you like, but it's all I have, it means everything in the world to me, and I can't give it up.[33]

With the collapse of the British Empire in the postwar period, a whole generation of colonial civil servants was returning "home" to try to live out that dream. Most of them would discover that it was impossible. That was the moment in which this film was made, and the impossibility of Lawrence's return must have been painfully clear to them.

For one thing, England had changed. In Osbourne's popular play *Look Back in Anger* (1957), a colonel retired from service in the Raj remarks to his daughter: "It was March, 1914, when I left England, and, apart from leaves every ten years or so, I didn't see much of my own country until we all came back in '47. Oh, I knew things had changed, of course. People told you all the time it was going—going to the dogs, as the Blimps are supposed to say. But it seemed very unreal to me, out there."[34] His daughter concludes, "You're hurt because everything is changed."

But there was also the other danger that nothing had changed, that they who had been thrust into the colonial service because they felt like outsiders to begin with were still treated like outsiders upon their return. There was always the class system, which created outsiders in the first place and ejected them into the colonial world: when they got back to the "home" country, it would reject them again.

In a subtle and very oblique way, Lean and Bolt picked up the theme of what happens to Lawrence when he returns to England in their movie *Ryan's Daughter,* though on the surface this film has nothing at all to do with Lawrence. One of the main characters, a decorated British war hero, severely shell-shocked in World War I, is sent to a remote and seemingly quiet outpost on the northern coast of Ireland at the time that the nationalist revolt against Great Britain is in full swing. There is an obvious parallel here to the Arab Revolt that occurred at the same time, but our "hero" has now been transformed from the leader of an anticolonialist, nationalist movement to its enemy. The major ends up catching one of the resistance leaders and confiscating contraband munitions. It is as if we now see enacted in the major the colonialist side of Lawrence's ambiguous role in nationalist rebellion. There are also some uncanny physical resemblances between the major and Lawrence: first of all, the actors Peter O'Toole and Christopher Jones have similar faces and eyes, though they are opposite in coloring. Furthermore, the major is exactly the sort of "burnt-out" case that Lawrence has become by the end of his Arabian campaign: though compelling in his own way, he is the merest shell of a human being. Both of them attract outcasts, the two servant boys who practically worship the ground Lawrence walks on, and the village idiot who follows the major like his shadow.

What might happen, then, the film asks, if this sort of man were to fall in love with a passionate woman? Would it revive him, change his life, "make a man of him" the way the war hadn't, even though it was supposed to (as General Murray had predicted of Lawrence)? His lover is Rosy Ryan, who is another kind of outsider, both within the village and within her conventional, unexciting marriage. Rosy is not simply there to "serve" the major, as it were, and rescue his masculinity; she is in fact the main character of the movie who falls in love with the romantic though enigmatic British officer in the hope of satisfying her grand passion for life, which her marriage to a well-meaning but stultifying schoolmaster had stifled. Toward the end of the movie the major realizes that his spiritual recovery is hopeless, however. Rosy, too, has her moment of self-revelation. She understands that the affair between them is over. In spite of a severe punishment inflicted upon her by the jealous villagers who falsely accuse her of betraying secrets about the resistance to the major, she fares better than her lover. We see him with a vial of nitroglycerin in his hand, standing on a beach, trying to decide whether he should toss it into the box of explosives confiscated from the resistance and end his life. Slowly the sun sinks over the horizon, and we realize that we have seen something like this take before. Startlingly, there is a cut to a match bursting into flame as the schoolmaster lights a kerosene lamp in a room where he is having a conversation with his wife, Rosy. Momentarily we are lulled into complacency until seconds later, when the couple hears a tremendous explosion. Its meaning is not simply that a man's life has ended, of course, but that such men as the major, and on another level Lawrence, cannot go home again after what they have experienced and seen. And now we realize that we have seen this sequence of scenes before. We saw them in *Lawrence of Arabia,* except that in that movie they were in reverse (Lawrence blows out the match, the sun rises, and a new life of adventure begins). We might even expect to be greeted by the lush romantic theme that is Lawrence's signature tune; instead, we are roused by the sound of an explosion.

Like other anthropologists leaving the field, I accepted or even welcomed the fact that I was going home, and yet when I returned to the States it was no longer that, if it ever was to begin with. Like the theme of "going native," anthropologists have little to say about the experience, perhaps because the "adventure" ends with the departure from the field, not the reentry into home. Yet it is primarily to our own culture that we inevitably return and to which we belong, if only halfheartedly.

I have been trying to demonstrate that the film *Lawrence of Arabia* talks about cross-cultural experience and ethnographic practice in ways that could serve as an allegory for anthropology and its criticisms in the 1990s. At the same time that I have been aligning myself fairly closely with a critical reading of anthropological texts begun by, among others, Marcus, Fischer, and Clifford, who attempt to destabilize the boundaries between anthropology and other fields of knowledge and between fieldwork and related practices such as travel, I have also tried to complicate that reading by making it more dialectical. That is, just as a film — intellectually complex, artistically compelling, and morally probing like *Lawrence of Arabia*— on the one hand colludes in the project of orientalism and on the other is aware of that project and critical of it, to the point where it calls its practices into question, so too anthropology has moved, and continues to move, dialectically from colonial representations to self-criticism and reform.

But here I would like to address the critical reading of anthropology on another point. While it is well and good to open the boundary between fieldwork and ethnography in anthropology and the practices performed by missionaries, intelligence officers, and colonial agents — in a way, anthropology's "repugnant" others — there is a danger in dissolving that boundary altogether. For example, no matter how deeply implicated my practices are in postcolonial or neocolonial politics, about which I can no longer afford to claim innocence, let alone ignorance, there are also times when I would strongly distinguish between what Lawrence did as an intelligence officer and a political agent, on the one hand, and what I did as an anthropologist. In fact, a comparison between Lawrence and myself did come up once in the course of my fieldwork under very upsetting circumstances.

In eastern Yemen, where I was studying oral tribal poetry in 1981, a war broke out and escalated to the point where it seemed to threaten the central state. As a lone American speaking Arabic in a politically troubled region and making contacts with a wide variety of people, I naturally came under suspicion of being a political agent, especially since the regime was embarking on a unification plan with communist South Yemen that was unpopular with the U.S. government. Around this time I was sitting in a large assembly hall on the formal occasion of a wedding celebration. A Baathist Syrian schoolteacher in the wedding party asked me whether I knew who Lawrence of Arabia was. "Of course," I replied, a little startled by the question. He then asked, "And did you know that he too wore tribal outfits?" The implication was, of course, obvious. Discussing privately the conversation with the village elder who overheard the Syrian's remarks, I tried to assure him that I was who I said I was, an anthropologist studying tribal poetry, not a political or espionage agent. He seemed less upset than I was, however. In the end, my efforts to allay suspicions failed, for national security police took me to the capital for questioning. I was still in Yemeni tribal outfit when I was hauled away. Though at first I may have been frightened, I can assure you that I had not met my Deraa. I was interrogated rather gently and released after a few days in detention. My research notes and other materials were eventually returned to me safely. I was even permitted to return to the village in which I had begun my project.

Not until something like this happens does one realize the very great difference between what anthropologists ought to do in the field and what Lawrence was doing in the Arab Revolt. This is where the convergence of the military war hero and the anthropologist, so fatefully conceived by Malinowski during World War I, must be resisted at all cost. The allegory of the film is precisely that if anthropologists do become political adventurers, like Lawrence, there will only be the desert for them.

CHAPTER 5

An Anti-Imperialist, Orientalist Epic

It would take the skills of a T. E. Lawrence to get these guys
to act in concert. . . . And I haven't noticed any Lawrences in
the corridors of the Pentagon.

An analyst speaking of the Arab multinational force,
assembled against Iraq in the Gulf War, New York Times,
August 11, 1990

Turning self-consciously this way and that, I couldn't help but
think of the film Lawrence of Arabia, in which Peter O'Toole
dressed in Arab garb for the first time, swirls slowly around
on the sand dunes admiring himself.

General H. Norman Schwarzkopf,
It Doesn't Take a Hero

Sometime in the late spring of 1979, just before I was beginning the
fieldwork I described in the previous chapter, a friend who was also an
anthropologist sent me a book. It was intended as a gift in exchange for
the theoretical texts I had dispatched to him while he was doing fieldwork in West Africa. He thought I would find it interesting as a criticism of the very thing the author might charge I was embarking upon
in North Yemen (now Yemen). The book was Edward Said's *Orientalism* (1978).

I recognized some of the stereotypes Said discussed in his criticism of
orientalist literature as ones I was trying to combat in my research in
Yemen. In particular, I was concerned with the so-called problem of tribal violence. It seemed to me that too much had been made of it by
scholars and journalists writing about this area of the world. The violence they were claiming to find in Arab societies might be the projection of a Hobbesian world onto that of another, rather different reality,
a point I made in the previous chapter. My anthropological training had
prepared me to be suspicious of (though, of course, not thereby immune

to) such assumptions about other cultures—a very old critique of ethno-centrism we owe to the Boasians.

When Said proceeded to analyze the structural nature of what he termed the "orientalist episteme," he argued that it draws distinctions of "us" versus "them" too starkly and inflexibly. Relying on the work of Lévi-Strauss and cognitive anthropologists who have investigated cul-tural schemata around the world, he observed that the structural con-cept of difference is built into the language of representation and clas-sification, and is hence universal. Said went immediately on to make a point that is another commonplace of structural linguistics as well as Boasian anthropology; namely, that "there is always a measure of the purely arbitrary in the way the distinctions between things are seen." [1] Difference is not given by nature (or, in today's parlance, "essentialized") but, as Émile Durkheim and Marcel Mauss argued at the beginning of this century, is constructed by society.[2] As Franz Boas noted at around the same time, though language may be structured in terms of formal categories, their meaning nevertheless varies from one language to the next and from one sociohistorical tradition to the other.[3] The us/them distinction was overdrawn, Said remarked, basing his claim on the work of anthropologists, because on some fundamental level human beings are alike, their representations of their worlds differing primarily because of contingent historical circumstances. An extreme relativist he is not. If I found anything odd in Said's project, it was his attempt to mitigate the "us" versus "them" distinction through a sort of European human-istic notion of the "human condition," an attempt that smacked a little of Eurocentrism.[4]

The link Said made between the orientalist episteme and colonialism, and his insistence on the historical responsibility that anthropology and other humanist disciplines bear for helping to forge it, were salutary interventions, though not novel by the late 1970s. Already in a volume of collected essays, anthropologist Talal Asad[5] and other contributors were interrogating anthropology's involvement in colonialism and its ef-fects on practices of fieldwork and ethnography.[6] I mention these criti-cal precedents in anthropology not to downplay Said's achievements, nor to enter into some sterile debate over who came first, but to stress something that Said tends to overlook or at the very least downplay in his examination of knowledge production, namely, the practices of *self-criticism* that practitioners of a disciplinary knowledge like anthropol-ogy may possess and deploy. So self-perpetuating and closed is the orien-talist episteme, in Said's view, that no one inside it has the chance to step back from and question it.[7] That questioning has to be initiated from the outside or, at the very least, by outsider/insiders like Said—intellectuals who for various reasons take up positions of criticism against the West. Place these kinds of intellectuals, or those inspired by them, in important sites of knowledge production, and you have the chance to create alternative narratives about places called the Orient. My aim is not to question that strategy, if such it is, to reconfigure our knowledge about the Orient. If I agree with it on political or economic grounds, that does not mean I find much intellectual justification for it. I want to ask a fundamentally different question concerning knowledge production and the possibilities of self-criticism within it—possibilities as well as limitations—for those who call themselves orientalists or who produce orientalist works like the film *Lawrence of Arabia*. In the introduction, I raised the possibility of what I call "dialectical criticism," in terms of which orientalist works are being increasingly examined by postcolonial critics.

Part of the reason for my raising this possibility is again autobiographical. When I returned to the United States in 1981 and then proceeded to teach in the academy, I was struck by the way in which anthropology was constructed by students outside the discipline. When I taught introductory courses in anthropology, I heard criticisms of the discipline that had been picked up elsewhere and were pronounced like revelations in which I clearly needed instruction. "I was told not to take anthropology because it's an imperialist discipline," one student informed a colleague of mine who was teaching at a prestigious liberal arts college. True enough, but was there a refuge from that accusation in other disciplinary knowledges? That that criticism has now become more widespread in fields such as literary criticism and history is, I think, salutary. The problem being more general, then, does one give up on all knowledge production that concerns the Other? My undergraduate teaching has been an attempt to respect the criticisms my students make of the discipline while at the same time teaching them the ways in which anthropology has also had a tradition of criticizing itself, not to mention Western society. On the basis of this kind of reflexivity, it is hoped, reformed practices of anthropological knowledge production might become possible.

Since the publication of *Orientalism*, examination of the many ways in which institutions of Western literature (and art more generally) were and continue to be tied to colonialist projects, not to mention the ways in which the representations of the world constructed through their texts are implicated in various projects of power, has continued apace.[8] By way of illustrating this kind of criticism, consider the way in which a very astute critic of film and text like Ella Shohat reads *Lawrence of Arabia*.[9] Her article makes the valuable point that "the critique of colonialism within cinema studies . . . has tended to downplay the significance of gender issues."[10] I will make use of this criticism in the next chapter. In keeping with the approach established by Said, however, Shohat reviews a tremendous number of films, spanning the birth of cinema to the contemporary age, in order to show the supposed persistence of an orientalist mode of representing the other:

> In most Western films about the colonies (such as *Bird of Paradise* [1932], *Wee Willie Winkie* [1937], *Black Narcissus* [1947], *The King and I* [1956], *Lawrence of Arabia* [1962], and even Buñuel's *Adventures of Robinson Crusoe* [1954]) we accompany, quite literally, the explorer's perspective. A simple shift in focalization to that of the "natives," as occurs in the Australian-Aboriginal *Nice Coloured Girls* (1987) or in the Brazilian *How Tasty Was My Frenchman* where the camera is placed on land with the "natives" rather than on ship with the Europeans, reveals the illusory and intrusive nature of the "discovery." More usually, however, heroic status is attributed to the voyager (often a male scientist) come to master a new land and its treasures, the value of which the "primitive" residents had been unaware. It is this construction of consciousness of "value" as a pretext for (capitalist) ownership which legitimizes the colonizer's act of appropriation. The "discovery," furthermore, has gender overtones. In this exploratory adventure, seen in such films as *Lawrence of Arabia* and the *Indiana Jones* series, the camera relays the hero's dynamic movement across a passive, static space, gradually stripping the land of its "enigma," as the spectator wins visual access to Oriental treasures through the eyes of the explorer-protagonist. *Lawrence of Arabia* provides an example of Western historical representation whereby the individual Romantic "genius" leads the Arab national revolt, presumed to be a passive entity awaiting T. E. Lawrence's inspiration. (Arab sources obviously have challenged this historical account.) The unveiling of the mysteries of an unknown space becomes a *rite de passage* allegorizing the Western achievement of virile heroic stature.[11]

I would argue that this kind of criticism is ultimately not dialectical enough. With regard to *Lawrence of Arabia,* it is true that the filmmakers give the impression that Lawrence was a "romantic genius" fashioning the Arab Revolt, but to leave that as the film's complete representation of him is to overlook the fact that they also indict him as a fascist. Bolt, as we have learned in chapter 3, even referred to his conceptualization of Lawrence as that of a "romantic fascist."[12] It is also to overlook the film's representation of the press (in the guise of the American reporter Jackson Bentley) as the source of this romanticism, which was intended to persuade the U.S. electorate to support the Wilson government in its war efforts (see the beginning of Part Two). Furthermore, by showing Lawrence to be a megalomaniac, a masochist, and a sadist, the film undermines his mythic-heroic construction. As we shall see in the next chapter on masculinity, these are only some of the criticisms that the film makes of its "hero" and the ambivalences it expresses toward the imperialist project. Thus, to what extent does the film in the end valorize "virile heroic stature"?

In the literature on *Lawrence of Arabia,* only rarely is there to be found a reading of the film's explicit criticism of imperialism. In the rush to show how this product of Hollywood has all the trappings of a hegemonic discourse, this point tends to get lost. While the "adventure" of British imperialism is clearly narrativized in the film, it is also debunked. This claim is justifiable on text-internal grounds but also gains cogency, as we shall see in a moment, in light of the historical context of the late 1950s and early 1960s that would in all probability have informed audiences' reactions to the film. However, it is not just British imperialism that is interrogated. The film also suggests that Feisal's dreams of an independent Arabia are connected with the vainglorious ambitions of former Arabo-Muslim empires (specifically, the Moorish empires of southern Spain). Furthermore, through the insertion of the American newspaper reporter Jackson Bentley, a veiled criticism is made of the United States' involvement in Southeast Asian independence movements during the late fifties and early sixties. In short, the film casts a far more interesting and complex glance at imperialism than we might at first suppose.

Recall the scene in which Prince Feisal is holding an audience in his tent with Brighton and Lawrence. The prince expresses his displeasure at the British for not sending ships to bombard the Turkish-controlled port of 'Aqaba, where he would like to set up a base of operations. The following heated exchange takes place between him and the British military adviser Colonel Brighton:

BRIGHTON: Put that out of your mind sir; the Navy's got other things to do.
FEISAL: Ah yes. Protecting the Suez Canal.
BRIGHTON: The one essential sector of this Front is and must be the Canal. You can see that, sir, surely?

FEISAL: I see that the Canal is an essential British interest. It is of little consequence to us.

BRIGHTON: I must ask you not to talk like that sir. The British and Arab interests are one and the same.

FEISAL: Possibly.

ALI: Ha! Ha!

For audiences of the early sixties, the most significant political event in the Middle East had been, of course, the Suez crisis of 1956. Gamal Abdel Nasser, president of Egypt, declared that the Suez Canal, the lifeline to Britain's former colony of India, would be nationalized. The irony of Brighton's assertion that "British and Arab interests are one and the same" in regard to the canal could not have been lost on audiences of the period. England and France, in conjunction with the relatively new state of Israel, declared war, while the United States intervened to stop the allies, fearing that the oil-producing countries would retaliate with massive embargoes. A majority of public opinion in England supported the government's defense of its imperial assets in the Middle East, in spite of the fact that they had dwindled to no more than a ludicrous symbol of British power, but the left and many of the country's leading artists and intellectuals raised objections, fearful of nuclear dangers that the use of force portended in the cold war world. In a sense, the crisis represented to the younger generation all that was wrong with Britain and its leadership of that day, committed as the latter was to outmoded and morally bankrupt imperialist agendas. But is Said correct, then, in faulting the criticisms of imperialism as really not being a criticism of the *system* of imperialism per se but of its economic costliness and political dangers in a cold war world? In fact, the British left was deeply concerned that the British withdrawal at Suez signaled the emergence of a new imperialism, represented by the United States and the forces of global capitalism, which used the anti-Communist scare as a tactic to squelch nationalist, anticolonialist uprisings in other places of the world.[13] It is important to bear in mind that Robert Bolt was part of the British left in the late fifties and early sixties. He opened his article in the *New York Times* that described his treatment of T. E. Lawrence with the revealing sentence: "I was brought up to disapprove of figures like T. E. Lawrence as being the colorful ornaments and stalking horses of imperialism."[14]

The conversation between Brighton and Feisal about the Suez Canal can be read as an allusion to the crisis. Though the crisis may have seemed remote in time from the year in which production for *Lawrence* began,

1960, historians of the period have noted that its significance—namely, that postwar Britain had lost its empire and its international preeminence in the modern world and that it seemed to be lacking a national purpose—did not actually sink into the national public consciousness until two years later. But the issues of imperialism and nationalism do not rest with the canal, as we are made to understand immediately following Ali's derisive exclamation.

> BRIGHTON: Fall back on Yenbo and we will give you equipment! We will give you arms, advice, training, everything!
>
> FEISAL (quickly): Guns?
>
> BRIGHTON: A modern rifle for every man.
>
> FEISAL (passionately): No! Guns! Artillery! Guns like the Turkish guns at Medina!
>
> ALI: (lounging, sneering) Yes; give us guns; and keep the training.

In other words, the "West" has the military technology that the "rest" of the world needs in order to fight its wars of independence. Without such hardware, the Third World cannot shrug off the yoke of imperialism. The diplomat Dryden warns General Allenby of the imminence of independence at the end of Part One when he remarks, "Given them artillery, sir, and you've made them independent."

Colonial dependence goes far beyond weaponry, however, and Lawrence understands this point only too well during the Arab nationalist meeting in Damascus:

> WHITE-HAIRED SHEIK: Let them [the electrical generators] burn. What needs telephones?
>
> LAWRENCE: The need is absolute!
>
> ALI: Then we need the English engineers.
>
> LAWRENCE: No! Take English engineers and you take English Government!

To build their infrastructures, developing countries required Western technology, but the catch was that such development once again placed them in a dependent position vis-à-vis the West. The lesson would be repeated for Feisal in Damascus by Dryden who mordantly expresses the political compromise imposed upon Arab nationalism: "Well, it seems we're to have a British waterworks with an Arab flag on it."

Let us now turn to the second part of the interview in Feisal's tent in which the problem of Arab nationalism/imperialism is constructed. To understand why Feisal's project is imperialist, we have to recall that his family, though descended from the Prophet Muhammad, represented only one kind of political legitimacy in the area, yet the royal family arrogated to itself the right to rule a vast Arab land vacated by the Ottomans. If in the conversation with Brighton the issue of British imperialism was raised and exposed, and in this scene continues to be explored, it is especially Feisal's imperialist longings that are constructed and, moreover, Lawrence who is now persuaded not only to identify with them but to become their agent. This is all done with the utmost compression of dialogue. The subtlety of visualization depends upon a sly exchange of glances and a choreography of body movements, all of which are performed in an atmosphere rendered eerie by a flickering candle in the foreground and a rising wind. According to Lean, this was technically one of the hardest scenes to shoot because of the complicated camera work.[15] Obviously, he was striving to achieve specific effects important to the development of the characters and the story; therefore, let us try to catch as many of these effects as we can.

The two men are now standing, in contrast to their position in the previous scene, but it is Lawrence who remains stationary throughout, almost like a passive receptacle, while the prince is active, moving to and fro, exerting a subtle psychological pressure upon the young Englishman. The camera is positioned in front and at a middle distance so that we can see them from the waist up.

Feisal confesses his fear of putting his men under British command because of the danger such an act would portend for Arab independence and sovereignty. One can hear the tent poles creak in the middle of the line "But I fear to do it—upon my soul I do," as if to manifest the insecurity of his position. A wind now picks up and continues to blow throughout the scene, causing the tent to sway slightly in the background.

Slowly the cameras move closer. We see Lawrence over Feisal's shoulder, as though from his perspective, and then vice versa. The prince ruefully observes to Lawrence, scrutinizing him all the while because he knows he is talking about him as well, that "the English have a great hunger for desolate places. I fear they hunger for Arabia." Lawrence urges him to resist British imperialism by telling him point-blank: "Then you must deny it to them." Feisal cannot quite believe his sincerity, for he reminds Lawrence that he is, after all, English and would have to be loyal to England. Is it possible, he asks the ingenuous or else hopelessly naive Englishman, to be loyal to England and Arabia both? Lawrence answers ambiguously, "To England and to other things," thinking that

Figure 14.   Lawrence in close-up, listening to Prince Feisal (his "subconscious")
in background shadows.

he can occupy a middle position that would not compromise his alle-
giance to either side.

Feisal is more skeptical. Now begins a careful staging of glances, body
movements, close-ups, and foreground-background positions that construct the deeper meanings of this scene. Feisal approaches Lawrence,
taking the measure of this strange young man—in effect testing him. He
looks straight into his eyes for a moment and concludes shrewdly that
he must be another of those "desert loving Englishmen"—Doughty, Stan-
hope, Gordon of Khartoum, in short, an incorrigible imperialist—and
he turns his back on Lawrence, literally and figuratively, walking out of
range of focus while the camera now frames Lawrence's face in close-up
(figure 14). Visible in the lighted foreground, he has a look of someone
listening intently and with slight consternation, as though he were eaves-
dropping. He is identifying so strongly with the other that he is inte-
riorizing his "voice" or point of view. This impression is enhanced by
making the figure behind O'Toole blurred and shadowy, as if he were
entering the Englishman's (un)conscious mind. That voice continues
gently to chastise Lawrence with the witty observation that "no Arab
loves the desert. We love water and green trees." The figure pivots to face
Lawrence's back, but though the prince is facing us, he is still in shadow
and outside the range of focus. We hear him say, in a remark that is
pointed directly at Lawrence, "There is nothing in the desert." In other
words, this identification with the desert that Lawrence shares with his
countrymen may in fact be perverse and therefore suspect. On that line,
Lawrence pivots to face the prince, and they look at each other.

Figure 15.   Feisal in close-up with Lawrence listening in the shadows.

The prince's test now turns into a taunt. Approaching Lawrence and coming back into focus, he repeats the self-righteous remark that Lawrence had made to Sherif Ali at the Masturah Well. "Or is it that you think we are something you can play with because we are 'a little people, a silly people; greedy, barbarous and cruel'?" An important moment of irony, it almost always amuses the audience. The seriousness lifts a little, and they both smile to enjoy this little joke at Lawrence's expense, after which Feisal begins to betray his own imperialist ambitions. "But you know, in the Arab city of Cordova were two miles of public lighting in the streets—when London was a village!" Once again, Lawrence shows his enthusiastic identification with the Arab cause. "Time to be great again," he urges. Feisal takes umbrage at the presumptuousness of this remark, for it was in order to become great again that his father had started the revolt against the Turks—"my father, Mr. Lawrence, not the English." The audience is reminded that the Arabs tried to take control of their own destiny, that they were not simply willing pawns in the hands of the British.

Now it is Feisal's turn to face the camera (figure 15). He moves to the foreground, leaving Lawrence behind him, thereby reversing their positions, with Lawrence backlit but out of focus. It is as though he is now in a position to be the prince's agent or instrument. We see the prince in remarkable close-up, his face dimly lit from below, which makes him look sinister, almost Mephistophelian. With a sigh, he confesses, "I long for the vanished Gardens of Cordova." He lingers wistfully for a moment over this vision of imperial grandeur, his face filling the screen, and then

Figure 16.   Feisal standing in his tent, looking in the direction of Lawrence,
who has just exited.

snaps out of his reverie. "However, before the gardens must come the
fighting." He turns around and approaches Lawrence.

The protagonists are now face-to-face, level with each other, and in
focus, united, as it were, in a common goal. Swiftly comes the climax.
Feisal quips, "To be great again, it seems we need the English or . . . ?"
Lawrence prompts him, "Or . . . ?" Feisal looks directly at him when he
says, "What no man can provide, Mr. Lawrence. We need a miracle."
He dismisses the lieutenant, whom we next see outside the tent flap, the
tent poles creaking in the wind. It is now Lawrence's turn to be seen at
an angle and with lighting that makes *him* appear diabolical, a look of
intense concentration on his face. This close-up so clearly parallels the
earlier one of Feisal musing over vanished Islamic glory that its composition cannot be accidental. He has identified with Feisal's cause and
tries to figure out how to work a "miracle" for him.

The wind that has been blowing outside the tent now picks up. As the
musical "dynamo theme" begins, we cut to Feisal inside the tent facing
in the direction of Lawrence, as though he could see him through the
tent flap, even though we know it has been lowered by the attendants
(figure 16). He is standing next to some sort of hanging, lit in a remark-
ably bright, almost sulfurish glow, as though he were standing on the
threshold of hell. The camera stays with this fiendish image for a couple
of seconds. Then there is an immediate cut to Lawrence walking through
the desert into the moonlit night. The implication is that he has become
the extension of Feisal's will.

What are the deeper, perhaps unconscious, meanings constructed by the camera work in this scene? Having realized that Lawrence is sympathetic toward the Arab cause, Feisal gets under his skin, so to speak, in order that Lawrence will take his identity, and ultimately his direction, from the Arabs. But, of course, Lawrence is also willing to be persuaded. As Bolt says of his conception of him, "I think we have to see a man made use of, but conniving at it." [16] If Feisal can manipulate him, it is because he suspects Lawrence to be supremely vulnerable: there is a void in him, a "desert," which the other can fill, and Lawrence is only too happy to become the receptacle for that other's will. This scene, presented at the very outset of Lawrence's involvement in the Arab Revolt, makes ambiguous his "will" to power. He seems to have the need to be dominated as much as he does to dominate. It is only possible to say that "Lawrence of Arabia provides an example of Western historical representation whereby the individual Romantic 'genius' leads the Arab national revolt" [17] by overlooking the subtleties of this scene. By the time Lawrence leaves the tent and wanders into an eerily beautiful desert, lost in thought on how to perform Feisal's "miracle," he has become the prince's pawn.

As for the selfishness of the British imperialist venture in Arabia, that is blatantly exposed in two interviews Lawrence has with General Allenby. In each one, Lawrence has come back with the intention of resigning. Realizing how important Lawrence is to him, the general persuades him both times to return to Arabia, in spite of the psychological toll that he realizes the campaign is having on the young officer. However, as in the interview with Feisal, we see that Lawrence is *willing* to be persuaded, susceptible as he is to Allenby's flattery. Let us look at the first interview with Allenby more closely to see how the filmmakers suggest that Lawrence is in the general's power.

In Allenby's office we see Lawrence in his slightly tattered Arab robes sitting next to a desk. The general's cap on the table is the focal point of the scene—a fetish, standing for the general's power, which is being subtly exerted on Lawrence. It is also, of course, a symbol of cultural identity in opposition to Lawrence's Arab headgear, which stands for "otherness," an interpretation that will become more obvious in a moment.

In the beginning of the scene, the camera pans slowly from Lawrence to Allenby sitting at the massive table and then is pulled back to reveal a gigantic room that is beautifully appointed—the very antithesis of Feisal's simple but elegant royal tent. Instead of tent poles, there are marble columns. Instead of floor cushions and a brass serving tray, solid oak chairs and a huge desk. Instead of the winds of the night, faint noises from daytime crowds in the street. Instead of a light, mobile structure, an edifice of weight and permanence. On the back wall is a framed map of Arabia, symbolic of colonial possession.

Lawrence tries to explain why he wants to be relieved of his assignment in Arabia. Having been placed away from the table, the camera now moves closer and assumes Allenby's perspective, thereby creating a more intimate relationship between the two antagonists. What was accomplished in the scene with Feisal by foreground-background movement, extreme close-ups distorted by lighting, and in/out focus is carried out in this scene primarily with props and camera angles.

As Lawrence confesses to his enjoyment of killing, the camera moves slowly but steadily closer, until only he and the cap are visible in the frame. It is as though Allenby himself were getting closer to Lawrence, peering into his soul, as Feisal had done earlier. This suggestion is made more overt by an exchange of close-ups between the two characters as Lawrence reveals the awful truth about himself. In response, Allenby blanches.

Trying to lighten the mood somewhat, the general now gets up, moves around the table, and approaches his junior officer, asking to see his Arab headgear. "Amateur theatricals?" he asks sarcastically, to which Lawrence responds facetiously, "Entirely." With the headdress in his hand, Allenby then turns to Colonel Brighton and asks how he, the general, would look in such an outfit. He is told, "bloody ridiculous, sir." Allenby silently agrees. He hands the headdress back to Lawrence and returns to his own side of the desk. A cultural divide has been crossed, but only for an instant. He is not about to shed one identity for another or become confused about his political loyalties. Make no mistake about it: the confusions are in Lawrence, not Allenby, who knows exactly who is, where he stands, what he wants, and how to get it.

What Allenby wants is to persuade Lawrence to rejoin the Arab Revolt, and so begins the transition into the next scene, a transition in which Allenby masterfully appeals to the young man's vanity. First, Allenby elicits high praise for Lawrence's achievements from Brighton and Dryden. Then a staff sergeant is called in. We do not see him, only his boots, with Lawrence seated in his chair in the foreground, wincing like someone struggling for composure. Lawrence almost appears to be listening to his own inner voice praising him—an echo of the scene with

Feisal in the tent—with the addition that the camera angle is Allenby's, so that we sense who is in control of the psychological manipulation and assessing its impact. Slowly, a stirring and somewhat pompous military march begins.

There is no need to repeat what happens next. The only point to emphasize is that the scene constructs the pomp of imperial splendor, a standard of epic films, and slyly mocks it. In the ensuing conversation around a beautiful tiled fountain, another conceit of Arabia, Allenby leads Lawrence on about British interests in the Orient. He is feeding the fish in the fountain, a symbolism that is almost heavy-handed in this scene of obvious duplicity. When Lawrence asks Allenby outright whether the British have imperial designs in Arabia, Allenby lies and says that they do not. Given that Lawrence has noticed the pointed exchange of glances between Dryden and Allenby, it is difficult to imagine that he cannot guess they are lying. It seems to be a case of self-deception where Lawrence once again is being made use of but, as Bolt says, is conniving at it.

This, like the interview with Feisal, is another scene of persuasion, but this time the power lies with the English general, who successfully lures Lawrence back into the Great Game. The general's exercise of his power over Lawrence, however, is more vicious than that of Feisal's, for he deliberately and unscrupulously lies to him about Britain's intentions and refuses to take seriously Lawrence's war trauma.

Let us bear in mind that this film originally was shown to American audiences at a time when U.S. imperialism, in contrast to that of its European counterparts, was expanding in the post–World War II period. America's view of Lawrence and of the British campaign in Arabia is provided in the film through the eyes of the American newspaper reporter Jackson Bentley, who makes his first appearance in Part Two. He tries to ingratiate himself with Feisal, but the latter has seen his type before and knows his number. When the cynical reporter remarks to Prince Feisal that "we Americans were once a Colonial people. We *naturally* sympathize with *any* people *anywhere* who are struggling for their freedom," the prince fixes him with such a withering look that Bentley gives up all pretense. For those of us who remember growing up in the 1960s with such slogans as "America, making the world safe for democracy," this little comic turn is deliciously titillating. To audiences of that time, however, the cynicism of the remark may have appeared a little shocking, for the notion of America fighting for other peoples'

freedom was still deeply ingrained in the country's political consciousness. It was popularly presented, though with quite different moral conclusions, by two best-selling books of the period: Graham Greene's *The
Quiet American* (1955) and William J. Lederer and Eugene Burdick's
The Ugly American (1958). The latter was also adapted for a movie in
1963, starring Marlon Brando. The contrast between these two contemporary works shows precisely the kind of heterogeneity of discourse
that I have been arguing for when examining Western representations of
the colonial project. *Lawrence of Arabia* would be situated much closer
to Greene's novel in terms of its representation of and attitude toward
colonialism.

Greene's novel anticipates with uncanny prescience the moral quag-
mire of America's future in Vietnam. The narrator is a cynical British
journalist by the name of Thomas Fowler who is stationed in Saigon,
where he is covering the French Indochina War. He prides himself on
the fact that "I have no politics" and "I'm not involved [in the war]." [18]
He meets up with his alter ego, a young, idealistic, earnest, enthusiastic,
and insufferably self-righteous American by the name of Arland Pyle.
Whereas Bentley is a cynic and therefore much closer in temperament to
his counterpart Fowler, Pyle is like the idealistic Lawrence—determined
to find a nationalist leader who is able not only to resist an errant colonialism but also set up an "independent" nation (allied, of course, to the
United States). Unable to convince Pyle of the wrongheadedness of his
clandestine political activities, the reporter sets him up to be murdered
after one of Pyle's interventions goes wrong and leaves many innocent
people dead or maimed and wounded. If the name Pyle has its unpleas-
ant associations, Fowler's are no more savory, for we have to suspect the
reporter's motives in getting rid of the meddling American when we realize that the latter has been successfully wooing Fowler's beautiful mistress. "Was I so different from Pyle, I wondered?" the reporter asks.[19]
As in *Lawrence of Arabia,* no one is left occupying the moral high
ground.

Though it is not clear how many Americans in 1962 were aware of
or much concerned about U.S. involvement in Southeast Asia—it is interesting to note, for example, that the Harris Poll did not start to sound
out public opinion on U.S. foreign policy in Vietnam until as late as
1964—it is not far-fetched to suppose that at least some people in the
audience could have interpreted *Lawrence of Arabia* as a parable about
American imperialism in places like Vietnam. And in the way in which
the character of Lawrence is represented, with strong allusions to the

flawed type of adventurer-diplomat that was being portrayed in literature and film, they could begin to explore the ambiguities of that imperialism. Indeed, if read as an allegory of Vietnam, the film, like Greene's
novel, is a warning. I will return to the question of U.S. imperialism at
the end of the chapter when I discuss a reading of the film in light of
events in the Gulf War.

I would argue that the critique of imperialism is fairly self-conscious.
Shortly before the film was released, Robert Bolt wrote about his conception of the main figure of the movie as one of those "stalking horses
of imperialism," and throughout the movie the British are portrayed
as ruthless and deceitful in their pursuit of imperial power. A broader
critique of the West, not unconnected to imperialism, concerns its technological superiority and the ways in which it can be perverted, a subject Lean had already explored far more deeply in *Bridge on the River
Kwai*. Although our look at political culture in Great Britain after World
War II was cursory, it is clear, I think, that there was a general questioning or criticism of Britain's imperial past—especially by its youth. Such
self-criticism as the movie provokes would not have seemed peculiar to
British audiences of that day. But where *Lawrence* differs from any previous Lean movie is in the unparalleled extent of its representation of the
Other, and here the orientalism that Said would criticize becomes most
pertinent. We have already seen that it is not that easy to say that the film
establishes a straightforward dichotomy between colonizer and colonized. To what extent, however, does it cordon "us" off from "them,"
reproducing on the plane of cultural representations the very power differences said to be characteristic of colonial discourses?

As in much orientalist discourse, "tribe" and "tribalism" become
metonyms for "Arab" in this film. For example, a central idea of the Arab
revolves around the concept of tribal blood feud that dominates all of
Part One. The first allusions occur during Lawrence's entry into Arabia
with his guide Tafas. At one point in their journey, Tafas halts and mo-
tions for Lawrence to crouch below the crest of a sand dune, from which
vantage point a huge plain is visible in the distance:

TAFAS: From here to Lord Feisal's camp is Harith Country.
LAWRENCE: I know
TAFAS: I am not Harith . . .
LAWRENCE: No, Hazimi, of the Beni Salem.

Tafas has a foreboding of trouble from enemy bedouin. It is not imaginary, as we soon discover at the Masturah Well. This is the first contact

in the movie between Arabs, and it is one of shocking brutality. "Your friend," Sherif Ali tries to explain to Lawrence, gesturing to the body on the ground, "was a Hazimi of the Beni Salem. The Beni Salem are blood enemies of the Harith. They may not drink at our wells." Lawrence then utters the famous rebuke, "Sherif Ali! So long as the Arabs fight tribe against tribe, so long will they be a little people. A silly people! Greedy, barbarous, and cruel—as you are!" The view of the "violent" Arab Lawrence expresses is only too painfully familiar from a long ethnographic and journalistic tradition representing the "other" in the Middle East. In anthropology, for example, one of the time-honored models of tribal society is the "segmentary lineage system," which presupposes that justice is served in parts of eastern and northern Africa by mobilizing kinsmen in actual or threatened feud against a criminal and his supporters, thus rendering society endemically violent in the absence of anything like a central state to maintain the peace.[20] To jump to a very different discourse, Thomas Friedman, in his highly acclaimed book *From Beirut to Jerusalem* (1989), has used tribal feud as a metaphor for understanding nearly all politics in the Middle East, from marauding nomads in North Africa to fighting urban militias in Beirut as well as political factions in the Knesset. And Charles Glass, a journalist kidnapped in Lebanon during that country's civil war, echoes the metonym by which tribe stands for Arab in the title of his memoir, *Tribes with Flags* (1990). The latter's subtitle is even more revealing: *A Dangerous Passage Through the Chaos of the Middle East.*

I am not interested in criticizing the filmmakers' narrative contrivance, by which the problem of violence is raised (it is, after all, unlikely that a guide would have been chosen who was in a state of blood feud with the very tribe to whom he was conducting the British officer), or their failure to consider law and dispute mediation as alternatives to violence in tribal politics. What I wish to discuss is whether *Lawrence of Arabia* at least expresses a certain unease or ambivalence with its pronouncements about "violently" tribal Arabs.

Let us consider whether Lawrence's remark might not be ironic. For one thing, some members of the audience would not overlook the irony that Lawrence is fighting in a war that pits nation against nation in the bloodiest and most barbaric conflict Europe had witnessed to date. The tribal trope, facilely projected onto the Other, appears uncannily like the return of the repressed. And, of course, in two subsequent scenes of the movie, Lawrence's exact words will be flung back at him by his

Arab hosts, first playfully by Feisal, then painfully by Ali, as the full horror of the war he has helped to unleash presses upon his and our consciousnesses.

But there is another way in which this scene works on American audiences—as an allusion to the violence and lawlessness of the American frontier depicted in western films, if, that is, the duel is thought of like a shoot-out in a western movie. By the time *Lawrence of Arabia* was released, of course, the American western had started to wane in popularity, yet Lean was shrewd in utilizing the genre as a frame of reference for understanding his epic. Allusions to the genre go beyond the "shoot-out." They include references to specific films as well. Consider, for example, the circulation of Lawrence's revolver throughout crucial scenes in the movie, a narrative device that allows the director to refer again and again to the problem of violence as issuing from the hands of the colonizer as much as it does from the colonized. The same device was used by the director Anthony Mann in a famous western, *Winchester '73* (1950), a story about two brothers, one of them an outlaw, the other trying to bring him to justice for having killed their father. The retributive agency is a magical rifle, a technological marvel of nineteenth-century weaponry, which we see passing through several hands—young and old, law-abiding citizen and outlaw, white and Indian—suggesting the spread of violence on the western frontier.

To say that the Other is in fact not that distant from the Self—a conclusion that may be anxiety-producing to audiences—comes dangerously close to collapsing difference altogether, which is not desirable either. The movie's ethnographic gaze, however, is unexpectedly subtle in its exploration of violence. In this regard, consider the feud that recurs in two other scenes of the movie with interesting twists and turns. In the first one, the Arab army, having crossed the Nefud Desert, meets up with Auda Abu Tayyi, sheikh of the formidable Howeitat. Once again the confrontation takes place at a well; once again the problem is construed as one of "stealing our water." The memory of the tragedy that befell Tafas now makes us catch our breath as in tense anticipation we watch the sheikh and his son descend upon the surprised raiders. Auda slowly makes his way through the hushed throng, challenging each one with a defiant look while facing the barrels of their rifles. He grabs a water skin from one of the bedouin, fixes the entire encampment with a withering look, and then dramatically empties the water on the ground. The men regard him warily, their firearms at the ready. We expect the scene to explode into violence at any moment. Instead of a bloodbath, however, we are treated to a verbal duel, a game of insult and counterinsult, that is supposed to test men's courage and symbolically construct their honor:

> AUDA: (as one who makes an effort of memory, politely to recollect an obscure name, thoughtfully) Harith . . . Ali (his face clears; with exaggerated delicacy) Does your father steal?

This much dialogue is in the production script, but during the filming it was decided to extend the dramatic interchange with the following ripostes:

> ALI: (stiffening slightly at the insult) Does Auda take me for one of his bastards?
>
> AUDA: (regarding his adversary with a sardonic smile) No, there is no resemblance. (He turns) Alas, you resemble your father. I knew your father well.
>
> ALI: (steadily fixing the challenger with a grim and determined look) Did you know your own?
>
> (Auda swings around as if to rush his opponent. Lawrence, dressed in his brilliantly white robes, immediately intervenes.)
>
> LAWRENCE: Auda! We are fifty; you are two. How if we shot you down?
>
> AUDA: Why then you have a blood feud with the Howeitat. Do you desire it?

Auda's mood becomes jocular, and the raiders, sensing that the moment of crisis has passed, let down their rifles with an almost audible sigh of relief and go about their business. Hostility is transmuted into hospitality as the great sheikh invites the Arab army to dine with him at his summer home in magnificent Wadi Rumm.

As in the shoot-out at the Masturah Well, the scene represents the "violence" of the Arab, but this time more subtly, as a *staging* of violence closely connected with notions of male honor. In fact, the practice of the challenge and counterchallenge is well known in tribal societies of the Middle East,[21] and the filmmakers were capturing it (perhaps intentionally, with the help of Omar Sharif, who would have known its cultural logic). The problem of the "honorable" man will become a central motivation of Auda's character: first, his willingness to attack ʿAqaba (on one level the gold he seeks in the strongbox is wealth, on another it is culturally coded as honorable); and then, his desperate search for "something honorable" to replace the junk he has retrieved from the train wreckage—and eventually finds in the prized possession of Arabian thoroughbred horses. Once his motivation in terms of the cultural system is understood (and it may very well not be understood by an audience that does not pick up the clues in the film), he appears less buffoonish.

Connected with blood feud, of course, is the supposed problem of unself-governability, which, according to a Western model of Arab politics, can be solved only by a peacekeeper from *outside* the tribe—that is, someone who transcends the context of the feud. This rhetoric is again an old one of colonial discourse. It is Lawrence, the great white hope, who must intervene between Auda and Ali to prevent the duel from escalating into a bloodbath. His problematical role as peacekeeper becomes pronounced in one scene in particular.

It is nighttime. In the phantasmagoric moonlight, the execution that follows takes on the quality of a nightmare, suggesting that violence is as much within Lawrence's psyche as it is, supposedly, in the society of the Other.

The Arab army assembled by Auda Abu Tayyi, Sherif Ali, and Lawrence pauses in the mountains to prepare for the final assault on 'Aqaba. Ali has taken Lawrence to the brim of the mountain overlooking the twinkling port city to gloat over the possession that seems to be within their grasp, when a shot rings out and the bedouin encampment is thrown into turmoil by murder. The culprit is held for execution, as the law requires. Trying to prevent the escalation of a feud, Lawrence takes the revolver from Sherif Ali's waistband (the same one Lawrence had given Tafas but Sherif Ali had confiscated at the Masturah Well) and then pronounces: "I will execute the Law! I have no tribe and no one is offended!" He turns to face the murderer, only to discover to his horror that he is Gasim, the same man he had saved from certain death in the Nefud Desert. The look of horror deepens on Lawrence's face as he shoots bullet after bullet into Gasim's body and realizes how much he enjoys his sadistic impulses. He flings the pistol away, as if it were an evil fetish, only to see the bedouin scrambling madly for possession of it: it is reintroduced in another round of violence. If the colonial European arrogates to himself the right to govern, on the assumption that peace cannot be obtained in any other way, he is at the same time the perpetrator of violence. Indeed, he may discover, like Conrad's Kurtz, that his high sense of compassion is a chimera.

But the movie is equivocal even on the question of Lawrence's leadership and power. Who has the real power: he or the Arabs? When he tries to assume power over them, do the Arabs accept him? For example, it is Auda who leads the charge on 'Aqaba the next day, and, as the script tells us, "Lawrence [is] following (with the other camel riders) in the wake of the tidal wave he has raised *but cannot lead*" (my emphasis). After the "miracle" of ʿAqaba has been accomplished and Ali tosses Lawrence a victory garland, the latter has trouble grasping it; it has fallen in the surf, where it swirls elusively in and out of his fingers—much to the amusement of his friend. Crossing Sinai with the facetious implication that he is like Moses with the children (an allusion that Auda vocally disapproves of), Lawrence becomes a delusional parent who in the end leads one of his beloved servant boys to his death. He becomes "blind" (by the horror of events that he, an oedipal king, has created) and has to be led by the other surviving boy out of the desert, their roles of "father" and "son" ironically reversed. And when Jackson Bentley accompanies Lawrence on one of his dynamiting missions of the Turkish railway, he is surprised to see that the tribesmen respond less to Lawrence's command than to Auda's to stop firing at the train.

If the movie slyly suggests that Lawrence was not the master of the Arabs, are the Arabs, by contrast, represented as the masters of their own destiny? Surely not, as a viewer of the 1962 film release understood very well in his letter to *The Times* of London:

Sir,

The distorted picture of Lawrence and Allenby in the film *Lawrence of Arabia* has naturally upset their relatives and friends. Equally alarming is the representation of the Arab leaders, except perhaps Feisal, as untrustworthy rogues whose only motive for fighting is greed, and who are so blinded by tribal hatreds that they have no concept of an Arab people for whose freedom they are fighting: indeed Lawrence has to expend much of his energy preventing them from killing one another. . . .

Arab disunity and pettiness reach their peak in the film with the farcical chaos in Damascus Town Hall, there being no hint of the speed with which the crisis was resolved and orderly government restored. The moral would seem to be that the Arabs were (and are?) incapable of any sort of self-government and that the Sykes-Picot Agreement was justified. . . .

It is deeply disturbing that so much money should be available for making a film out of a script which has so little regard for historical truth and for personal or national feelings.

Yours faithfully,
Philip J. Stewart
St. Anthony's College, Oxford[22]

Where I would disagree with the viewer is in his conclusion that the film considers the Sykes-Picot Agreement (i.e., colonialism in the Middle East) "justified." In the film's view, Arab nationalism was frustrated by British refusal to provide heavy artillery in the campaign against the Turks, not to mention technical assistance when it was badly needed in Damascus. As in the earlier *Bridge,* the Other is made to appear dependent on Western technology and therefore vulnerable to colonial domination. We also learn that Allenby has deliberately delayed the arrival of Feisal's train so that the charismatic leader, son of the sharif of Mecca who raised the revolt in the first place, will miss the opening of the town hall meeting and will therefore be unable to rally the Arabs. In other words, the British are seen as conniving mightily to prevent Arab self-rule. Nor is it true that the film singles out greed as the motive for fighting, for we have just seen how "greed" is complicated by the cultural system of honor. But I think it is true, as the viewer sensed, that the film depicts Arab nationalism as being deeply problematical, regardless of extenuating circumstances. In the context of the late 1950s and early 1960s, when the Arab world from Nasser to Arafat was trying to assert its independence from colonial rule, this representation becomes disturbing.

The idea that the Arabs are incapable of self-rule is reinforced in the conversation Ali has with Bentley when the raiders rest briefly in the desert after arduous campaigning against the Turks. Bentley is chuckling over a child's primer on the British Parliament, which Ali has set himself to read. Ali explains that he is trying to learn politics in order that the Arabs might form a democracy, an idea that Bentley finds preposterous. In the Western view, Arabs must put themselves in a tutelary relationship vis-à-vis the outsider, the westerner, the colonizer, in order to learn democracy. (This, after all, was one of the things the "Protectorates" were supposed to accomplish after World War I). Ali adds that Lawrence is his "teacher." The comment is highly ironic, for in the immediately preceding scene Lawrence has been depicted in fascist colors. On top of a dynamited train which the bedouin are looting, he is seen striding in his boots, the cheers of "Aurens! Aurens! Aurens!" reverberating all around him. This is the man who says to Bentley that he will obtain "freedom" for the Arabs.

In the absence of any hopeful representation of Arab nationalism, the final image of Sherif Ali—the one who will "try politics"—disappearing into total darkness is both arresting and deeply disturbing, as are the words of Auda flung after him: "Being an Arab will be thornier than you think!—Harith!" Factionalism is the last word. Banish hope, Lean and

Bolt seem to say, cynically: the Arabs are as incapable of self-rule as the British are of renouncing their colonial possessions.

I sat in a darkened movie theater, watching and listening to the audiences as much as I did the screen. They laughed out loud at the sly gibes at colonialism when Brighton, for example, explained why Britain is a "great" country or when Feisal deflated Bentley's rhetoric about America's support for colonial peoples. To me, however, it was uncanny how the story on the screen seemed to have parallels to the Gulf War. Stormin' Norman as a combination of Allenby and Lawrence, with His Royal Highness Prince Khalid bin Sultan al-Saud, commander of the Multinational Joint Combat Group, taking the role of Sherif Ali! In fact, as we would later find out from reading Schwarzkopf's memoirs, the general liked to think of himself (only half humorously) as Peter O'Toole cavorting in Lawrence's desert robes, thus inviting the comparison between a narrative about the Gulf and this particular movie.

In fact, the press generated a fair amount of interest in Lawrence during the Gulf War. Besides the *New York Times* article quoted at the beginning of this chapter, editorials in a number of newspapers placed the blame for the crisis in the Middle East on the political settlements established in the area by none other than T. E. Lawrence. The November 1990 issue of a national magazine catering to men, *M, Inc.: The Civilized Man,* included the Augustus John portrait of Lawrence on its front cover along with the headline: "Desert Warriors: Why Are We in Saudi Arabia? Blame Lawrence." On the television news millions of people could hear a soldier flatteringly compare himself to Lawrence of Arabia trudging in the desert. It is plausible, then, to assume that an analogy had been established, whether negative or positive, in the minds of some of the public between the Gulf War and Lawrence's involvement in the Near East. It happened at this time that the reconstruction of the movie *Lawrence of Arabia* was still playing in select movie houses around the country. What follows is an admittedly speculative reading of the movie as an allegorical text on the events and personalities of the Gulf War.

Take, as a first parallel, the problem of atrocities. During the height of the Gulf War there were conflicting and unconfirmed reports about Iraqi treatment of civilians and prisoners of war. Downed allied pilots were shown on television, and it was not clear whether their bruises and battered faces were the result of crash landings or of punishment inflicted by Iraqi interrogators. And what happened to the female POWs? We imagined the worst because of the grizzly stories that had already come out of Kuwait of rape, torture, and execution of civilians.

Until now, I have not remarked on the extent to which the representations of the Turks in this movie are more Other than those of the Arabs. Hauntingly, the movie constructs the malevolence of the Turks in the same way that we demonized the Iraqi soldiers. Already in Bentley's interview with Feisal, their cruelty is foreshadowed by dire warnings about the Turkish treatment of Arab prisoners. Thus, as Feisal informs the reporter, the Arabs prefer to kill their own wounded rather than have them captured alive. These fears are acted upon when we later see Lawrence execute Farraj, who has been mortally wounded by an exploding detonator, and our fears are then confirmed when we see Lawrence brutally beaten and presumably raped in the Turkish Citadel.

From the very beginning of the Gulf War air offensive, we were aware of the fact that Iraqi military positions in Kuwait were being "pounded" more heavily than any army in history. The aim was to kill tens of thousands of Iraqi troops, hopefully of the elite Republican Guard, in order to make it easier for our allied forces to penetrate defensive positions at a minimum loss of life to *our* side. Meanwhile, photographs appeared in U.S. papers showing Iraqis surrendering with their hands high in the air to "merciful" U.S. soldiers (figure 17).

Again, the parallels in the movie are uncannily exact with the addition, however, of irony to undercut the Western moral position. During General Allenby's "big push" to Damascus, he holds a briefing in which artillery officers are ordered to keep Turkish defenses under constant bombardment. His fists hit the blackboard on which the positions of the armies have been drawn in chalk, and he exhorts the artillery general, "Pound them, Charley, pound them." There is a cut to a horizon flashing with artillery fire, and we hear the distant, thunderous sounds of explosions. Our moral attitude toward this strategy of saturated bombing is complicated by what we see next—Lawrence looking at the horizon with an indifferent stare, all the while spinning the bullet chamber of his revolver. It is the Arab Sherif Ali, not the Englishman, who shows compassion:

ALI (softly): God help the men who lie under that.
LAWRENCE (flippantly): They're Turks!
ALI (stubbornly): God help them.

Figure 17.   Iraqi soldier in Gulf War surrendering to an American soldier
(courtesy of the Department of Defense).

After the beating and rape in the Turkish Citadel, Lawrence may not be
in a compassionate mood, but that fact does not excuse his racist remark.

In his interview with Prince Feisal, Bentley commits the faux pas of
implying that the Arabs' compassion toward the Turks must be due to
Lawrence's influence. Feisal is furious at the suggestion that Arabs have
to learn compassion from a westerner. He cynically observes: "With Major Lawrence, mercy is a passion. With me it is merely good manners.
You may be the judge which motive is the more reliable." Of course, all
of Part Two is directed toward showing Lawrence (and the British) to be
the opposite of what Bentley presumes them to be.

The climax of Lawrence's journey into his heart of darkness comes in
the massacre of a Turkish column. We see a bedouin village recently laid
to waste in its wake. While Lawrence is importuned by Sherif Ali to go
around the column in order to beat the British in the race to Damascus,
his cutthroat mercenaries want him to attack and take "no prisoners."
Though a struggle with his conscience ensues, he eventually succumbs
to his sadomasochistic impulse and his desire to avenge his humiliation

in Deraa. What follows is one of the most gruesome scenes in the film. Most horrible of all—completely undercutting the construction of compassion—are the images of Lawrence laughingly committing wanton acts of killing, culminating in the shooting at point-blank range of a Turkish soldier surrendering to him with his hands held high in the air (see figure 10).

A slight digression is worth pursuing here regarding the filmmakers' representation of this scene. Lawrence's biographer Liddell Hart criticized Robert Bolt for his interpretation of the events described in *Seven Pillars of Wisdom*, claiming, "You seem to me to have been unduly influenced by his account of the [no prisoners] sequel to the Turkish atrocities in [the village of] Tafas."[23] Replying to Hart in a letter dated November 22, 1962, Bolt defended his decision: "One of the things that have most irritated me in accounts of Lawrence has been the tendency of writers to put this Tafas business down as one incident among others and walk away from it. It simply won't do. . . . It seems to me to do less than justice to the man to whitewash this; all this whitewashing belittles; it denies the man his whole stature and by implication lessens the pain (the inner pain I mean) which he must have borne. And as you say, he suffered revulsion afterwards. Of course he did. And before, too. That is my point."[24] What Bolt is getting at, it seems to me, is that moment of self-knowledge when Lawrence understands the worst about himself, a moment captured at the end of this scene when he peers at his own image in the bloody blade of his dagger. This is the visual equivalent of Kurtz's moment of truth in *Heart of Darkness:* "He cried in a whisper at some image, at some vision—he cried out twice, a cry that was no more than a breath: 'The horror! The horror!'"[25]

Perhaps no other images coming out of the Gulf War echoed this scene of massacre in the movie more profoundly than the televised pictures of the "Highway of Death"—a four-lane road in Kuwait used by the Iraqis to flee the allied advance. We saw smoldering heaps of metal, the remains of thousands of vehicles in which many Iraqis had died. General Schwarzkopf later tried to mitigate the magnitude of the carnage by claiming that "most [Iraqi soldiers] had jumped out of their vehicles and run away."[26] He "thought, but didn't say, that the best thing the White House could do would be to turn off the damned TV in the situation room."[27] Whatever consternation these images may have engendered in the public's conscience was soon dissipated. Denial set in.

The official number of Iraqi dead was a matter of political controversy for many months, and our nation as a whole has still refused to come to terms with the devastating aftermath of the war. "Smart bombs" supposedly hit military targets with pinpoint precision (except when they didn't, of course, which is when the Iraqis were blamed for having moved civilians into range of military targets). But the virtual collapse of the country's infrastructure produced tremendous strains on the provision of health care, sanitation, food and water supplies, and other essentials, no doubt endangering the health and lives of many civilians, especially children. The echo of such heartlessness comes in the movie when Allenby refuses to give technical assistance, particularly of the medical kind, to help the wounded in Damascus, his aim being to cause a general collapse of the infrastructure and thereby exacerbate the crisis in the political system. Lawrence is not to be spared the sight of the wretches in the fly-ridden Turkish hospital, one of whom—already more a ghost than a live human being—begs him for water.

The movie ends with a soldier returning home, a soldier whose face is obscured by a dusty windscreen. How many U.S. soldiers returned from the Gulf War, having seen the worst happen to Iraqi soldiers, surrounded and badly outgunned, but unwilling or unable to talk about their nightmares with their loved ones and friends who would want to deny the extent of devastation? It was, sadly, as though this movie spoke more honestly and painfully of this war than any representations of it emanating from the government or the press.

The title of this chapter, "An Anti-Imperialist, Orientalist Epic," was meant to be paradoxical. How can an orientalist discourse be "anti-imperialist" when Edward Said has argued that orientalism is imperialist by definition because its discourses inevitably and ineluctably represent other peoples in ways that legitimate and hence facilitate the West's domination over them? I have not doubted the validity or importance of Said's criticism, as much as I have tried to amend it by suggesting ways in which discourses produced in the imperial culture—and, even more surprisingly, discourses such as Hollywood epic film—are capable of criticizing the very hegemonic projects they represent. This capacity for self-criticism, I argue, should be taken seriously.

To some postcolonial critics, Lean and Bolt's film will not have gone far enough in its critique of the colonialist venture, precisely because it does not question its representation of the Other as rigorously as it may expose the moral ambiguities of the Western heroic self and the baseness of the Great Game. They might aver that the critiques of the filmmakers are no more than a symptom of a late liberal conscience trying to assuage its guilt over Europe's imperialist past. I obviously would disagree with that assessment as being too easily dismissive of the political complexities of discourse and representation. To be sure, the film is anti-imperialist within the constraints of the historical (post-Suez) and cultural (angry young men) contexts from which it emerged. Sadly enough, as we saw in the Gulf War, it continues to have moral relevance to our colonialist involvement in the Middle East today.

CHAPTER 6

Maskulinities

Puzzling for some, our tradition of girls being boys and men
being women as they are in our old ways of Christmas pan-
tomime. Deliciously sexy, though, a man's doublet and hose
when filled with the limbs and body of a fine woman . . .
Deeper, yet more playful still, the gorgeous sexual ambivalences Shakespeare so saltily, sweetly gives us with his Viola,
say, or his Rosalind; girls played by boys playing women playing men, romantically confounding both women and men
alike, telling us, the audience, to see what we will and to take
it as we like it. Delightful, sublimely funny, moving glimpses
of the frailties of our human condition.

> *Peter O'Toole,* Loitering with Intent

The older men in the American military establishment and
government did betray the younger men in Vietnam, lying
about the nature of the war, remaining in safe places themselves, after having asked the young men to be warriors and
then in effect sending them out to be ordinary murderers.
And so the demons have had a lot to work with in recent
American history. The demons urge all young men to see
Lawrence of Arabia . . . [because it reminds] us how corrupt all men in authority are and how they betray the
young male idealist.

> *Robert Bly,* Iron John

The fact that Lawrence was represented in this movie as a complex person, not conventionally masculine in the way that American culture
tends to straitjacket boys, was deeply, if probably also only unconsciously, satisfying to me when I was a teenager. Those attitudes that my
older sisters inculcated in me—compassion, an appreciation for beauty,
an emotional openness risking vulnerability—were not culturally coded
as masculine in the early 1960s, just the reverse perhaps; and yet they

were ambiguously incarnated in the character who kept my attention riveted on the screen. Like him, I had little interest in sports and did not play them hard, which, I admitted ruefully to myself, already marked me as slightly less than a "man." I overheard my father once ask my mother with chagrin, "Always his head in a book: why doesn't he play sports with the other boys?" My father had been an avid reader all his life and could appreciate my immersion in a good read, but he had also been a star football player in high school. "Because he finds sports boring," my mother answered him very much to the point, if not to his satisfaction. My flair was for the stage, not the gridiron, which is one reason I found the sheer theatricality of Peter O'Toole's performance in the starring role so exhilarating. But I had developed my talent, such as it was, ambivalently, suspecting that it tarnished my masculine image more, not less. When I looked into the mirror, it seemed to me that I was plagued with something worse than acne. Without the benefit of the classic lines defining culturally coded "masculine strength"—square-cut jaw, straight nose—which made O'Toole's face masculine, I seemed feminine by comparison. Since *Lawrence of Arabia* was planned and executed in a period of increased questioning of male identity and sexuality, it is reasonable to suppose that the movie can be read on one level as being about the issues of gender and sexuality that occupied the imaginations of the British (and American) male and female moviegoing public.

In this chapter I offer speculative readings of men and women caught in different historical moments of Euro-American culture who might have seen the movie and reacted to it. They are *my* constructions of their audience positions based as much as possible on available data from reviews by critics, letters from individual viewers, interviews with specific spectators, my ethnographic observations in theaters where the movie was shown, and hints provided by fashions or parodies the film has inspired over the years.

The readings are intended to be dialectical in the sense discussed more fully in previous chapters. The spectator position of someone informed by a particular ideology (be it feminism or gay liberation) may lead to a particular criticism of the culture industry as producing works representing a socially hegemonic worldview. While I am sympathetic to such criticisms, I do not find them always to be adequate readings of particular works in question, especially works that are intellectually complex, artistically ambitious, and morally engrossing like *Lawrence of Arabia*. Such works may contain profound ambivalences toward their hegemonic projects, sometimes even detailed criticisms of them, that destabilize dominant representations of gender or sexuality and open up rather than shut down the possibilities of contesting dominant positions. I contend that *Lawrence of Arabia* has to be read dialectically where gender and sexuality are concerned, at one and the same time representing certain dominant forms of masculinity and yet distancing itself from them, as if to critique them. The possibilities as well as limits of that criticism intrigue me.

O'Toole's performance, which embodied the ambiguities and anxieties of a "warring" masculinity (captured by his "hysterical male" look), had a history in the cinema. According to Marcia Landy, the post–World War II period through the 1950s saw "British cinema's increasing concern with the problematic nature of masculinity and of male relationships."[1] She points out that the male protagonists of the melodramas dating from that period were conflicted in their loyalties to class, honor, and duty and tormented psychologically by questions of their male identity and sexuality. "Marginal types" (such as working-class men, toughs, Don Juans, and, in a more disguised way, gays) became representative of men in the cinema. "In many of the postwar films, in particular," Landy comments, "the motif of troubled male identity manifests itself . . . in films that increasingly explore, if only covertly, men's relationships with each other."[2]

The character of Lawrence is also both like and unlike the representations of conventional masculinity in American film.[3] On the one hand he stands for the white bourgeois ideal of manhood: tall, blond, blue-eyed, and handsome; not to mention, of course, also courageous and hardy. He is of a tough-man type we are familiar with in Hollywood cinema through the performances of such actors as John Wayne, Jimmy Stewart, and Clint Eastwood. However, Landy points out a difference between American and British epic or historical films that is important in grasping the way the heroic male would have been received by culturally different audiences, at least in the postwar period through the 1950s:

> As we have seen in the films of empire, the British cinema of the 1930s reveals very few instances of the physically forceful, supervirile male hero so characteristic of American cinema. Ruggedness would seem out of place in the upper-middle-class dramas, in which too much brawn is vulgar, perhaps because associated with the working-class male. . . . The emphasis is more on wit and ingenuity than on physical prowess, owing in part to censorship strictures governing representations of violence, but even more to the British cin-

ema's overwhelming focus on middle-class protagonists, in contrast to Holly-wood cinema.[4]

Lean's *Bridge on the River Kwai* exemplifies these culturally distinct representations through two kinds of heroes: the American William Holden, whose muscular torso is photographed shirtless throughout much of the movie and is subtly coded as "natural" or "virile"; and the British Alec Guiness, who is possessed of endurance more than physical strength, always in uniform, relentlessly principled, the very icon of the "civilized" man (though this last reference becomes heavily ironic by the end of the movie). The character of Lawrence is coded more in line with British conventional cinema's notion of the heroic gentleman, and as a result American audiences might interpret him as being more, not less, effete or "feminine."

In the movie Lawrence rebels against hierarchy and rigid conventions, a trait that was marked in the characters played, for example, by James Dean (especially in *Rebel Without a Cause* [1955]) and Marlon Brando. *Lawrence of Arabia* begins with a famous motorcycle scene, and one suspects that *MAD Magazine,* in its 1964 parody "Flawrence of Arabia," was not the first or last to interpret this as an allusion to Marlon Brando's *The Wild One* (1953). British cinema had its counterparts, of course. One of the most intriguing was Dirk Bogarde (who in fact came very close to playing Lawrence in an aborted film project of the mid-fifties). In the same period the notion of the "angry young man" was constructed in British theater, as in John Osbourne's immensely popular play *Look Back in Anger* (1957). Its protagonist, Jimmy Porter, rails against bourgeois conventionality and conformism, as represented by his hapless wife's family, and laments the fact that a man has no significant role to play in a world where "great causes" (for example, imperialism) no longer exist. He execrates the class system and excoriates the button-downed emotions of middle-class society. While we might well be dismayed by the misogyny he betrays, the fierceness of his attack on what would come to be known as the "establishment" anticipated the sentiments of the countercultural generation, male and female, of the sixties.

The angry young man was not the only important masculine construct to emerge in the postwar period that questioned and threatened masculine ideals of conventionality, emotional self-containment or invulnerability, classism, and so forth; there were the equally potent cul-

tural icons of the "outsider" and the "stranger" or the "alienated self."
A number of important literary works were responsible for these constructions: Colin Wilson's *The Outsider* (1956), a runaway best-seller,
was one, as were also Jean-Paul Sartre's plays, such as *No Exit*, or Albert
Camus's *The Stranger,* which became compulsory reading in many college and even high school courses in the late fifties through the sixties.
Wilson's book, for example, professes to explore in literature and philosophy a type of person (always male), the outsider, who considers
everyday life to be unreal and alienating, and who searches vainly for
some spiritual purpose. Interestingly, T. E. Lawrence becomes an icon
in the book for Wilson's outsider. Echoes of the "outsider" and the
"stranger" can be heard throughout Robert Bolt's screenplay of the
movie. Lawrence, as we already know, does not see himself as fitting
into conventional society, or British culture, because he thinks he is "different." Others, too, see him as a social misfit. While serving in the army
he deliberately flouts hierarchical rules and regulations, thereby earn-
ing the hearty contempt of his commanding officers. "You're a clown,
Lawrence," one of them pronounces. And he makes himself unpopular
not only by trying to challenge the racist prejudices of his fellow officers
but also by identifying with the cultural, subaltern Other, as when in
conversation with Brighton in the officers' mess he explains, with a heavy
note of irony, who has taken ʿAqaba. "The wogs have. *We* have," and
he then pointedly defends the boy Farraj against the abuse of the other
officers in the bar. In the beginning of the movie, Lawrence may appear
to embody the Sartrean vision of the 1950s existential hero who can
choose freely and take responsibility for his actions (after all, he proudly
asserts to his Arab friends that "nothing is written," to counteract their
supposedly fatalistic Muslim beliefs), but with accelerating panic he begins to realize that he is being manipulated by psychological and historical forces he only dimly discerns, much less can control. He is nearly
driven insane by the contradiction between two images that might
equally represent him: the hero who fashions his own destiny and the
puppet whose strings are pulled by its imperial masters.

There is also a certain "feminizing" of the male in this film that, as I
will argue more fully, complicates issues of sixties masculinity. Obviously, differences in and problems of reception loom large here. Some
male and female spectators would have culturally coded the traits of in-
tellectualness, sensitivity, introspection, and passivity in men as "feminine" (as I did in the early sixties), while others would have simply placed
them within an alternative model of manhood. Some male and female

spectators, myself included, would have found some validation for these traits in O'Toole's sensitive and nuanced screen performance. Others would have found his performance unnerving and would have distanced their own male identity from its implications, as I think, for example, the creators of the special issue of *MAD Magazine* expected their readers to do. There is the added complication of what happened to cultural constructions of male and female from the 1970s through the 1980s. The previously mentioned traits may have seemed more "feminine" in men for audiences of the early sixties, still caught up in fairly rigidly polarized conventions of masculinity, than for audiences of the seventies who had by then experienced women's and gay men's liberations, as well as some talk in the immediate aftermath of Vietnam of developing the "feminine" and "maternal" in men as a corrective to the homicidally violent "masculine." For example, it is often forgotten that the guru of the men's "mythopoetic" movement, Robert Bly, was one of the most ardent proponents of this "feminizing" of the male in the late seventies. In the 1980s, as these ideological movements gained momentum and strength, they were greeted, as some feminists have argued, by backlashes of various sorts, which manifested themselves in the cinema through a "remasculinized" image of America, as seen, for example, in the *Rambo* series.[5] The male was still tough, and in the figure of the Vietnam vet he was certainly marginal, but the ambiguously masculine, ambiguously heroic character had all but vanished. At the end of this chapter I will examine the possibility that the 1990s may bring another transformation of the cultural conception of the masculine. There I will try to "read" the character of Lawrence in terms of the spectator position of men involved in the contemporary men's movement.

On the surface, of course, this movie is not like the predecessors Landy describes, particularly in its glaring absence of female characters (women are fleetingly seen only four times, though one of these occasions is also one of the movie's most moving and visually beautiful scenes—the farewell of the desert raiders as they journey toward 'Aqaba). One could argue that a story about Lawrence among the bedouin in the desert would not leave much room for women in the first place, but that is to bind the moviemakers to a literalism they never scrupled to obey. To some women (and men) in the audience, this absence can be a source of either consternation or simply boredom, as heard in the complaint that it may be hard for women to identify with a movie in which female characters are absent. The subtler and more interesting point can be made that the category "woman" is always present—and not less so in narratives produced and controlled by men. As Eve Kosofsky Sedgwick, for one, has pointed out, the male homosocial world may in fact on some unconscious level be all about women.[6]

In what, perhaps oblique ways, then, might the "female" be present in this movie? Some male and female spectators, myself included, have commented that they can identify with the main character as portrayed by Peter O'Toole because he is feminized. "In a film where women are conspicuous by their absence, Lawrence—pale, effeminate, a blond and blue-eyed seraph—becomes a surrogate woman, a figurative white goddess," observes one of this film's most astute critics.[7] One wonders to what extent women of the early sixties could have placed themselves imaginatively *in* his figure and his narrative. Take, for example, the 1962 comments of the respected critic of the *Sunday Observer,* Penelope Gilliat: "In the performance Peter O'Toole gives, there seem to be at least ten incompatible men living under the same skin, and two or three women as well. . . . When he puts on a Sherif's robes for the first time and does an entranced ballet with himself in the desert, it made me think more than ever that one of the reasons for Lawrence's passion for Arab life might well have been that it allowed him to wear a skirt."[8] Here a woman, and one suspects she was not alone, could see a "woman" inside O'Toole's performance.

What traits in O'Toole's characterization of Lawrence might have been culturally coded for (some) American and British audiences as "feminine" in the early sixties? He is, for example, intensely aesthetic (it is implied that he writes poetry, appreciates fine art) and intellectual, even academic (he knows several languages and has memorized the Qur'an), a fact noted by General Murray with barely concealed contempt ("I know you've been well educated, Lawrence; it says so in your dossier. . . . You're the kind of creature I can't stand"). Above all, he is deeply, one might even say morbidly, introspective, and as he comes to understand the darker aspects of his nature, particularly his sadomasochism and megalomania, he sinks into horror and despair, becoming not simply vulnerable but supremely passive.

Other aspects of his character are even more unequivocally stereotyped as womanly or girlish in American culture. For example, O'Toole delivers his lines in a soft-spoken voice, a feature of his performance that did not go unnoticed by critics at the time of the film's release. Nor did it go unnoticed by me. I have always had a soft voice, a drawback in the theater or in a debate tournament, for which I compensated by develop-

ing a very clear enunciation, thus in a sense redoubling the effect of fem-
ininity, or so I thought when it would sometimes be greeted as "speaking like a girl." Of Peter O'Toole's voice in his performance as Lawrence
a critic said, "His voice is . . . lowpitched, curiously flat, and repressed,
more in a feminine than in an effeminate way." [9]

Many critics and moviegoers uniformly praised O'Toole for his good
looks while acknowledging that he was not handsome in a conventional
sense. Stanley Kaufman, for one, noted that O'Toole has "an interesting, expressive face—a face that is strong yet, *in a valuable sense,* feminine." [10] Presumably, "effeminate" would imply homosexual and something not necessarily positive to this reviewer at that time (the early
sixties), whereas "feminine"—which both critics emphasize in their description of O'Toole's physiognomy—would be "valuable," though in
just what sense of that word is unclear. To be noted, too, is the bottle-
blond hair O'Toole is given in certain scenes, particularly in the desert,
and the mascara around his eyes. Both of these cosmetic touches can
be justified on grounds of verisimilitude—after all, the desert sun does
bleach hair to an abnormal paleness, and the bedouin do line their eye-
lids with antimony for protection against flies and dirt—but the point
is the reception of his appearance for a movie audience: the effect of the
makeup is, I think, to feminize him.

For one critic, the voice, appearance, and mannerisms were so ambiguous, and presumably threatening, that he spoke disparagingly of
"O'Toole's tormented hermaphrodite." [11] O'Toole admitted when filming was completed, "The clothes were so comfortable I practically turned
into a transvestite! I thought I'd literally end up running around in a
nightie for the rest of my days." [12] The remark is both defensive, playful,
and deep. As an emerging international movie star, he must have known
that he was taking risks with audience receptions in his sexually ambiguous interpretation of Lawrence. In the interview he was obviously
distancing his identity from that of the character on the screen. If one
bears in mind the epigraph to this chapter, however, the remark becomes deeper than one might suppose. In it O'Toole suggests that cross-
dressing not only was part of the history of the English stage of which
he, at the time, was one of its emerging stars, but also was deeply woven
into British culture. "Puzzling for some," he muses, "our tradition of
girls being boys and men being women," and then mischievously adds
the admonition "to see what we will and to take it as we like it."

One way to view gender, as Penelope Gilliat sees it, is that Lawrence
was a man who wanted to play at being a woman. However, it is not just

a question of O'Toole wearing flowing robes that would appear feminine, at moments even bridal, to a Western (though not an Arab) audience; he poses and exhibits himself in them like a model, and exclusively
for his admiring *male* companions—thus placing himself in the subject
position of the female whose image is constructed in the controlling gaze
of the male spectator.[13] Whatever one might think of the psychological
explanation for the male gaze, the insight is important, and I mean to
appropriate it anthropologically. Mary Ann Doane has argued convinc-
ingly, for example, that the look in cinema carries with it *culturally*
constructed gender differences.[14] That is, men arrogate for themselves
the power of gazing at women, and female gender in turn is constructed
by them as "to-be-looked-at-ness" (to quote Mulvey). At least until
the late 1960s, perhaps even later, it has been the male look in the cinema that has been challenging and controlling. The female's, with the
possible exception of the vamp's, has been culturally constrained from
looking at men. At best the female could gaze at her own reflection
(i.e., narcissistically)—hence the prevalence of mirrors with female characters—or to look away; literally to stare into (empty) space. In her
study of Rudolph Valentino, Miriam Hansen shows how this movie star's
roles were ambiguously male insofar as his look could gain mastery over
female characters, while his body simultaneously enacted an exhibitionism, a "to-be-looked-at-ness," that is culturally coded as female.[15]

One of the most famous scenes in *Lawrence of Arabia* encapsulates
all of these gender codes to perfection. Lawrence has just been given his
white Arab robes by Sherif Ali and is encircled by tribesmen who gaze
admiringly at his slowly turning figure, uttering their heartfelt compli-
ments. There "she" is: the female, and a fetishized object she certainly
appears to be in her brilliantly white robes that simultaneously place
Lawrence among their kind and yet set him apart and elevated. There
"she" is, constructed in the gaze of the encircling males. When Sherif Ali
tells Lawrence that the robes are "good for riding" (as though an excuse
were needed for him to indulge in exhibitionism), he tries them on and
then canters off on his mount. As soon as he thinks he is out of eye-
shot, he alights from his camel and strides across the desert floor. Now
O'Toole renders the metaphor of a cross-dressing performance more
blatant. He turns around, takes out his dagger, and then admires his
reflection in the blade, adjusting his headgear in a kind of vain after-
thought. Here is embodied the culturally encoded gesture of the narcissistic female gazing at her own reflection. However, the fact that the mirror is displaced onto a dagger links the narcissism with specifically male

anxieties about sexual potency. Satisfied with what he sees, O'Toole decisively slaps the dagger back into its sheath, as though masculinity, endangered by gender ambiguities, may nevertheless be put securely back in its place.

From gazing at his reflection, he now turns to admire his shadow on the ground, giving a deep bow and saluting it. The image is of Narcissus kissing his own reflection. When O'Toole then spreads out his cloak as if to fly off into the wind and sun, enacting another mythical image of the male, he is embarrassed to be caught playacting by Sheikh Auda Abu Tayyi, who has obviously been observing his antics all along. The camera angle, which aligns the audience's viewing with the perspective of the sheikh, deeply implicates us in this act of voyeurism. The audience may be constructed as "male" by the cinema apparatus (according to Mulvey's formulation), insofar as we gaze upon the fetishized object from a male point of view represented quite specifically in this scene by Auda, but since we have been identifying with Lawrence, an anatomical male, while at the same time becoming attracted to *her* image, does not a dominant or hegemonic representation of the masculine become suddenly unstable?

If my interpretation is correct, we might look for some evidence of audience reception to this destabilizing of the hegemonically masculine. Such evidence is a line of women's haute couture suggested by the film. It is in fact quite common for major films to inspire imitations in the fashion industry. What is interesting in this example is that an all-male film should inspire a line of women's fashions. One costume combined the turban and flowing lines of the Arab outfit, emphasizing what would appear to be more sensually "feminine" (figure 18). The other is a mannish army/colonial look complete with topee hat, khaki uniform, and—appropriately enough for this movie about sadism—a whip (figure 19). On the one hand, these fashion statements impute a (dominant, powerful) masculine to the female; on the other, they incarnate an orientalizing representation of the Arab as feminine. What is muted, it seems to me, is the gender anxiety the film might arouse in white, Euro-American males (unless one reacts to these fashions as high camp), an anxiety that I think becomes more obvious in the next example from popular culture, the parody of the film made by *MAD Magazine* (figure 20).[16] The cartoon shows Peter O'Toole playing Lawrence "in drag," with two Arabs watching his performance in the background. Here we have an influential satire magazine of 1950s and 1960s American popular culture constructing Lawrence's character as "feminine," and even more obvi-

Figure 18.   Fashions inspired by
Lawrence of Arabia.

Figure 19.   More fashions inspired by *Lawrence of Arabia.*

ously as "homosexual," by its reference to an ingenue in a famous Broadway musical whose supposedly narcissistic and feminine character she expresses in song. Whereas the male cartoonists at *MAD Magazine* and their primarily male, teenage audience seemed unable to contain their gender panic, displacing their hysteria onto a caricatured Lawrence and a homosexual Arab, O'Toole, I think bravely, resisted succumbing to the temptation of high camp, in order to treat seriously the question of gender ambiguity.

If we accept this interpretation—that Lawrence is like "women" in some important respects—then what does this profoundly androgynous figure "do" for or to hegemonic representations? It has, of course, been

Figure 20.   *MAD Magazine*'s parody "Flawrence of Arabia" (MAD Magazine and all related elements are trademarks of E. C. Publications, Inc. © 1964. All rights reserved. Used with permission.)

remarked before that the representations of male heroes sometimes incorporate feminine traits in order that they might triumph all the more completely in their projects of conquest and domination. Tania Modleski, for example, has made this point about Sir John Menier, the protagonist in Alfred Hitchcock's *Murder!,* when she remarks that "Sir John immerses himself in the 'feminine' element and allows it to control him so that he can achieve the appropriate mastery over appearances." [17] A somewhat similar observation was made about the representations of Lawrence as they appeared in Lowell Thomas's best-selling boys' adventure book.[18] In his perceptive study of that work, Graham Dawson notes, "These evocations of a feminine Lawrence—which perform no necessary narrative function—add another dimension to the fantasy of Lawrence as the man who has everything." [19] It is difficult to apply such an interpretation to the representations of Lawrence in the film, however, for the simple reason that we see him destroyed in the end rather than triumphant. In other words, there is nothing to suggest that the feminine is particularly empowering. Could, then, Lawrence's feminization be construed as a contributing cause to his downfall? Could a male audience console itself with the thought that if Lawrence had only kept his gender narrowly male, he would not have gotten himself into such trouble in the first place? There is very little question, I think, that that *is* the way the cartoonists of a magazine like *MAD* intended their readers to respond, and yet the film allows for subtler spectator reactions. I remember my own, which I briefly sketched in the beginning of this chapter. At that time in my life I thought of myself as more introspective than other boys of my age, a result I attributed to the influence of my much older sisters. One could argue that by the end of the movie Lawrence's feminine side as evinced in his introspection is his only redeeming feature, even though it is not enough to "save" him or make him whole again, one of the female's thankless roles in traditional male narratives.

What might be the possible ways in which women could identify with O'Toole's Lawrence? On one level, of course, there is no reason to suppose that they would see O'Toole's performance as anything but masculine, his attractiveness enhanced by the fact that he offers an alternative to the tough, silent, and invulnerable John Wayne image: handsome but delicate, aggressive but sensitive, a man of action yet articulate and reflective, able to confess his weaknesses and his sufferings, and so forth. For some women in the early sixties, ambitious to assume new roles both in the workforce and at home, it might be easier to imagine their lives with such a man for a partner or lover. To other women, expecting and relishing a more conventionally masculine characterization, the feminine side of O'Toole's portrayal might appear less appealing than odd. But suppose that there might be some women who could identify his character as a "woman" (in opposition to a feminized male); what, then, does gender ambiguity do for such women spectators of a film about war and politics, the classical preserves of the male story? The movie would suggest that wo/men—striding as conquerors across the world—should take heed of their fate, for s/he will be betrayed, brutalized, and possibly raped by men.

There is a way of developing such a reading—of Lawrence as a woman moving through a malevolent male world—by examining a text that in many ways suggests the same possibility. The text is *She Went to War* (1992), by Major Rhonda Cornum, who served in the Gulf War and was captured by Iraqi soldiers, one of whom, she later charged in congressional testimony on sexual harassment, had attempted to rape her.

Rhonda Cornum represents herself in her book as an "independent" though not radically feminist woman ("Women in our family did not burn their bras, they just went out and did what they wanted to do")[20] and "masculinized" female ("The women, as well as the men, were to be strong and in control").[21] By her own admission, she loves "to go fast" in cars and airplanes, and is intrigued rather than intimidated by complex machinery. Like Lawrence in the first third of the movie, she romanticizes war as an "adventure": "The entire experience of the war was a challenge that will be tough to match: deploying to the desert, caring for so many soldiers, fighting a war, and surviving as a prisoner. When I was a girl, I remember fantasizing about being lost in the wild and having to survive. . . . In my imagination I was like Robinson Crusoe, and being stranded alone was not horrible; it was fun, a challenge. I wanted the ultimate challenge, something where the stakes were higher than a game of cards." [22] She worries that if she had stayed at home during the Gulf War, her daughter would have thought her a "wimp." [23] Indeed, when her husband, also a medical officer serving in the air force during the Gulf War, calls home to speak with his daughter, she petulantly complains, "You and Mother are over there having fun and getting to play war, and I'm up here." [24] One is inevitably reminded of the scene early in the movie when Lawrence is given his assignment to go to Arabia and says to his mentor, "Thanks, Dryden. It's going to be fun." Cornum's mother confesses to having been scared at the thought of war even though everyone, her daughter included, thought her to be too "macho." [25] She declares, "I wanted to go to war to test myself," [26] and indeed, if there is one thing that seems to characterize a "constant" in her life it "has been a burning desire to do the best, to seek new challenges and conquer them." [27] As feminist critic Jean Bethke Elshtain has pointed out, there is a long though not well-known history of women warriors who, like Rhonda Cornum, have also been loving wives and devoted mothers. [28]

In spite of the fact that the terms in which she describes herself have been traditionally coded as masculine, [29] Cornum nevertheless claims to be a gender-neutral soldier in a more or less gender-neutral army—a claim that might well stretch our credulity. "That's how the army is: when we're busy doing our jobs, it doesn't matter to anyone if I'm a woman or a man. We're all soldiers; or as they say in the army, we're all green." [30] It is interesting to note that the same argument about neutrality could not and would not be made for sexuality by people representing the army's views. For instance, the assertion would not work if one substituted "if I'm gay or straight" in place of "if I'm a woman or a man."

Of course, as Cornum observes with regret, this supposed gender neutrality does not extend to combat, where women are still not allowed to serve "equally" with men and share in the glory as well as in the danger and pain. This presents her with a paradox, for, as she explains in a letter to her mother, "going into combat is the real reason people stay in the army. . . . it is a personal test to see if you have the 'right stuff.'" [31] In other words, there is not necessarily anything wrong with war except for the fact that women have not been allowed to test themselves in it as men have. She carries this gender-neutral tale (which in my view is really a hypermasculinist saga of self-fashioning to which all, male and female, are supposed to conform) to extreme lengths.[32]

The story that Rhonda Cornum tells, a story about a highly intelligent and superbly trained woman, a gung ho soldier in Arabia, encapsulates in depressingly complete fashion one way of reading women into the film *Lawrence of Arabia,* but to stop there would be to ignore the introspection of the main character as well as the reflexivity the movie evinces. It is precisely the introspection that marks a supposedly "feminine" side to Lawrence's character that leads him to doubt not only his masculine exploits but, more important, the militaristic and political projects to which they are harnessed. Both are missing in *She Went to War.* Rhonda Cornum is unable to ask whether what she calls "gender-neutral" is in fact masculine through and through, and like a good soldier she rarely betrays any doubts about her mission or the correctness of her nation's policies. By invoking *Lawrence of Arabia* we can subvert this story of the "masculinized" female, arguing that such a narrative of war and the army will be no more viable for women than it has been for men.

When I saw *Lawrence of Arabia* for the first time, I did not know that he was gay. In fact, had I read the biographies the issue would have still been left cloudy, given that the subject of his homosexuality was treated neither widely nor well. Some biographers, and there is no good reason I can see for assuming a priori that they are homophobic, say that Lawrence was less homosexual than asexual. But whatever we may decide about his sexuality, our question has to do with the movie's representation of him. It seems to me that I thought at the time I saw the film in 1963 that he *could* be gay as indicated by the way O'Toole played the role. When I discussed the movie with my parents and friends, however, this question of his homosexuality was not something I felt could be broached. If I showed an interest in the subject, which I certainly did, must I not also be gay or at least have homosexual inclinations? This line of questioning was too terrifying for a teenager like myself in the homophobic climate of that day.

But the film industry's commentary on the movie did discuss Lawrence's alleged homosexuality. Indeed, it seems to have been fascinated by it. Both the filmmakers and the critics commented on it. Together they oriented the adult reading public to a certain kind of reception of the film as having to do with homosexuality. I know that it is no longer fashionable to give much weight to authorial intent, but when through

the public sphere such intent becomes widely known, it inevitably informs the way the nonacademic public reads or views artistic works and
becomes important in constructing audience receptions.

One of the ways in which the filmmakers' intentions became known
publicly was through a vitriolic exchange between the movie's producer
and the heirs of the Lawrence estate. Here is Sam Spiegel replying in
the *New York Times* to an editorial written by Arnold Lawrence, the
younger brother of the military hero, who complained that "the film
tries to tell an adventure story in terms of a psychological study which
is pretentious and false."[33] Spiegel caustically observed in the same newspaper article:

> I quite understand what the movie must mean to someone who has lived in
> the shadow of a legend of an older brother for some 50 years.
> Professor Lawrence did not want family skeletons rattled. He wanted to
> preserve the Lawrence of Arabia legend in Victorian cleanliness. But anyone
> who dramatizes the life of Lawrence of Arabia cannot ignore that he was il-
> legitimate or avoid the conflict of this man who was aware of homosexual-
> ism [sic]. This was a man who became involved in all sorts of masochism as
> the result of his conflicts.[34]

Even before the release of the movie, however, the screenwriter Robert Bolt felt compelled to explain his representation of Lawrence in the
Sunday magazine of the *New York Times*:

> *The question I am asked most often now* is whether I think Lawrence was
> homosexual. Whether he was homosexually active I have no idea. That he
> was more or less homosexual by nature I think almost certain. He, himself,
> seems to me to make small bones about it.
> His references to homosexual practice among his young Bedouins are de-
> liberately lyrical. His punishment by the Turks when he was captured is
> specifically homosexual and described in the same soaring style. His house
> was kept full of young soldiers. He seems always to have been with men when
> he was not alone, never with women. . . . *But I can't see the importance of it.*
> It seems more important to know whether a man was brave or cowardly,
> clever or stupid, noble or ignoble. . . . There does seem to have been in his
> psyche an element of sadism, or sado-masochism (dreadful terms; what is one
> to call it?), some special regard for suffering, inflicted or received. . . . But as
> for the other business: a very great many people are homosexual; there was
> only one Lawrence of Arabia.[35]

The opening statement clearly indicates that public interest in the question of Lawrence's sexuality was already considerable in 1962. This is

not to say that Bolt didn't treat the theme in the script or that treating it ambiguously, as he did, was inappropriate, given Lawrence's ambivalence about his homosexuality, the censorship code of the time or the hoped-for appeal of this movie at the box office. But in the view of some people, he overlooked the connection between Lawrence's homosexuality and his politics.[36]

Rather than faulting Bolt for sharing certain liberal assumptions of the 1960s that today we might find reprehensible, I prefer to examine the ways in which homosexuality is, in fact, treated in the film, noting along the way that its treatment is more complex than reviewers have appreciated. The critic for *Time Magazine* made reference to a "sadomasochist, hemi-homosexual [*sic*], self-publicizing charlatan,"[37] but apart from mentioning allegations about Lawrence's sexuality, little about the film's treatment of the subject is discussed. Among the critics who did broach this subject, there was agreement that the treatment was either insufficient or incoherent. For example, Peter Barker noted that the film "carefully avoids the issue of homosexuality which he [Lawrence] at least condoned, almost praised publicly, in his book."[38] And according to Roger Sandall: "Bolt may well have seen a pattern uniting aestheticism, sadism, and homosexuality and hoped to examine it in a coherent character. But for the producer [Sam Spiegel] these were just spectacular paradoxes to be exploited for whatever millions they might be worth."[39] Stanley Weintraub, a perceptive literary critic of Lawrence's writings, shrewdly noted that censors and the prevailing cultural climate may have prohibited a frank discussion of Lawrence's sexuality. "Nevertheless," he adds, "it was far more significant in terms of the motivation of T.E.'s later behavior than can be understood from a suggestive pinch and a beating, followed by being tossed into the street."[40]

It is noteworthy that these reviews focus on the scene with the Turkish bey as almost the only instance in which the film attempts to represent Lawrence's homosexual impulses, while little mention is made of O'Toole's appearance, voice, or movements. They are also silent on the way audiences might interpret relationships between males such as the friendship between Farraj and Daud or between Lawrence and Ali. They took, in other words, the movie's most explicitly homosexual scene as the extent of its treatment of homosexuality rather than exploring subtler manifestations of it. However, as Michael Anderegg has noted: "Homoeroticism is simultaneously repressed and exhibited by the text. For many reviewers, this coyness probably resolves itself into an assertion of Lawrence's homosexuality. Since sexual 'deviancy' has nearly always been

treated obliquely and ambiguously in the mainstream cinema, oblique-
ness and ambiguity themselves signify the presence of what is absent." [41]
Aside from the critics, it is much more difficult to gauge the reactions of
moviegoers. Though there were some letters to the *Times* protesting the
movie, none fulminated against or even commented much on the subject
of homosexuality. Anything one says on this point is necessarily speculative. To repeat, there is Bolt's comment that "the question I am asked
most often now is whether I think Lawrence was homosexual," which
would presuppose strong, if closeted, public interest in the subject. Insofar as they can be trusted, there are also retrospective accounts of moviegoers who can remember their adolescent reactions: one lesbian said to
me that it was one of the most powerful movies she had ever seen, precisely because of the subtlety with which it treated, in the context of the
early 1960s and the film industry, Lawrence's homosexuality. A gay man
who was also coming of age at this time, if not yet out of the closet, told
me that his fascination with the performances of O'Toole and Omar
Sharif was more than skin-deep: their friendship had an emotional vi-
brancy and a repressed sexual charge that he found exciting and desirable. And in my undergraduate classes only one student, a female
unidentified according to sexual preference, commented on the film's
treatment of homosexuality, and in terms as subtle as Anderegg's: "I
had . . . heard that Lawrence was a homosexual though I did not expect
any hint of this in the film. I was surprised—sort of—by some of the nuances that indicated this fact [?]. Though now that I think about it, [it]
would have been hard to avoid the sexual, male quality of Arabia." As
she rightly suspects, the "nuances" of the homosexuality theme are to
be found in the homosocial world that the movie constructs.

   To gauge another kind of reaction of moviegoers, let us return to
MAD Magazine's satire (see figure 20). In a segment next to O'Toole
dancing in the desert there is a close-up of two Arabs. The one says, "Go
ahead, Khalil! Don't be bashful! *Ask* him to dance with you!" To which
the bashful one replies, "I don't know! I think he's a little too tall for
me!" The other urges him on. "Listen, you're just going to *dance* with
him! You're not going to *marry* him!" No, indeed, for as we continue
reading the satire to the end we discover that Lawrence sees an apparently Jewish shrink who gives him the motherly advice of settling down
with a "nice Egyptian girl." Lawrence seems to have heeded his psychia-
trist's advice. His flirtation with homosexuality is supposedly at an end
when we see him in the final frame nuzzling up to Cleopatra, played vo-
luptuously enough by Elizabeth Taylor, who by 1963 of course had al-

ready made her blockbuster epic. The distancing from and condemnation of homosexuality the movie refuses to perform for its audiences (within the censorship strictures of mainstream cinema, of course), *MAD Magazine* reinstates with a vengeance. That the Arab (and the British), but not the American, is homosexual is defensively suggested in the segment re-creating the famous conversation in Feisal's tent. Lawrence is explaining his plan to the prince: "So I'll take 50 men across the desert, and attack the Turks from the *rear!*" The prince dryly remarks, "Attack from the *rear?* That's Un-American." To which Ali quips, "That's okay! None of us here are Americans!"

It is important to bear in mind when trying to understand the homophobic climate of the 1950s that this decade in particular witnessed intense police activity against homosexuals conducted in Britain and the United States, activity that continued almost unabated into the beginning of the next decade. In Britain, for example, plainclothes policemen sought to entice and entrap suspected homosexuals, and in the United States the McCarthy Senate hearings waged a relentless witch-hunt against alleged Communists and homosexuals. We have to bear in mind, too, the tormented images that many gays had of their own sexuality before the advent of the gay liberation movement, having internalized the hatred their society felt for them. By the late 1980s the acceptance of homosexuality and its representation by the public, if not exactly satisfactory according to the standards of many gay people, had certainly increased. In addition, something had been appropriated openly in popular culture, a "gay look" that is thought to be distinctive and attractive to gay and non-gay audiences alike and therefore commercially exploitable. Consider, for example, the advertising surrounding the promotion of *Lawrence of Arabia*. As Janet Maslin of the *New York Times* has pointed out: "The 1962 advertising art for the film presented a strong, shadowy figure with a lantern jaw, a much more rugged image than that of the supremely edgy, fine-tuned Mr. O'Toole in the role. Today's ads, by contrast, show a Lawrence so fashionably fey that he appears to be modeling his flowing costume."[42] Maslin is referring to the poster for the 1989 reconstruction and its androgynous representation of Lawrence (figure 21). The face is recognizably O'Toole's. He stands on a sand dune and is blown by the wind, the robes fluttering behind his body. Examining the image more carefully, one will notice that it looks like a composite. As was pointed out to me (Scott Morgensen, personal communication), one half looks very much like a man's body—the robes outlining a slim but strong physique, the arm hanging down at the side, and the foot struck

Figure 21.   Poster advertising the 1989 release of *Lawrence of Arabia* (from author's collection; photo by Jon Kersey).

confidently outward—while the other half looks like a woman's, with the headdress streaming in the wind like long hair, the robes billowing out like a skirt, the arm crooked and held at the waist as though clutching a purse, and the foot demurely in front. Clearly, the advertising art was pushing a reading of the movie that would pique the gender-blurring interests of audiences of the late 1980s.

We have seen to what depths O'Toole's androgynous characterization plumbs, and we have read it as opening up possibilities for destabilizing a more conventional masculinity. But another, perhaps even more obvious, way to read this androgyny is as a sign of homosexuality. "Although there have been and still are competing understandings of homosexuality," Harriet Whitehead reminds us, "a recurrent one stresses the 'intermediate' sexuality or androgynous character of the homosexual practitioner."[43] Further caveats may be necessary, if, as I have suggested for British culture, androgyny can become a cultural practice associated not only with gays but also with straight people who enjoy exploring gender reversal. But I think it is safe to say that Lawrence's cross-dressing can be read as something in addition to this—that is, as Whitehead suggests, it can be interpreted as a sign of his gayness.

As for reading homoerotic desire in this movie, one has to attend closely to the diegetics (narrative-internal system) of looking. If Lawrence is "feminized" by being caught exhibitionistically in the gaze of other men, the men who are looking at Lawrence in hero worship and affection in their turn become ambiguous sexual figures. The gaze of Sherif Ali, seemingly unmotivated by the narrative, is explicable largely in terms of male desire mediated through what we might call the "rhetoric of friendship," a common representation of gay relationships in pre-Stonewall gay film and fiction. In the beginning, Ali dislikes Lawrence because of his self-righteousness at the Masturah Well, a hostility that subsequently hardens in their rivalry to determine who is the "better" man in the crossing of the Nefud. This display of one-upmanship is of course familiar in competitive male culture, adolescent or adult, Western or Arab, and can sometimes be a displacement for homoerotic attraction. It is more obviously, even humorously, drawn in *The Wild One*, in which Lee Marvin's character, head of a rival motorcycle gang, picks a fight with Marlon Brando's character. Although he gets thoroughly beaten, he nevertheless brawls, "I love you Johnny, I love you." As Lawrence seems to demonstrate in excellent Sartrean fashion that he can "write" his will in whichever way he chooses, Ali's hostility begins to melt and is transmuted into hero worship. This sort of male admiration,

Figure 22.   Sherif Ali gazing longingly in the direction of Lawrence.

too, is a cliché. But when Ali gives Lawrence his Arab attire, which look to a Western spectator rather more like a bridal gown than a manly uniform, and then watches Lawrence ride off in them, his hardened look dissolves into something quite different (figure 22). Neither hostile nor hero-worshiping, it is nevertheless intense and utterly absorbed, as if Ali were lost in contemplation of a desired object. Omar Sharif hints at the quickening of this response, and its suppression, when he shakes his head slightly, as if recalling himself from a reverie.

With these reflections in mind, we might do well to recall Omar Sharif's account of the film production, according to which he and O'Toole developed a close friendship. Sharif claimed rather grandiosely that "this close friendship was what actually made *Lawrence of Arabia* a success."[44] Of course, he meant much more by this statement than that the two actors helped each other in practical ways. Their real-life affection was projected into their screen relationship. As Wayne Kostenbaum has pointed out in a study of male literary collaboration entitled *Double Talk*, "Collaborators express homoeroticism and they strive to conceal it."[45] Having made this point, I resist reducing the rhetoric of friendship to some sort of homoeroticism that is constructed as being more "real." Rather, the two dialectically enhance each other. Homoeroticism can give male friendship a certain passion, whereas friendship in turn can bestow homoeroticism with profoundly moving social resonances.

There is also a way in which Lean's directorial style unintentionally, even ironically, intersects with what might be called a certain gay sensibility toward movie reception. David Lean was born to Quaker parents. He once said, "I think Quakers, being very keenly aware of the passions and trying to keep them under control, wanted to put a cap on those actresses and the wickedness that went on backstage."[46] This attitude may have influenced not only the subjects he chose for some of his films but also his emotionally restrained directorial style. His fear in his movies, expressed again and again in interviews, was of "going over the top." I think it may have influenced the way he directed his actors, particularly O'Toole in his edgy but also highly controlled, emotionally button-down performance that is seething under the surface. The emotional tone of that performance may sound a homosexual undertone for some gay audiences. In his perceptive remarks on Lean's *Brief Encounter,* Richard Dyer argues that beyond the melodramatic story of frustrated and illicit love, there is also an emotional style of acting that gay audiences, at least of a certain generation, could identify with.

Finally, let us look at the scene in Deraa where Lawrence does become the object of *openly* expressed homosexual desire on the part of the Turkish bey (Jose Ferrer), the scene on which most 1960s moviegoers and critics fixated when they thought about the film's treatment of Lawrence's homosexual desire.

T. E. Lawrence described the incident in chapter 80 of *Seven Pillars of Wisdom.* He was taken prisoner while on secret reconnaissance to Deraa, a garrisoned town in what is now southern Syria, and was hauled up before the commander referred to in the text as the "Bey." Supposedly, Lawrence's identity as a British officer was never discovered, even though he underwent intense interrogation. Lawrence claims the bey to have made homosexual advances toward him, which he rebuffed. In retaliation, he was ordered to be savagely beaten and was probably also raped by the guards. The chapter ends with the sentence: "In Deraa that night the citadel of my integrity had been irrevocably lost." Though he does not admit of homosexual feelings, Lawrence does reveal masochistic pleasure in the beating. "I remembered smiling idly at him [the corporal kicking his groin], for a delicious warmth, probably sexual, was swelling through me." Lawrence, however, was too bloody for the bey's liking and was thrown into a room from which he eventually made his escape.

In the film the opening of this scene is yet another variant of the play-acting motif. Lawrence's dress is no longer conspicuously white but plain and slightly soiled, in keeping with the negative image of Arabs that he has now internalized. He wants to be caught and to be punished, and thereby be purged of these identifications. In order to attract attention, he "deliberately" acts the madman, appropriately enough, given what we

Figure 23.   Lawrence, Christlike, "walking on water" while entering Deraa.

have seen of his megalomania, by invoking the image of Christ. He walks
in a puddle of water with arms outstretched, eyes cast heavenward, although with a most unpious giggle on his lips (figure 23). Eventually he
succeeds in being stopped and is seized by a Turkish patrol, who apparently are unaware of the identity of their prisoner. His companion Sherif
Ali is dismissed as unworthy.

We next see Lawrence standing in a lineup of men whom the bey walks
over from his desk to inspect. From the glances he exchanges with the individual men, it is clear not only what he wants from them but also what
he thinks of them. He lingers for a moment over the face of a young,
good-looking man who smiles tentatively. When he gets to Lawrence, the
guards smirk knowingly, and it takes the bey only a second to make up
his mind. He coughs and says to Lawrence "You." The rest of the men in
the lineup are hustled out.

What now transpires is the reverse of an earlier scene in which Lawrence received his white robe from Sherif Ali. In that scene Lawrence,
too, was surrounded by men; friendly, not hostile, ones. The glances he
received were also admiring but not lascivious. Then he was dressed, now
he is stripped. If earlier he was encouraged to perform a masquerade,
here he is unmasked. And most important of all, the bey has displaced
Ali, who faithfully waits outside the Citadel, hoping his friend will survive the ordeal.

Lawrence's body is subjected to a total assault. The bey admires his
blue eyes, surmising that he is Circassian. As happens again and again
in this movie, Lawrence is misrecognized, thus multiplying his identities
as if he were caught in double reflecting mirrors. That Lawrence is mis-

taken for a Circassian saves him from one fate, only to subject him to another (the Circassians are a light-skinned people from the Caucasus whose women, it is significant to know in this context of seduction, were renowned for their beauty and therefore favorites in the Sultan's harem). Lawrence's vulnerability is conveyed in part by having the camera focus not on his face but on the bey's highly polished boots, next to which we see Lawrence's headdress. He discovers Lawrence's blond hair with evident astonishment. Brutally he rips apart the shirt of the robe to expose Lawrence's torso. The bullet wound inflicted on the right shoulder by the Turkish officer firing from the train wreck is discovered, and the bey pokes at it as if he were inspecting a slab of beef. Lawrence now has reason to be alarmed, since he knows how harshly a rebel will be treated. Fixing him with a knowing gaze, the bey concludes, "You are a deserter." Then more archly he asks, "But from *which* army?" Clearly, the bey has his suspicions that Lawrence might be working for the British or at least fighting in the Arab army. It is important for us to bear this suspicion in mind, for his intention to have Lawrence beaten becomes ambiguous— as both a political and a sexual act. He then quips, "A man cannot be *always* in uniform." In other words, the masquerade is over and a moment of truth has arrived.

The bey admiringly kneads Lawrence's pectoral muscle between his fingers, remarking "Your skin is very fair." It is the whiteness of his skin above all that is desirable. In light of my earlier interpretation of Lawrence as a woman, this could be read as the white woman being the object of desire of the Asian potentate. Yet in being disrobed (or no longer being able to hide in his skirts), he is revealed as an anatomical male; hence desire is constructed as primarily homosexual. To bring home that point we next see a huge close-up of the bey's moist lips, followed by a close-up of Lawrence's frightened eyes. Lawrence strikes out in homophobic panic.

In retaliation the bey gives the order to have Lawrence beaten. In chapter 80 of his memoir, Lawrence writes, "Somewhere in the place a cheap clock ticked loudly, and it distressed me that their beating [i.e., the beating of the soldiers] was not in its time." Throughout the beating, the bey coughs. It is a symbolic equivalent of the ticking clock. The bey slinks off in a castrated walk and then goes into another room but pointedly leaves the door ajar so that he can watch the beating (figure 24). This is a voyeurism that Lawrence himself can see—at one point he cranes his neck around to spot the bey in the next room—and as such it is an exact parallel of previous scenes of exhibitionism in which someone else (Brigh-

Figure 24.   The Turkish bey (Jose Ferrer) watching Lawrence's beating from
the open doorway.

ton, Auda, the wounded Turkish officer in the train wreck) is a silent
spectator to his playacting.

The soldiers force Lawrence face down on a long bench, holding his
arms outward, in a Christlike position. The violence's buildup is slow
and highly ritualized, the point of which is to show the crushing of a
man's will, not simply the destruction of his body. It has resemblances to
a sadomasochistic rite.

Nighttime. Ali is seen haunting the shadowy precincts of the Citadel,
which he watches in horrified fascination. The bey and Ali are positioned
alike in this scene as voyeurs. Now Ali slowly moves toward the camera
and into the moonlight, his huge eyes dimly illuminated (figure 25). It is
at this moment that the audience (the third set of voyeurs) realizes, if it
realizes it at all, that Lawrence is being raped. But it is not allowed to sit
comfortably distanced from the scene of violence, for when Ali's eyes
are illuminated we realize that they are looking *directly* into the camera,
and therefore at us. This is the second of only two times in the movie
when a character does look into the camera, the other being at the beginning of the scene at the Masturah Well, another climax of psychological projection. It is as though Ali peers into our psyches to see a sexual
drama not unlike the one he imagines unfolding behind him inside the
Citadel. To be emphasized is the fact that the audience is brought into
the scene through the mediating look of Ali in order to disturb, not assuage, its complacency. The look is a challenge thrown at us: What about
the nature of *our* sexual desires? Are they, too, perhaps homosexual or
sadomasochistic?

Figure 25. Close-up of Ali, at night, voyeuristically watching the scene of male trauma outside the Citadel.

Next, we see the Citadel from Ali's perspective. The door is flung open, Lawrence's body is pitched into the darkness, where it lands in a dirty puddle, a bitter conclusion to a scene that opened with him walking on water. One by one the windows of the Citadel become dark as though they symbolize the lights within Lawrence's soul having become extinguished. Seeing that the coast is clear, Ali goes over to comfort him.

In his important book on the representation of homosexuality in cinema, Vito Russo singled out this scene in *Lawrence of Arabia* as evidence for his argument that "the allowance of the American dream of staunchly heterosexual heroes to coexist with visible homosexuality [was possible] so long as the two fought the classic battle and homosexuality and heroism did not occur in the same person." [47] In addition, some of my students have complained that the scene is racist because the Other, and not Lawrence, is shown to be homosexual.

The trouble with Russo's interpretation is, first of all, that it is unclear whether Lawrence has in fact distanced himself from his homosexuality. Lawrence's self-projection has been examined and criticized throughout the movie (especially in the Masturah Well scene) and is problematized again in the scene with the bey. The latter's discovery of a fresh bullet wound on Lawrence's arm recalls an earlier scene of projection when a Turkish officer tried to assassinate Lawrence, who stands suicidally in the path of his revolver. In the Turkish garrison he meets his double once again, only this time Lawrence has reached ground zero, for now the double can no longer be conveniently dispatched by the patriarchal

Sheikh Auda. In fact, the double *is* the patriarchal father who simultaneously tries to seduce and castrate the son. Above all, however, the system of looks implicates us in both homosexual desire and its sadistic
punishment. Sherif Ali is watching the Citadel and then looking directly
at us, suggesting that we are also caught in this circle of desire.

The movie confronts us as well with our (male) fears of rape. The
interesting twist in Major Cornum's testimony on Capitol Hill came
in the opinion she expressed that the proceedings were focusing more
on the abuse suffered by women in the military than by men. Captured
along with Major Cornum in the Gulf War was Specialist Troy Dunlap.
In prison, she would hear him being beaten by Iraqi interrogators, but
nothing is said about how far they might have gone in their punishment
of him. He would try to clarify matters later: "If it would have happened
to me, rape I mean, I probably wouldn't be here today; I probably would
have done something to get myself killed. . . . But if for some strange reason I survived, I would never tell anyone, no one, never. To me, that's
the worst thing that a guy could have done to him." [48] Is it not precisely
Dunlap's fears that the scene in the movie arouses for many men in the
audience?

As always, the problem with this movie is knowing which version the
audience has seen that would affect its reception. By 1963 deep cuts had
been made, and in some versions the scene with Ali skulking in the shadows of the Citadel is cut, so that after Lawrence is beaten he is seen tossed
out into the street. Unless the audience knew Lawrence's story about
sexual assault, they would have missed the implication that anything
more than a beating had transpired. It was important, therefore, to re-
store Ali's gaze at the audience in the 1989 reconstructed version, if the
themes of homosexuality and male rape were to be understood at all.
And the impact, as we can infer from what Specialist Dunlap said about
men being raped, is disturbing, and not just to women. It threatens the
sense that males in particular harbor of being in control and powerful.

I have been arguing that a figure, like Lawrence, who combines disparate
masculine traits becomes ambiguous in complex ways to different audiences at different historical periods. In this final section I will explore the
ways in which he could be interpreted as being emblematic of a masculinity constructed by the contemporary mythopoetic men's movement.

Sometime in the summer of 1991, I was watching *Lawrence of Arabia* on a big movie screen with a friend whom I knew to be active in the
men's movement. According to his own story, he grew up a "latchkey"

kid in a family whose father had been absent from the start, fighting a losing battle with schizophrenia, and whose mother could not spend much time with her son and daughter when trying to raise children on meager resources and, as it turned out, in terrible pain from a mortal illness of her own. Bright, talented, hardworking, and disciplined, my friend has managed to keep his head above water, though haunted by various demons from his past. Along the way, college counselors and therapists have helped, but he felt that he had reached a real turning point in his "healing" when he started to attend men's conferences in which he felt "empowered." On the one hand it was a relief, my friend said, to be with men like himself who were "wounded," who had severe psychological problems and wanted to talk about them rather than keep them under wraps, who did not subscribe to the myth of invulnerable, all-powerful males and yet at the same time were vivid, complex, and interesting. It was important for him to be around men who communicated their emotions rather than keeping them under wraps, who were compassionate and showed strength of character. In reference to the movie, he said, "It's good to experience an all-male world like Arabia."

My friend took me to San Francisco to attend a conference with seven hundred other men on July 27, 1991. Robert Bly, along with Michael Meade and Robert Moore, two other leaders of the "mythopoetic" men's movement, were speaking on the subject of violence, and as it turned out, unbeknownst to the general audience, the Gulf War. Relying on a romanticized construct of the primordial "native" borrowed, I regret to say, from anthropological writings, the speakers told us what was "right" about "them" and "wrong" about "us," and that we had to change to become more like them. What was "right" about "them" was that they could supposedly confront their violence and channel it in ritual ways that were more creative and ultimately more constructive than our sports or wars. One had only to consider the Gulf War to understand that point, Bly claimed. Only at the end of the conference did he remind us that this construction of the native other should be taken as metaphor, not literal truth, but by then perhaps it was too late to correct the naturalizing effect of the discourse. These problems aside, what emerged in the course of the day was a heated discussion between the key speakers on one side and articulate members of the audience on the other regarding central issues of the Gulf War—in fact, one of the few and certainly the most interesting public discussions I heard about the war in a politically mixed group. The audience was made aware of its racism toward Arabs and the widespread denial among Americans of the destruction the allied armies had wrought. As Bly sometimes does at his gatherings, he proceeded to recite Arabo-Muslim poetry, commenting on the importance of verbal art in Arab male society, a phenomenon I had experienced in Yemen and Saudi Arabia, and then remarking dryly, "You see, that's the culture we've been busily destroying over there." Disgruntled, I was nevertheless moved. When I thought about what moved me, I realized that the last time I had been in a company of men whose emotional level was that high, whose conversations were that intense and interesting and, yes, disturbing, and whose bodily articulateness was that beautiful and compelling was in Yemen.

In some of the discourses of this movement, it is said that men are "wounded" by a patriarchal and ultimately capitalist system that ejects the father from the family—if not literally, then figuratively, as an alienating (because alienated) member of the household. While the girl supposedly has her mother close to hand as a female role model, the boy has to look for male role models outside the family—the (essentialist) assumption being that a woman cannot adequately represent a male figure for the boy, just as, presumably, a man cannot be a "mother" to his son or daughter. In any case, the boy is raised by the mother or by other well-intentioned women but will almost inevitably grow up a "soft male," one who supposedly has been feminized or, to put it differently, has not yet come into contact with his "deeper masculinity." In O'Toole's performance one can almost see embodied Bly's idea of the "soft male."

A search is initiated in the boy for a "wild man" or, as Bly explains, a mentor who will teach the boy what it means to be a man who is not destructive but is at the same time in the fullness of his psychological powers—confident, energetic, and spontaneous, or what Jungians would call an "individuated" self—in other words, the opposite of a "soft male."[49] The boy reaches out to father surrogates in the form of teachers, sports coaches, and army sergeants, the latters' influence being more baleful than benign, according to Bly. In the absence of effective initiation by such elders, including his father, the boy will search for initiation into manhood through other means, the most dangerous of which is initiation through war. Such an initiation—one that General Murray approves of when he remarks, "Who knows, it might make a man of you"—such an initiation is inevitably destructive, leading not to the cultivation of the "wild man" within but of the "savage," the darker side of the Jungian warrior archetype.

The movie, by parodying certain stereotypes of white masculinities, simultaneously calls attention to their inadequacies and implicitly critiques them. Nowhere is this parody more apparent than at the beginning of the film, when the officers in the mess are seen lounging around in a bored state of relaxation, leaning a little unsteadily at the bar, immersed in their ritualized afternoon tea, absorbed in the reading of a newspaper, or playing a game of billiards. We cannot overhear their conversation, but imagine it to be banal—probably about sports or women. This sort of scenario would be rife for Bly's satirical gibes about male bourgeois society. In the middle of this elegant but dull and rather lifeless tableau charges Lawrence like a bantam rooster, disrupting the staid atmosphere of a severely masculine world. The parody returns at various moments in the movie, with sports as the butt of the humor. When Lawrence goes to headquarters in Jerusalem after arduous campaigning in the desert, he asks an officer, "What's doing here?" and is told "We're settling in, sir. We've built a squash court." In the context of war, the pursuit of sport is made to appear absurd and even somewhat evil, as in the scene where General Allenby, cynically biding his time until the Arab Council collapses so that he can take over Damascus, is seen casting an imaginary reel and line while absorbed in a book about trout fishing. "I'm going to take this up after the war," he comments to the diplomat Dryden.

As portrayed in Part One of the movie, the world of men is intensely hierarchical, riddled by class and racism. We see Lawrence for the first time in the map room, which is significantly located in the basement (among the underlings) of a huge palace, bantering with his Cockney chums. As soon as he is with his fellow officers in the upstairs mess, his demeanor changes, for he is now in a different space with "gentlemen" who are stuffily self-conscious of prerogative and propriety. Their pretentiousness seems to bring out his most mischievous side. It is clear that he can't stand them, and they in turn feel the need of putting him in his place because of the way he ignores or flouts social codes and thereby upsets class barriers. But above all, it is their racism that Lawrence and we find shocking, though wholly unsurprising. That racism is apparent not only in the scene in which General Murray contemptuously dismisses the bedouin as a "nation of sheep stealers" but also when Lawrence, dressed in his sheikh's robes, is treated abusively for having hauled the youth Farraj with him into the officers' mess, thereby violating the color bar. In no uncertain terms, he is told to get rid of the little "wog."

Not finding a positive image of manhood (the wild man) among his own kind, Lawrence must embark upon a quest, a journey, into the fairy-tale kingdom of the Other. Here the parallel to the wild man myth would seem to be complete. I would claim that the movie is more subtle in its rhetoric, however. Lawrence is not made whole again through contact with the noble savage, the wild man in the form, say, of Sherif Ali, the reverse ethnocentrism that says we can learn from the Other in order to heal ourselves and thereby regain our position of supremacy. By the end of the movie, Lawrence does not become a man who, in Bly's words, "has taken the way down and out [and] has become a descended man," [50] for Lawrence is a burnt-out case, a hollow man, a man more wounded than healed.

Let us now examine more closely some of the male relationships portrayed in the movie that bear on men's movement's concerns. No single male bond has come under closer scrutiny or been subjected to harsher criticism by Bly and others than the father-son tie. There are deep feelings of resentment in many sons toward their fathers for having been absent, literally or emotionally, for most of their lives and for failing to teach them what manhood or masculinity might mean. At the same time that they are distanced from their fathers, men are said to be isolated and alienated from each other, and thereby incapable of deep friendships, partly as a result of a ruthlessly competitive economic system, partly because they have been taught to maintain instrumental rather than emotional relationships with each other. Both kinds of relationships are explored in surprisingly subtle and complex ways in the movie.

Though there are plenty of metaphoric patriarchal relationships, the movie's only explicit father-son tie is that of Sheikh Auda and his boy. Auda tests his son's knowledge with a series of questions about Lawrence's bedouin clothing when they meet for the first time in the desert:

AUDA: Son, what fashion is this?
  BOY: Harith, father.
AUDA: And what manner of Harith?
  BOY: A Beni Wejh Sherif, father.
AUDA: And *is* he Harith?
  BOY: No father. English.

Next, the father tests the son's courage. "Son, they are stealing our water. Tell them we are coming." The boy rides off without questioning his father's command, while the patriarch laughs approvingly at such a display of obedience and then immediately rushes off to join him. I suggest that one can read this scene as a kind of critique, often expressed by the postwar generation, of the fathers who ordered their young sons to the front, as they did at Paschendale and the Somme, without, however, sharing their dangers in battle, as Auda clearly does.

Because it is a brief scene, it is unwise to make too much of it, and yet it sticks out because of its oddity. We will not see the boy after the well scene, nor will there be any reference to him. Why, then, introduce a son of Auda at all? Let us recall that the immediately preceding scene shows Lawrence being "adopted" into the tribe and becoming an "Arab." As a bastard, Lawrence would naturally look on with wonder and a certain wistfulness at the pride the sheikh takes in the paternal relationship. He has traveled to the land of the Other to find a father. What he has to confront with considerable consternation in the scene with Auda and his son, however, is the falseness of his own claims to authenticity.

The paternal relationship so subtly exhibited in the brief scene between Auda and his son colors the relations between Lawrence and two other figures, Prince Feisal and General Allenby. Historically, Prince Feisal was in fact approximately the same age as Lawrence, yet in the movie he is portrayed as being much older. To appreciate this interpretation of Feisal as a father figure, one need only contrast the movie with the television production *Lawrence After Arabia* (1992), which depicts Feisal and Lawrence (Ralph Fiennes) as being much closer in actual age, thereby implying a different relationship and a different sort of devotion between them, akin to an affection that is fraternal, possibly even erotic.

It is above all the scenes with Allenby that render this paternalistic relationship with subtlety and considerable villainy. This is all much clearer in the script than in the various versions of the movie. Here is a dramatic instance of the authorial intentions of Lean and Bolt being obfuscated by severe cutting. What *is* clear on the screen is that Allenby is desperately trying to persuade Lawrence to go back into battle in the desert one last time in order to help in the final push to Damascus. We can see Allenby show concern and sympathy for Lawrence's wounds, which are visible on the blood-soaked back of his uniform. We next see Allenby without his jacket, a cigar in hand, treating Lawrence more as an equal than a subordinate. He tries to work on Lawrence's vanity, as he had done successfully in a previous scene in Part One, but when he prophetically remarks that Lawrence's name will become a household word whereas the public shall have to go to the War Museum to find out who Allenby was, Lawrence recoils in horror, as though facing the temptation of the Devil himself, and pleads to be left alone. Allenby then shows Lawrence a photograph of his family and says, "That's my lad. You must come and see us, afterwards." The thrust meets its mark. To be

clasped in the paternal embrace, to be assured some sort of domestic in-
clusion is all that Lawrence, the illegitimate son, wants, and in exchange
for which he is willing to pay any price, even if it amounts to his sanity
and possibly his life. Lawrence answers, "I'd like to."

The production script notes that "it is almost like a physical object he
has handed to ALLENBY—the keys of his *citadel*" (my emphasis). This is
a clear allusion to the scene in Deraa where Lawrence is beaten and raped
at the orders of the Turkish general, in which the "citadel"—literally and
metaphorically—figures importantly. What we next hear is that Lawrence has agreed to the general's opportunings, but we assume, because
we have not heard the immediately preceding dialogue, that Lawrence
had succumbed merely to the general's flattery, a much less interesting
motive than a craving for paternal approval and affection.

Let us now pick up the hint dropped in the script that Allenby and the
Turkish general are symbolic equivalents. This surmise is supported by
an interchange between Bentley and Sherif Ali as they await the arrival
of Lawrence and his bodyguard to lead the march to Damascus:

BENTLEY: What did the Turkish General *do* to him, in Deraa?
ALI: . . . What did the *English* General do to him, in Jerusalem?

Not only is there the suggestion that Allenby's psychological manipulation and betrayal are comparable to the physical abuse of the Turkish
bey but also that Lawrence underwent his suffering in *Jerusalem,* with
all the religious associations this name stirs. Could the father figure assume grander and simultaneously more evil associations?

As a bastard Lawrence was betrayed by his father, which instilled in
him a yearning for a surrogate—Feisal, Allenby, even the Turkish bey.
They all betray him in the end. Of course, Lawrence is not guileless, for
he seems to wish these betrayals upon himself, perhaps as a way of inflicting another form of self-punishment. Lawrence tries to assume a fatherly
role with the orphan boys Daud and Farraj, but he betrays them too, thus
repeating the evil of the fathers. For example, when they accompany him
at his insistence through the Sinai Desert, they complain of fatigue; yet
he pushes them relentlessly beyond the limits of their endurance (just as
Allenby will push Lawrence beyond his), with the result that Daud loses
his life. Recall the scene: Daud does not have the strength to hold onto
the lifeline Lawrence throws out to him and thus sinks over his head into
"quicksand." In Part Two Farraj will be mortally wounded in a dynamite
accident, and it is Lawrence who executes him before the Turks get their

hands on him. The ironic fade into that scene reveals Lawrence with a paternally protective arm across the young boy's shoulder.

There are haunting echoes of this traumatic theme of the father-son relationship in Lean's life. As mentioned earlier, Lean was in his early teens when his father left his wife and more or less walked out on his two sons. Lean's estranged relationship with his father was obviously painful and would continue to bother him throughout his life:

> You know . . . it's one of my great regrets now that my father never really realized that I've made a success of it. He lived well into his nineties. I don't know precisely how old he was when he died, but I know he was past ninety-five. He got, we became, very distant, and, I remember, I was terribly hurt. I sent him an invitation to the premiere of *Lawrence of Arabia,* and he said it was too far to come.
> And I've often thought of this.[51]

In his direction, Lean may have fixated on this scene between Auda and his boy, which he redid many times in part because of his own psychological needs, but we will never know this. Nor do I wish to suggest that he intended this scene to be read in the ways I have chosen. I am suggesting that in watching his own film, the scene would no doubt have a certain poignancy for Lean because of his relationship with his own father, and that insofar as men in the audience had similar experiences with their fathers, they might fixate on it as well.

Also uncanny is the way in which the paternalistic relationship represented and critiqued in the film would be reenacted by Lean with his metaphoric sons and daughters, the actors and actresses who worked for him, a relationship that in the best of times led to considerable strain, in the worst to complete and nearly permanent rupture. Peter O'Toole, for example, made no secret of the fact that he found almost sadistic the demands Lean made on him in a physically arduous location. By the end of nearly two years of filming, the director and his star were barely on speaking terms—one suspects more out of O'Toole's choosing—and they supposedly did not meet again until 1988, while working on the film's restoration. Could one ask for a more precise parallel between the relationship of Allenby and Lawrence on the one hand and the director forcing his star to remain in the desert on the other? The women stars, as one might suspect, fared no better. Julie Christie, who played Lara in *Doctor Zhivago* (1965), held more charitable feelings toward her director than did O'Toole, though she too hints at her resentment of Lean's autocratic style: "David's presence on *Zhivago* was more paternalistic than that of many directors. The whole vision of the film was in *his* head, and he used us [actors] like colors on his painting. This . . . admirably suited the very insecure young actress I was." And she deepened the last point by adding, "I . . . felt a closeness based on paternalism." [52] For Judy Davis, however, the experience of working with such a paternalistic director was more galling. According to her, Lean did not care for the film *My Brilliant Career,* a movie about an "independent" woman, in which Davis starred and first gained international prominence. As an actress on the set of *Passage to India,* Davis too saw herself as a fairly independent woman, a habit that apparently interfered with Lean's controlling style. [53]

The point I wish to emphasize is that Lean regarded the patriarchy rather wistfully, as in the idealized scene between Auda and his son, and at the same time much more ambivalently, as in the relationship between himself and his father or between Lawrence and Allenby. His patriarchal relationship with his actors, male and female, was fraught with tension and at times very disagreeable. Yet in spite of these problems, the hunger for the father and the need to reinstate him, or become him, persisted. Confused as these feelings might seem, they are not unusual for men of the middle to late twentieth century, as evidenced in the testimony of more than one text from the burgeoning men's movement, and as such they might evoke powerful and troubled responses in some male members of the audience.

Lawrence is depicted as not having British friends. In the beginning of the movie, at the service in Saint Paul's cathedral, we might think otherwise, for a number of admirers turn up to pay their respects to his memory, not the least being a teary-eyed Brighton, who says that Lawrence was the most extraordinary man he had ever met. This sentimentality is ironic, however, for although it is true that Lawrence got closest to Brighton of all the officers on the British staff, their relationship did not flower into a full-blown friendship. Only when Lawrence is on his way to leave Arabia in the next to last scene does Brighton realize how much he cared for the upstart young lieutenant, but by then a demonstration of affection is too late. The poignancy of that moment, when Brighton runs to the entrance of the palace only to find Lawrence swallowed up in the crowd, is not in his losing a friend but in his learning too late that he had one.

Another source of friendship might have been the lower-class and lower-ranked soldiers whom the historical figure professed to prefer over the company of his fellow officers, but after an early scene with Lawrence and some Cockney chums, this possibility of developing friendship across class lines is not explored. As for his relations with his fellow commanding officers, they are tense, at times extremely hostile, especially when Lawrence attempts to go native and implicitly attacks their racism. The only real possibility of friendship for Lawrence, if it is a possibility at all, lies with cultural, not class, "others," with the Arabs, not the British.

We sense this possibility almost immediately, when Lawrence enters the Arabian desert with Tafas. He is more than a guide, as Lawrence reminds Ali after the killing at the Masturah Well. The relationship of Farraj and Daud exemplifies an ideal of friendship, underpinned by loyalty, devotion, and affection, that is highly romantic and seemingly unselfconscious. Some American audiences in the early 1960s, especially white middle-class ones, would have had little cultural precedent for an emotionally charged, romantic relationship between boys, perhaps unlike their English and German counterparts. While Lawrence's memoir explicitly states that this was the case, the movie, unsurprisingly in the sixties, is vague, if not silent, on that subject. Keeping the eroticism low-key, if not absent, left open a certain space, however, for those same audiences to imagine passionate attachments among men that were nonerotic and hence nonthreatening. To put the same point differently, one did not have to be a gay man to feel, or at least to want to feel, passionately about other men.

In the movie, the friendship between Farraj and Daud becomes an interesting foil for the relationship between Lawrence and Sherif Ali. The adult friends have some of the others' charm, but theirs is a far less innocent relationship, one that is troubled by a complex politics. *Lawrence of Arabia* is in some respects a "truer" adaptation—in spirit at least— of E. M. Forster's *Passage to India* than the movie Lean would later make of the same novel. I mean by this perhaps odd-sounding statement that *Lawrence* probes the possibilities and limits of male friendship between colonial unequals in a cross-cultural encounter much more deeply than does the film adaptation of Forster's book. For the movie sentimentally rejoins Fielding and Aziz at the end, thus refusing to acknowledge the difficulties, if not impossibilities, of such friendship in the colonial situation. But it may not be just the colonial situation that hinders such friendships, as men in our society engaged in struggles of one sort or another have learned to their cost.

When I saw this movie at thirteen, it articulated in complex ways fa-

ther hunger, patriarchal dilemmas, and the yearning for but seeming impossibility of male friendships, all of which were a stressful part of my
growing up in the 1950s and 1960s. The problems of these relationships
have not been alleviated in thirty years, nor have their representations
become more reassuring, at least in my view. Once again, what it means
to be a man, a father, and a friend is cast into doubt. As I have already
suggested, the movie distances itself from the men's movement's comforting hope that white, middle-class, and middle-aged men, deeply disturbed about their own insufficiencies, can redress them by finding the
wild man within. Nothing is more unnervingly pessimistic than the final
image of Lawrence, listless, numb, all but dead, speeding out of Arabia
in a jeep that is being covered in dust by a passing motorcycle, the motorcycle we had seen at the beginning of the movie and which is the har-
binger of his death at the end.

Epilogue

In Williamstown, Massachusetts, on a cold, gray morning in mid-January of 1997, I waited outside the town's only movie theater, "Images," to see a 35 mm print of the film *Lawrence of Arabia* and to talk to junior high and high school students about it. They had come from nearby North Adams, a town of about fourteen thousand working-class people whose economic fortunes had suffered a steady decline since the 1970s with the closings of the textile mills and other businesses. They were participating in a pilot project, the brainchild of an energetic, tough, and affable New York arts consultant named Alyce Dissette who was working with the Massachusetts Museum of Contemporary Art (Mass-Moca) to bring artworks and artists that would be of interest to the local community. Alyce thought that movies and moviemakers would certainly be as interesting as paintings by Dali or Henry Moore sculptures, perhaps more so, and it was even part of her long-range plans to renovate a former movie palace, now boarded up and deteriorating in the downtown area, and to equip it with wide-screen projection as well as stereo sound equipment.

"How does *Lawrence of Arabia* fit into this?" I asked Alyce when she first spoke about the possibility of my coming to Williamstown.

"I didn't want to show only contemporary works and artists. I also wanted to show a film that was an important part of the history of filmmaking. And of the films on my list, *Lawrence* was the one about which

239

people had only positive things to say. Teachers, parents, the mayor of the town, the director of MassMoca, my colleagues in the industry: they all agreed that *Lawrence* was the most suitable." The fact that these people, admittedly from a variety of walks of life, had "only positive things to say" about a film that has disturbed some, especially Arab Americans, made me pause.

The hall was so crowded with high school students by the time I got in that no seat was available, and so I watched from the back of the central aisle, standing for most of Part One. From there I could look straight at the center of the screen in spite of bobbing heads and kids scurrying up the aisle to go to the bathroom or to sneak a smoke outside the theater. They laughed at several of the scenes, especially the high jinks of the two boys Daud and Farraj. I tried to catch their stray comments, at least the ones that had anything to do with the movie they were watching. "I didn't know they had rifles in those days," said one boy. His friend hissed back at him, "It's the twentieth-century, you moron." When Auda tells Lawrence and Ali that they trouble him like women, one girl clucked to her companions, "Ah! Did you hear that? That's sexist!" They giggle, delighted with her astuteness.

When the lights go up at intermission, there is a small ripple of applause. Lunch is served, and then Alyce introduces me. "I've tried to lay some of the groundwork with the students," she had explained when she contacted me by phone. "I've met twice with four groups of fifty to talk a little bit about the geography and history of the modern Middle East as well as Arab bedouin culture. I've also explained to them who Lawrence was and why he is considered important in World War I and to British colonialism. I showed them the opening and final scenes from the movie to give them a sense of the pacing, and alongside it showed an edited version that is closer to the rhythm they are used to. They were fascinated." She had to admit, with a laugh, that they were a lot of work. "But they're great kids, and I think you'll like them too."

I still wasn't sure how I could contribute. "You've been to the Middle East, to some of the places in the film. You've studied it. Speak to them for a few minutes about what you appreciate in *Lawrence of Arabia* and then answer their questions. The whole thing shouldn't take more than forty minutes."

It sounded so simple, but when I was in the movie theater with the kids, I wasn't sure. It was a long, narrow room, and it was impossible to be heard in it when people were whispering to each other and clowning around, as they had to be after two hours of straining to understand a complex, slow-moving picture. Crowd control is how I described the situation to myself. I would have no choice but to move up and down the central aisle, speaking directly to the audience in back as well as in front. I had prepared something that I had wanted to read but gave that up as hopeless under the circumstances.

I tried to get them to talk about the images in the film. They were polite but also restless and rambunctious, and it was all I could do to keep them focused on the questions. "From what you've seen, how does the desert strike you?" It's big, it's empty except for the Arab tribes, it's hot, it's dangerous. "It's also mysterious," said one girl.

"Yes, it is," I agreed, "and what do you see in the desert that gives you that impression?"

"When Lawrence's friend—what's his name?—"

"Ali?"

"Yeah, when Ali appears, there's this mirage."

"Good! That is mysterious. Anything else that gives you a sense of mystery?"

"Well, there are those little tornadoes."

"You mean the whirlwinds?"

"Yeah, and I thought when he got to those ruins with only one of the two boys left—"

"You mean when he was crossing the Sinai Desert to get to Cairo?"

"—Yeah, I guess so, anyway those ruins were spooky."

"So you get a sense of this place we call a 'desert,' don't you? Good. And what about the people who live in it? The bedouin? What do you learn about them?" Several different people now spoke up.

"They fight over water because there isn't enough to go around."

"Okay, and what else?"

"Well, they're fighting the Turks. They want to get rid of them so that they can be free."

"Excellent. They want to form their own nation, right? And what else do you learn about them?"

"They ride camels." There was a snigger in the room.

"They do . . . And what do they believe in?"

"They're Muslims." I asked for a definition and was given a good one.

"Excellent. And how does the movie show their religion?"

"You see what's-his-name reading from their book. . . . What's it called?"

Somebody else provided the answer.

"Good. And what else do you learn about their society?"

No one seemed able to answer the question. I coaxed them a bit. "What about the chief or sheikh, Auda Abu Tayyi? When he talks about his honor, what does he mean?" Silence. I attempted an explanation and then an illustration. "You remember when Ali and Auda spar with each other by the watering hole? They're not really fighting. They're challenging each other, and if you're a man of honor, you have to show that you're equal to someone else's challenge."

I decided to switch to a discussion of Lawrence. "What kind of impression does he make on you?" I asked the students. Various ones told me that he's smart, brave, handsome, and so forth.

"He also seems to be conceited," said one girl. "And he's kinda nuts," volunteered another.

"How do you know that?" I asked her, encouragingly. After a pause, another girl raised her hand and piped up, "Because he says he likes to kill."

"That's right, he likes to kill. And in the next part of the movie you'll see that he seems to get worse, becoming more and more egotistical and crazy. You're going to see a different kind of movie in Part Two. It's no longer a celebration of Lawrence as hero. . . . Now, do you have any questions for me?"

A boy raised his hand. "What happened to the little boy when he disappeared in the desert?"

"Do you mean when he fell into quicksand?" He nodded. I proceeded to give an elaborate answer about its symbolism. I looked at Alyce in the back of the auditorium for help. She was smothering her giggles and pointing to the dial of her watch to indicate that my time was up.

When I went up to her a few seconds later, she told me laughingly, "He wanted to know *literally* what happened to the boy."

"You mean that he died?"

"Yup, that he was smothered. They're kids, you know. They're fascinated and horrified by death. I tell you, you earned your honorarium."

In conferences with Alyce, the teachers had said they doubted the students would be able to sit still for a movie that was almost four hours long. "Well, you know, learning to sit that long is good for all of us," she had replied sharply. The students were surprisingly still, in fact, losing their patience only toward the end, in the last half hour. When Lawrence is being beaten in the Turkish prison, I was anxious to see whether the students would understand the full extent of his punishment. My doubts were laid to rest when I heard a boy whisper to his neighbor, "It's *sod-omy*, you jerk."

At two in the afternoon, they spilled out of the auditorium. Alyce and I were at the door saying good-bye. "It was long," many of them commented. Some of them added, "I liked it."

Six weeks later, I went with Alyce to North Adams to conduct some focus groups in the junior high school. She wanted to know more about the students' taste in movies generally. I wanted to know more about their reception of the film.

I was pleased to learn that it was the thirteen-year-olds we were going to speak to rather than the high school kids. I felt a special affinity with them because I had been their age when I first saw the movie, but they also seemed more responsive and less self-conscious than their high school counterparts. The teachers had hand-picked the students in advance, and so we got some very bright and articulate kids, divided for the purposes of our interview into three groups of about twelve each.

We started each session by trying to summarize the plot of the movie, writing it down on a large sheet of paper. It had been a long time since they had seen the movie, and we weren't sure if they remembered much of it. The exercise also helped to get the conversation going.

After about ten minutes a brief outline of the plot had been scrawled on the notepad as follows:

LAWRENCE OF ARABIA, A SOLDIER IN WORLD WAR ONE, GOES TO THE DESERT TO TALK TO PRINCE FEISAL, LEADER OF THE ARABS, TO HELP HIM FIGHT THE TURKS. SHERIF ALI, HIS FRIEND DRESSED IN BLACK, HELPS LAWRENCE AND TOGETHER THEY TAKE ʿAQABA BY CROSSING THE GREAT NEFUD DESERT. AFTER AQABA, LAWRENCE DYNAMITES THE TURKISH TRAINS AND MOVING NORTHWARDS WITH HIS ARMY TAKES DAMASCUS. DURING THE CAMPAIGN LAWRENCE GOES CRAZY. HE LIKES TO KILL. HE WANTS TO BECOME AN ARAB BUT CAN'T. AND HE WANTS TO DIE. HE FEELS REJECTED BY BOTH THE BRITISH AND THE ARABS. THE MOVIE ENDS WITH HIM NOT KNOWING WHO HE IS.

I asked them, "Why, by the way, does he want to become an Arab? Why, as they say in the movie, does he want to 'go native'?"

In a very quiet voice, a girl explained, "He felt lonely because the English people didn't really like him?"

"And why didn't they like him?" I prodded.

"They talked about him as though he was kinda stupid."

I laughed. "Yeah, or else he was acting like a clown, a fool. Good. And why else does he go crazy? What's your impression of him? Did you like him?"

A boy said, "I think he wanted to die. He was, like, takin' all these chances. Like when he was rushin' into battle and the time the train flipped over and the guy was shootin' at him."

I was taken aback by the astuteness of this observation. "So you're saying he was suicidal, he wanted to die. And by the end of the movie, how does he seem to you, and how is he different from the way he was at the beginning?"

The boy drew back and said nothing. After a few moments, a girl volunteered an answer. "He feels rejected by both the British and the Arabs."

Alyce tried to get to the same thing by another tack. "Do you remember the last scene of the movie, the very last scene?" The silence lasted a long time. We reminded them of the ending.

"What does that last scene seem to say about Lawrence?" Alyce asked.

We had almost given up trying to get an answer when another voice piped up tentatively, "He doesn't seem to know who he is anymore?"

"He doesn't seem to know who he is anymore," I agreed emphatically.

I now asked the focus group whether they understood what the filmmakers were trying to say about Lawrence and his situation. One girl said she found it annoying that he seemed to be one thing in one scene and another in a different one, as if they couldn't make up their minds. That was a problem, I agreed.

"You kinda feel sorry for him," said another girl. "He's rejected by the British and he's rejected by the Arabs and no one likes him in the end."

"Yeah," I added, "he doesn't even seem to have a home to go back to in the end, does he? Can you identify with this? Or is this so removed from your own experience that you don't understand it?"

"No, I can understand it," said a boy. "Being rejected by people— that happens." I had an intuition that, at his age, he was not talking abstractly.

Now Alyce tried to get them to think more deeply about this notion of rejection. "Does the word betrayal come to mind?" she asked. "Does anyone know what betrayal means?" After a bit of coaxing a boy explained the difference between betrayal and rejection by saying that in the case of the former, "Your friends stab you in the back." But they didn't seem to think that Lawrence had been betrayed. Or else it was more ambiguous. Perhaps he brought his destruction on himself.

I asked them if they noticed anything else about the film that was interesting.

The same boy who had talked about Lawrence's suicidal tendencies now observed, "I noticed that he didn't seem to have any feelings. He didn't seem to feel any pain or sadness or happiness or anything."

"And was that disturbing to you, this sense that he's dead inside?" The boy nodded to me.

It seemed as though we'd run out of steam, so I shifted gears and asked them if they had any favorite scenes from the movie. Alyce added that it didn't have to be a scene, it could be just a vivid image.

"The guy dying in quicksand," said one of the girls. Several students raised their hands to indicate that they remembered that scene. They thought it stuck in their minds because it was such a horrible way to die.

Someone else remembered the moment when Lawrence and his other servant boy arrive at the Suez Canal and see the smokestacks of a ship behind the sand dunes. A boy liked the canyons of Wadi Rumm.

The same boy who was so perceptive about Lawrence's suicidal character remembered the scene in which he kills Farraj, accidentally wounded by a detonator explosion. Someone else liked the desert journey with Tafas, another the charge of 'Aqaba, a third the demolition of the train at the beginning of Part Two, yet another the lemonade scene with Farraj in the officers' mess back in Cairo, and so on.

I was about to wrap up this segment when someone mentioned the scene in the Turkish prison where Lawrence is beaten. "What about before the whipping scene, when one of the guys comes on to him," a girl said between giggles.

"Do you want to watch that scene again?" I asked. "The one where Lawrence is whipped in the prison?"

Some hands went up. Alyce asked, "Is this peer pressure, or are we being sincere here?" They agreed that they wanted to watch it.

We watched the scene. They laughed at Lawrence's clowning around when he enters Deraa. They watched the rest of it in silence but with rapt attention. There was a slight gasp when the bey rips off Lawrence's shirt.

"Well, what's going in that scene?" I asked at the conclusion. One student wanted to know why the general pinches Lawrence's breast. It was hard to know whether she really didn't understand the significance of the gesture or was simply being coy. Another girl said she didn't understand why the general walked up to the different men and looked them up and down. Finally, a boy said that one of the teachers explained to the class that Lawrence had been sexually attacked.

Alyce asked the class, "How many of you think that's what happened?" Almost all the hands went up.

"How many of you thought that that's what happened the first time you saw the movie?" Only a couple of hands went up.

Alyce and I both admitted that we didn't get it the first time we saw the movie at thirteen or so. Alyce laughed when she told us that even Bob, the owner of the Images Theater in Williamstown, didn't know that that's what the scene was about. "It's all about what you happen to notice, what you're thinking about. Don't you think that is interesting? That some people get something out of a movie that's different from what other people get out of it"?

I added, "It's not as if you missed something if you didn't get it. You might notice other things about the scene that someone else didn't get. After all, the general is talking about how white Lawrence is, how fair, a reminder that he isn't an Arab after all. So this scene could also be about that—about Lawrence not being able to pass for an Arab or to go native."

Alyce now asked them if they liked the movie. It was hard to follow, said some. It was hard to tell one person apart from another. They didn't like *Star Wars* for the same reason, a reaction that came as a surprise.

I now asked the class whether it bothered them that there were no women in the movie. One girl admitted that she hadn't thought about it until her friend pointed it out to her, and then she thought, you're right. Her friend explained, "If you think about it, the film is kinda sexist because it's saying that women weren't really back there, weren't really important."

A boy agreed, "Even in the camps or the cities, you don't see much of the women."

The same girl who had called the movie sexist pointed out that it could have shown more of family life in the camps and how the women felt about their husbands leaving them. She was interrupted by her friend, who mischievously suggested a parting love scene between husband and wife.

Changing the subject, Alyce asked the class, "How many of you think you know something about the Middle East after having seen this film?"

A couple of students pointed out that they saw the Arab tribes fighting and not being able to get along. If they seemed aware of the "sexism" of the film, they were far less attuned to criticisms of its "orientalism." Furthermore, they hadn't picked up the film's references to different aspects of Arab life. They didn't understand, for example, that Auda is a paragon of Arab hospitality. Instead, we got bogged down in details that they found odd or inexplicable. "Why don't the Arabs wear pants?" asked one girl. I pointed out to them that in bedouin society often the women wear the pants, the men the robe. "How did they know where to go in the desert with no markings?" asked a boy. "By the stars," a girl explained.

Alyce now asked whether the students would have appreciated knowing more about the story and the society before they had seen the movie. Wouldn't they have been bored? A girl disagreed. She had a hard time following the story, and when she had figured out the end, she had forgotten the beginning. She also didn't understand why the teacher was laughing at many of the lines. The rest of the class agreed. What was so funny about the things that Lawrence said or did? Almost all of them agreed that they would go to see it again because they understood it better now.

By way of wrapping up, Alyce pointed out that every generation seems to have a movie or a couple of movies that defines their film experience. *Lawrence of Arabia* was hers and mine. But we wanted to know about their favorite movies. *Caspar, Clueless, Annie, Independence Day, Forrest Gump,* and *Braveheart* were some of the titles that came up. *Clueless* was mentioned most often. Alyce focused on *Independence Day* and asked them if they thought it was a "serious" movie. They agreed that it seemed to be making fun of things. "Don't you think that the whole thing defies logic?" Alyce suggested.

A girl pointed out, however, "It's a movie. It's supposed to defy logic. *Snow White* defies logic. All those other movies defy logic—"

"That's true," Alyce agreed.

"That's the fun of a movie, to see something that you know really can't happen," the girl concluded.

The second focus group met with us at ten. It was a lot livelier, in part because of the later morning hour and also because the students were less shy. They not only had no trouble summarizing the movie but also could remember scenes more fully and vividly. There was some disagreement about the beginning of the film. Some students were of the opinion that Lawrence had killed himself in the motorcycle accident by purposively driving recklessly. Others thought he simply didn't care whether he lived or died. Some of the students also didn't like him by the end of the movie, but one girl did. She explained, "The way Allenby would send him back to do that work and everything when he was crazy and really needed help—I felt bad for him."

"What made you think he was crazy?" I asked.

Several students reminded me that Lawrence likes killing people.

There was much discussion of the scene in which he kills the same man that he had rescued from the desert, shooting him repeatedly as though he were getting a kick out of it. They also pointed out that he is power hungry and egotistical.

When I asked what they thought the movie was about, one boy said he thought it had to do with the way things can change quickly and unexpectedly. After a bit of coaxing he concluded that he meant fate. That was why his favorite scene was the one in which the boy dies in quicksand. It happens so quickly and unexpectedly, showing not only the treacherousness of the desert but also how fickle Lawrence's fate can be.

For another boy, the scene in which the trains get derailed was exciting because he liked the "action." For yet another, it was the one in which Lawrence orders lemonade in the British officers' lounge. I asked the class what they thought about this scene. They explained that Lawrence is protecting Farraj from the insults of the officers. Why are they insulting them? After kicking that question around a bit, they pointed out that the British officers are racist in their attitudes toward Arabs.

"Does this scene remind you of anything in our society? Do we have places where whites can go but not blacks?" asked Alyce.

The boy who began to dominate this class talked about the civil rights movement of the sixties. I reminded him that the movie came out in the sixties: people might have identified with Lawrence and the situation he finds himself in.

As the discussion proceeded, the class focused on Lawrence's character, and the match scene was discussed as revelatory of his love of pain and his need to control his body. One girl added something new to the analysis of the character, namely, that he wants to make people think he's someone else. As if he were wearing a mask? I asked. "Yeah," she agreed. Another girl made the point even more subtly: "I think he wasn't only hiding something—like you say, wearing a mask—I think he also was trying to change who he was because he didn't like that person."

"You mean that the mask stood for someone else?" I asked.

She nodded in agreement. "Give me an example of a scene," I asked the class, "in which Lawrence makes himself appear as though he were someone else." The dominant boy brought up the scene in which Lawrence tells Brighton, "Didn't you know? I can only be killed by a golden bullet," making himself out to be someone special, a magical being.

"And is there a scene in which Lawrence seems to be unmasked, in which he is revealed to be an ordinary person?" I asked. Without hesitation, another boy in the class referred to the scene in which Lawrence is whipped by the Turks. At first he could not explain why he thought this is a scene of unmasking, but the dominant student offered the suggestion that in it Lawrence is revealed to be a "white" person and not an Arab as he wants others to believe he is. "He said to some guy before he went into the town where the Turks nab him that he has lived so long with the Arabs that he knows their culture." I asked the class if there was anything else about the scene that was revealing. The girl whose insight into masking started this part of the discussion responded, "It shows that in fact he can't stand pain. He's an ordinary person after all." I prodded them a bit more to discuss the meaning of the scene in the Turkish prison, but unlike the previous group they did not come up with the theme of sexuality.

It was the scene in which Lawrence puts on Arab clothes for the first time that left an impression on another girl. She thought the scene showed that he was pleased at being "accepted" into Arab society. "And why does he crave acceptance?" I asked. The boy who had been irrepressible but also quite perceptive throughout told us, "Because he wasn't accepted by the British, and here he had a chance to be this great hero, which flattered his ego." But a girl pointed out that he wasn't accepted in Arab society by the end of the movie, and that's why he leaves to go back to Britain. The boy tried to synthesize the two points by observing, "It's like he went around in a circle: he started out being rejected by the British and was nothing; then he became this great hero among the Arabs but was rejected by them too; and finally went back to the British, but was rejected a final time. It's like he had nothing to live for." The boy referred back to the scene at the beginning of the movie on the steps of the cathedral where a reporter gets one story from one group of people, then a different story from another group.

"So do you think there are several ways in which you could look at this man called Lawrence, and that no one way is correct or preferred?" I asked him. He nodded his head.

When we started talking about memorable scenes, the class was full of mischief. They wanted to watch the scene of the two little boys begging a cigarette from one of the British soldiers (when the soldier tricks them, they shove a stick up the camel's rear, making it toss the soldier to the ground); or the one in which the boys sneak into camp by hiding behind the legs of the camel and then are caught by Qasim. But Alyce persuaded them to combine them with another, the scene in which Lawrence wears his Arab outfit for the first time.

They watched it intently and laughed at the end when Auda Abu Tayyi appears. I asked the class what they noticed in the scene. "Lawrence is happy that he finally has some friends," ventured one girl. The dominant boy in the class said that Lawrence now realizes what he wants to become. I asked him what, exactly, he thought that was. "I think he wants to be an Arab, to be recognized as one," he replied. And why did the class laugh? "Because he looks like Superman the way's he flying around there," the boy once again blurted out.

Wrapping up this segment of our conversation, the class admitted that they had a hard time understanding *Lawrence of Arabia*. It was difficult to relate to, said one girl, because it's not about people or places they knew much about. Another said that it was hard to follow what was going on, to tell one character apart from another, or to remember who was what. But they did understand a lot of what was going on, I protested: they could tell me the plot; they even gave me quite subtle interpretations of the character and his situation. In fact, I knew they understood the movie better than I did when I saw it for the first time. Yes, said the boy who had monopolized the discussion, but he had to think a lot about it afterward; it wasn't like most movies you see today that click as soon as you've watched them. Alyce now objected, pointing out that that's okay, isn't it, that you have to think about a movie afterward or maybe even see it more than once before you understand it. But we're not used to it, the boy emphasized.

The third focus group was less rewarding. My energy was flagging, and I also caught Alyce once or twice with her eyes closed. The students were torn between wanting to stay for the whole period or go to biology lab, where they would dissect frogs. Besides, the lunch hour was approaching, and everyone was getting hungry. Rather than fight this inertia, Alyce and I tacitly agreed to let the session stop a few minutes before it was supposed to.

Leaving North Adams by car a few hours later, we held a postmortem. It had been a lot of work, much more so for Alyce than for me. She had had to prep the classes for the film and then arrange for the projection of a 35 mm print, whereas I had only to show up for the screening and then run the focus groups. We were glad about both experiences, however. It was surprising how much of a film that was alien in sensibility and daunting in length had been absorbed by these teenagers. No matter that it was not their favorite or that they didn't even like it very much in the end. As Alyce put it, even if these kids don't remember the movie years from now, they'll remember having seen it on a special field trip and that they talked to us about it afterward.

Alyce toyed with the idea of doing this again with different groups of students, perhaps in different parts of the country. Would I be interested in joining her "roadshow"? she asked recently. We have both gone on to different things by now, and the idea lies dormant.

That same winter I had the occasion to watch *Lawrence of Arabia* a second time, however. Fellow anthropologist Michael Gilsenan and I decided to show it at one sitting of both of our classes, his being a course on the Middle East at New York University and mine on cultural studies at the New School for Social Research. We had rented a 35 mm copy, at considerable expense, but when it came time to show it in a special auditorium, it turned out that the student film projectionists had never had training on this format and therefore were unable to exhibit it. Our students were disappointed, of course, and it was difficult to get them to arrange their schedules for another evening showing later in the week; nor was it clear to us that we could afford to extend the lease from the film distributor, even if our students agreed to come. We asked the projectionists, all five of whom, one after the other, had been struggling bravely to get the show on the road, to pack up the fourteen canisters of film, which we then lugged on a handcart back to Michael's office, trying to keep them dry by covering them with our raincoats as we slithered across Washington Square.

The showing of the film was in fact rescheduled. This time around, the NYU Film School took charge of the exhibition in one of its own auditoriums. A competent young man busily slicing the reels together said that everything seemed to be all right, except for some mysterious wetness around the edges of the reels, which he hoped would not damage the film. "Do the best you can," muttered Michael, as he slunk out of the projectionist booth, not having the heart to bring up the fiasco of a few nights ago, which would have explained the telltale wetness. After a few trials to get the sound and image in synch and to work out some focus problems, we were ready to roll. It was Michael's birthday, and as the house lights dimmed, I broke out some champagne and dessert. But when they heard the cork pop, our students might have thought we were celebrating the fact that *Lawrence of Arabia* was being shown on the screen at long last.

I was teaching at Eugene Lang College, the undergraduate institution of the New School for Social Research. I had been asked to teach the cultural studies course at the last minute, and I agreed, but only on the condition that I could base it on my book. I didn't have time to prepare anything else, I explained. Though I welcomed this opportunity to test some of the book's ideas, I was still apprehensive about the prospect of basing a whole course on it. For some people cultural studies has become an arena of "multiculturalism," in that it not only critiques mass media representations of the Other but also explores the ways in which subaltern groups, excluded or marginalized in hegemonic cultural works, manage to express their own experiences and political struggles in "alternative" media. Basing a whole course on a film like *Lawrence of Arabia* would allow us to explore some of these issues but not others. Nevertheless, it was a complex film, and by analyzing it almost frame by frame, I hoped to explore topics such as basic film techniques, transnational aspects of film production, questions of realism, complexities of genre, and narrative and editing, and finally to introduce students to cinematic theory, helping to clarify the latter's points by making reference to a film they would know inside out.

When the class finally did see *Lawrence of Arabia,* students were well prepared to follow the film. I had put together a reader with excerpts from all the major biographies on Lawrence—British, French, and Arab—including Thomas's famous travelogue as well as Lawrence's memoir. From these readings, they analyzed how the constructions of Lawrence had shifted over time, and in relation to what historical circumstances, and they realized that the film was part of a particular moment of revisionist history surrounding his legend. I also asked them to make maps of the region, and some responded with a cartography of their feelings. One student created a beautiful gouache and watercolor over pencil, with warm, inviting yellows for the land masses and a bright, swirling blue for the seas, lakes, and rivers. Another student's creation was self-consciously modeled after Jasper Johns's paintings, an exhibition of which she had just seen at the Museum of Modern Art. She had painted bold, agitated strokes of gray onto cardboard—the national borders in black, the names of countries and cities in white, the Damascus-Medina Railroad looking like a lurid scar across the Arabian plateau—with the entire map split apart horizontally, the halves held loosely together by thick cord. This was a schizophrenic space of violence and fear, the very opposite of the inviting, secure, wholesome, romantic setting of the gouache and watercolor. I remarked to the artists on how much these two maps encapsulated the film's (and our) subconscious attitudes toward the Near East.

Frustrations began to build about a month into the course and were politely conveyed to me. A talented artist from the Parsons School of Design wondered whether we could also see some films that were "contemporary." My reply was that as long as the topic of the course was *Lawrence of Arabia,* we could watch some films that owe an obvious debt to it, such as *The English Patient,* but I wanted to stick to a particular historical period of film production and reception and to understand as much of its richness and complexities as possible. Although the class went along with it, I don't think it ever completely reconciled itself to this historical perspective.

Another student who acknowledged the need to examine critically films such as this one, which told stories about male power and colonialism, nevertheless felt we were spending too much time on them. What about other kinds of films, talking about other kinds of experiences, particularly those of marginalized groups? This, too, was a reasonable and, in terms of the logic of cultural studies, even compelling request, though I asked that we stick to films of the time period of the 1950s and 1960s or one that had something to do with the epic film genre we were studying.

As a result of her intervention, we watched *Salt of the Earth.* Unfortunately, the only students to attend this extra class, which was made voluntary, were the three students of color, and of course the absence of the white students did not go unnoticed. The latter rented the video and saw it at their own convenience, but as a result they did not catch the reactions of the students to the film, let alone the discussion we had about it directly after the showing. The students of color loved the film, and the Latina woman who had asked me to open up the course in showing some films made by alternative filmmakers was particularly moved by it. I did not tell her until the film was over that the scriptwriter was Michael Wilson, who of course had worked on *Lawrence of Arabia.* A man, I remarked teasingly, writing this sensitively about feminist issues! A white man, to boot, daring to put into the mouths of his Chicano actors and actresses feelings that you describe as heartachingly familiar! I added that the film had been unofficially banned during the McCarthy period, not only because of its portrayal of socialist labor organizing against rapacious capitalist bosses but also because most of the filmmakers had been blacklisted. An alternative to precisely the kind of film that *Lawrence of Arabia* represented had been rendered invisible by a particular constellation of political forces in the 1950s.

Thus, we spent a good deal of the course trying to understand the political conditions of censorship (external and internal to the industry)

that historically constrained U.S. film production and reception. I needed
to make this context clearer for *Lawrence of Arabia,* which bridged, after all, the United States and Great Britain, in order to explain the possibilities and limits of its own critique of power and colonialism. In regard
to the latter claim, however, lay the source of yet another strain or tension in the class; that is, some of the students were unwilling to concede
that the film was in fact critical of colonialism. The person most resis-
tant to this idea and most eloquent in arguing against it was an African-
American woman. Her views became more nuanced as she developed
her defense. It's nothing but the typical story about the great white man
who comes to save a poor and feuding people, she averred in the beginning. Isn't this what epics always claim? she asked. It was pointed out to
her that Lawrence is portrayed as demonic, even insane, that in the end
he does not save anybody, least of all himself—the point at which the
North Adams students had arrived in their interpretation of his character. Furthermore, the epic weight and thrust of the first part of the film
is contradicted by the second, turning it into an anti-epic epic. She again
held her own by saying that all the film showed is that colonialism was
inevitable, whether because of the machinations of the British or the
supposed inabilities of the Arabs to govern themselves, but it made no
critique of colonialism per se. The fact that the moral arguments that
had underpinned imperialism were subverted by the film made no impression on her. Many of the white students disagreed, though the differences in view did not fall out easily along a color line, for one of the
Latinas, also one of the most articulate students—at least in her papers—
could see how the movie took a position against colonialism, while at
the same time she concurred with the African-American woman that it
did not go far enough in that regard. I let the disagreement remain unresolved, telling students that in the end an interpretation is after all an
interpretation.

However, I had obviously not taken adequately into account the fact
that my "dialectical criticism" of a film like *Lawrence of Arabia* might
be threatening to certain students while it was welcome to others. Some
of the white students seemed to insist that the film was to a certain degree critical of colonialism and that this was important to note. But why
was it important to note? I asked. Because not all films from the period
were the same, some being more racist or colonialist and some less, and
it is interesting to know what makes the latter kinds of films possible.
They had been watching *Four Feathers, Gunga Din, Sanders of the River,*

and other films of the colonial period, and they could clearly see differences among them as well as between them and *Lawrence of Arabia*. However, I'm sorry that we didn't discuss much more the stakes involved for students of color that might make them anxious about my approach to the course. Was I saying that works from the center such as *Lawrence of Arabia* were sufficient in both their critiques of colonialism and their representations of the Other to render unnecessary representations coming from nonhegemonic positions? I thought I had been clear in saying just the opposite, though the example of *Salt of the Earth* also brought home the point that one cannot simply bring these to light but also must try to understand the broader political contexts that limit their reception. Nonetheless, the fear that other points of view might be suppressed, I think, persisted.

Partly in response to that fear, I had the class watch Spike Lee's *Malcolm X,* a film of epic proportions and therefore within the bounds of the genre we were considering, a film about an individual who is ensnared in historical forces larger than himself and therefore not unlike the treatment of Lawrence in Lean's film. This time I showed the film during regular class periods so that the students would have no scheduling conflicts that would prevent them from seeing it together. When it was over, the African-American woman was crying. Though everyone was clearly moved by the film, if more silent in their testimony, her tears seemed to preclude any serious criticism of what they had seen. One white woman said that she was disturbed by the way in which white women were portrayed in the film and then mentioned that she once had a terrible argument with her black boyfriend about it. Get used to it, was the response of the Latina woman and the African-American, for now you know how women of color have been represented in the mainstream cinema. But if it's not excusable in mainstream cinema, was she saying that it's all right if Spike Lee does it? Does this really matter so much that it detracts from the film's significance? was the rejoinder. She wasn't saying that the film isn't powerful or that its subject matter is unimportant, explained the white woman, but for someone like her that aspect of it is problematic. A white male later confided in me that he didn't think the film was very reflexive or self-critical. It seemed as though we were deadlocked.

In the following month, I introduced the class to postcolonial theories of orientalism (Said, Bhabha, Suleri) and to feminist film theory (Mulvey, Studlar, Modleski, Clover), showing how, in my view at least, they had been moving more toward what I have called in the introduction of my book "dialectical critique." There was more resistance on the part of the two of the students of color to ideas of ambivalence, irony, and so forth when it came to studies of orientalism and representations of the Other than there was to the same ideas when it came to studies of gender, particularly masculinity. But there was a moment of epiphany when these same students read Kobena Mercer's article "Skin Head Sex Thing," in which the black British cultural studies critic explains how he came to revise his opinion of Robert Mapplethorpe's photographs of black men. At first, as he explains, he argued that these photographs were racist in the way they fetishized black male bodies by familiar stereotypes, all in order to advance Mapplethorpe's reputation and career, but then he reconsidered his criticism in light of the photographer's gayness and the political context surrounding the reception of his art in the early 1990s—particularly the assault by the American right on various controversial artists as well as public agencies such as the National Endowment for the Humanities that supported them and public museums that exhibited them. Now Mercer was arguing that the photographs were still disturbing in the messages they sent out about black men, but that it was important to note how they were also subverting the white body as the "classic" nude, long at the heart of the white Western canon of "high" art.

The whole class enjoyed the article and especially liked the fact that Mercer was not only able to change his mind but that he was willing to talk about it honestly. It was the two students of color who told me that what I had been trying to do was now clearer. My approach had been validated because it was authorized by someone whose motives they could trust, whose stakes were presumably similar to theirs. Of course, it was at this time, too, that I talked about how I could relate to the ambiguous treatment of homosexuality in *Lawrence of Arabia* because of my sexuality. I had waited to bring it up at the end because I didn't want it to dominate the class or lead to a reductionist reading of the film. Foucault says, "Do not ask who I am and do not ask me to remain the same." [1] Now I feared that I was trusted by the students of color because I was marked as a marginalized person, something I have never felt or claimed for myself. If I seemed, finally, to get my students to read the film dialectically, the "victory" was not without its ironies: I had to construct myself in a certain way that sounded persuasive to them but somewhat false to myself.

But the feeling of having won on one front was soon dispelled. A young white woman who had had poor class attendance came to me at the end, very much in tears, to say that she felt awful about not coming to class but that she had hated its dynamics. I knew her to be bright and serious, so I believed the confession. She felt like she couldn't speak up without seeming to appear retrograde or worse, and yet she had been in tense multicultural situations before, such as women's groups in which the dynamics had been quite different. In large part I took the blame for the dynamics, but I also pointed out that coming to class had not been so easy for the students of color either, who had been dubious about my approach in the first place, and yet theirs was probably the best attendance. But the truth was that I didn't know the answer to the more fundamental question she was asking: In this country, how does one have conversations in the classroom across race and ethnic boundaries about subjects as fraught as cultural difference and the history of white oppression and still keep everyone in the boat paddling together to another shore? The choices prevailing today seem too stark: either a celebration of the other or a reviling of the self. The complexities of positions and their histories seem not to count at all. We are not there yet, but I have to hope that that day will not be far off.

Let me return to the end of *Lawrence of Arabia*.

Lawrence is in a jeep speeding away from Damascus. The terrain is flat, featureless, and dusty. He sees ahead a party of mounted bedouin and thinks he might know them. Standing up to get a better look, he discovers that they are strangers and sits down. From misrecognition, his encounter with the Other has turned into nonrecognition.

A truck transporting troops singing a World War I song approaches, the soldiers' husky voices raised in song. Lawrence is no longer part of that world, the world of power and war, and it rushes past him, trailing in the wind. The world around Lawrence returns to silence. He is absorbed in his own brooding thoughts.

"It'll be good to go 'ome, sir," says his driver cheerfully. Lawrence has not heard. "Huh?" and he looks at him. "'ome, sir." Britain was never Lawrence's home. It won't be now. He looks away and says nothing.

A speeding motorcyclist now passes, kicking up dust on the windshield. He, as we now know, is the premonition of death, a death awaiting Lawrence on a narrow, shady, country road less than two decades hence. The camera stays on the dusty windshield. We can barely discern the outline of Lawrence's head, his features obscured as though covered by a shroud. We hear the wind. Faintly, tentatively, the Lawrence theme starts up. We continue to see him obscured behind a dusty windscreen but being moved as though propelled through space.

After this meditation on the perils of talking about colonialism and cultural difference, to close on this fearful image of uncertainty and dread may seem bleak but also somehow true.

Notes

INTRODUCTION. THE TEATRO DEL LAGO AND AFTER

1. To glean some of the atmosphere of these movie houses, though it is a social history of the cinema of Britain between the wars, see Jeffrey Richards, *The Age of the Dream Palace* (London: Routledge and Kegan Paul, 1984).

2. Janet Maslin, "'Lawrence' Seen Whole," *New York Times,* January 29, 1989, sec. 1, 1.

3. Allen Barra, "At Long Last, the Real Lawrence," *American Film* 14 (5) (1989): 44.

4. Stephen Farber, "Look What They've Done to 'Lawrence of Arabia,'" *New York Times,* May 2, 1971, sec. 2, 11.

5. For a witty and insightful discussion of the problems of credibility facing the academic critic who would today take the study of epic seriously, I recommend the article by Vivian Sobchack, "'Surge and Splendor': A Phenomenology of the Hollywood Historical Epic," *Representations* 29 (Winter 1990): 24–29.

6. Tania Modleski, *The Women Who Knew Too Much: Hitchcock and Feminist Theory* (New York: Routledge, 1988), 120.

7. Linda Williams, *Hard Core: Power, Pleasure and the "Frenzy of the Visible"* (Berkeley: University of California Press, 1989), xi.

8. The term "postcolonial" is relatively new but has fairly quickly become common in literary and cultural criticism. Various meanings are attributed to it, none of which is unproblematical. One such meaning, fairly prevalent in academic discourse, is that this criticism of texts has been emergent since the decolonization of the Third World in the post–World War II period, even though it is understood that that world is still dominated by the West through new modes of economic and technological "colonialism." Sometimes this meaning is accompanied by a Foucauldian notion of power as it is attached to the production of

knowledge, with the result that colonial texts would be read as advancing Western imperial projects. For a discussion of some of these and other issues, see Ella Shohat, "Notes on the 'Post-Colonial,'" *Social Text* 31–32 (1993): 99–113; and Kwame Anthony Appiah, "Is the Post- in Postmodernism the Post- in Post-colonial?" *Critical Inquiry* 10 (Winter 1991): 336–57.

9. Laura Mulvey, "Visual Pleasure and Narrative Cinema," *Screen* 16 (3) (Autumn 1975): 6–18

10. Laura Mulvey, "On *Duel in the Sun:* Afterthoughts on 'Visual Pleasure and Narrative Cinema,'" *Framework,* nos. 15–17 (1981): 12–15.

11. For some of the ways in which Mulvey's formulations have been retheorized, particularly with respect to the concept of the "gaze," see the two articles by Gertrud Koch, "Ex-Changing the Gaze: Re-Visioning Feminist Film Theory," *New German Critique* 34 (Winter 1985): 139–53; and Gertrud Koch, "Comment," *Camera Obscura* 20–21 (May–September 1989): 209–17; and in particular, D. N. Rodowick, "The Difficulty of Difference," *Wide Angle* 5 (1) (1982): 4–15; and Gaylyn Studlar, "Masochism and the Perverse Pleasures of the Cinema," *Quarterly Review of Film* 9 (4) (Fall 1984): 267–82. For a discussion particularly of the male gaze, see Edward Snow, "Theorizing the Male Gaze: Some Problems," *Representations* 25 (1989): 30–41.

12. Modleski, *Women Who Knew Too Much,* 116–17.

13. Ibid., 120.

14. Carol J. Clover, *Men, Women, and Chain Saws: Gender in the Modern Horror Film* (Princeton, N.J.: Princeton University Press, 1992).

15. Edward Said, *Orientalism* (New York: Vintage,1978). See also Edward Said, "Orientalism Reconsidered," in *Europe and Its Others,* vol. 1, ed. Francis Barker, Peter Hulme, Margaret Iversen, and Diana Loxley, Proceedings of Essex Conference on Sociology and Literature (July 1984) (Colchester: University of Essex, 1985), 14–27.

16. See the following works by Homi K. Bhabha: "The Other Question," *Screen* 24 (6) (1983): 18–36; "Difference, Discrimination and the Discourse of Orientalism," in *Politics of Theory,* ed. Francis Barker, Peter Hulme, Margaret Iversen, and Diana Loxley (Colchester: University of Essex, 1983), 194–211; "Of Mimicry and Man: The Ambivalence of Colonial Discourse," *October* 28 (1984): 125–33; and "Signs Taken for Wonders: Questions of Ambivalence and Authority Under a Tree Outside Delhi, May 1817," in *Europe and Its Others,* vol. 1, ed. Francis Barker, Peter Hulme, Margaret Iversen, and Diana Loxley, Proceedings of Essex Conference on Sociology and Literature (July 1984) (Colchester: University of Essex, 1985), 89–106.

17. Sara Suleri, *The Rhetoric of English India* (Chicago: University of Chicago Press, 1992).

18. Bhabha, "The Other Question," 24.

19. Ibid.

20. Ibid., 22.

21. Ibid., 25.

22. Ibid.

23. Sigmund Freud, "Fetishism" (1927), in *Sexuality and the Psychology of Love* (New York: Macmillan, 1963), 204–9.

24. Bhabha, "Of Mimicry and Man."

25. Ibid., 126.

26. In the mimicry piece, and even more so in his "Signs Taken for Wonder," Bhabha introduces the possibility of resistance by the colonized of the representations imposed by the colonizer, a resistance that takes the form of difference, or continual slippage in the mimicry between what is demanded by the colonizer and what is granted by the colonized. In other words, just as the colonizer might insist on there being a difference between "self" and "other" by way of establishing hegemony (i.e., the "other" never quite measuring up), so might the colonizer by resisting the constraining system of the colonial regime.

27. Sigmund Freud, "The 'Uncanny,'" in *Sigmund Freud: The Standard Edition of the Complete Psychological Works* 17 (1917–19), trans. James Strachey (London: Hogarth Press, 1925), 235.

28. Suleri, *The Rhetoric of English India*, 2.

29. Ibid., 3.

30. Ibid., 5.

31. Edward Said, *Culture and Imperialism* (New York: Knopf, 1993), 146.

32. Ibid., 159.

33. Suleri, *The Rhetoric of English India*, 116.

34. Ibid., 130.

35. Ibid., chapters 2 and 3.

36. Sadeq al-'Azm, "Orientalism and Orientalism in Reverse," *Khamsin* 8 (1981): 5–26.

37. Aijaz Ahmad, *In Theory: Classes, Nations, Literatures* (London and New York: Verso, 1992).

38. The most comprehensive history of the Frankfurt school is Rolf Wiggershaus, *The Frankfurt School: Its History, Theories, and Political Significance,* trans. Michael Robertson (Cambridge, Mass.: MIT Press, 1994). It is especially useful in clarifying the position of this school after Horkheimer and Adorno moved back to Germany in the postwar period, not to mention the role of Jurgen Habermas as its last great but also quite ambiguous representative. For years, the standard history has been Martin Jay's *The Dialectical Imagination: A History of the Frankfurt School and the Institute of Social Research, 1923–1950* (Boston: Little, Brown, 1973), which is still indispensable reading. That work, but also in particular Susan Buck-Morss's *The Origins of Negative Dialectics: Theodor W. Adorno, Walter Benjamin, and the Frankfurt Institute* (New York: Free Press, 1977) are particularly important for the idea of "dialectical" criticism developed by the Frankfurt school, which has influenced my thinking as well.

39. Theodor W. Adorno, *Negative Dialectic,* trans. E. B. Ashton (New York: Continuum, 1973).

40. Although other of Benjamin's studies on these subjects could be cited, I am thinking especially of his Paris "arcades project," which he never lived to complete and which exists only in the form of notes and scattered drafts. There have been various reconstructions of the project, and the reader should at least consult Susan Buck-Morss's *The Dialectics of Seeing: Walter Benjamin and the Arcades Project* (Cambridge, Mass.: MIT Press, 1989).

41. Max Horkheimer and Theodor W. Adorno, "The Culture Industry: Enlightenment as Mass Deception," in *Dialectic of the Enlightenment,* trans. John Cumming (New York: Continuum, 1989), 120.

42. Ibid., 127.

43. Theodor W. Adorno, "Perennial Fashion—Jazz," in *Prisms,* trans. Samuel Weber and Shierry Weber (Cambridge, Mass.: MIT Press, 1981), 227–42.

44. Walter Benjamin, "The Work of Art in the Age of Mechanical Reproduction," in *Illuminations,* ed. Hannah Arendt and trans. Harry Zohn (New York: Schocken, 1969), 217–51.

45. The notion of the "optical unconscious" is mentioned in only a few places in Benjamin's oeuvre. See his "A Small History of Photography," in *One-Way Street and Other Writings,* trans. Edmund Jephcott and Kingsley Shorter (London: NLB, 1979), 240–57, and "The Work of Art in the Age of Mechanical Reproduction." Of course, as with many of Benjamin's ideas, there has been controversy over what he meant by it. For recent uses of the concept, sometimes deliberately at cross-purposes with what is construed to have been Benjamin's intentions, see Rosalind E. Krauss, *The Optical Unconscious* (Cambridge, Mass.: MIT Press, 1993); and Michael Taussig, *Mimesis and Alterity: A Particular History of the Senses* (New York: Routledge, 1993).

46. Kenneth Burke, *A Grammar of Motives* and *A Rhetoric of Motives* (Cleveland: World Publishing, 1962).

47. Horkheimer and Adorno, "The Culture Industry," 126.

48. E. Ann Kaplan, "E. Ann Kaplan Replies," *Cinema Journal* 25 (1) (1985): 52.

49. Miriam Hansen, *Babel and Babylon: Spectatorship in American Silent Film* (Cambridge, Mass.: Harvard University Press, 1991).

50. Elizabeth G. Traube, *Dreaming Identities: Class, Gender, and Generation in 1980's Hollywood Movies* (Boulder, Colo.: Westview Press, 1992).

1. "TRAVELLING CIRCUS"

1. Irving Bernstein, *Hollywood at the Crossroads: An Economic Study of the Motion Picture Industry* (Hollywood: Hollywood AFL Film Council, 1957), 48.

2. See, for example, H. Schiller, *Mass Communication and American Empire* (Boston: Beacon, 1971); A Mattelart, *Corporations and the Control of Culture* (Brighton, England: Harvester Press, 1979); N. Graham, "Contribution to a Political Economy of Mass Communication," *Media, Culture and Society* 2 (April 1979): 123–46; T. Guback, "Film as International Business," *Journal of Communications* 24 (1) (Winter 1974): 90–101; Thomas Guback, "Hollywood's International Market," in *The American Film Industry,* ed. Tino Balio (Madison: University of Wisconsin Press, 1985), 463–86; T. Guback, *International Film Industry* (Bloomington: Indiana University Press, 1969); and Janet Wasko, *Movies and Money: Financing the American Film Industry* (Norwood, N.J.: Ablex, 1982).

3. Arjun Appadurai, "Global Ethnoscapes," in *Recapturing Anthropology,*

ed. Richard Fox (Santa Fe, N.M.: School of American Research, 1991), 191–210; and Liisa Malkki, "Citizens of Humanity: Internationalism and the Imagined Community of Nations," *Diaspora* 3 (1) (Spring 1994): 41–68.

4. See Tino Balio, ed., *The American Film Industry* (Madison: University of Wisconsin Press, 1976); David Bordwell, Janet Staiger, and Kristin Thompson, *The Classical Hollywood Cinema* (New York: Columbia University Press, 1985), especially parts 2 and 5; and Bernstein, *Hollywood at the Crossroads*. As far as I am aware, a comprehensive history of the economics of the film industry has yet to be written and in fact is badly needed.

5. Andrew Sinclair, *Spiegel: The Man Behind the Pictures* (Boston: Little, Brown, 1987), 17.

6. Donald Nelson, "The Independent Producer," in *The Motion Picture Industry,* ed. Gordon Watkins, *Annals of the American Academy of Political and Social Science* (1947): 49–57; Frederic Marlowe, "The Rise of the Independents in Hollywood," *Penguin Film Review* 1 (1946–49): 72–75; and Richard Dyer MacCann, "Independence, with a Vengeance," *Film Quarterly* 15 (3) (Summer 1962): 14–21.

7. Bernstein, *Hollywood at the Crossroads,* 21–22.

8. Ibid., 45–70.

9. Ibid., 47.

10. Ibid., 47–48.

11. A similar argument is made by Ruth Vasey, "Foreign Parts: Hollywood's Global Distribution and the Representation of Ethnicity," in *Movie Censorship and American Culture,* ed. Francis G. Couvares (Washington, D.C.: Smithsonian Institution Press, 1996), 212–36.

12. Bernstein, *Hollywood at the Crossroads,* 69.

13. Ibid., 69–70.

14. Ibid., 67.

15. Armand Mattelart, *Transnationals and the Third World,* trans. David Buxton (South Hadley, Mass.: Bergin and Garvey, 1983), 16.

16. See Uriel Dann, *King Hussein and the Challenge of Arab Radicalism: Jordan, 1955–1967* (New York: Oxford University Press, 1989); Peter Snow, *Hussein: A Biography* (Washington, D.C.: R. B. Luce, 1972); King Hussein I, *Uneasy Lies the Head* (New York: Random House, 1962).

17. See L. Robert Morris and Lawrence Raskin, *Lawrence of Arabia: The Thirtieth Anniversary Pictorial History* (New York: Doubleday, 1992), 46.

18. Ibid., 62–63.

19. See Howard Kent, *Single Bed for Three: A "Lawrence of Arabia" Notebook* (London: Hutchinson, 1963), 173.

20. Ibid., 64.

21. Omar Sharif, with Marie-Thérèse Guinchard, *The Eternal Male,* trans. Martin Solokinsky (New York: Doubleday, 1977), 23.

22. See Morris and Raskin, *Lawrence of Arabia,* 65–66.

23. Ibid., 80.

24. Jeffrey Richards and Jeffrey Hulbert, "Censorship in Action: The Case of Lawrence of Arabia," *Journal of Contemporary History* 19 (1984): 153–70, es-

pecially pp. 161–62. This is also a very interesting case of the way in which state politics can influence foreign film production.

25. Morris and Raskin, *Lawrence of Arabia,* 24 (details about Korda's alleged espionage done through his international film company).

26. Ibid., 77.

27. The model of segmentary tribal politics was first enunciated by E. E. Evans-Pritchard in his *The Nuer* (Oxford: Oxford University Press, 1940) and has since influenced generations of anthropologists working not only in the Middle East but also in Africa and elsewhere.

28. The good, in-depth studies of Lean's oeuvre are few. The most detailed examination to date of Lean's life and work is Kevin Brownlow's *David Lean: A Biography* (New York: St. Martin's Press, 1996). Substantial portions of the text are based on interviews with Lean and his close associates, though the book lacks analysis and narrative. I also highly recommend the following works: Alain Silver and James Ursini, *David Lean and His Films* (Los Angeles: Silman-James Press, 1991); and Michael Anderegg, *David Lean* (Boston: Twayne, 1984). They are both insightful, analytically interesting works. For a more chatty but beautifully illustrated volume, which also contains a wealth of useful anecdotal information culled from numerous interviews with associates of Lean, see Stephen M. Silverman, *David Lean* (New York: Abrams, 1989). For a useful reference work on David Lean, which contains film synopses and other information, see also Gerald Pratley, *The Cinema of David Lean* (London: Tantivy Press, 1974). For a listing of writings on David Lean, Louis P. Castelli and Caryn Lynn Cleeland's *David Lean: A Guide to References and Resources* (Boston: G. K. Hall, 1980) is indispensable. For an earlier commentary on Lean, see the articles by Steven Ross, "In Defense of David Lean," *Take One* 3 (1972): 10–18, and Douglas McVay, "Lean—Lover of Life," *Films and Filming* 9 (1963): 12–15, which are both quite favorable. James Holden, "The Best Technical Man in the Business: A Study of David Lean," *Film Journal* 1 (April 1956): 1–5, and Ron Pickard, "David Lean: Supreme Craftsman," *Films in Review* 25 (May 1974): 265–84, are more negative. A retrospective on Lean that is useful for explaining his varying reception by film critics is Hollis Alpert, "The David Lean Recipe: A 'Whack in the Guts,'" *New York Times Magazine,* May 23, 1965, 32–33, 94, 96, 98, 110.

Lean has also been interviewed, though not extensively, and has talked about his views on filmmaking. Extremely useful in this regard is his own *David Lean: A Self-Portrait,* produced and directed by Thomas Craven, Pyramid Films (1971), and an interview with David Lean, entitled "Out of the Wilderness," *Films and Filming* 9 (1963): 12–15. Also consult the interviews with Gerald Pratley, "Interview with David Lean," in *Interviews with Film Directors,* ed. Andrew Sarris (Indianapolis: Bobbs-Merrill, 1967), 263–67, and with Melvyn Bragg, "Lean and Bolt," *The South Bank Show,* produced and directed by David Thomas, London Weekend Television (1990).

29. Richard Dyer, *Brief Encounter* (London: British Film Institute, 1993), 41.

30. See Andrew Sarris, *The American Cinema: Directors and Directions, 1929–1968* (New York: Dutton, 1968).

31. See Ross, "In Defense of David Lean."

32. Betty Spiegel quoted in Silverman, *David Lean,* 121.

33. Lean, "Out of the Wilderness," 12–15.

34. Silverman, *David Lean,* 20.

35. Brownlow, *David Lean,* 46.

36. Ibid., 40.

37. Ibid., 130.

38. Ibid., 239.

39. Malkki, "Citizens of Humanity," 41.

40. Ibid., 49.

41. Roland Barthes, "The Great Family of Man," in *Mythologies* (New York: Hill and Wang, 1972), 101–2.

42. Dyer, *Brief Encounter,* 10.

43. For an interesting review of the restored version, see Michael Sragow, "David Lean's Magnificent Kwai," *Atlantic Monthly,* February 1994, 104–9.

44. Sinclair, *Spiegel,* 81.

45. Sharif, *Eternal Male,* 15–16.

46. Ibid., 12.

47. Ibid., 11.

48. Ibid., 120.

49. Ibid., 23–39.

50. Ibid., 14.

51. See Roy Armes, *Third World Film Making and the West* (Berkeley: University of California Press, 1987), 243–53, for information on Youssef Chahine.

52. Sharif, *Eternal Male,* 66.

53. Ibid., 101.

54. Ibid., 15.

55. Alpert, "The David Lean Recipe," 96.

56. Sharif, *Eternal Male,* 13.

57. Anonymous, "Brother Rejects Lawrence Film," *New York Times Western Edition,* January 5, 1963, 7.

58. See A. W. Lawrence, "Letter to the *Times,*" *Times,* December 14, 1962, 13.

59. Daisy Allenby, "Letter to the *Times,*" *Times,* December 27, 1962, 7.

60. Vasey, "Foreign Parts," 221–22.

61. Roy Frumkes, "The Restoration of 'Lawrence of Arabia,'" *Films in Review* 1 (May 1989): 286.

62. See Morris and Raskin, *Lawrence of Arabia,* 179.

63. See the statement in al-Jarīdah al-rasmiyyah l-il-mamlikah al-ʿurduniyyah al-hāshimiyyah (The Official Journal of the Hashimite Kingdom of Jordan), no. 1739 (10 Shibat 1964), p. 134. "The Council of Ministers decided in a meeting convened on January 13, 1964 [to discuss] the film production [Lawrence of Arabia] that it would forbid its exhibition in Jordan."

64. Morris and Raskin, *Lawrence of Arabia,* 124.

65. I have never been able to find the article in which this report is gone into in detail, however, much less a copy of the official protest itself.

2. LEAN'S LENS

1. All quotations, unless specified otherwise, are from David Lean's letter to Michael Wilson, dated April 24, 1960, which is on deposit in the Michael Wilson Papers, Arts Library–Special Collections, Library of the University of California, Los Angeles.

2. Photographs can be found in Morris and Raskin, *Lawrence of Arabia,* 47. There are two superb books on the production. One of them is by Morris and Raskin. Also excellent is Adrian Turner, *The Making of David Lean's LAWRENCE OF ARABIA* (Limpsfield, England: Dragon's World Book, 1994). Omar Sharif has talked extensively about the making of the movie throughout his memoir *The Eternal Male.* At various times during the shooting, critics visited the set and reported back on the production. See Robert Emma Ginna, Jr., "The Return of Lawrence of Arabia," *Connoisseur,* May 1989, 156–63, which contains his reminiscences of watching and talking with O'Toole and Lean on the set. Also of interest is the brief article by John Knowles, "All-Out in the Desert," *Horizon Magazine,* July 1962, 109–11, and by correspondent John R. Woolfenden, "Desert Caravan on the Trail of 'Lawrence,'" *New York Times,* June 25, 1961, sec 2, 7. A publicist for the film who was responsible for cataloging all the production stills visited the set or accompanied the filmmakers in one or another expedition and wrote an anecdotal account. See Kent, *Single Bed for Three.* David Lean has spoken about the filming in several places, the most interesting being his interview with Melvyn Bragg, "Lean and Bolt." There has also been a Bravo Channel examination of the production through interviews with surviving crew, in particular the cinematographer Fred Young, which, I regret to say, I have not yet been able to see.

3. Vivian Sobchack has observed that this self-referentiality is typical of the epic genre, in which the production seems to be enacting the story it is filming; for example, the "(male) heroism" required of the filmmakers to carry out the production. See her article "'Surge and Splendor,'" 24–49. For a similar but more pointedly feminist critique of the narratives of film productions, particularly of those associated with the "big" screen, see Tana Wollen, "The Bigger the Better: From Cinemascope to IMAX," in *Future Visions: New Technologies of the Screen,* ed. Philip Hayward and Tana Wollen (London: British Film Institute, 1993), 10–45. A similar critique could be made of the production accounts for *Lawrence of Arabia.* Take this passage as just one example of the way in which masculinity is constructed. "'Peter broke his back for only one reason,' says one member of the cast. 'That was David Lean. Somehow word got around that Lean didn't think Peter was tough enough. One time Lean made him run up and down a sand dune 25 times just to see if he could do it, and he did.'" See Trevor Armbrister, "O'Toole of Arabia and O'Toole: Oscar Winner?" *Saturday Evening Post,* March 9, 1963, 28.

4. T. E. Lawrence, *Seven Pillars of Wisdom: A Triumph* (Garden City, N.Y.: Doubleday, Doran, 1935), 351.

5. Andre Bazin, "Fin du montage," *Cahiers du cinéma,* no. 31 (January 1954): 43. For an excellent overview of wide-screen processes, see John Belton, *Widescreen Cinema* (Cambridge, Mass.: Harvard University Press, 1992).

6. For a technical explanation of this effect, see Freddie Young and Paul Petzold, *The Work of the Motion Picture Cameraman* (New York: Communications Arts Books, 1972), 196.

7. Ibid., 196–97.

8. Lorin D. Grignon, "The Sound for CinemaScope," in *New Screen Techniques,* ed. Martin Quigley, Jr. (New York: Quigley Publications, 1953), 159–70.

9. Bazin, "Fin du montage," 43

10. Charles Barr, "CinemaScope: Before and After," *Film Quarterly* 16 (4) (1963): 22. His article is one of the best early discussions of wide-screen processes and their artistic implications for filmmaking and film viewing. Some of these claims have been considered in an excellent overview of wide-screen processes by David Bordwell in David Bordwell, Janet Staiger, and Kristin Thompson, *The Classical Hollywood Cinema* (New York: Columbia University Press, 1985), 358–64.

11. Barr, "CinemaScope," 18.

12. Andre Bazin, "Un peu tard," *Cahiers du cinéma,* no. 48 (January 1955): 46.

13. Ibid., 47.

14. Bazin's notions of realism have been subject to considerable comment. J. Dudley Andrew's discussion of Bazin's theory of realism in his *The Major Film Theories* (London: Oxford University Press, 1976) is one of the best I have found, acknowledging its incompleteness but also appreciating its depth and subtlety. For a more critical view of the writings of this controversial film theorist, besides the articles by MacCabe cited in the bibliography, see Christopher Williams, "Bazin on Neo-Realism," *Screen* 14 (4) (Winter 1973–74): 61–68.

What realism may be is a vexed question and has, of course, been central to many disciplines for quite a long time. It is becoming pressing once again as a result, among other things, of technologies that purport to manufacture "simulacra" of the world (for example, the technology of "virtual reality"). For a very good general introduction to the question in the history of art, see Linda Nochlin, *Realism* (New York: Penguin, 1971). Perhaps the classic modern text is E. H. Gombrich's *Art and Illusion,* The A. W. Mellon Lectures in the Fine Arts 5, The Bollingen Series 35 (Princeton, N.J.: Princeton University Press, 1969). It puts forward the thesis that whatever passes for realism among critics and viewers is always dependent upon psychological "schemata," deeply embedded within human consciousness, which are not "innate" as much as they are conventional and traditional. In other words, what might be given as "natural" is in fact "constructed" according to certain schemas that may have a long and powerful hold on our viewing practices.

In film theory, the question of realism is discussed in depth and with great subtlety by Bill Nichols, *Representing Reality* (Bloomington: Indiana University Press, 1990). His discussion of realism includes a concern for both the representation—granting its construction according to conventions—and what is construed by the viewer to be its relationship to the context (or world) outside the representation. Surely, this must be one of the deepest and most problematical questions in a whole host of disciplines. In the genre he is most concerned with, documentary film, this relationship is construed to be "truthful," or at least criticizable according to (perhaps contested) arguments, but the important point is that attention to and judgment of the relationship cannot be ignored or backgrounded by the viewing public. Speaking of the more conventional photograph, for example, but including also film, television, and video, Nichols points out that in the documentary genre the viewer expects the photographer to have been "coexistential" with the thing in the world that is being represented by the images in the photograph. Or, as Peirce would have said, there is an "indexical" relationship between the image and the thing that is imaged in the photograph.

15. The concept of "embodiment" has become current in some circles today for discussing questions of representation and realism. For the project of realism discussed in this chapter, I find particularly helpful the phenomenologically inspired approach of Vivian Sobchack, as presented in her challenging work on film, *The Address of the Eye: A Phenomenology of Film Experience* (Princeton, N.J.: Princeton University Press, 1992).

16. Leon Shamroy, "Filming 'The Robe,'" in *New Screen Technologies,* ed. Martin Quigley, Jr. (New York: Quigley Publications, 1953), 177.

17. Jean Negulesco, "New Medium—New Methods," in *New Screen Technologies,* ed. Martin Quigley, Jr. (New York: Quigley Publications, 1953), 175.

18. Sobchack, *The Address of the Eye,* especially chapters 1 and 2.

19. David Bordwell concludes that "Hollywood's widescreen filmmaking was but another instance of trended change, a new set of stylistic devices brought into line with the classical schemata." See Bordwell, Staiger, and Thompson, *The Classical Hollywood Cinema,* 361.

20. Silverman, *David Lean,* 28.

21. Ibid., 42.

22. For a critical look at Lean, see Holden "'The Best Technical Man in the Business.'"

23. Henry Koster, "Directing in CinemaScope," in *New Screen Technologies,* ed. Martin Quigley, Jr. (New York: Quigley Publications, 1953), 173.

24. Ibid., 171.

25. Shamroy, "Filming 'The Robe,'" 180.

26. Negulesco, "New Medium—New Methods," 176.

27. Shamroy, "Filming 'The Robe,'" 180.

28. Ibid.

29. Only one major biography has been written of O'Toole. See Nicholas Wapshott, *Peter O'Toole* (New York: Beaufort Books, 1983). The actor has written two volumes of a projected multivolume autobiography entitled *Loitering with Intent* (New York: Hyperion, 1992). The first volume, subtitled *The Child,* stops at the point at which O'Toole is about to embark on his acting career; the second volume covers his years at the Royal Academy of Dramatic Art; not yet in print at publication of this book is presumably the volume or volumes that will speak of his acting career in film.

30. Wapshott, *Peter O'Toole,* 44.

31. Ibid., 45.

32. Ibid.

33. Ibid.

34. Ibid.

35. He had done some musical stage work (*O Mein Papa*), appeared in a few television programs, and had a small part in the film *Kidnapped* (1960), followed by a more substantial role in *The Day They Robbed the Bank of England* (1960), in which he portrayed a British lieutenant of the guards. He had the choice of playing the Irishman but shrewdly declined it, fearing typecasting. See Armbrister, "O'Toole: Oscar Winner?" 28. Of course, this was the "playing against type" that would work for him politically in his role of Lawrence.

36. Kent, *Single Bed for Three*, 99.

37. Ibid., 81–82.

38. For this argument, see Ella Shohat, "Gender and Culture of Empire: Toward a Feminist Ethnography of Cinema," *Quarterly Review of Film and Video* 13 (1–3) (1991): 45–84.

39. Bob Fisher, "Freddie Young, BSC: An Epic Trail of Achievement," *American Cinematographer* 74 (3) (March 1993): 50–54.

40. Ibid., 52.

41. Ron Magid, "In Search of the David Leans Lens," *American Cinematographer* 70 (4) (April 1989): 95–98.

42. Silverman, *David Lean*, 137.

43. Ibid., 136.

44. Ibid., 137.

45. Benjamin, "A Small History of Photography," 243.

46. Ibid.

47. Benjamin, "The Work of Art in the Age of Mechanical Reproduction," 236–37.

48. Benjamin, "A Small History of Photography," 243–44.

49. Ibid., 244.

50. Colin MacCabe, "Theory and Film: Principles of Realism and Pleasure," in *Narrative, Apparatus, Ideology,* ed. Philip Rosen (New York: Columbia University Press, 1986), 179–97.

51. See Dudley, "Andre Bazin," 158.

52. See MacCabe, "Theory and Film."

53. I would like to thank Karen Kelly, a student in my class "Lawrence of Arabia," which I taught at Eugene Lang College (New School for Social Research) in 1997, for the articulation of the point in terms of the sublime.

54. Sinclair, *Spiegel,* 103.

55. Morris and Raskin, *Lawrence of Arabia,* 108.

56. Pratley, "Interview with David Lean," 263.

57. Maslin, "'Lawrence' Seen Whole," 13.

58. Frumkes, "The Restoration of 'Lawrence of Arabia,'" 208.

3. RIDING THE WHIRLWIND

1. David Robb, "Credit, at Last, for 'Lawrence of Arabia," *New York Times,* September 14, 1995, D7.

2. For an analysis of the *Lawrence of Arabia* screenplays done by Wilson, see especially Turner, *The Making of David Lean's LAWRENCE OF ARABIA,* chap. 4 ("The Screenplay"); and Joel Hodson, "Who Wrote *Lawrence of Ara-*

bia? Sam Spiegel and David Lean's Denial of Credit to a Blacklisted Screen-writer," *Cineaste* 22 (4) (1994): 12–17.

3. For the British Writer's Guild ruling, see especially Turner, *The Making of David Lean's LAWRENCE OF ARABIA.*

4. René Chateau, "Entretiens avec Michael Wilson et Dalton Trumbo," *Positif* 64–65 (1964): 90–94.

5. Erich Fromm, *The Working Class in Weimar Germany: A Psychological and Sociological Study,* ed. Wolfgang Bass, trans. Barbara Weinberger (Cambridge, Mass.: Harvard University Press, 1984).

6. Andrew Parker, Mary Russo, Doris Sommer, and Patricia Yaeger, eds., *Nationalisms and Sexualities* (New York: Routledge, 1992).

7. Kaja Silverman, "White Skin, Brown Masks: The Double Mimesis, or with Lawrence in Arabia," *Differences* 1 (3) (Fall 1989): 3–54.

8. See articles by Homi Bhabha, especially "The Other Question" and "Of Mimicry and Man."

9. Hodson, "Who Wrote *Lawrence of Arabia*?" 12–13.

10. Unless indicated otherwise, all quotations are from Michael Wilson, *I Am the Sum of My Actions,* an oral history of his life and career by Joel Gardner, done shortly before Wilson's death. It remains unpublished but is available at the library of the University of California, UCLA. For information on Bolt's life and career, see Robert Bolt, "First Interview," in *Contemporary Playwrights: Robert Bolt,* interviewed and edited by Ronald Hayman (London: Heineman, 1969), 1–15; and also Bragg, "Lean and Bolt."

11. Lawson was the author of a number of plays, including *Success Story* (1932), and screenplays, among which can be counted *Dynamite* (1929) for Cecil B. de Mille, *Sahara* (1943), directed by Zoltan Korda and starring Humphrey Bogart, and *Blockade* (1938), directed by William Dieterle with Henry Fonda in the lead role.

12. Chateau, "Entretiens avec Michael Wilson et Dalton Trumbo," 95–96.

13. Wilson Papers, Arts Library–Special Collections, UCLA. This statement has been printed in Gary Crowdus, "The Writers Guild of America vs. the Blacklist," *Cineaste* 21 (4) (1995): 29–34.

14. Unless indicated otherwise, all citations are from "LAWRENCE OF ARABIA: Elements and Facets of a Theme," Wilson Papers, Arts Library–Special Collections, UCLA.

15. This document of Lean's is to be found in the Wilson Papers, Arts Library-Special Collections, UCLA.

16.This document is to be found in the Wilson Papers, Arts Library–Special Collections, UCLA.

17. See Hodson, "Who Wrote *Lawrence of Arabia*?"; and Turner, *The Making of David Lean's LAWRENCE OF ARABIA.*

18. See Hodson, "Who Wrote *Lawrence of Arabia*?" 12.

19. Roman Jakobson, "Concluding Statement: Linguistics and Poetics," in *Style in Language,* ed. Thomas A. Sebeok (Cambridge, Mass.: MIT Press, 1960), 351–77.

20. Steven C. Caton, "Contributions of Roman Jakobson," *Annual Review of Anthropology* 16 (1987): 223–60.

21. David Bordwell and Kristin Thompson, *Film Art: An Introduction* (Reading, Mass.: Addison-Wesley, 1979), 79–80.

22. Bolt, "First Interview," 13.

23. See Hodson, "Who Wrote *Lawrence of Arabia*?" 12.

24. E. R. Wood, "Introduction," in *The Tiger and the Horse: A Play by Robert Bolt* (London: Heinemann), vi.

25. Bolt, "First Interview," 7.

26. Robert Bolt, "The Playwright in Films," *Saturday Review*, December 29, 1962, 16.

27. For a general discussion of Brechtian theater, see Martin Esslin, *Brecht: A Choice of Evils* (London: Methuen, 1984), especially p. 120, for a clear description of alienation technique. See also Walter Benjamin, "What Is Epic Theater," in *Illuminations: Essays by Walter Benjamin,* ed. Hannah Arendt and trans. Harry Zohn (New York: Schocken, 1969), 147–54.

28. Lawrence, *Seven Pillars of Wisdom,* 563.

29. Peter O'Toole and Rebecca West. "A Redbook Dialogue," *Redbook* 122 (5) (1964): 148.

30. A nearly slapstick sense of this obsession with Hitleriana can be gleaned from Melvyn Bragg's interview with Peter O'Toole on the *South Bank Show,* which shows O'Toole and a friend prowling around in Hitler's old neighborhoods and scaling ladders in order to peer into his apartment windows. During the show, particularly at the end, O'Toole begins to question, however slightly, the possible motives for this obsession, wondering whether it implicates him, too, in evil and madness. Indeed, these qualities color his interpretation of many of his film roles, including *Night of the Generals* (1967) and *The Ruling Class* (1972).

31. O'Toole, *Loitering with Intent,* 153.

32. Ibid., 154.

33. Ibid., 150.

34. Kenneth Burke, "The Four Master Tropes," in *A Grammar of Motives* (Cleveland: World Publishing, 1962), 503–17.

35. Ibid., 514

36. Frumkes, "The Restoration of 'Lawrence of Arabia,'" 287.

37. Farber, "Look What They've Done to 'Lawrence of Arabia,'" 11.

38. Ibid.

39. Maslin, "'Lawrence' Seen Whole," 13.

40. See text by Sam Spiegel in Roger Manvil, ed., "Lawrence of Arabia," *Journal of the Society of Film and Television Arts Limited* (Special Issue), no. 10 (Winter 1962–63): 5; emphasis added.

41. Robert Bolt, "Clues to the Legend of Lawrence," *New York Times Magazine,* February 25, 1962, 16.

42. See Andrew Sarris, "Notes on the Auteur Theory in 1962," *Film Culture* 27 (Winter 1962–63): 1–8. Sarris was to respond to his critics in the introduction of his book *The American Cinema,* where he explains what he meant by the use of the term "auteur" in application to film criticism:

> Ultimately, the auteur theory is not so much a theory as an attitude, a table of values that converts film history into directorial autobiography. The auteur critic is obsessed

with the wholeness of art and the artist. He looks at film as a whole, a director as a whole. The parts, however entertaining individually, must cohere meaningfully. This meaningful coherence is more likely when the director dominates the proceedings with skill and purpose. . . . The cinema is both a window and a mirror. The window looks out on the real world both directly (documentation) and vicariously (adaptation). The mirror reflects what the director (or other dominant artist) feels about the spectacle. It would seem that a theory that honored the personality of a director would endorse a cinema in which a director's personality was unquestionably supreme. Paradoxically, however, the personalities of modern directors are often more obscure than those of classical directors . . . [who] knew its audience and their expectations, but it often provided something extra. This something is the concern of auteur theory. (pp. 31–32)

43. Sarris, *The American Cinema,* 159–60.

44. I recommend highly the article by Vivian Sobchack, "'Surge and Splendor,'" one of the first academic works in recent times to have taken the study of epic seriously. Another excellent study on the epic, which does not apologize either for its interest in this genre, is Bruce Babington and Peter William Evans, *Biblical Epics: Sacred Narrative in Hollywood Cinema* (Manchester: Manchester University Press, 1993). See also Marc Ferro, *Cinema and History,* trans. Naomi Greene (Detroit, Mich.: Wayne State University Press, 1988). See also the following works: Allen Barra, "The Incredible Shrinking Epic," *American Film* 14 (5) (1989): 40–43, 45, 60; Louis Castelli, "Film Epic: A Generic Examination and an Application of Definitions to the Work of David Lean" (Ph.D. diss., Northwestern University, 1977); Raymond Durgnat, "Epic," *Films and Filming* (December 1963): 9–12; Derek Elly, *The Epic Film: Myth and History* (London: Routledge and Kegan Paul, 1984); Stephen Farber, "The Spectacle Film: 1967," *Film Quarterly* 20 (4) (Summer 1967): 12–22; Foster Hirsch, *The Hollywood Epic* (New Brunswick, N.J.: A. S. Barnes, 1978); and Jacques Siclier, "L'Age du Peplum," *Cahiers du cinéma,* no. 131 (May 1962): 26–38.

45. Martin Green, *Children of the Sun: A Narrative of "Decadence" in England After 1918* (New York: Basic Books, 1976).

46. Bolt, "Clues to the Legend of Lawrence," 16.

47. See Bragg, "Lean and Bolt."

4. AN ALLEGORY OF ANTHROPOLOGY

1. It is interesting that as a student of the Middle East, I am not alone in thinking that the movie had an impact on my professional interests. Ann Mayer, a distinguished historian of Islamic jurisprudence, said in an interview for the alumni magazine of the University of Pennsylvania that she had first contemplated working on the Middle East when as a teenager she had seen the film. A friend and anthropologist at Williams College, David Edwards, also said something of the sort in conversation with me. Although we grew up in the same suburb, we never met as children, though we probably saw the movie at approximately the same time and probably even in the same movie theater. While David ended up doing fieldwork in Afghanistan, I went to North Yemen.

2. Smadar Lavie, *The Poetics of Military Occupation: Mzeina Allegories of Bedouin Identity Under Israeli and Egyptian Rule* (Berkeley: University of California Press, 1990).

3. James Clifford, *The Predicament of Culture: Essays by James Clifford* (Cambridge, Mass.: Harvard University Press, 1988).

4. Stephen J. Greenblatt, ed., *Allegory and Representation* (Baltimore, Md.: Johns Hopkins University Press, 1981).

5. Stephen Farber, "Lean and Lawrence: The Last Adventurers," in *Favorite Movie: Critic's Choice,* ed. Philip Nobile (New York: Macmillan, 1973), 80–81.

6. Ibid., 81.

7. Ross, "In Defense of David Lean."

8. A literary work that became a best-seller in England and was important in shaping the public's view of the "alienated" individual in the late 1950s was Colin Wilson, *The Outsider* (Boston: Houghton Mifflin, 1956). For a good social history of England of this period, see Robert Hewison, *In Anger: Culture in the Cold War, 1945–1960* (London: Weidenfeld and Nicolson, 1981).

9. Michael A. Anderegg, "Lawrence of Arabia: The Man, the Myth, the Movie," *Michigan Quarterly Review* 21 (2) (Spring 1982): 281–309.

10. Claude Lévi-Strauss, *Tristes Tropiques,* trans. John Weightman and Doreen Weightman (New York: Atheneum, 1955), 383.

11. Clyde Kluckholn, *Mirror for Man* (New York: McGraw-Hill, 1949), 4.

12. Hortense Powdermaker, *Stranger and Friend: The Way of an Anthropologist* (New York: Norton, 1966), 20.

13. Although, see Anne Roe, "A Psychological Study of Eminent Psychologists and Anthropologists, and a Comparison with Biological and Physical Scientists," *Psychological Monographs* (American Psychological Association), no. 352 (1953): 1–55, for interesting data that corroborate this view.

14. Georg Simmel, "The Stranger," in *On Individuality and Social Forms,* ed. Donald N. Levine (Chicago: University of Chicago Press, 1971), 143–49.

15. Lean, *David Lean: A Self-Portrait.*

16. Farber, "Lean and Lawrence."

17. Bronislaw Malinowksi, *A Diary in the Strict Sense of the Term* (Stanford, Calif.: Stanford University Press, 1967), 180.

18. General H. Norman Schwarzkopf, with Peter Petre, *It Doesn't Take a Hero: The Autobiography* (New York: Bantam, 1992), 96.

19. Ibid., 108

20. For an interesting discussion of some related themes, see Marianna Torgovnick, *Gone Primitive* (Chicago: University of Chicago Press, 1990). There is, however, something to be said for distinguishing between "going native" and "gone primitive." When one goes "native," the "other" may be perceived as civilizationally "inferior" to the space one occupies, but on the other hand the movement may also be understood as occurring between civilizationally equivalent spaces, as when someone said of me after five years in California, "Oh, so you've gone native."

21. Schwarzkopf, *It Doesn't Take a Hero,* 110.

22. Victor Turner, *A Forest of Symbols* (Ithaca, N.Y.: Cornell University Press, 1969).

23. Marjorie Shostak, *Nisa* (New York: Random House, 1981).

24. Vincent Crapanzano, *Tuhami* (Chicago: University of Chicago Press, 1980).

25. See, for example, Steven C. Caton, *"Peaks of Yemen I Summon": Poetry as Cultural Practice in a North Yemini Tribe* (Berkeley: University of California Press, 1990).

26. Freud, "The 'Uncanny,'" 234.

27. Ibid.

28. Evans-Pritchard's classic statement about feud in "stateless" societies is to be found in his book *The Nuer*. His theory of segmentation and opposition has served as a jumping-off point for elaborations on "feud-addicted" tribes in the Middle East.

29. I am indebted to Richard Randolph and Anna Tsing for pointing out to me the significance of Maugham's writings in this regard. See in particular his short stories.

30. See Torgovnick, *Gone Primitive*, and Abigail Solomon-Godeau, "Going Native," *Art in America* 77 (7) (July 1989): 118–29. The dialogue between anthropologists is beginning somewhat with an exchange between Barbara Jones and Carolyn Martin Shaw, "Going Native or Becoming Native: A Joint Study" (manuscript). The distinction of "going" versus "becoming" native is discussed in terms of the anthropological production of knowledge and power relationships in the field.

31. Bolt, "Clues to the Legend of Lawrence."

32. Dorinne K. Kondo, "Dissolution and Reconstitution of Self: Implications for Anthropological Epistemology," *Cultural Anthropology* 1 (1) (February 1986): 76.

33. W. Somerset Maugham, *Collected Short Stories*, vol. 4 (London: Penguin, 1978), 267.

34. John Osbourne, *Look Back in Anger* (New York: Criterion Books, 1957), 68.

5. AN ANTI-IMPERIALIST, ORIENTALIST EPIC

1. Said, *Orientalism*, 54. The previous page is a discussion of Lévi-Strauss's "logic of the concrete." One might add that Saussure, in his *Course in General Linguistics* (1915), had defined the linguistic sign in relational terms, as something constituted through difference with something else, and not merely a content. In the work of Roman Jakobson and other structural phonologists, however, this arbitrariness of the "substance" in which sign differences are marked was called into question. A relatively small set of distinctive phonetic features (the functionally relevant sound differences in a given language) could define the sound systems of all the languages in the world. Thus, how differences are marked (or by what sound features) may not be as arbitrary as was once thought. See Roman Jakobson and Morris Halle, *The Fundamentals of Language* (The Hague: Mouton, 1956).

2. Émile Durkheim and Marcel Mauss, *Primitive Classifications*, trans. Rodney Needham (Chicago: University of Chicago Press, 1963).

3. Franz Boas, "On Alternating Sounds," in *A Franz Boas Reader*, ed. George F. Stocking, Jr. (Chicago: University of Chicago Press, 1974), 72–76.

4. A similar criticism of humanism, and of all universalist as well as relativist

schemas, was made by Homi Bhabha in his discussion of diversity and difference. See Homi Bhabha, "The Third Space: Interview with Homi Bhabha," in *Identity,* ed. Jonathan Rutherford (London: Lawrence and Wishart, 1990), 207–21. "The difference of cultures cannot be something that can be accommodated within a universalist framework," he remarks (p. 209), going on to specify "being human," "class," and "race" as kinds of universalist concepts. I take his "being human" to be a reference to humanist ideologies, among other things. For a critical examination of Said's ambivalent relation to European humanism (at once critiquing humanist texts as orientalist, yet at the same time seeking escape from orientalism through some notion of European humanist values such as tolerance, accommodation, and so forth), see Ahmad, *In Theory,* 163–64.

5. Talal Asad, ed., *Anthropology and the Colonial Encounter* (New York: Humanities Press, 1973).

6. Dell Hymes, ed., *Reinventing Anthropology* (New York: Pantheon, 1972). See also Johannes Fabian, *Time and the Other: How Anthropology Makes Its Object* (New York: Columbia University Press, 1983), who was writing his critique of anthropology at about the same time that Said's book came into print.

7. "[The orientalist attitude] shares with magic and with mythology the self-containing, self-reinforcing character of a closed system, in which objects are what they are because they are what they are, for once, for all time, for ontological reasons that no empirical material can either dislodge or alter." See Said, *Orientalism,* 70.

8. See Linda Nochlin, "The Imaginary Orient," reprinted in *The Politics of Vision: Essays on Nineteenth-Century Art and Society* (New York: Harper and Row, 1989), 33–59; and Solomon-Godeau, "Going Native," 118–29.

9. See Shohat, "Gender and Culture of Empire."

10. Ibid., 45.

11. Ibid., 52.

12. Bragg, "Lean and Bolt."

13. See, for example, Peter Worsley, "Imperial Retreat," in *Out of Apathy,* ed. E. P. Thompson (London: Steven and Sons, 1960), 101–40.

14. Bolt, "Clues to the Legend of Lawrence," 16.

15. See Melvyn Bragg's interview with David Lean in "Lean and Bolt" on *The South Bank Show,* in which the director talks about the complexity of the camera work, which involves having Alec Guiness moving in and out of focus.

16. Bolt, "Clues to the Legend of Lawrence," 48.

17. Shohat, "Gender and Culture of Empire," 52.

18. Graham Greene, *The Quiet American* (London: Penguin, 1955), 199, 151.

19. Ibid., 185.

20. Evans-Pritchard, *The Nuer;* Ernest Gellner, *Saints of the Atlas* (London: Weidenfeld and Nicolson, 1969).

21. See Pierre Bourdieu, "The Sentiment of Honour in Kabyle Society," in *Honour and Shame: The Values of Mediterranean Society,* ed. Jean G. Peristiany (Chicago: University of Chicago Press, 1966), 191–242.

22. Philip J. Stewart, "Letter to the *Times," Times,* January 7, 1963, 9g.

23. Morris and Raskin, *Lawrence of Arabia,* 149.

24. Ibid., 151.

25. Joseph Conrad, *Heart of Darkness* (1902; Toronto: Dover, 1990), 64.

26. Schwarzkopf, *It Doesn't Take a Hero,* 468.

27. Ibid.

6. MASKULINITIES

1. Marcia Landy, *British Genres: Cinema and Society, 1930–1960* (Princeton, N.J.: Princeton University Press, 1991), 263.

2. Ibid., 234.

3. A number of studies have recently been published on this topic. By far the most interesting are Steven Cohan's "Masquerading as the American Male in the Fifties: *Picnic,* William Holden and the Spectacle of Masculinity in Hollywood Film," *Camera Obscura,* no. 25–26 (January/May 1991): 43–72; and selected essays from Steven Cohan and Ina Rae Hark, eds., *Screening the Male: Exploring Masculinities in Hollywood Cinema* (London: Routledge, 1993). See also Kaja Silverman's "White Skin, Brown Masks," 3–54, and the final chapter of her book *Male Subjectivity at the Margins* (New York: Routledge, 1992). For earlier work on the constructions of masculinity in film, see also John Caughie and Gillian Skirrow, "Ahab, Ishmael . . . and Mo: Sample Cult Readings of a Cult Movie," *Screen* 23 (3–4) (1982): 54–59; Pam Cook, "Masculinity in Crisis? Identification in 'Raging Bull,'" *Screen* 23 (3–4) (1982): 39–46; Richard Dyer, "Don't Look Now: The Instabilities of the Male Pin-Up," *Screen,* 23 (3–4) (1982): 61–72; Steve Neale, "'Chariots of Fire,' Images of Men," *Screen* 23 (3–4) (1982): 47–53; Steve Neale, "Masculinity as Spectacle: Reflections on Men and Mainstream Cinema," *Screen* 24 (6) (1983): 2–16; and Paul Willemen, "Looking at the Male: Anthony Mann," *Framework,* no. 15–17 (1981): 16–20.

4. Landy, *British Genres,* 239.

5. Susan Jeffords, *The Remasculinization of America: Gender and the Vietnam War* (Bloomington: Indiana University Press, 1989); Traube, *Dreaming Identities.*

6. Eve Kosofsky Sedgwick, *Between Men: English Literature and Male Homosocial Desire* (New York: Columbia University Press, 1985).

7. Anderegg, "Lawrence of Arabia."

8. Cited in Morris and Raskin, *Lawrence of Arabia,* 158.

9. Henry Hart, "Lawrence of Arabia," *Films in Review* 14 (1) (January 1963): 44.

10. Stanley Kaufman, "A Passion in the Desert," *New Republic,* January 12, 1963, 28; emphasis added.

11. Roger Sandall, "Lawrence of Arabia," *Film Quarterly* 16 (3) (Spring 1963): 57.

12. See Morris and Raskin, *Lawrence of Arabia,* 120.

13. Mulvey, "Visual Pleasure and Narrative Cinema," 6–18; and also her "On *Duel in the Sun,*" 12–15.

14. See Mary Ann Doane, "Film and the Masquerade: Theorising the Female Spectator," *Screen* 23 (3–4) (1982): 74–87; and her "Masquerade Reconsid-

ered: Further Thoughts on the Female Spectator," *Discourse* 11 (1) (Fall–Winter 1988–89): 42–54.

15. Hansen, *Babel and Babylon.*

16. "Flawrence of Arabia," *MAD Magazine,* no. 86 (April 1964): 43–48.

17. Modleski, *The Women Who Knew Too Much.*

18. Thomas, *With Lawrence in Arabia.*

19. See Graham Dawson, "The Blond Bedouin," in *Manful Assertions: Masculinities in Britain Since 1800,* ed. Michael Rooper and John Tosh (London: Routledge, 1991), 113–44.

20. Rhonda Cornum, as told to Peter Copeland, *She Went to War: The Rhonda Cornum Story* (Novato, Calif.: Presidio Press, 1992), 90.

21. Ibid., 91.

22. Ibid., 202.

23. Ibid., 20.

24. Ibid., 127.

25. Ibid., 22.

26. Ibid., 62.

27. Ibid., 89.

28. Jean Bethke Elshtain, *Women and War* (New York: Basic Books, 1987).

29. Carol Cohn, "Wars, Wimps, and Women: Talking Gender and Thinking War," in *Gendering War Talk,* ed. Miriam Cooke and Angela Woollacott (Princeton, N.J.: Princeton University Press, 1993), 227–46.

30. Cornum, *She Went to War,* 68.

31. Ibid., 133.

32. Stanley D. Rosenberg, "The Threshold of Thrill: Life Stories in the Skies over Southeast Asia," in *Gendering War Talk,* ed. Miriam Cooke and Angela Woollacott (Princeton, N.J.: Princeton University Press, 1993), 43–66.

33. Anonymous, *New York Times Western Edition,* January 5, 1963, 7.

34. Murray Schumach, "'Lawrence of Arabia' Producer Defends Film Story of Hero," *New York Times Western Edition,* January 26, 1963, 5.

35. Bolt, "Clues to the Legend of Lawrence"; emphasis added.

36. See Silverman, "White Skin, Brown Masks."

37. Anonymous, *Time,* January 4, 1963, 58.

38. Peter Barker, "'Lawrence of Arabia,'" *Films and Filming* 9 (5) (1962): 32.

39. Sandall, "'Lawrence of Arabia,'" 57.

40. Stanley Weintraub, "'Lawrence of Arabia,'" *Film Quarterly* 17 (4) (Summer 1964): 53.

41. Anderegg, "Lawrence of Arabia," 288.

42. Maslin, "'Lawrence' Seen Whole."

43. Harriet Whitehead, "The Bow and the Burden Strap: A New Look at Institutionalized Homosexuality in Native North America," in *Sexual Meanings,* ed. Sherry B. Ortner and Harriet Whitehead (Cambridge: Cambridge University Press, 1981), 96.

44. Sharif, *The Eternal Male,* 21.

45. Wayne Kostenbaum, *Double Talk: The Erotics of Male Literary Collaboration* (New York: Routledge, 1989), 3.

46. Silverman, *David Lean,* 21.

47. Vito Russo, *The Celluloid Closet* (New York: Harper and Row, 1981), 133.

48. Elaine Sciolino, "Female P.O.W. Is Abused, Kindling Debate," *New York Times,* June 29, 1992, A13.

49. Robert Bly, *Iron John: A Book About Men* (Reading, Mass.: Addison-Wesley, 1990), 36.

50. Ibid., 102.

51. Silverman, *David Lean,* 24.

52. Ibid., 166.

53. Ibid., 189–90.

EPILOGUE

1. Michel Foucault, *The Archaeology of Knowledge,* trans. A. M. Sheridan Smith (New York: Pantheon, 1972), 17.

Bibliography

Adorno, Theodor W. *Negative Dialectic.* Translated by E. B. Ashton. New York: Continuum, 1973.

———. "Perennial Fashion—Jazz." In *Prisms: Essays by Theodor W. Adorno,* translated by Samuel Weber and Shierry Weber, 227–42. Cambridge, Mass.: MIT Press, 1981.

Ahmad, Aijaz. *In Theory: Classes, Nations, Literatures.* London: Verso, 1992.

Al-ʾAzm, Sadeq. "Orientalism and Orientalism in Reverse." *Khamsin* 8 (1981): 5–26.

Aldington, Richard. *Lawrence of Arabia: A Biographical Enquiry.* Chicago: Henry Regnery Company, 1955.

Allenby, Daisy. "Letter to the *Times.*" *The Times,* December 27, 1962, 7

Alpert, Hollis. "A Great One. Review of *Lawrence of Arabia.*" *Saturday Review,* December 29, 1962, 29–30.

———. "The David Lean Recipe: A 'Whack in the Guts.' " *New York Times Magazine,* May 23, 1965, 32–33, 94, 96, 98, 110.

Anderegg, Michael A. "Lawrence of Arabia: The Man, the Myth, the Movie." *Michigan Quarterly Review* 21 (2) (Spring 1982): 281–309.

———. *David Lean.* Boston: Twayne, 1984.

Andrew, J. Dudley. *The Major Film Theories.* London: Oxford University Press, 1976.

Anonymous. "All-Star, All-Good. A Review of *Lawrence of Arabia.*" And "Talk with the Star: An Interview with Peter O'Toole." *Newsweek.* December 24, 1962, 64.

Anonymous. "Full-length Portrait of Lawrence in the Desert." *The Times,* December 11, 1962, 13.

Anonymous. "Hail Quinn of Arabia." *Sunday Times,* May 21, 1989, B20.

Anonymous. "The Spirit of the Wind. A Review of *Lawrence of Arabia." Time,* January 4, 1963, 58.

Appadurai, Arjun. "Global Ethnoscapes: Notes and Queries for a Transnational Anthropology." In *Recapturing Anthropology,* edited by Richard Fox, 191–210. Santa Fe, N.M.: School of American Research, 1991.

Appiah, Anthony. "Is the Post- in Postmodernism the Post- in Postcolonial?" *Critical Inquiry* 10 (Winter 1991): 336–57.

Armbrister, Trevor. "O'Toole of Arabia and O'Toole: Oscar Winner?" *Saturday Evening Post,* March 9, 1963, 22–26, 28.

Asad, Talal, ed. *Anthropology and the Colonial Encounter.* New York: Humanities Press, 1973.

Babington, Bruce, and Peter William Evans. *Biblical Epics: Sacred Narrative in Hollywood Cinema.* Manchester: Manchester University Press, 1993.

Balio, Tino, ed. *The American Film Industry.* Madison: University of Wisconsin Press, 1976.

Barker, Peter. "Lawrence of Arabia." *Films and Filming* 9 (5) (1962): 32–33.

Barr, Charles. "CinemaScope: Before and After." *Film Quarterly* 16 (4) (1963): 4–24.

Barra, Allen. "At Long Last, the Real Lawrence." *American Film* 14 (5) (1989): 44.

———. "The Incredible Shrinking Epic." *American Film* 14 (5) (1989): 40–43, 45, 60.

Barthes, Roland. "The Great Family of Man." In *Mythologies,* 100–102. New York: Hill and Wang, 1972.

Bazin, André. "Fin du montage." *Cahiers du cinéma,* no. 31 (January 1954): 43.

———. "Un peu tard." *Cahiers du cinéma,* no. 48 (January 1955): 45–47.

———. *What Is Cinema?* Vol. 1. Translated by Hugh Gray. Berkeley: University of California Press, 1967.

Belton, John. *Widescreen Cinema.* Cambridge, Mass.: Harvard University Press, 1992.

Benjamin, Walter. "What Is Epic Theater?" In *Illuminations: Essays by Walter Benjamin,* edited by Hannah Arendt and translated by Harry Zohn, 147–54. New York: Schocken, 1969.

———. "The Work of Art in the Age of Mechanical Reproduction." In *Illuminations: Essays by Walter Benjamin,* edited by Hannah Arendt and translated by Harry Zohn, 217–51. New York: Schocken, 1969.

———. "A Small History of Photography." In *One-Way Street and Other Writings by Walter Benjamin,* translated by Edmund Jephcott and Kingsley Shorter, 240–57. London: NLB, 1979.

Bernstein, Irving. *Hollywood at the Crossroads: An Economic Study of the Motion Picture Industry.* Hollywood: Hollywood AFL Film Council, 1957.

Bhabha, Homi K. "Difference, Discrimination and the Discourse of Colonialism." In *The Politics of Theory,* edited by Francis Barker, Peter Hulme, Margaret Iversen, and Diana Loxley, 194–211. Colchester: University of Essex, 1983.

————. "The Other Question." *Screen* 24 (6) (1983): 18–36.

————. "Of Mimicry and Man: The Ambivalence of Colonial Discourse." *October* 28 (1984): 125–33.

————. "Signs Taken for Wonders: Questions of Ambivalence and Authority Under a Tree Outside Delhi, May 1817." In *Europe and Its Others*, vol. 1, edited by Francis Barker, Peter Hulme, Margaret Iversen, and Diana Loxley,, 89–106. Colchester: University of Essex, 1985.

————. "The Third Space: Interview with Homi Bhabha." In *Identity*, edited by Jonathan Rutherford, 207–21. London: Lawrence and Wishard, 1990.

Bly, Robert. *Iron John: A Book About Men*. Reading, Mass.: Addison-Wesley, 1990.

Boas, Franz. "On Alternating Sounds." In *A Franz Boas Reader*, edited by George F. Stocking, Jr., 72–76. Chicago: University of Chicago Press, 1974.

Bolt, Robert. "Preface." *A Man for All Seasons: A Play in Two Acts*, vii–xx. New York: Random House, 1960.

————. "Clues to the Legend of Lawrence." *New York Times Magazine*, February 25, 1962, 16–17, 45, 48, 50.

————. "The Playwright in Films." *Saturday Review*, December 29, 1962, 15–16.

————. *Lawrence of Arabia*. Script. Hollywood: Script City, 1962.

————. "First Interview." In *Contemporary Playwrights: Robert Bolt*, interviewed and edited by Ronald Hayman, 1–15. London: Heineman, 1969.

Bordwell, David. *Narration in the Fiction Film*. Madison: University of Wisconsin Press, 1985.

Bordwell, David, Janet Staiger, and Kristin Thompson. *The Classical Hollywood Cinema*. New York: Columbia University Press, 1985.

Bordwell, David, and Kristin Thompson. *Film Art: An Introduction*. Reading, Mass.: Addison-Wesley, 1979.

Bourdieu, Pierre. "The Sentiment of Honour in Kabyle Society." In *Honour and Shame: The Values of Mediterranean Society*, edited by Jean G. Peristiany, 191–242. Chicago: University of Chicago Press, 1966.

Bragg, Melvyn, editor and presenter. "Lean and Bolt." *The South Bank Show*. London Weekend Television. Production. David Thomas, producer and director. Nigel Wattis, executive producer, 1990.

————. "Peter O'Toole." *The South Bank Show*. London Weekend Television Production. Frances Dickenson, producer and director. Nigel Wattis, executive producer, 1992.

Brownlow, Kevin. *David Lean: A Biography*. New York: St. Martin's Press, 1996.

Buck-Morss, Susan. *The Origin of Negative Dialectics: Theodor W. Adorno, Walter Benjamin, and the Frankfurt Institute*. New York: Free Press, 1977.

————. *The Dialectics of Seeing: Walter Benjamin and the Arcades Project*. Cambridge, Mass.: MIT Press, 1989.

Burke, Kenneth. *A Grammar of Motives and A Rhetoric of Motives*. Cleveland: World Publishing, 1962.

Castelli, Louis. "Film Epic: A Generic Examination and an Application of Definitions to the Work of David Lean." Ph.D. diss., Northwestern University, 1977.

Castelli, Louis P., with Caryn Lynn Cleeland. *David Lean: A Guide to References and Resources*. Boston: G. K. Hall, 1980.

Caton, Steven C. "Contributions of Roman Jakobson." *Annual Review of Anthropology* 16 (1987): 223–60.

———. *"Peaks of Yemen I Summon": Poetry as Cultural Practice in a North Yemeni Tribe*. Berkeley: University of California Press, 1990.

Chateau, René. "Entretiens avec Michael Wilson et Dalton Trumbo." *Positif* 64–65 (1964): 90–94.

Clarke, Charles G. "CinemaScope Photographic Techniques." *American Cinematographer* 36 (6) (1955):336–37, 362–4.

Clifford, James. *The Predicament of Culture: Essays by James Clifford*. Cambridge, Mass.: Harvard University Press, 1988.

Clover, Carol J. *Men, Women and Chain Saws: Gender in the Modern Horror Film*. Princeton, N.J.: Princeton University Press, 1992.

Cohan, Steven. "Masquerading as the American Male in the Fifties: *Picnic*, William Holden and the Spectacle of Masculinity in Hollywood Film." *Camera Obscura*, no. 25–26 (January/May, 1991): 43–72.

Cohan, Steven, and Ina Rae Hark, eds. *Screening the Male: Exploring Masculinities in Hollywood Cinema*. London: Routledge, 1993.

Cohn, Carol. "Wars, Wimps, and Women: Talking Gender and Thinking War." In *Gendering War Talk*, edited by Miriam Cooke and Angela Woollacott, 227–46. Princeton, N.J.: Princeton University Press, 1993.

Combs, Richard. "Enigma Variations." *Times Literary Supplement*, May 26–June 11, 1989, 583c.

Conrad, Joseph. *Heart of Darkness*. 1902; New York: Dover, 1990.

Cornum, Rhonda, as told to Peter Copeland. *She Went to War: The Rhonda Cornum Story*. Novato, Calif.: Presidio Press, 1992.

Crapanzano, Vincent. *Tuhami*. Chicago: University of Chicago Press, 1980.

Crowdus, Gary. "Lawrence of Arabia: The Cinematic (Re)Writing of History." *Cineaste* 17 (2) (1989): 14–21.

———. "The Writers Guild of America vs. the Blacklist." *Cineaste* 21 (4) (1995): 29–34.

Crowdus, Gary, and Alan Farrand. "Restoring Lawrence: An Interview with Robert Harris." *Cineaste* 17 (2) (1989): 22–23.

Crowther, Bosley. "Review of *Lawrence of Arabia*." *New York Times*, December 17, 1962, sec. 5, 2.

Dann, Uriel. *King Hussein and the Challenge of Arab Radicalism: Jordan, 1955–1967*. New York: Oxford University Press, 1989.

Dawson, Graham. "The Blond Bedouin." In *Manful Assertions: Masculinities in Britain Since 1800*, edited by Michael Roper and John Tosh, 113–44. London: Routledge, 1991.

Doane, Mary Ann. "Film and the Masquerade: Theorising the Female Spectator." *Screen* 23 (3–4) (1982): 74–87.

———. "Masquerade Reconsidered: Further Thoughts on the Female Spectator." *Discourse* 11 (1) (Fall–Winter 1988–89): 42–54.

Drucker, Mort, and Larry Siegel. "Flawrence of Arabia." *MAD Magazine*, April 1964, 43–48.

Durgnat, Raymond. "Epic." *Films and Filming* (December 1963): 9–12.

Dyer, Richard. *Brief Encounter*. London: British Film Institute, 1993.

Elly, Derek. *The Epic Film: Myth and History*. London: Routledge and Kegan Paul, 1984.

Elshtain, Jean Bethke. *Women and War*. New York: Basic Books, 1987.

Esslin, Martin. *Brecht: A Choice of Evils*. London: Methuen, 1984.

Evans-Pritchard, E. E. *The Nuer*. Oxford: Oxford University Press, 1940.

Fabian, Johannes. *Time and the Other: How Anthropology Makes Its Object*. New York: Columbia University Press, 1983.

Farber, Stephen. "The Spectacle Film: 1967." *Film Quarterly* 20 (4) (Summer 1967): 12–22.

———. "Look What They've Done to 'Lawrence of Arabia.'" *New York Times*, May 2, 1971, sec. 1, 11.

———. "Lean and Lawrence: The Last Adventurers." In *Favorite Movie: Critic's Choice*, edited by Philip Nobile, 76–86. New York: Macmillan, 1973.

Ferro, Marc. *Cinema and History*. Translated from the French by Naomi Greene. Detroit, Mich.: Wayne State University, 1988.

Fisher, Bob. "Freddie Young, BSC: An Epic Trail of Achievement." *American Cinematographer* 74 (3) (March 1993): 50–54.

Fixx, James F. "The Spiegel Touch." *Saturday Review*, December 29, 1962, 13–15.

Foucault, Michel. *The Archaeology of Knowledge*. Translated by A. M. Sheridan Smith. New York: Pantheon, 1972.

Freedland, Michael. *Peter O'Toole*. New York: St. Martin's Press, 1982.

Freud, Sigmund. "The 'Uncanny.'" In *Sigmund Freud: The Standard Edition of the Complete Psychological Works*, vol. 17 (1917–19), translated by James Strachey, 219–52. London: Hogarth Press, 1925.

———. "Fetishism" (1927). In *Sexuality and the Psychology of Love*, 204–9. New York: Macmillan, 1963.

Frumkes, Roy. "The Restoration of 'Lawrence of Arabia.'" *Films in Review* 1 (April 1989): 204–10; 1 (May 1989): 285–92.

Fussell, Paul. *Abroad: British Literary Traveling Between the Wars*. New York: Oxford University Press, 1980.

Gellner, Ernest. *Saints of the Atlas*. London: Weidenfeld and Nicolson, 1969.

Ginna, Robert Emma, Jr. "The Return of *Lawrence of Arabia*." *Connoisseur*, May 1989, 156–63.

Gombrich, E. H. *Art and Illusion*. The A. W. Mellon Lectures in Fine Art 5; The Bollingen Series 35. Princeton, N.J.: Princeton University Press, 1969.

Graves, Robert. *Lawrence and the Arabian Adventure*. Garden City, N.Y.: Doubleday, Doran, 1927.

Green, Martin. *Children of the Sun: A Narrative of "Decadence" in England After 1918*. New York: Basic Books, 1976.

Greenblatt, Stephen J., ed. *Allegory and Representation*. Baltimore, Md.: Johns Hopkins University Press, 1981.

Greene, Graham. *The Quiet American*. New York: Penguin, 1955.

Grignon, Lorin D. "The Sound for CinemaScope." In *New Screen Techniques,* edited by Martin Quigley, Jr., 159–70. New York: Quigley Publications, 1953.

Guback, T. *International Film Industry.* Bloomington: Indiana University Press, 1969.

Gunning, Tom. *D. W. Griffith and the Origins of American Narrative Film.* Urbana: University of Illinois Press, 1994.

Hansen, Miriam. *Babel and Babylon: Spectatorship in American Silent Film.* Cambridge, Mass.: Harvard University Press, 1991.

Harris, Robert. "The Reconstruction of *Lawrence of Arabia.*" Liner notes for laser disc production of *Lawrence of Arabia* (Criterion Collection). Santa Monica, Calif.: The Voyager Company, 1989.

Hart, B. H. Liddell. *Colonel Lawrence: The Man Behind the Legend.* New York: Halcyon House, 1935.

Hart, Henry. "Lawrence of Arabia." *Films in Review* 14 (1) (January 1963): 42–44.

Hartung, Philip T. "The Screen: The Lawrence Legend." *Commonweal,* January 18, 1963, 439–40.

Hatch, Robert. "Review of *Lawrence of Arabia.*" *The Nation,* January 19, 1963, 58–59.

Heath, Stephen. "Film and System: Terms of Analysis." Part I. *Screen* 16 (1) (1975): 7–77. Part II. *Screen* 16 (2) (1975): 91–113.

Held, David. *Introduction to Critical Theory: Horkheimer to Habermas.* Berkeley: University of California Press, 1980.

Hewes, Henry. "All the King's Camels. A Review of *Lawrence of Arabia.*" *Saturday Review,* January 5, 1963, 31.

Hewison, Robert. *In Anger: Culture in the Cold War 1945–60.* London: Weidenfeld and Nicolson, 1981.

Hirsch, Foster. *The Hollywood Epic.* New Brunswick, N.J.: A. S. Barnes, 1978.

Hodson, Joel. 1994. "Who Wrote *Lawrence of Arabia*? Sam Spiegel and David Lean's Denial of Credit to a Blacklisted Screenwriter." *Cineaste* 22 (4) (1994): 12–17.

Holden, James. "'The Best Technical Man in the Business': A Study of David Lean." *Film Journal* 1 (April 1956):1–5.

Horkheimer, Max, and Theodor W. Adorno. "The Culture Industry: Enlightenment as Mass Deception." In *Dialectic of Enlightenment,* translated by John Cumming, 120–67. New York: Continuum, 1989.

Hussein I, His Majesty King. *Uneasy Lies the Head.* New York: Random House, 1962

Hymes, Dell. *Reinventing Anthropology.* New York: Pantheon, 1972.

Jacobs, Jay. "Fraud and Freud. A Review of *Lawrence of Arabia* and Freud." *Reporter,* January 31, 1963, 48–49.

Jakobson, Roman. "Concluding Statement: Linguistics and Poetics." In *Style in Language,* edited by Thomas A. Sebeok, 351–77. Cambridge, Mass.: MIT Press, 1960.

Jarre, Maurice. "Maurice Jarre on *Lawrence of Arabia.*" An interview by

William H. Rosar and Vincent Jacquet-Francillon. *The Cue Sheet: Journal of the Society of the Preservation of Film Music* (April 1990): 13–23.

Jay, Martin. *The Dialectical Imagination: A History of the Frankfurt School and the Institute of Social Research, 1923–1950*. Boston: Little, Brown, 1973.

Jeffords, Susan. *The Remasculinization of America: Gender and the Vietnam War*. Bloomington: Indiana University Press, 1989.

Joyaux, Georges. "*The Bridge over the River Kwai:* From the Novel to the Movie." *Literature/Film Quarterly* 2 (Spring 1974): 174–82.

Kael, Pauline. "The Flawed Hero. A Review of *Lawrence of Arabia*." *New Yorker,* December 22, 1962, 77.

Kaplan, E. Ann. "E. Ann Kaplan Replies." *Cinema Journal* 25 (1) (1985): 52–54.

Kaufman, Stanley. "A Passion in the Desert." *New Republic,* January 12, 1963, 26–28.

Kent, Howard. *Single Bed for Three: A "Lawrence of Arabia" Notebook*. London: Hutchinson, 1963.

Kipling, Rudyard. *Kim*. Toronto: Bantam, 1983.

Kluckholn, Clyde. *Mirror for Man*. New York: McGraw-Hill, 1949.

Knowles, John. "All-Out in the Desert." *Horizon Magazine,* July 1962, 109–11.

Koch, Gertrud. "Ex-Changing the Gaze: Re-Visioning Feminist Film Theory." *New German Critique* 34 (Winter 1985): 139–53.

———. "Comment." *Camera Obscura* 20–21 (May–September 1989): 209–12.

Kondo, Dorinne K. "Dissolution and Reconstitution of Self: Implications for Anthropological Epistemology." *Cultural Anthropology* 1 (1) (February 1986): 74–88.

Konigsberg, Ira. *The Complete Film Dictionary*. New York: Penguin, 1987.

Kostenbaum, Wayne. *Double Talk: The Erotics of Male Literary Collaboration*. New York: Routledge, 1989.

Koster, Henry. "Directing in CinemaScope." In *New Screen Techniques,* edited by Martin Quigley, 171–73. New York: Quigley Publishing, 1953.

Krauss, Rosalind E. *The Optical Unconscious*. Cambridge, Mass.: MIT Press, 1993.

Landy, Marcia. *British Genres: Cinema and Society, 1930–1960*. Princeton, N.J.: Princeton University Press, 1991.

Lavie, Smadar. *The Poetics of Military Occupation: Mzeina Allegories of Bedouin Identity Under Israeli and Egyptian Rule*. Berkeley: University of California Press, 1990.

Lawrence, A. W. "Letter to the *Times*." *The Times,* December 14, 1962, 13.

Lawrence, T. E. *Revolt in the Desert*. Garden City, N.Y.: Garden City Publishing, 1926.

———. *Seven Pillars of Wisdom: A Triumph*. Garden City, N.Y.: Doubleday, Doran, 1935.

Lean, David. "Possible Scenes, Sequences, Characters or Visuals." Document to filmmakers of *Lawrence of Arabia*. Bombay, October 1959. Michael Wilson Papers. Arts Special Collection, University Research Library, University of California, Los Angeles. Los Angeles, California.

————. Letter to Michael Wilson, 24 April 1960. Michael Wilson Papers. Arts Special Collection, University Research Library, University of California, Los Angeles. Los Angeles, California.

————. "Out of the Wilderness: Interview with David Lean." *Films and Filming* 9 (1963): 12–15.

————. *David Lean: A Self-Portrait.* Produced and directed by Thomas Craven. Pyramid Films, 1971.

Lederer, William J., and Eugene Burdick. *The Ugly American.* New York: Fawcett Crest, 1958.

Leonard, John. "Novel Colonies." *The Nation,* March 22, 1993, 383–90.

Lévi-Strauss, Claude. *Tristes Tropiques.* Translated by John Weightman and Doreen Weightman. New York: Atheneum, 1955.

MacCabe, Colin. "Realism and the Cinema: Notes on Some Brechtian Theses." *Screen* 15 (2) (Summer 1974): 7–27.

————. "Theory and Film: Principles of Realism and Pleasure." In *Narrative, Apparatus, Ideology,* edited by Philip Rosen, 179–97. New York: Columbia University Press, 1986.

MacCann, Richard Dyer. "Independence, with a Vengeance." *Film Quarterly* 15 (3) (Summer 1962): 14–21.

MacGowan, Kenneth. "The Screen's 'New Look'—Wider and Deeper." *Quarterly of Film, Radio, and Television* 11 (Winter 1956): 109–30.

————. "The Wide Screen of Yesterday and Tomorrow." *Quarterly of Film, Radio, and Television* 11 (3) (Spring 1957): 217–41.

Magid, Ron. "In Search of the David Lean Lens." *American Cinematographer* 70 (4) (April 1989): 95–98.

Malinowski, Bronislaw. *A Diary in the Strict Sense of the Term.* Stanford, Calif.: Stanford University Press, 1967.

Malkki, Liisa. "Citizens of Humanity: Internationalism and the Imagined Community of Nations." *Diaspora* 3 (1) (Spring 1994): 41–68.

Mankiewicz, Herman J., Orson Welles, and Pauline Kael. *The Citizen Kane Book.* London: Methuen, 1989.

Manvil, Roger, ed. "*Lawrence of Arabia.*" Comments by Sam Spiegel, Robert Bolt, Peter O'Toole, John Box, F. A. Young, Anne V. Coates, and David Lean. *Journal of the Society of Film and Television Arts Limited* (Special Issue), no. 10 (Winter 1962–63): 1–24.

Marcus, George, and James Clifford. *Writing Culture.* Berkeley: University of California Press, 1986.

Marcus, George, and Michael Fischer. *Anthropology as Cultural Critique.* Chicago: University of Chicago Press, 1986.

Marlowe, Frederic. "The Rise of the Independents in Hollywood." *Penguin Film Review* 1 (1946–49): 72–75.

Maslin, Janet. "'Lawrence' Seen Whole." *New York Times,* January 29, 1989, sec. 1, 1, 13.

Mattelart, Armand. *Transnationals and the Third World.* Translated by David Buxton. South Hadley, Mass.: Bergin and Garvey, 1983.

McVay, Douglas. "Lean—Lover of Life." *Films and Filming* 9 (1963): 12–15.

Metz, Christian. *The Imaginary Signifier. Psychoanalysis and the Cinema.*

Translated by Celia Britton, Annwyl Williams, Ben Brewster, and Alfred Guzzetti. Bloomington: Indiana University Press, 1977.

Modleski, Tania. *The Women Who Knew Too Much: Hitchcock and Feminist Theory.* New York: Routledge, 1988.

Morgan, Kenneth O. *The People's Peace: British History 1945–1989.* Oxford: Oxford University Press, 1990.

Morris, L. Robert, and Lawrence Raskin. *Lawrence of Arabia: The Thirtieth Anniversary Pictorial History.* New York: Doubleday, 1992.

Moynahan, Julian. "Seeing the Book, Reading the Movie." In *The English Novel and the Movies,* edited by Michael Klein and Gillian Parker, 143–54. New York: Frederick Ungar, 1981.

Mulvey, Laura. "Visual Pleasure and Narrative Cinema." *Screen* 16 (3) (Autumn 1975): 6–18.

———. "On *Duel in the Sun*: Afterthoughts on 'Visual Pleasure and Narrative Cinema.'" *Framework,* nos. 15–17 (1981): 12–15.

Musser, Charles. "Toward a History of Screen Practice." *Quarterly Review of Film Studies* 9 (1) (Winter 1984): 59–69.

Neale, Steve. "Masculinity as Spectacle: Reflections on Men and Mainstream Cinema." *Screen* 24 (6) (1983): 2–16.

Negulesco, Jean. "New Medium—New Methods." In *New Screen Techniques,* edited by Martin Quigley, Jr., 174–75. New York: Quigley Publications, 1953.

Nelson, Donald M. "The Independent Producer." In *The Motion Picture Industry,* edited by Gordon Watkins. *Annals of the American Academy of Political and Social Science* (1947): 49–57.

Nichols, Bill. *Representing Reality.* Bloomington: Indiana University Press, 1991.

Nochlin, Linda. "The Imaginary Orient." Reprinted in *The Politics of Vision: Essays on Nineteenth-Century Art and Society,* 33–59. New York: Harper and Row, 1989.

Nutting, Anthony. *Lawrence of Arabia: The Man and the Motive.* New York: Signet, 1961.

Osbourne, John. *Look Back in Anger.* New York: Criterion Books, 1957.

O'Toole, Peter. *Loitering with Intent: The Child.* New York: Hyperion, 1992.

Perry, George. "Dusting Off the Definitive Epic." *Sunday Times,* April 16, 1989, C8a.

———. "Hero's Return for Lawrence." *Sunday Times,* May 28, 1989, C11b.

Pickard, Ron. "David Lean: Supreme Craftsman." *Films in Review* 25 (May 1974): 265–84.

Powdermaker, Hortense. *Hollywood: The Dream Factory.* Boston: Little, Brown, 1950.

———. *Stranger and Friend: The Way of an Anthropologist.* New York: Norton, 1966.

Pratley, Gerald. "Interview with David Lean." In *Interviews with Film Directors,* edited by Andrew Sarris, 263–67. Indianapolis: Bobbs-Merrill, 1967.

———. *The Cinema of David Lean.* London: Tantivy Press, 1974.

Rattigan, Terence. *Ross: A Dramatic Portrait.* New York: Random House, 1962.

Rescher, Gayne. "Wide Angle Problems in Wide Screen Photography." *American Cinematographer* 37 (5) (1956): 300–301, 322–23.

Richards, Jeffrey. *The Age of the Dream Palace*. London: Routledge and Kegan Paul, 1984.

Richards, Jeffrey, and Jeffrey Hulbert. "Censorship in Action: The Case of *Lawrence of Arabia*." *Journal of Contemporary History* 19 (1984): 153–70.

Robb, David. "Credit, at Last, for 'Lawrence of Arabia.'" *New York Times*, September 14, 1955, D7.

Robinson, David. "Desert Epic Finds Its Length." *The Times*, May 25, 1989, 20a.

Rodowick, D. N. "The Difficulty of Difference." *Wide Angle* 5 (1) (1982): 4–15.

Rosenberg, Stanley D. "The Threshold of Thrill: Life Stories in the Skies over Southeast Asia." In *Gendering War Talk*, edited by Miriam Cooke and Angela Woollacott, 43–66. Princeton, N.J.: Princeton University Press, 1993.

Ross, Steven. "In Defense of David Lean." *Take One* 3 (1972): 10–18.

Rushdie, Salman. "Outside the Whale." In *Imaginary Homelands: Essays and Criticisms of Salman Rushdie, 1981–1991*, 87–101. London: Granta Books (in association with Viking), 1991.

Russell, Francis. "How to Write a Screen Play." *National Review*, February 26, 1963, 167–69.

Russo, Vito. *The Celluloid Closet*. New York: Harper and Row, 1981.

Said, Edward. *Orientalism*. New York: Vintage, 1978.

———. "Orientalism Reconsidered." In *Europe and Its Others*, edited by Francis Barker, Peter Hulme, Margaret Iversen, and Diana Loxley, 14–27. Proceedings of Essex Conference on Sociology of Literature (July 1984). Colchester: University of Essex, 1985.

———. "Representing the Colonized: Anthropology's Interlocutors." *Critical Inquiry* 15 (2) (1989): 205–25.

———. *Culture and Imperialism*. New York: Knopf, 1993.

Sandall, Roger. "Lawrence of Arabia." *Film Quarterly* 16 (3) (Spring 1963): 56–57.

Sarkisian, Jeanette A. "'Lawrence' Inspires the ARAB LOOK." *Saturday Evening Post*, March 9, 1963, 30–31.

Sarris, Andrew. "Notes on the Auteur Theory in 1962." *Film Culture* 27 (Winter 1962/63): 1–8.

———. *The American Cinema: Directors and Directions, 1929–1968*. New York: Dutton, 1968.

———, ed. *Interviews with Film Directors*. Indianapolis: Bobbs-Merrill, 1967.

Scherer, Maurice. "Vertus cardinales du Cinemascope." *Cahiers du cinéma*, no. 31 (January 1954): 36–40.

Schumach, Murray. "'Lawrence of Arabia' Producer Defends Film Story of Hero." *New York Times Western Edition*, January 26, 1963, 5.

Schwarzkopf, H. Norman, with Peter Petre. *It Doesn't Take a Hero. The Autobiography*. New York: Bantam, 1992.

Sciolino, Elaine. "Female P.O.W. Is Abused, Kindling Debate." *New York Times*, June 29, 1992, A1, A13.

Sedgwick, Eve Kosofsky. *Between Men: English Literature and Male Homosocial Desire*. New York: Columbia University Press, 1985.

———. *Epistemology of the Closet*. Berkeley: University of California Press, 1990.

Segal, Lynne. *Slow Motion: Changing Masculinities, Changing Men*. New Brunswick, N.J.: Rutgers University Press, 1990.

Shaheen, Jack. "Lawrence of Arabia: Memorable for What It Is, Regrettable for What It Might Have Been." *Washington Report on Middle East Affairs* 3 (11) (November 1989): 15, 56.

Shamroy, Leon. "Filming 'The Robe.'" In *New Screen Techniques,* edited by Martin Quigley, Jr. 177–80. New York: Quigley Publications, 1953.

Sharif, Omar, with Marie-Thérèse Guinchard. *The Eternal Male*. Translated by Martin Solokinsky. New York: Doubleday, 1977.

Shohat, Ella. "Gender and Culture of Empire: Toward a Feminist Ethnography of Cinema." *Quarterly Review of Film & Video* 13 (1–3) (1991): 45–84.

———. "Notes on the 'Post-Colonial.'" *Social Text* 31–32 (1993): 99–113.

Shostak, Marjorie. *Nisa*. New York: Random House, 1981.

Siclier, Jacques. "L'Age du Peplum." *Cahiers du cinéma,* no. 131 (May 1962): 26–38.

Silver, Alain, and James Ursini. *David Lean and His Films*. Los Angeles: Silman-James Press, 1991.

Silverman, Kaja. "White Skin, Brown Masks: The Double Mimesis, or with Lawrence in Arabia." *Differences* 1 (3) (Fall 1989): 3–54.

———. *Male Subjectivity at the Margins*. New York: Routledge, 1992.

Silverman, Stephen M. *David Lean*. New York: Abrams, 1989.

Simmel, Georg. "The Adventurer." In *On Individuality and Social Form,* edited by Donald N. Levine, 187–98. Chicago: University of Chicago Press, 1971.

———. "The Stranger." In *On Individuality and Social Form,* edited by Donald N. Levine, 143–49. Chicago: University of Chicago Press, 1971.

Sinclair, Andrew. *Spiegel: The Man Behind the Pictures*. Boston: Little, Brown, 1987.

Snow, Edward. "Theorizing the Male Gaze: Some Problems." *Representations* 25 (1989): 30–41.

Snow, Peter. *Hussein: A Biography*. Washington, D.C.: R. B. Luce, 1972.

Sobchack, Vivian. "'Surge and Splendor': A Phenomenology of the Hollywood Historical Epic." *Representations* 29 (Winter 1990): 24–49.

———. *The Address of the Eye: A Phenomenology of Film Experience*. Princeton, N.J.: Princeton University Press, 1992.

Solomon-Godeau, Abigail. "Going Native." *Art in America* 77 (7) (July 1989): 118–29.

Sragow, Michael. "Lawrence of Arabia." *Film Society Review* 6 (9) (1971): 35–38.

———. "David Lean's Magnificent *Kwai*." *Atlantic Monthly,* February 1994, 104–9.

Stewart, Philip J. "Letter to the *Times*." *The Times,* January 7, 1963, 9g.

Studlar, Gaylyn. "Masochism and the Perverse Pleasures of the Cinema." *Quarterly Review of Film* 9 (4) (Fall 1984): 267–82.

Suleri, Sara. *The Rhetoric of English India*. Chicago: University of Chicago Press, 1992.

Taussig, Michael. *Mimesis and Alterity: A Particular History of the Senses.* New York: Routledge, 1993.

Thomas, Lowell. *With Lawrence in Arabia.* New York: Century, 1924.

Tompkins, Jane. *West of Everything: The Inner Life of Westerns.* New York: Oxford University Press, 1992.

Torgovnick, Marianna. *Gone Primitive.* Chicago: University of Chicago Press, 1990.

Traube, Elizabeth G. *Dreaming Identities: Class, Gender, and Generation in 1980's Hollywood Movies.* Boulder, Colo.: Westview Press, 1992.

Turner, Adrian. *The Making of David Lean's LAWRENCE OF ARABIA.* Limpsfield: Dragon's World Book, 1994.

Turner, Victor. *A Forest of Symbols.* Ithaca, N.Y.: Cornell University Press, 1969.

Vasey, Ruth. "Foreign Parts: Hollywood's Global Distribution and the Representation of Ethnicity." In *Movie Censorship and American Culture,* edited by Francis G. Couvares, 212–36. Washington, D.C.: Smithsonian Institution Press, 1996.

Walsh, Moira. "Lawrence of Arabia." *America,* January 5, 1963, 26–28.

Wapshott, Nicholas. *Peter O'Toole.* New York: Beaufort Books, 1983.

Wasko, Janet. *Movies and Money: Financing the American Film Industry.* Norwood, N.J.: Ablex, 1982.

Watt, Ian. "Bridges over the River Kwai." *Partisan Review* 26 (Winter 1959): 83–94.

Weintraub, Stanley. "Lawrence of Arabia." *Film Quarterly* 17 (4) (Summer 1964): 51–54.

Whitehead, Harriet. "The Bow and the Burden Strap: A New Look at Institutionalized Homosexuality in Native North America." In *Sexual Meanings,* edited by Sherry B. Ortner and Harriet Whitehead, 80–115. Cambridge: Cambridge University Press, 1981.

Wiggershaus, Rolf. *The Frankfurt School: Its History, Theories, and Political Significance.* Translated by Michael Robertson. Cambridge, Mass.: MIT Press, 1994.

Will, George. "Seven Faces of Lawrence." *The Times,* July 30, 1988, 10b.

Williams, Christopher. "Bazin on Neo-Realism." *Screen* 14 (4) (Winter 1973–74): 61–68.

Williams, Linda. *Hard Core: Power, Pleasure and the "Frenzy of the Visible."* Berkeley: University of California Press, 1989.

Wilson, Colin. *The Outsider.* Boston: Houghton Mifflin, 1956.

Wilson, Michael. "LAWRENCE OF ARABIA: Elements and Facets of the Theme." A treatment for a screenplay of T. E. Lawrence's memoir *Seven Pillars of Wisdom.* 20 September 1959. Michael Wilson Papers. Arts Special Collection, University Research Library, University of California, Los Angeles. Los Angeles, California.

———. "Outline of *Seven Pillars of Wisdom.*" Paris, 10 December 1959. Michael Wilson Papers. Arts Special Collection, University Research Library, University of California, Los Angeles. Los Angeles, California.

———. *Seven Pillars of Wisdom: A Screenplay.* First draft, August 1960. Third draft, January 1961. Michael Wilson Papers. Arts Special Collection, University Research Library, University of California, Los Angeles. Los Angeles, California.

———. *I Am the Sum of My Actions*. Interviewed by Joel Gardner. Oral History Program. Los Angeles: University of California, 1983.

Wollen, Tana. "The Bigger the Better: From Cinemascope to IMAX." In *Future Visions: New Technologies of the Screen*, edited by Philip Hayward and Tana Wollen, 10–45. London: British Film Institute, 1993.

Wood, E. R. "Introduction." *The Tiger and the Horse: A Play by Robert Bolt*, v–xxii. London: Heinemann, 1963.

Woolfenden, John R. "Desert Caravan on the Trail of 'Lawrence.'" *New York Times*, June 25, 1961, sec. 2, 7.

———. "'Lawrence of Arabia': Theater Brochure." New York: Richard Davis, 1962.

Worsley, Peter. "Imperial Retreat." In *Out of Apathy*, edited by E. P. Thompson, 101–40. London: Steven and Sons, 1960.

Young, Freddie, and Paul Petzold. *The Work of the Motion Picture Cameraman*. New York: Communication Arts Books, 1972.

Zambrano, A. L. "Great Expectations: Dickens and David Lean." *Literature/Film Quarterly* 2 (Spring 1974): 154–61.

Index

Compositor:	G & S Typesetters, Inc.
Text:	10/13 Sabon
Display:	Sabon
Printer & Binder:	Thomson-Shore, Inc.